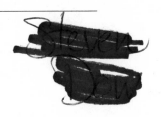

A CRITIQUE OF ADJUDICATION

{fin de siècle}

Duncan Kennedy

HARVARD UNIVERSITY PRESS
Cambridge, Massachusetts
London, England

For my mother and father

First Harvard University Press paperback edition, 1998

LIBRARY OF CONGRESS CATALOGING-IN-PUBLICATION DATA
Kennedy, Duncan, 1942–
A critique of adjudication : fin de siècle / Duncan Kennedy.
p.   cm.
Includes bibliographical references and index.
ISBN 0-674-17760-6 (cloth)
ISBN 0-674-17759-2 (pbk.)
1. Judge-made law—United States.   2. Critical legal studies—
United States.   3. Law and politics.   4. Postmodernism—United
States.   I. Title.
KF8700.K46   1997
347.73—dc21   96-48671

ACKNOWLEDGMENTS

This book is one of the by-products of a collective intellectual endeavor, the critical legal studies movement, and the ideas in it developed during the course of our intense debates over the last twenty years. I am deeply grateful for what these debates have taught me, although the positions I take here are sometimes at variance with those that prevailed within the movement. These ideas also developed in the classroom, and I owe a heavy debt to several generations of students who have challenged and inspired me. Nathaniel Berman, Brian Bix, Wayne Eastman, Karen Engle, Aeyal Gross, David Kennedy, Karl Klare, Frank Michelman, Kerry Rittich, and Joseph Singer read all or parts of this manuscript in its various stages, and I thank them for their comments. Thanks also to Eugene Paige and Kevin Vosen, to Patricia Fazzone, and to Mopsy Strange Kennedy.

Chapter 8 has appeared in a somewhat expanded form as "Strategizing Strategic Behavior in Legal Interpretation" in 1996 *Utah Law Review* 785.

CONTENTS

I

Introduction

This essay proposes a theory of the political effects of the American social practice of organizing law making through distinct adjudicative and legislative institutions. It is a work of general social theory written from a leftist and a modernist/postmodernist point of view. It represents adjudication and legislation as parts of political and cultural life, in the hope that the picture presented will be both convincing and unsettling.

The main question addressed is the role of political ideology, in the simple sense of, say, "liberalism" and "conservatism," or "states' rights" and "abolitionism," in the part of judicial activity that is best described as law making. I argue that judicial law making has been the vehicle of ideological projects of this familiar kind and of other kinds, but that ideologically oriented legal work is different from ideologically oriented legislative work. I address the grand question of the meaning and effects of adjudication in society through the development of these differences.

The main vehicle of my analysis is a detailed account of adjudication that employs a variety of methodologies. The law-making activity of judges takes place in the context of a structure of legal rules, in the face of a particular gap, conflict, or ambiguity in the structure. Judges resolve interpretive questions through a form of work that consists in restating some part of this structure and then deploying a repertoire of legal arguments to justify their solutions. The most important mode of influence of ideology in adjudication comes from the interpenetration of this specific, technical rhetoric of legal justification and the general political rhetoric of the time.

It is sometimes plain that judges experience themselves as constrained by the materials to reach particular solutions, even if they work in a medium saturated with ideology. But they *always* aim to generate a particular rhetorical effect through this work: that of the legal necessity of their solutions without regard to ideology. They work for this effect against our knowledge of the ineradicable possibility of strategic behavior in interpretation, by which I mean the externally motivated, ideological choice to work to develop a particular restatement and a particular solution rather than another. As a matter of fact, they seem often to engage in a form of denial of their own strategic behavior that puts them in bad faith.

On the basis of this model, I propose three answers to the question of the effects of adjudication. First, we can at least guess at the difference it makes to the total corpus of law that so much of it is made by judges pursuing ideological projects under these peculiar interpretive constraints. The diffusion of law-making power reduces the power of ideologically organized majorities, whether liberal or conservative, to bring about significant change in any subject-matter area heavily governed by law. It empowers the legal fractions of intelligentsias to decide the outcomes of ideological conflict among themselves, outside the legislative process. And it increases the appearance of naturalness, necessity, and relative justice of the status quo, whatever it may be, over what would prevail under a more transparent regime. In each case, adjudication functions to secure both particular ideological and general class interests of the intelligentsia in the social and economic status quo.

A second way in which adjudication functions in our politics is through its relationship to the general idea of rights. The belief that rights exist is both sustained and threatened by their role in legal discourse. I will try to show, from my own "post-rights" perspective, how the belief in rights has sustained belief in adjudication, and how the critique of adjudication has sometimes been implicated in the loss of faith in rights.

Finally, our ambivalent belief in the possibility of legal rationality is one of the models, along with scientific rationality, for the general institution of "rightness" in our society. At the most general level, the notion that there are expert discourses to which a practitioner can pledge faith, not just outside but against ideology, supports a multitude of depoliticizing practices of role specialization. "It's not my job," and "don't politicize your workplace," are maxims that make sense, at least in part, because judges model neutrality for all of us. The concluding chapter teases out some implications for workplace politics of the critique of adjudication taking place in the distant realm of legal theory.

Iconology of constraint

The figure of the Judge is important in American culture, carrying multiple resonating meanings and associations, under- and overtones of mystic power. Among the things that define the figure are the duty of interpretive fidelity and the experience of constraint to which it gives rise. Judges are supposed to "rise above" and "put aside," to "resist" and "transcend," their personal interest, their instinctive or intuitive sympathies, their partisan group affiliations, and their ideological commitments. They are supposed to "submit" to something "bigger" and "higher" than "themselves."

The Judge is a mythic figure in part because this is understood to be a struggle, much like a religious or monastic struggle, to renounce what is natural and also corrupt and banal in human conduct, to depersonalize him- (or her)self. The Judge has to struggle to achieve his (or her) own constraint. Anyone can try and succeed at this to some extent, but it is one of the domains in which we recognize the possibilities of talent, greatness, and genius, in which we have an auteur theory of culture.

Constraint is not the only thing we look for. Two other deep images are those of the Judge as wielder of trained moral intuition and the Judge as the scourge of corruption. The first sees at a glance the awful complexity of the most trivial interaction, can't sleep for pondering the quandary of justice in the particular case. The second cuts through the screen of technicalities, roots out the truth, punctures the arrogance of arbitrary power, appeals to first principles and equity, raises up the oppressed, and restores the just and natural order of things. The first suffers deeply, in silence, his (or her) responsibility for the blood he (or she) must let with no guide but frail reason. The second stands up on behalf of all of us to the Klan bombing of his (or her) house and to obscure warnings from friends in high places.

The Judge can go wrong by becoming a petty dictator, by surrendering to corruption, by becoming a bureaucrat, or by failure of heroism. Some of the Judge's mythic role models are God, the good Father of a large family, the King, and Solomon. His (or her) more mundane comrades are the clergyperson, the police officer, the doctor, the therapist, and even the airline pilot. Describing the Judge in gender-neutral language distorts the figure, because he is one of the multiple archetypes of virtuous male power, defined by semiotic contrast with the Mother, the Sybil, the Nurse, the Virgin Sacrifice, and other images of female virtue and power.

We won't be able to figure out the political consequences of constraint in adjudication unless we acknowledge its role in this symbolic complex. The experience of constraint is real and frequent and must often involve struggle. Our sense that judges struggle for constraint is one of the things that lets us "believe in" them. Because they are under strong norms to behave this way and often do behave this way, we (I) admire and respect and fear them, and willingly give them power to determine our (my) fate.

But within the very political culture that inculcates this set of feelings about judges, there is a countercurrent, a worm in the apple, a *trahison des clercs,* a subversive or "nihilistic" doctrine aiming to delegitimate judges, dispel their aura. And then there is a defense, a counter to the critique. This book is part of the critique, in dialogue with the defense.

Because judges operate under a norm of fidelity to the materials, it is a fault or a sin or a breach of contract for them to adopt the attitude of "writing on a clean slate." This distinction between attitudes retains its importance even though no one ever writes on a clean slate. It seems likely that judges who operate under a norm of interpretive fidelity will make, in many and important cases, different rules of law than would judges who did not see themselves as constrained in this way, and will make different rules than they would make as legislators.

But my thesis is that some part of judicial law making in adjudication is best described as ideological choice carried on in a discourse with a strong convention denying choice, and carried on by actors many of whom are in bad faith. What difference does it make that so much of our law making is made under these conditions rather than under those of some more transparent alternative?

My idea is that real experiences of constraint, represented (by song and story) in culture, legitimate and reinforce judicial authority in law-making situations where the imagery of constraint gets at only part of what is going on. In other words, one of the consequences of the *reality* of constraint is the mystification of choice, controversy, and ideology in adjudication, of situations in which constraint is only part of the story.

In Western Europe, including Britain, the Judge is a far less potent figure than in the United States. His (or her) resonance, mythic and daily companionship, and charismatic power are real but notably less than here. But there is a paradox in the comparison. On the one hand, Europeans live with something much closer to legislative supremacy than Americans, and this seems to undermine the figure of the Judge, to make him less like the Father and more like an agent. On the other, the subordination of the judge seems to function to sustain rather than undermine the power of an hypostasized image of the law.

Subversive doctrine has progressed less far, and perhaps as a consequence the subordinated judge can function in politics as a criminal prosecutor with a kind of mystified authority that is hard to imagine here. There is nothing natural or inevitable about the quantum here or there, and at the same time we have no simple explanation of the complicated cultural difference. But that the difference exists is an invitation to speculate about the way in which the factors that are common or not common in the cultures play within the judicial persona.

Critical social theory, leftism, modernism, postmodernism

This will be an exercise in a particular kind of social theory. It is descriptive, one might say hypothetico-descriptive. It tries to describe a large hunk of social life, without respecting social science disciplinary boundaries. It psychologizes social phenomena and interprets psychological phenomena sociologically. The perspective is unrelentingly "critical," both in the sense of attacking existing social and cultural arrangements and in the sense of internal critique of texts and practices. Some recent practitioners, obviously at a much more ambitious level than that here, are Jean-Paul Sartre,[1] Herbert Marcuse,[2] and Michel Foucault.[3]

The sensitive reader will detect two tensions in my attempt to perform in this genre. First, while my presentation certainly falls recognizably within the tradition and deploys most of its familiar categories, it is a severely chastened version. My focus includes only a fraction of the totality at which the masters aimed. The elements from which I construct my scheme include ideology and legitimation, but in mundane forms: American liberalism and conservatism, reinforcing the status quo rather than "capitalism." My conclusions are only hypotheses, and even if all proved correct they would be neither strikingly counterintuitive nor of obvious use.

In part, this modesty is the consequence of the extensive debate between the proponents of the critical project and the proponents of Liberalism (which I capitalize to indicate that I mean to indicate the larger worldview that includes both American conservatism and American liberalism, both discussed at length in Chapter 3). As in any debate, I have tried to defuse or evade what seem the most effective objections from the traditional adversary, and stolen techniques and characteristic ways of talking whenever they suit my rhetorical purposes. I grew up in the atmosphere of American progressive pragmatism and find it difficult to take either the claims or the methods of the Continental critics at face value. I'm happy to moderate them as long as I don't have to abandon them altogether.

Second, and more serious, the theory of the consequences of adjudication, and critical legal studies in general, seem to exist at an uneasy juncture of two distinct, sometimes complementary and sometimes conflicting enterprises, which I will call, for the duration, the left and the modernist/postmodernist projects. I use the word "project" here as a term of art, a term of art that is also a fudge.

A project is a continuous goal-oriented practical activity based on an analysis of some kind (with a textual and oral tradition), but the goals and the analysis are not necessarily internally coherent or consistent over time. It is a collective effort, but all the players can change over time, and people at any given moment can be part of it without subscribing to or even being interested in anything like all its precepts and practical activities.

The situated practice part has as much influence on the theory part as vice versa, but the two never fully conform to one another. It isn't a project unless people see it as such, but the way they see it doesn't exhaust what outsiders can say about it. Liberalism and conservatism are "projects of ideological intelligentsias," and so are modernism/postmodernism, leftism, and critical social theory.

The goals of the left project are to change the existing system of social hierarchy, including its class, racial, and gender dimensions, in the direction of greater equality and greater participation in public and private government. The analysis includes a critique of the injustice and oppressiveness of current arrangements, a utopian part, and a positive theory of how things got so bad and why they stay that way. The practical activities cover the range from very cloistered intellectual work, through participation in electoral or administrative processes, to the micropolitics of organizing and the micropolitics of family life.

The left project overlaps—that is, is in part the same thing as and in part different from—the liberal and conservative projects I describe in Chapter 3, as well as the "radical" projects of Marxist revolutionaries, anarchists, black nationalists and radical integrationists, radical feminists, and gay liberationists. Its relationship to each, and to similar others, is contested, as is its very existence. One connecting thread is oppositionism, which is important to leftism in a way it is only sometimes important to

Liberalism and Marxism. Another is universalism, which differentiates it from the political movements based on identity. I don't think it important for my purposes to try for a tight definition.

But I will try to make myself more intelligible through a few hints about my personal relationship to the enterprise, meaning to situate myself among the more or less familiar leftist types or characters. My political identity has changed a number of times, but it emerged or was induced in adolescence in the experience of listening to stories of *other people's* oppression, stories to be sympathized with and outraged about, with a sense of guilt, but without implications for action. Direct experiences of oppression occurred in the family (no sisters), a progressive elementary school, a boarding school, and the neighborhood. In school, there was generational conflict, tyranny within small groups of boys, and battles/seductions of the sexes. In the neighborhood, the basic paradox was the reversal of class hierarchy: lower-middle- and working-class white Catholic kids oppressed upper-middle-class white Protestants and Jews.

The oppression that happened to other people in the public and economic spheres was theorized along a liberal/conservative axis. McCarthyites oppressed communists (the most "like us" of victim groups); Southern whites oppressed blacks; communists oppressed liberals and everyone else in the Soviet Bloc. Nearer to home, blacks and working-class people we knew or almost knew deserved unlimited sympathy and unquestioning respect because their lives were harder than ours and because many people other than ourselves were prejudiced against them.

Oppression in daily life occurred along confusingly cross-cutting, largely untheorized generational, gender, and neighborhood class axes. The genteel progressive tradition seemed more a cultural and class attitude, the creation and possession of a fraction of the intelligentsia, than a program (say of the Adlai Stevenson wing of the Democratic Party).

Modernism/postmodernism (mpm), a no less contested concept, is a project with the goal of achieving transcendent aesthetic/emotional/intellectual experiences at the margins of or in the interstices of a disrupted rational grid. The practical activity of mpm centers on the artifact, something made or performed (could be high art, could be the most mundane object, could be the deconstruction of a text, could be the orchestration of dinner).

Making and appreciating artifacts are two paths toward transcendent experience, but they regularly upset the theory of the experience. The analytics, which in modernism are always ex post, are incorporated into the performance by postmodernists and emphasize the omnipresence of repressed or denied "primal forces" or "dangerous supplements" and the plasticity of formal media that presuppose that they are not plastic.

Mpm overlaps (both includes and doesn't include) therapeutic ideology; avant garde movements within modern literature, painting, music, dance, and so on; French poststructuralism; literary theory; and many others. Women, people of color, and gays have been numerous in the personnel of mpm. It shares with leftism the unifying trait of oppositionism but directed at "official" or "bourgeois" culture, "phallogocentrism," and rationalism generally, rather than at the political, social, and economic status quo. Another unifying thread is the attitude of "postness," which I render prosaically as "loss of faith," toward the rationalizing, universalizing claims and aspirations of modern elites, whether left or right, personal or political, intellectual or practical.

I will try later to distinguish this modernism from a number of others. But an autobiographical snippet may clarify my usage. My parents socialized me into the tradition of revolt against bourgeois repression and into the cult of formal innovation, rather than into the tradition of political radicalism. The keys were yearning . . . originality . . . the artist. Originality meant refusal of the claims of convention and group life, and therefore loneliness (alienation). Education meant learning to reject bourgeois essences like "individual," "man," "nation," "class," "race," "family," even or especially "humanity." E. M. Forster's two aphorisms—"Only connect," and "If I had to choose between betraying my country and betraying my friend, I hope I should have the guts to betray my country"—say it all, as long as we are willing to turn them back against "connect" and "friend."

The critique of bourgeois life extended to radical politics. There was a strand of dandyism, aestheticism—and political quietism. Art is compromised and interstitial, as well as oppositional and contemptuous, with respect to the bourgeoisie. Modernists broke with the revolutionary and communist traditions because the leftists turned out to be hyperbourgeois in cultural matters (socialist realism, revolutionary puritanism). They turned out to hate both the anarchic primal underforces and the formal play of critique, experiment, and innovation.

Critical legal studies

I have pursued my own version of a left/mpm project in the context of American critical legal studies (cls), which I'd better describe briefly here.

Cls has existed for me in four quite distinct modes. First, there was once a "movement" called cls; there still exist a cls "school" and a "theory of law" called cls; and there is from time to time a media "factoid" called cls.

By the "movement" I mean a "project" in just the sense I described above—a goal-oriented practical activity of a loosely identifiable group carried out in light of an analysis contained in a literature of shifting content. The people in the cls project were overwhelmingly legal academics; the goals were contested within the group, but my version was that we were trying to create a left legal academic intelligentsia as a new social grouping that would influence both its own workplaces and the general political culture.

Two practical activities were reforming law faculties, in a left/mpm direction, and creating a legal academic literature that would develop left ideas within legal scholarship. Cls was a movement rather than just a project because the ideas of "change," "growth," and "opposition" were built into it, in the sense of being conscious collective purposes. A third practical activity was "building the movement" by recruiting new people, doing public relations, and developing relationships on the inside. The social/political/intellectual network that "was" cls in the late 1970s and early 1980s came apart in the late 1980s, for reasons I have tried to describe elsewhere (including discipline and seduction by the mainstream, gender and race politics, intergenerational tensions, the advent of postmodernism, and, doubtless, failures of nerve and leadership).[4] But there are various successor networks that are as active as ever.

Cls as a school of thought is like the movement in that it is a project, but it is the strictly academic project of developing a network of writers and teachers who share a set of ideas, rather than the academic/political project of transforming society by transforming legal education. The members of the school share the goal of expanding its membership and influence, and they critique mainstream legal scholarship more or less aggressively, but they do so without trying to challenge the rules of the game or the balance of power in their institutions.

The social organization of the school is based on teacher-student and mentor-mentee relations. Characteristic activities include recruiting and then helping to advance careers to build the school, the organization of scholarly events where the far-flung members of the network can exchange ideas and build collegial relationships, and "representing" cls on academic occasions when it is seemly that the different schools established in legal thought should all be present.

The internal politics are generational and professional. They involve the anxiety of influence as between and within generations, rivalry for the ownership of ideas, and dramas of success and failure, heroism and opportunism, on the ladder of academic appointments. The school, unlike the movement, is institutionalized at a small number of law faculties and continues to reproduce itself socially and to develop intellectually over time.

Cls as a theory of law exists in the very different form of a canon, a list of texts that "are" cls, along with commentaries and critiques. You can be the author of a canonical text without ever having participated in the movement, and you can help define cls as a theory of law by producing an interpretation that is influential mainly because it is discrediting. Like many others, I tried to write articles that would constitute a cls canon and that would "strengthen" it in its competitive relationship with other theories. Cls as a theory of law is very much alive, "on the map" of generally recognized rival theories, and it continues to develop as people write "cls articles" and others comment on and critique "the" theory.

Now that a canon is constituted, I have to struggle like other authors to get my current ideas included. Only texts and not people can be "in" the canon, and a person's relationship to the historical movement or the current successor networks doesn't guarantee, though, of course, it does strongly affect his or her ability to get a new writing canonized. This book is an attempt to add to the canon and thereby to change what the theory "is," by developing it, strengthening it, and inflecting understanding of it in the directions I favor. This implies critiquing and trying to displace the many ideas found in canonical cls texts that I think are wrong.

Finally, cls existed recently, and may exist again, as a factoid, that is, as an entity in the "spectacle" that the mass media provide for our amusement and edification.[5] In the spectacle, cls "is" what journalists decide it is. A network participant or theoretician of cls can affect what it is like and what it does as a character in the spectacle only by meeting the rigid criteria for what counts as a "story."

The elements in a story within the spectacle have to be both familiar and simple, at the same time that the narrative as a whole has to be novel, or at least interesting to the mass audience, and has to be edifying. So cls could be "scanned" or "parsed" by the media as "sixties radicals at Harvard in the eighties," for example, but not as "a few people interested in a combination of New Left, neo-Marxist, cultural modernist, and feminist ideas inspiring unease among liberal mainstream law professors" (not that the latter would be "true").

The spectacle is a continuing current history of the world, and the journalists who construct it obey narrative constraints. Once cls developed a factoid or virtual existence in the spectacle, later accounts of cls "doings" had to preserve the earlier character (journalists research only what earlier journalists have said about cls), though in the narrative the character can change ("cls has lost its combative edge with age," for example). I felt quite a bit of pride when we early participants in the movement managed to get into the "real world" of the spectacle. But I was surprised by how little events on the screen corresponded to what I thought was happening in the "real world" I had access to off-screen, and by the increasing divergence as narrative constraint took hold. This just shows that I was myself a typical member of the audience of the spectacle.

Leftism and modernism/postmodernism in cls

The notions of leftism and mpm are helpful in understanding many of the debates that occurred within cls when it was a live movement and that still arise about cls understood as a school and a theory of law. Attacks from the left, internal and external, often focus on its mpm quality. "Being right" in the rationalist sense has been a crucial part of leftism, and the mpm strand in the project is hostile to rightness in all its forms. Other critiques of the project from the left come from the demand that theory contribute to a particular model of action in the world, whereas the dandyish, aestheticist, politically quietist mpm strands rebel against that image.

Many critiques of the project from the other direction come from mpm maximalism—from the demand to be right in the total rejection of rightness, and thereby justify quietism. The reaction is against the project's apparent *demand for commitment.* Other mpm criticisms (revalidation of the subject, failure to see that everything is already within a structure) are also provoked by its leftism. In mpm, there is often a sense that critique should be aimed at achieving negative liberty, against various kinds of bourgeois moralism and hypocrisy. The left strand in the project seems as much of a threat as the Right.

The reason for the chastened character of current American critical social theory may be that within it mpm seems to have a "hypercritical" direction that threatens to annihilate the left strand. Within critical legal studies, in particular, the critique of adjudication has figured in a development of ideas that paradoxically reverses its original function, turning it from a workhorse obviously useful against Liberal legalism into a Trojan horse.

Loosed from its host (adjudication), critique has spread through the project, attacking all the "precritical" elements that seem necessary to give the whole a left-wing character.

I will try to show that there is still something both tenable and left wing in critical legal theory, in spite of mpm critique, though the showing requires abandoning or scaling down many left-tending claims that would have seemed plausible a generation ago. The outcome, as I'm sure the reader knows already, will be analysis that sometimes seems afraid of its own implications. So, in Chapter 14, I'll let the left and mpm elements clash head on. Working on the conflict between them involves changing the traditional meanings of each, in the hope that the sacrifices will be repaid in new energy (a typically modernist revivification project).

Subversion

This book is part of the long-running project of the critique of judges, and for that reason has subversive aspirations. In the argument between the critics and the defenders, most of what gets said presupposes a common moral and intellectual framework between the disputants. Nonetheless, it is not uncommon for defenders to charge critics with betrayal of the ideal of the rule of law, or with betrayal of Reason itself. (We are no less nasty from our side, as in the allegations of "apology" I will be leveling shortly.) These charges have a particular quality, in legal academic debate, somewhat like accusations of heresy among believers, with an undercurrent of disapproval, even condemnation, going well beyond the rather dry, even abstrusely intellectual issues that seemed to be all that was under discussion.[6]

I tend to be surprised, and my feelings are often hurt by this kind of attack, when it is aimed at me personally, since I most of the time consider myself to be at heart a "good boy," though rebellious and disrespectful, and hope to persuade and even to impress, rather than to provoke moral repulsion. Arguments come to the aid of wounded narcissism. One is that, as a 1950s liberal, I abhor loyalty oaths and consider it a point of pride to refuse them. Another is that the idea that some ideas have a bad tendency is an idea with a bad tendency, to be rejected a priori.

Yet I do think that both the rule of law as an ideal and the ideal of Reason are deeply implicated in these technical legal discussions. And I am one of those who see the twentieth as a century of collective devotion to the shedding of innocent blood, much inspired by evil, including evil ideas. So here are some thoughts, first about the rule of law, and second about Reason, or at least about "objectivity." In each case, I want to say that, yes, I am a "believer" *but* that, in my versions, the ideals in question have only a little of the radiant authority that Liberal theorists have hoped for from them.

The rule of law

A legal system plays an important part in the systems of government, production, and social order in general in democratic capitalist countries like the United States, Belgium, the Czech Republic, Japan, and Australia. But it doesn't play the *same* part in each of them, and it plays quite different parts *within* each, according to the sector in question. The notion of the rule of law that I "believe in," in the sense of supporting it as a matter of political morality, is broad enough so that one can say that it prevails, though honored sometimes only in the breach, in all of these countries.

This broad notion of the rule of law requires:

That there be justiciable legal restraints on what one private party can do to another, and on what executive officers can do to private parties;
That judges understand themselves to be enjoined to enforce these restraints independently of the views of the executive and the legislature, and of political parties;
That judges understand themselves to be bound by a norm of interpretive fidelity to the body of legal materials that are relevant to whatever dispute is before them.

Under the rule of law, citizens automatically have "rights," in the limited but important sense that they can appeal to judges against other private parties and against executive officers when they feel that they have been injured in violation of legal norms. Rights, in this sense, are the logical corollaries of justiciable restraints on private and public action, and they "exist," even if there is no Bill of Rights, no institution of judicial review of legislation, and no legal recognition of the particular rights that particular countries consider "fundamental."

In other words, this is a procedural or institutional definition of the rule of law, rather than a definition that builds in or entails a particular substantive legal regime. I am happy to raise my right hand and swear that I think that such a procedural/institutional arrangement is a good thing, by comparison with the arrangement that has prevailed in modern capitalist, fascist, or communist regimes without meaningful separation of governmental powers, or without meaningful separation between governmental and political party power, or without an effective norm of interpretive fidelity in judging.

But I have two reservations. First, I don't think the rule of law is an absolute value. It's not an implication of a foundational notion of some kind, but an instrumental thing. Its value depends on a context of other modern Western Liberal institutions, so it doesn't make sense to prescribe it for another kind of society without knowing a lot about it. It sometimes has to be compromised with ideas like emergency, national security, or just "substantial justice."

Second, the institution has had and still has—not as a matter of its internal logic, but as a matter of its contingent evolution in Western society and culture—a serious down side, the side I will be exploring in this book. In all the Western systems, the discourse that judges, legal authorities, and political theorists use to legitimate the application of state power denies (suppresses, mystifies, distorts, conceals, evades) two key phenomena: *(a)* the degree to which the settled rules (whether contained in a Code or in common law) structure public and private life so as to empower some groups at the expense of others, and in general function to reproduce the systems of hierarchy that characterize the society in question; *(b)* the degree to which the system of legal rules contains gaps, conflicts, and ambiguities that get resolved by judges pursuing conscious, half-conscious, or unconscious ideological projects with respect to these issues of hierarchy.

These alleged defects of the rule of law as practiced in the West are not, I repeat, inherent in the procedural/institutional definition given above. We might have the benefits of judiciality without its current drawbacks. The notion of "counterfactual legislative supremacy," a situation in which judges would make less law and legislatures more, will allow us to explore the down side of the rule of law as we currently practice it, without calling into question (or for that matter further discussing) its abiding virtues.

Objectivity

My project is to represent adjudication as an aspect of what one might call "socio-legality," using the conceptual media made available by diverse methodologies. I want the representation to attract an audience and to have a left/mpm political and cultural impact on it. There is a theory of objectivity, or of Reason, if you will, that's implicit in these buzz words.

Socio-legality. This is the chaotic mass of data or inputs or phenomena that I register (observe, collect, measure) and then reconfigure as parts of my representation of adjudication. It includes legal rules, legal discourse, the behaviors of legal institutional actors, and social behavior in general that seems significantly impacted by or to have a significant impact on the phenomenon of adjudication—in short just about anything is grist for my mill.

My representation of adjudication is "a very selective picture." This means that I've experienced lots of choice in deciding about what to include and how to include it. It means I look for what I want to find and keep at it until I find it, often changing my criteria of what it is that I'm looking for when what I find initially doesn't fit the picture I'm trying to make.

But socio-legality also has, some of the time, in particular aspects, the quality of the objective. When I've registered something, sometimes I can't help seeing it in a particular way, even if I don't want to see it that way. What I register as I search can force changes in the representation. The data don't support the hypothesis. I just can't find what I thought would be there. The representation doesn't ring true. Things happen that disprove my theory. Other people come up with representations that "fit the facts better" or just come up with lots of facts that destabilize my representation.

The conceptual media made available by methodologies. This book is methodologically eclectic. It uses concepts, techniques, and models of performance drawn from technical legal analysis, jurisprudence, neo-Marxism, Weberian sociology, semiotics and structuralism, psychoanalysis, historicist narration, Lewinian field theory, phenomenology, modernist fiction, and deconstruction.

I have chosen eclecticism in part out of the conviction that each method that I know at all how to use, and methodology in general, have been subjected to a critique that undermines any claim their practitioners might have to get at the truth of the objects they represent. So I don't believe that my object (adjudication) corresponds, in fact, only and truly, to a representation made in the "correct" medium. It will transcend or surpass my representation, and indeed my understanding, no matter what method(s) I adopt, and that's fine with me. Nevertheless, I don't think the critique of methodology has come close to invalidating any of my own collection of methods in a way that would establish that what I do with them is necessarily a lie.

Second, eclecticism expresses modernist commitment to representation as a two-way street—I want to get at all of my object, to appropriate it, eat it, incorporate it into my artifact so it can do its work on my audience. But I don't want to annihilate its exteriority by reducing it to what can be represented in any particular method.

Third, I think eclecticism is politically correct. Many believe that each methodology has a particular political slant built into it (deconstruction is demobilizing, for example), but I don't agree. I think I can best pursue my political goals sometimes through one and sometimes through another, and that others can, too. Using supposedly politically incorrect methods in ways that show they can be politically correct is a de-reifying move, increasing practical freedom of action but also affirming freedom in general.

A final reason for eclecticism is the iron law of methodology, which I will try to state in a moment.

Representations. A representation of adjudication is a text that describes or analyzes or models a part of socio-legality. It makes sense to me to say that adjudication exists as an objective reality "out there," in the sense described above: "it" is something that I, as the knowing and representing subject, am at the mercy of. It makes sense to criticize particular representations (other people's) on the grounds that they are false. It doesn't make sense to me to speak of the representation as objective.

My notion is that the most you can hope for is that your representation won't suffer the fate of falsification. That happens through external or internal critique. Your or someone else's references to the object, behind the back of or around the representation, produce the experience of "doesn't fit," "won't budge," "there was not in fact any train scheduled to leave at that hour," that I discussed earlier. Or, the internal logic of the model is contradictory. But that your representation doesn't get falsified doesn't mean that it is "true" or that it won't soon be falsified in spite of your best efforts and good faith.

Given the critique of each methodology that I use, and of methodology in general, there is no other available meaning for objectivity than "a representation that hasn't been falsified (yet)." At least that's the conclusion I draw from the critiques.

What the audience can hope for from (as yet) unfalsified socio-legal studies is not objectivity, but a "hit," generated by putting ourselves in relation to the trio of an object (such as adjudication), an author, and a representation by the author of the object. The goal of modernist representation is to produce an artifact, a representation that can produce ecstasy in, inform, and perhaps change the audience without having to be accepted as true in the mirror sense, indeed often by playing on the limits of representation (that is, of methodology).

The representation as artifact in this modernist mode presupposes that the audience and the object have their own relationship—the audience has its own access to the object (and maybe vice versa, if the object is someone's behavior). The audience is trying to increase its own understanding, rather than depending on the representation for everything. It's all in the triangulation.

Contrast the traveler who wants to know when the train will leave and has no way of knowing except through a schedule. The traveler cares only whether the representation is true or false. The audience for the artifact, by contrast, has its own version of the object to check against the representation and, if the artifact "works" (big if), understands itself to gain rather than lose by radical discontinuities as well as by striking similarities between the two. (The artifact is in a metonymic relation to the object.)

Political/cultural impacts. My project for changing the world through artifact production is left wing and culturally modernist/postmodernist. I work on the assumption that the things that seem wrong and dead about the social world are that way in spite of people's deep longing for justice and liveliness. Also that belief systems constitute all of us in ways inconsistent with our own longings and impede our efforts to realize justice and liveliness by falsely making it appear that they can't be realized or that they have already been realized. My idea is to participate with others in producing representations that will be inconsistent with these "legitimating" but also "constitutive" belief systems.

The test of this practice is whether the representations get appreciated by an audience that incorporates them into left/mpm political and cultural projects. This goal has a massive impact on the choice of what to represent and how to do it, including on the choice of methodology. The reason for this is the iron law of methodology: *The more "hard"* (capable of being counted, highly verifiable and replicable, intersubjectively "valid"), *the more "narrow"* (partial, fragmentary, meaningless). The things that interest me are "broad," like justice and liveliness, so they can be grasped in their totality only by means that are "soft" (contestable, subjective, vague).

I think the way to respond to this dilemma is by using the hard/narrow methods of representation strategically, in the interest of making the soft/broad methods plausible, and in order to poke threatening holes in what seem to me false as well as legitimating and deadening representations of others. We don't believe only statistics, and we don't believe only prose that sings totality. Why not use both?

To my mind, none of this "undermines objectivity." The object quality of that which is represented is accessible to the audience, and the representation works only to the extent that the audience can hold it and the object and the author in mind together without experiencing the representation as falsified or inert. The artifact is effective not because it is constructed following procedures that guarantee that it represents objectively (though much of it may be empirical or deductive), but because by juxtaposing the representation, the author, and the object the audience experiences a "revelation."

The model of alienated powers

It would be nice to begin (at last!) with a simple revelatory model along the following lines. Imagine that all questions of law either have or do not have a "determinate correct answer" when approached as questions of interpretation. A question that does not have a determinate answer will be decided, but the best way to understand the outcome is as a choice by the judge between rival ideological projects rather than between better and worse interpretations. Then imagine that the participants in the system believe in the naive rule-of-law theory, according to which judges apply but do not make law.

What would be nice about this way of looking at it is that it would fit in with the critical project of Ludwig Feuerbach[7] and Karl Marx.[8] In such a critical project, we begin with supposedly conclusive demonstrations of the internal incoherence of arguments for the existence of an omnipotent God, or for the claim that the capitalist system operates through inexorable laws to reward each participant according to his or her social contribution. But people believe the opposite—that an omnipotent God does exist and that the market distributes according to contributions. In each case, there is a false appearance of determinacy in the social world, and the false determinacy hides a true determination by human agency. In other words, people "alienate their powers."

One then analyzes the consequences of belief in the false appearance of determinacy secure in the knowledge that whatever may be going on it is not what the participants think it is. The next move is to show that things are really determined by something else. Thus determination by God's will hides determination by, say, the need for food; determination by the market hides determination by class power; determination by law hides determination by, say, ideology.

The illusion, and the alienation of human powers, contribute to or influence or partly cause the patterns of social life rather than just mystifying them. The claim of the classical theories is that people would be less likely to accept the patterns if they understood that the appearance of determination by God's will or the market is just a mask for determination by human beings like themselves. Revealing that the apparent determination is an illusion or fraud, and that an alternative determination (the need for food, the logic of capital) is what is really going on, ipso facto discredits the way things are.

The representation thus includes not only an alternative analysis of what is really going on but also an appeal to an ethic that discredits what is really going on. Communism as an affirmative ideal was cast as an application of the reigning Judeo-Christian ethic to the world as it looked when the precepts of classical political economy had been revealed as fraudulent. The ethical move is thus a second determination: it correctly applies to the world rendered transparent the principles that had functioned, in the mystified world where people alienate their powers, as apology.

That left-wing project is the model for this one, in the following sense. I argue that ideology influences adjudication, by structuring legal discourse and through strategic choice in interpretation. I argue that the denial of the presence of ideology in adjudication leads to political results different from those that would occur in a situation of transparency. And I suggest that it would be in some sense "better" to determine our fates without alienating our powers.

But my version of the critical project is modified in ways intended to deprive it of pretensions to truth. The first modification is to get rid of the idea that there is an objective boundary line we can draw between questions of law that have correct determinate answers and questions that can be resolved only through ideological choice. The second is to propose an understanding of the rules that dispose ideological stakes as products of the interaction between the legal materials, understood as a constraining medium, and the ideological projects of judges. The rule choices that emerge from the interaction should be understood neither as simply the implications of authority nor as the implications of the ideological projects, but as a compromise.

The third is to reject the idea of simple illusion, or false consciousness, in favor of the more complex idea that judges are in bad faith. They "deny" their ideological projects rather than either putting them aside or lying about them, so that there is a discontinuity between two levels of their consciousness rather than between truth and illusion. The fourth is to explore the ideological consequences of law making through adjudication in bad faith, without proposing either a substitute determination of what is "really" going on or an ethical determination of how we must respond to the revelation of error.

PART ONE

Ideological Stakes in Adjudication

2

The Distinction between Adjudication and Legislation

This chapter takes up one of the "great dichotomies"[1] of political theory in general and legal theory in particular, that between adjudication and legislation. I have already suggested that the ideological element in adjudication is "denied" by many, and that judges operate in "bad faith." The denial is in part a response to the critique of judging, the "viral" element in American legal thought. Jurisprudence theorizes denial by explaining how adjudication can be nonideological, and it is now time to examine the variety of ways in which it does this.

It is important to distinguish at the outset between denying the ideological element in judging and denying that judges make decisions that are important to ideological intelligentsias. I don't think many people would deny that liberals and conservatives care about what rules the U.S. Supreme Court adopts about abortion, and care in a way that is well described as ideologically motivated. I don't think many people would deny that ideological intelligentsias care ideologically about which rule courts adopt when they are working out the details of products liability.

But it is a different matter to claim that the discursive process by which the rules are made, here appellate adjudication, has ideological content and significance in its own right. It is different because many liberals and conservatives believe, some of the time, to some extent, usually in bad faith, that although there are ideological stakes in rule definition, the discursive process that disposes the stakes by choosing the rule (appellate decision) is not or ought not to be ideological. Judges, moreover, always claim that they themselves are proceeding according to a discursive procedure that positively excludes ideology, though of course it is commonplace for them to accuse other judges of failing to make this exclusion.

There are two quite different conventional ways to state the idea that appellate court discursive practices for choosing rules do or should exclude ideology. These will figure heavily in the future discussion. One is to say that the rule-making process is or ought to be "objective"; the other is to say, much more modestly, that it ought not to be "personal."

Within legal culture, since the late nineteenth century, there has been debate about the objectivity of the procedures that judges use in choosing rules of law. *For lawyers,* I assert, the main thing at stake in these discussions has been whether or not judges are, or have to be or ought to be, ideological actors. To say that judicial law making produces rule choices that are objectively correct is simply to say that it produces rule choices that cannot be attributed to the ideological sympathies of the judges. It is sometimes asserted that there are other stakes, like the nonpolitical value of certainty as a facilitator of legal transactions, but these turn out to be makeweights in the legal debate, though occasionally appealing to outsiders.

An amusing sideshow to this debate has been staged by philosophers (of many persuasions and ideologies) who have been interested in objectivity "in general" and who address the question in law as an analogue to the question as it arises elsewhere. Often, they haven't understood the lawyers' stakes, and so propose that law is objective according to an account of objectivity that doesn't respond to the issue of the preclusion of ideological determination, thinking they are thereby clarifying things for us philosophical illiterates.[2] Because they miss the point, these interventions don't usually get incorporated into the lawyers' debate.

Stanley Fish made the opposite mistake in his debate with Ronald Dworkin.[3] He seemed to think it should comfort us that, though law is certainly not objective, there is no way for judges to escape control by their context. But the mode of "always already constrained" that he proposed was patently a constraint that couldn't exclude ideology.

The parallel debate about whether legal decision making is not or ought not to be "personal" has the same stakes. Nonlawyers sometimes interpret the exclusion of the personal as aimed at corruption, or at the random preferences of judges, say, for litigants wearing blue shirts. But the only real issue is the personal understood as the ideological. The following passage is highly typical, not least in its equivocation as to whether judges "really do not" decide on the basis of personal values, or are only "deterred" from so doing, so that they can make "massive doctrinal shifts" only "rarely."

[T]he fact that judges are protected in significant ways from the popular will . . . make[s] it inappropriate for them to reach outcomes on the basis of their personal (and possibly idiosyncratic) values. Despite all the palaver that this is what judges really do, *the truth is that they really do not.* The institutional constraints I have already mentioned—combined with the requirement of reasoned decision and a moral obligation of candor—are *checks that deter* the imposition of judges' personal values and that confine the courts to "molecular motions." *Massive doctrinal shifts are rare.* When they do occur, they are *usually* a long time building, and, if they touch sensitive moral nerves, are at least as long a time commanding the general acceptance needed to make them effective.[4]

I want to state forcefully that at the present time in American legal culture this version of adjudication (David Shapiro's) is not "mainstream" because there isn't a mainstream view of the issue. Lawyers vary from perfect cynicism to perfect late-nineteenth-century Langdellianism, with a surprisingly large and idiosyncratic range of variations in between. Legal academics are the same. Legal theorists, who are often professionally concerned with the issue, unanimously reject "nihilism" (whatever that means) but equally unanimously reject any kind of "formalism." Their range of intermediate variants is more organized into schools than the random variants of lawyers but no less baroque.

Shapiro's article does represent an orthodoxy, a view that was once merely common sense but that has become tradition, embattled but faithful to first principles amidst a sea of heretics, backsliders, and cranks.

I will not be arguing about whether judges do or should reach outcomes (make rules) on the basis of their personal or idiosyncratic values, if we take personal in the sense of "preference between chocolate and vanilla ice cream," or preference for litigants wearing blue shirts or carrying bribes. What I am interested in is the way in which judges' ideological commitments (including the commitment not to be ideological) enter into rule making, and the consequences of their presence, if they are present, under erasure or denial. It seems clear to me that *sometimes* judges choose rules on the basis of deduction from other rules, and that *sometimes* they are (I'm happy to say "improperly") influenced by truly idiosyncratic factors. But ideological orientation, in the conception I will develop at some length in the next chapter, is never something "merely personal."

Adjudication versus legislation

The distinction between adjudication and legislation is closely related to a number of others, and it is impossible to explain it without reference to them. They include the distinctions between a court and a legislature, between applying and making law, between law and politics, between objective and subjective questions, between rights and powers, and between professionally and electorally accountable officials. In one way of looking at it, adjudication is what courts do and legislation is what legislatures do. In this version, the distinction is parasitic on the prior one between the two institutions of court and legislature and is merely descriptive. Whatever courts do is adjudication; whatever legislatures do is legislation.

It is much more common, however, to see the two as *methods of decision* that might or might not characterize any given activity of a court or a legislature. In the oldest and simplest version of this view, though not in the current understanding of lawyers, what legislatures do when they legislate is make law, and what courts do when they adjudicate is apply law to facts. But it is perfectly possible for a legislature to adjudicate and for a court to legislate. In this version of the distinction, adjudication and legislation are mutually exclusive concepts—an actor cannot be doing both at the same time, deciding a question in one way precludes deciding it in the other, applying existing law to existing facts is different from making new law to apply to future (or past) facts.

The distinction remains sharp even if we recognize that application will often require reformulation of the rule before it can be applied to the facts. We are unsure at first blush how to apply the rule to the facts; we resolve the question by appealing to the definitions of the words. As long as the process of reformulation is understood to be "semantic," or "deductive," in the sense of looking for the "meaning" of the words that compose the rule to be applied, it is not, in this understanding, rule making, even if the case is a hard one. "Questions of law," as conventionally distinguished from "questions of fact," fall within the judge's province, in this view, because they involve objective questions of meaning rather than the subjective judgments that are required when we make the political choice to apply one rule or another to a given fact situation.

The distinction between adjudication and legislation has often been a building block in the larger normative theory of Liberalism (capitalized to distinguish it from "liberalism," the political ideology that is opposed to conservatism). By "Liberalism" I mean belief in individual rights, majority rule, and the rule of law. Liberal theories of the rule of law require the separation of powers as one means to protect individual rights in a regime of majority rule. The separation between legislative and judicial institutions corresponds exactly to the distinction between legislation and adjudication as methods of decision. Legislatures *should* legislate and only legislate; courts *should* adjudicate and only adjudicate, even though they may in fact violate these role constraints.

In this normative view, the law-making process requires value judgments, which are inescapably subjective, and therefore political. Because law making is political, it should be done by elected officials (possibly subject to constraints imposed by the people as whole through constitutional law making), operating under a norm of accountability to their constituents.

Conversely, legislatures should not adjudicate. Adjudication (law application) determines the rights of the parties to disputes. Liberals of both the positivist and natural rights schools agree that the rule of law means that the parties have a right to determination of their rights, however established, by a process that is not tainted by the subjective political preferences of the majority. As I noted above, these writers are concerned not so much with the eccentric, the truly "personal," as with the ideological, what James Madison called "faction."

Adjudication, in the old view, need not be political, because it involves questions of meaning and questions of fact that are independent of value judgments (objective). Since the determination of questions of right can be done objectively, rather than ideologically, it seems obvious that it should be. Therefore it should be entrusted to trained professionals operating under a norm of "independent" fidelity to law. Courts constituted to perform this function should not legislate because they are not elected.

Within this normative vision, the phrase "judicial legislation" has an invariably negative normative meaning, as in this sentence from a sophisticated journalist commentator on a Supreme Court nominee: "Although Breyer's instincts are moderate rather than activist, his pragmatism raises questions about judicial legislation that might be useful to explore."[5] This theory takes the rule of law to mean that the exercise of force or violence against citizens must be justified in two ways: first, by appeal to a norm produced by the democratic decision-making process that is embodied in the legislature or the process of constitution making; second, by the application of the norm to the facts in a process that is independent of the very decision process that generated it. Judicial legislation is problematic because it violates the first requirement, just as the trial of cases in the legislature would violate the second.

This version of the distinction between legislation and adjudication and of its place in Liberal theory plays a substantial role in American popular political culture, but it has little credence among the intelligentsia and even less in the specifically legal intelligentsia. The reason is that it seems implausible to describe the actual activity of judges as nothing more than applying law, at least as the notion of law application is generally understood.

Of course, judges do apply law all the time, in the sense of taking a norm that everyone involved understands to be "valid" and asking whether its factual predicates have been proved. But it seems equally obvious that judges constantly have to do something better described as making than as applying law. At a minimum, judges often have the job of resolving gaps, conflicts, or ambiguities in the system of legal norms. In some cases, no amount of reformulation based on the underlying definitions of the words composing the arguably applicable rules produces a deductively valid resolution. When it is agreed that there is a gap, conflict, or ambiguity in this sense, then it is also agreed that the judge who resolves it "makes" a new rule and then applies it to the facts, rather than merely applying a preexisting rule.[6]

When identified with the contrast between law making and law application, the legislation/adjudication dichotomy seems to admit of no middle term. But as soon as we shift to this broader notion of legal interpretation, it follows that adjudication involves both making and applying. But it does not follow, and is controverted, that judicial law making must be or is in fact "judicial legislation" and therefore abhorrent to the part of the theory of the rule of law that requires a democratic (legislative) legitimation for the use of force against the citizen.

American judges vigorously deny that what they do even in "hard cases" has to be or is in fact judicial legislation, though they often concede that they make law. They argue for particular rule choices in a rhetoric of nonpolitical necessity. I think it fair to say, however, that their case-by-case claims that they are constrained by the legal materials to reach results to which their politics are irrelevant are not convincing.

First, it is a convention of judicial opinion writing, and a political requirement of popular culture, that judges represent themselves as neutral with respect to the content of the law they make. Second, any individual judge making any particular rule has an interest, an interest in his or her rule prevailing, in presenting the rule choice as not judicial legislation. Third, many particular claims of legal necessity in judicial opinions are unconvincing on their face, and therefore raise the question of what is "really" determining the outcome.

In stark contrast with the view that judges present in their opinions, the standard practice of sophisticated journalism treats judges, at least of the Supreme Court, as political actors whose views and alignments can be analyzed through the conventional vocabulary of politics. Indeed, as in the following quotation, the journalistic treatment of the Court uses the language of ideology with more confidence than would a parallel treatment of legislative disputes, given the prevailing sense that straightforward left-right divisions only partially describe legislative politics. Linda Greenhouse is describing the 1993 Supreme Court term for the Sunday *New York Times* "News of the Week in Review":

> [M]any of the decisions [the justices] produced revealed deep divisions and some bore the marks of raw ideological combat . . .
>
> . . . [T]he exchange . . . highlighted the Court's current dynamic: Justices Thomas and Scalia at the extreme conservative end of the Court's spectrum, and Justices Blackmun, Stevens, Souter and Ginsburg occupying a place that, while certainly not classically liberal, can be defined as liberal relative to where the Court is today . . .
>
> . . . Justice Kennedy occupied the gravitational center of the Court.[7]

It is worth noting that in the only substantive argumentative exchange she mentions, the "liberal" wing attacks the "conservatives" for making "a 'radical' attempt to argue policy rather than law." The judges, in other words, attack one another for judicial legislation even as the commentators tell the story in strict ideological terms. A week later, a *Boston Globe* journalist portrayed the "general ideological makeup" of the Court on a spectrum including the categories liberal, moderate liberal, moderate, moderate conservative, and conservative, and predicted that Stephen Breyer would be a moderate liberal.[8]

A large part of American legal academic work is concerned with whether there is a politically legitimate method of judicial law making through the interpretation of legal materials—in other words, a middle term between law application and judicial legislation. This literature is both descriptive and normative. A good deal of it might be described as simultaneously reassuring and celebratory. It presents famous judges, for example, as paragons exactly because they manage to contribute mightily to law (that is, make a lot of "good" law) without falling into the trap of ideology. Here is John Noonan, a judge who was first a law professor, reviewing, for the general intelligentsia readership of the *New York Times Book Review,* a law professor's celebratory biography of Judge Learned Hand:

> The craftsman was committed to neither a conservative nor a liberal agenda, but to a creed of judicial restraint . . . reinforced by his own experience of democracy. Judicial restraint was the watchword of liberals when conservatives dominated the courts; it continued to be the watchword of judges like Hand and Felix Frankfurter even after liberals were in judicial ascendancy. The result is that Hand's opinions do not wholly please either left or right . . . Political correctness was not his concern. He sought to produce the right decision.[9]

A few months later, Vincent Blasi, also a law professor, reviewed a biography of Justice Lewis Powell in exactly the same vein:

> In an age that generated fierce pressures to interpret the Constitution to serve one or another partisan agenda, Lewis Powell probably did as much as anyone to keep alive the ideal of judicial independence. Few Justices in history have succeeded so well at separating their political predilections from their judgments regarding what the Constitution means. Justice Powell's performance disappointed many conservatives . . . Because his view prevailed in a large number of closely contested decisions, Justice Powell's independence had a major impact on the development of the law.[10]

A letter writer was concerned that the review might mislead the "educated layman" into thinking that "independence" was rare rather than the rule on the Supreme Court, but agreed that Powell's "ability to place the law ahead of any ideological or political considerations is what made him a noteworthy jurist."[11]

The jurisprudence of adjudication

Though in neither the reassuring nor the celebratory mode, this chapter addresses the anxiety implicit in these reviewers' particular choice of praise. If what makes a judge great is his ability to resist not only other people's but also his own ideological predilections, then it seems to follow, as the letter writer sees, that lesser judges don't manage this. In building their

normative theories, legal philosophers take positions about what it is possible for judges to do and appeal constantly to ideas about what they do
in fact. In the process, they provide a typology of approaches to the ideological "underside" of adjudication.

We can distinguish no fewer than five general strategies for dealing
with the problem. The first, associated with classical positivism through
H. L. A. Hart,[12] is to deny or at least to ignore the possibility of a middle
term, arguing that what is not law application is for all intents and purposes judicial legislation. A basic problem with this approach is that there
is a large number of cases in which the judge at least reformulates the
existing rule of law.

Is it plausible that whenever the judge's reformulation is other than a
deduction from the "core meanings" of words in an earlier valid formulation, we should understand him as behaving as he would if he were a
legislator? No one interested in the political analysis of the content of the
legal system would adopt such a hypothesis. It seems too obvious to argue
that the institutional contexts of adjudication and legislation are so different that identical ideological motives in judges and legislators will produce very different substantive rule-making outcomes. But the question
is, different in what way?[13]

The second position, which I associate with Hans Kelsen,[14] Roberto
Unger,[15] Mark Tushnet,[16] Gary Peller,[17] and James Boyle,[18] collapses the
distinction between rule making and rule application by showing that rule
application cannot be insulated from "subjective" influence, including
ideological influence. It seems to follow a fortiori that the far less structured activity of resolving gaps, conflicts, and ambiguities is similarly
porous. There are a number of arguments as to why rule application "cannot be objective," relying on linguistic philosophers as diverse as John
Locke, Ludwig Wittgenstein, Richard Rorty, and Jacques Derrida, but one
example will suffice here.

It is often asserted that "no rule can determine the scope of its own
application," meaning that applying, say, "close the door at five" will require judgments about whether particulars in the order of events correspond or don't correspond to the concepts "close," "door," and "five." As a
logical matter, the basis for these judgments can't be found in the concepts
themselves. But there are no "objective" tests of correspondence outside
the text of the rule, once one agrees that language is not the mirror of
nature.

It is common to respond (as Owen Fiss[19] has) that when the rule applier acts, he does so according to something other than a deductive process, relying on "practical reason," the consensus of the "interpretive community," or whatever. The critics reply that whatever method one chooses as a solution to the "application problem," that is, however one grounds rule application, that method will not have the demonstrable or objective quality that would be necessary to guarantee that the decision maker's ideology played no role in the choice of an outcome.[20]

The collapse of even the hardest core of rule application into rule making, and its consequent opening to ideological influence, were important events in the general cultural contests about role constraint and about "being right." But the collapsing strategy is less important to the enterprise we are pursuing here—that of trying to assess the particular character of judicial as opposed to legislative law making.

It is already widely recognized in our legal culture that judges make law through legal interpretation. Moreover, it is obvious that in many or most cases the application process is experienced by all involved not just as unproblematic, but also as unproblematizable, no matter how clearly nondeductive. And we have a choice in formulating norms between using terms that will be "easy" ("you can vote at age 21") and those that will be "hard" ("when you achieve good character") to apply. The experience of core meanings survives the loss of its metaphysical grounding.[21] Although problematic cases of rule application remain common in spite of our best efforts, they pose less of a problem for the claim of ideological neutrality in adjudication than does the acknowledged openness of the interpretive process.

Judges' choices among new rules proposed to resolve gaps, conflicts, and ambiguities are contestable (and contested) within a distinct normative discourse of statutory and constitutional interpretation, precedent, and "policy." This discourse may sometimes falsely presuppose that whatever rules judges adopt can be applied "neutrally," and it is certainly true that how rules get applied is sometimes as important as what they "are." In a common law, but not in a code system, when judges reformulate rules in the process of applying them in particular cases, the reformulations become part of the body of "sources" of law in later cases. Common lawyers interested in judicial law making have always been interested in this process and in how we might compare it with the legislative process. Showing that law is made even in the most routine application of rule to facts is important, but it seems more important to try to figure out how the rules get made in the first place.

The third position is that while there is no middle term, in the sense of a method distinct from both application and legislation, judicial law making is nonetheless distinct from legislation because it is bounded in its substance. A classic statement would be Oliver Wendell Holmes's: "I recognize without hesitation that judges do and must legislate, but they can do so only interstitially; they are confined from 'molar to molecular motions.' "[22] Another would be Felix Frankfurter's list of the doctrines that confine constitutional adjudication and thereby restrain its political impact (standing, case or controversy, political question doctrine).[23] Yet another would be Joseph Raz's list of institutional constraints on adjudication.[24]

A solution of this kind accepts that what is not rule application is methodologically indistinguishable from judicial legislation, and perhaps acknowledges that the nondemocratic character of judging makes this problematic. A further concession would be that the second-level rules that confine judicial law making within a "sphere" are open to the same critique as the judge's first-order rule making. In other words, what guarantees a nonideological distinction between "interstitial" and "macro" law making, or between "political" and "judicial" questions? The minute the judge is doing something more than applying (searching for the meaning of) the rules that confine the scope of his legislative law making, he is engaged in judicial legislation about the scope of judicial legislation.[25]

The fourth solution addresses this problem by proposing a genuine middle term between law application and judicial legislation. This is the method of "coherence" or "fit," through which the judge can make new rules of law without consulting his own legislative preferences. I associate this solution with the work of Benjamin Cardozo,[26] Karl Llewellyn,[27] Lon Fuller,[28] Henry Hart and Albert Sacks,[29] Neil MacCormick,[30] J. M. Finnis,[31] and Ronald Dworkin.[32] Fit or coherence rule making is distinct from the method of developing the definitions of the words in legal rules as an aid to applying them, because it is focused on the choice among different rules proposed to resolve a gap, conflict, or ambiguity in the legal system seen as an ensemble of rules. It is clear that the judge is making law. He does so by treating the whole existing corpus of rules (rather than the words of a particular rule) as the product of an implicit rational plan, and asks which of the rules proposed best furthers that plan. If he employs the method of coherence, he will make law that is not influenced by his personal convictions, simply because he will follow the rational plan even when he doesn't agree with it.

The method of coherence permits the judge to do ideological work when he furthers a particular legal regime by developing it in the face of a gap, conflict, or ambiguity. The regime may be incomprehensible except as the working out of an ideological conception, in the sense of a liberal or conservative conception. In the familiar case, the legislature has enacted a comprehensive statute, say the National Labor Relations Act, which self-consciously rejects a preexisting conservative regime of labor relations and equally self-consciously adopts a rival liberal regime. The judge who wants to resolve a case in a way that "fits" the statutory scheme has to pursue the liberal conception. But it is not his "personal" ideology but that of the legislative (or constitutional) boss that guides him. The coherence conception permits similar analysis of bodies of case law. The judge does the ideological bidding of the prior judges, relying on the legislature to change that ideology if it wants to.

A coherence theorist might believe, as does Dworkin, that the legal regime taken as a whole is intelligible only as the expression of a particular combination of political theoretical conceptions. If this is the case, coherence requires the categorical exclusion from the interpretative process of *other* political conceptions: "A judge who accepts this constraint, and whose own convictions are Marxist or anarchist or taken from some eccentric religious tradition, cannot impose these convictions on the community under the title of law, however noble or enlightened he believes them to be, because they cannot provide the coherent general interpretation he needs."[33] I find this statement odd (possibly because of my own combination of Marxist, anarchist, and eccentric religious convictions) but typical of the narrowing aspirations of coherence theorists (explored below).

The position that there is a middle methodology between law application and judicial legislation is consistent with the idea (the third solution above) that there are rules that constrain the scope of judicial law making and thereby serve to limit the impact of ideology on adjudication. Indeed, the method of coherence provides a response to the fear that such rules only push the problem of judicial legislation back from the interpretation of substantive norms to the interpretation of the supposedly constraining rules. The judge who interprets the political question doctrine or the vaguer notion of "interstitiality" through the requirement of coherence with prior cases and other rules of the system is enacting "the system's" ideology of judicial constraint or judicial activism, rather than his personal view.

One can distinguish two variants of the position that there is a methodological middle term. The English version remains true to its Benthamite positivist heritage by positing that there is a limit to the range of cases that correspond to the method of coherence. The judges are obliged to decide all cases that come before them, and some of these are beyond the middle range—in other words, the law "runs out" and the judge must legislate. Of course, he does so subject to the various constraints, such as the requirement of a case or controversy, described above.

In this version, there are two forms of judicial legislation, only one of which has a negative connotation. If, on the one hand, the judge fails to perform his function of judicial law making according to the method of coherence, and particularly if he makes a rule that corresponds to his legislative preference rather than to the preference implicit in the legal materials, then the rule of law is in jeopardy. On the other hand, where the law "runs out," he is simply the victim of a contradiction between the role constraints proposed by popular political culture. He is supposed to decide the case without judicial legislation, but this is impossible. Since not deciding is also impossible (walking away means that the defendant wins), the right thing for him to do is what he thinks is right, leaving it to the legislature or (in the United States) to the constitutional amendment process to correct him if he is wrong.

In the American version, the method of coherence will give a "right answer" to any dispute over which the judge has jurisdiction. There may be types of cases for which the adjudicative method is inappropriate (Fuller,[34] Hart and Sacks[35]), but legal doctrine itself defines these cases and forbids the judge deciding them, rather than requiring him to do so. The defendant wins "as a matter of law," rather than by refusal of justice. The judge never has to legislate, and judicial legislation is *always* bad. The conventional judicial rhetoric of constraint by law can be honored, rather than treated in the positivist manner as a pious fraud. In this version, the judge can do his job.

With the passage from Cardozo to Fuller and Llewellyn through Hart and Sacks to Dworkin, there is a noticeable evolution of this position. It moves in the direction of blurring the difference between the middle term of coherence and judicial legislation, while at the same time vigorously affirming its importance. Dworkin and many other modern American legal theorists concede (even affirm) the political character of adjudication. They affirm the possibility of "rightness" in even the "hardest" cases, while progressively abandoning any claim that this rightness is "objective," or demonstrable in the sense that any rational practitioner of legal reasoning would have to accept it, let alone noncontroversial within the canons of good legal reasoning. They nonetheless retain a sharp distinction between judging and legislating:

> [L]egal practice is an exercise in interpretation not only when lawyers interpret particular documents or statutes but generally. Law so conceived is deeply and thoroughly political. Lawyers and judges cannot avoid politics in the broad sense of political theory. But law is not a matter of personal or partisan politics, and a critique of law that does not understand this difference will provide poor understanding and even poorer guidance.[36]

For Dworkin, a hard case may require judgments of "political theory" because there may be more than one solution that meets the requirement of coherence or fit. Moreover, the operation of investigating whether a proposed solution passes the initial test of fit will be influenced by the same political theories that the judge appeals to if at the end of the day he has to choose between outcomes that are equally coherent. There is no metacriterion for choosing between political theories, or between versions of coherence influenced by those theories, other than the judge's conviction that a given theory is the best.

As Gerald Postema points out,[37] this is an extreme "protestant" version of "rightness" in interpretation. In hard cases, the judge cannot rely on external authority or even on the idea of objectivity, and cannot hope to compel the agreement of others; but he is never to succumb to doubt as to whether the truth he seeks "really exists" outside himself. "[J]udges deciding difficult constitutional cases are [not] simply voting their personal political convictions as much as [*sic*] if they were legislators or delegates to a new constitutional convention."[38] If the judge is doing "ordinary politics in disguise," he is "incompetent or in bad faith."[39]

Contrast, finally, the civil law version of adjudication, a fifth strategy that combines all of these elements in yet another way. On the Continent, the official story is that the role of the judge is to apply the relevant Code to the facts of the case using a presumption of gaplessness. If the case cannot be resolved by semantic or deductive analysis of the meanings of the terms in a validly enacted rule, the judge deploys interpretive techniques based on the presumption that the Code is the coherent working out of a particular conceptual structure. He does the best he can but does not entertain the possibility that "there is no right answer." In the official version, the judge can always do his job, though some cases are harder than others. In this respect, Dworkin is a Continental.

But the official version[40] denies, first, that the judge will ever have to go beyond coherence, or fit, into Dworkin's realm of personally held general political theory, and, second, that these general theories legitimately influence the operation of determining coherence in the first place. The more radical Continental thinkers suggest that it may sometimes be necessary for the judge to appeal beyond the conceptual form of coherence to the notion of "progress" or "social evolution," but they underplay rather than emphasize the controversial character of these ideas. Even the Continentals of the free law school took the convention of judicial necessity far more seriously than does the current American academic mainstream.[41]

Typology of Theories of Adjudication

Deduction + judicial legislation	Hart
Judicial legislation	Unger
Deduction + limiting rules + judicial legislation	Raz
Deduction + coherence + judicial legislation	MacCormick
Deduction + coherence + personal political theory	Dworkin
Deduction + coherence	Civilians

It is pretty plain that the development of each of these theories of adjudication has been part of a broader political project. As soon as we shift from understanding adjudication as rule application to understanding it as interpretation, we threaten to destabilize the larger Liberal conceptual structure that distinguishes courts from legislatures, law from politics, technical from democratic decision making, and the rule of law from tyranny. The larger structure, whether understood as a prescription or as a description of reality, plays a central role in ideological controversies among various conservativisms, liberalisms, and radicalisms, including the Marxist variants. The question of the role of ideology in adjudication is an ideological question.

The theory I propose in Chapter 7 is closer to the American model of a third term between law application and judicial legislation, and to its Dworkinian variant, than to any of the others in this typology. But I don't think Dworkin's central distinctions, between "political theory" and "partisan or personal politics," and between rights and policies, can do the work he wants them to do. Because it affirms the presence of ideology in all aspects of adjudication, my account resembles the "crit" strategy of collapsing the distinction between rule making and judicial legislation, while rejecting that strategy's reliance on a merely logical (rather than "internal") critique of judicial practice.

My argument will be that the peculiar American jurisprudential solution to the problem of judicial legislation is a response to a situation in which the ideological stakes disposed by judicial law making are very high, while the internal critique of legal regimes and the judicial opinions that rationalize them is highly developed. As a preliminary to this political account of the critique of adjudication, the next chapter offers more precise definitions of the notions of ideology and ideological stakes than has seemed necessary up to this point.

3

Ideological Conflict over the Definition of Legal Rules

My overall project is to examine the place of adjudication in an ideologically divided society. A basic idea is that much ideological conflict is about the rules of law. Judges play a large role in developing the rules of law. But whether they are ideological actors is disputed. To the extent that they are ideological actors, there has been little attention paid to the question of how the organization of a significant amount of rule-making activity through actors whose ideological role is disputed, sometimes denied and sometimes affirmed, affects the outcome of ideological dispute.

All of these terms are fuzzy. I want to make them considerably more precise by proposing a vocabulary corresponding to a model. First, I define an ideology as a universalization project[1] of an ideological intelligentsia[2] that sees itself as acting "for" a group with interests in conflict with those of other groups, and specify liberalism and conservatism as two primary examples of American ideology. I assert that an important characteristic of these American ideologies is that they have both a similar general structure and similar argumentative elements, so that the difference between them is in the way the elements are deployed or "spoken" with respect to a range of issues.

When the issues are legal, as they often are, the legal representatives of the ideological intelligentsia argue them to legislatures, executive and administrative officers, judges and juries. We can classify legal issues in a rough way as involving either rule making (and interpretation) or fact finding, with a significant intermediate category of "mixed" questions (was the defendant "negligent").

With respect to any particular legal question, we can identify the "stakes" for the participants who understand the question in ideological terms. These may or may not be distinct from the stakes as the legal parties

39

understand them (defining the rules governing police searches may be a minor aspect of the defendant's strategy but the major question for "civil libertarians").

This study is about "questions of law" rather than "of fact," and about the place in the court system, the appellate level, where judges have final formal authority to decide them. The activity of appellate courts is most clearly an instance of law making that disposes ideological stakes but is carried out in a situation of dispute as to whether the decision makers are (or should be) ideological actors.

The rest of this chapter elaborates the elements of the model, discussing (*a*) groups, interests, and conflicts, (*b*) ideologies and ideological intelligentsias, (*c*) liberalism and conservatism, (*d*) the kinds of ideological stakes liberals and conservatives see in legal rules, and (*e*) the way appellate rule making through adjudication disposes those stakes in practice.

Groups, interests, conflicts

The three concepts of groups, interests, and conflicts are not fully distinct from one another. Groups are composed of people, and they are continuous but not identical through time. The idea includes communities in the strong sense but also groups that have only ideal interests in common— such as civil libertarians. Interests are enduring orientations of groups to outcomes for conflicts. The interest may be one held by all groups, something they compete over, like income or wealth or space; or it may be an interest in doing something that another group doesn't want done, as abortion. It may be a large or small aspect of group existence. Conflicts are situations in which it looks as though interests are "at stake," rather than just the object of discussion or disagreement.

Interests in common can bring people to consider themselves a group. A group will enter into conflict with another group to protect its interest, but a conflict between two individuals can cause others to redefine their interests, or others to come into being as a group. There are no ontological priorities among the concepts.

Group interests in the evolution of legal rules

Rules of law play an important role in many different conflicts that people conceive as "between groups." When these conflicts become lawsuits, the plaintiff and defendant are understood to be stand-ins for groups, even if they themselves have no desire for this to be true and do their best to avoid it. The group focuses not on the total complex of the parties' good and bad behavior, extended back in time and implicating everything in life, or on their guilt or innocence, but on a particular rule that has played a role in the way the dispute evolved. This rule is a situational element, quite possibly minor, in the dispute, but it is also part of the permanent structure of group conflict. The choice of a definition or interpretation of the rule may be insignificant for the parties, but because the rule appears again in many other, distant contexts of similarly structured group conflict, it is significant enough for the groups to fight about.

Ideology is universalization of group interests

When do we call a conflict over the definition of a rule of law an "ideological" conflict? First, it has to implicate the interests of many people beyond the litigants, at least in the eyes of the representatives of the many. Second, the groups must restate their interests in universal terms, present them as something more than "selfish." The claim must be that other groups "ought" to yield on the issue of rule definition.

Third, there must be something recognizable as a "body of thought," a discourse, a sequence of texts, that can be "applied" or brought to bear over and over again to produce arguments in favor of rule definitions that will favor the interest. This means an intelligentsia. The intelligentsia consists of those people who operate the ideology, who develop it, apply it, and change it sometimes radically, over time.

In this conception, the ideology is independent of the interests with which it is "associated," though not so independent as to be altogether distinct. Dependence and independence operate both on an ideal level and on a social level. At the ideal level, the body of ideas, the textual tradition, once constituted has a "life of its own" in the sense that people using it experience it as capable of going against the interests, and even of reshaping them. What gives ideology its particular character is the tension between group commitment—with its elements of psychological identification, shared feelings and wants, and self-conscious solidarity—and these requirements or directions or suggestions of the body of texts.

At the social level, the group that develops the ideology, the intelligentsia, is always ambivalently related to the larger group that has the interests. It has its own interests that arise from the position of ideological developer, and these can conflict with the general interest of the group.

These intelligentsia interests may themselves be ideologized (the intelligentsia may see itself as having a loyalty to "truth" that is fully independent of any loyalty to group interests as perceived by others).

They may also be classic examples of "selfish" interests, like that in the power within the group that the intelligentsia obtains by virtue of its monopoly of the universalization project, or in privileges that the society grants to intellectuals at the expense of others, including those who share the ideological commitment or the group interest in question.

An ideology is a "project," in the sense defined above. It is not just a translation of interests into another medium. Rather, it is a mediation between interests and universal claims. People's understanding of their interests comes about in the context of universalization into ideology, as well as vice versa, so ideology can shape interests, as well as vice versa. Ideology is not a superstructure responding to interests that are "materially based" or otherwise just "given," nor is it a "pure" domain of ideas.

In this conception, one may be an ideologist without being rigid or doctrinaire, without understanding the ideology as "correct theory" in a scientistic manner, or being fanatical. One is an ideologist because one has made a commitment to working within a complex body of texts, a discourse, and accepted the blinders and limitations that inevitably go along with the advantages of such a commitment, and because the commitment to the texts goes along with, and sometimes conflicts with, a commitment to a group or groups in conflict with others.

The "interminable" character of ideological conflict

Ideologies exist not only in relation to group interests but also in relation to other ideologies. A defining characteristic of an ideology is that it is "contested." This means that there is more going on in a debate than a quarrel over the outcome of a particular interest conflict, and more also than a focused disagreement in which it is clear to the parties exactly what is at stake and how one might go about establishing the truth or falsity of a position. In ideological conflict, it is common to hear things like, "I disagree with everything you said; I disagree with your whole approach." Often the two sides will propose different criteria of truth and falsehood or of verification, so that it is hard to see how either side could possibly convince the other.

Because the contest of ideologies is "deep" in this sense, we experience it as interminable, at least in the sense that we think the opponents will go on arguing in complete good faith indefinitely. Each contender has sufficiently numerous and complex resources that it seems always possible to repair a damaged position by restatement. If the proponents are committed as well as in good faith, they will never have to admit final defeat, though the judgment of others may be that they have been decisively refuted. The line between a mere ideology and a cult or sect is as blurry as that between a mere ideology and the disinterested pursuit of knowledge.

The interminable conflict of ideologies at the discourse level is fueled by the interminable conflict between groups pursuing their interests at the practical level. The kind of ideological conflict we are interested in here is over the definition of legal rules. Whether the forum is an administrative agency, the legislature, or an appellate court, the goal is to achieve an outcome—a particular rule definition—and this outcome is a "stake."

Conflict over stakes is "institutionalized" in the sense that all the participants expect there will be an indefinitely extended series of such conflicts. The players will remain roughly the same (the opposing intelligentsias, rather than individual litigants), past debates and past outcomes are relevant to future ones, and when circumstances change, the intelligentsias will modify their positions to respond, without abandoning their projects altogether. The intelligentsia is a Neurathian "crew reconstructing the boat out in the ocean" or in a Lévi-Straussian "bricolage" situation. Except that there are several boats out in the ocean at the same time . . .

Ideological conflict versus dialogue and bargaining

Long-run ideological conflict over the stakes of rule definition therefore needs to be distinguished quite sharply from two other types of discursive situation. It is different from the notion of a Socratic dialogue and also from the notion of "arms-length" bargaining. In a dialogue, we imagine that the parties are interested *only* in deciding the truth of some question. In bargaining, we imagine that each party is interested in achieving the most favorable possible consensual division of an object of dispute, but *only* in order to avoid the bad consequences of failing to agree.

What long-term ideological conflict over stakes (legal rules) has in common with dialogue is that the parties have universalization projects, rather than merely raw demands for satisfaction of their interests. Each claims that the other ought to agree to its proposed rule definition because its definition is right in terms of a shared higher order set of norms. The difference is that both sides expect that a decision will be made—the stakes will be disposed, the rule defined one way or another—before there is a consensus on whose view of the truth of the matter is better. And each party believes that, at the practical level of the stakes in question in each particular dispute, its group's interests deserve protection *whether or not* it is possible to achieve consensus on the truth before a decision is made.

Because the stakes will probably be disposed without agreement of all affected, the ideological participants have an interest that is merely "strategic" from the point of view of the truth seeker. They enter in good faith into the dialogue trying to persuade and open to being persuaded, but they have to keep always in mind that they are responsible for the concrete interests of the groups they are representing. They need to win even when they can't persuade, rather than defining winning as persuading.

Ideological conflict shares with bargaining the situation of having to decide one way or the other, whether or not the parties can achieve consensus on what is right or fair, and therefore the element of the "strategic" (versus the dialogic). But in contrast with arms-length bargaining, the crucial fact of ideological conflict is the existence of neutrals and potential converts, whether in the electorate, legislature, administrative agency, jury, or judicial panel. The ideologists assume that over the long run the project will succeed or fail according to its ability to affect these "swing" people. In arms-length bargaining, we take it for granted that you know what your interests are and I know what mine are; in ideological dispute, each side tries to persuade some, "enough," of the others that what is involved is a misunderstanding rather than a "true" conflict of interests.

The very universalizing of ideological intelligentsias presupposes that something more than mere "settlement" is a possible outcome of the conflict. But it most definitely does not presuppose even the possibility of consensus. Indeed, the most common structure for ideological conflict in modern society seems to be that each side is internally heterogeneous, with its members arrayed on a spectrum from "completely closed to persuasion by the other side" to "practically no ideological loyalty at all," and that there is in most disputes a significant "center" that *defines* itself as ideologically neutral (of course, this turns out to be an ideology, too). Ideological conflict presupposes the possibility of persuasion but also, typically, the probability that when persuasion has proceeded a certain distance the definition of the rule, or indeed the overall shape of society, will be decided against the will of a large number of the participants in the society.

The subjects of ideologized group conflict over the definition of rules in our particular society

A list of the stakes of ideologized group conflict in appellate courts is a list of the claims of groups, cast in universal terms, that groups have tried to get resolved in their favor in the courts. There is no list of issues that are by their nature ideological or that are by their nature legal. The tentative list below of issues that are understood and argued this way is the product of the particular history of American society and American law. Although I've organized it into a typology, I don't mean it to be exhaustive; rather, it should be evocative of what "everyone" knows about American politics.

    1. The legal treatment of groups and their practices:
   (*a*) A status group is a group that is formally identified by law for different, inferior treatment, or whose former identification is understood to underlie nongovernmental discrimination. The issue is that of the boundaries of the domain of formal legal equality. It has to do with the preliberal hierarchical organization of society, and also with the use of the preliberal model to constitute new status groups.

     Some status groups of the old order were women, wives, children, servants, the insane, the poor, slaves, blacks, Native Americans, aliens, homosexuals, students, and indentured labor. Representatives of the formerly hierarchically inferior groups argue against "discrimination." They are answered in terms of "protection," or in terms of "difference" in the group that justifies different treatment, or in terms of the autonomy of the discriminators.

   (*b*) The issue of tolerance (cultural pluralism) has to do not with the legal treatment of groups but of practices, ideas, or behaviors that are important, sometimes even defining, for some group, but disapproved by others. Some examples are Mormon polygamy, German in the schools, bilingualism, cult child-rearing practices, homosexual acts, pornographic speech, abortion, and communist speech. The terms of argument are free speech and freedom of religion, assembly, association, privacy, and sometimes property, against the police power, national security, the state's interest in reproduction, and so on.

2. A second category of ideologized group conflict over the rules concerns the design of the market, bureaucratic (public and private) and family systems, and their impact on the relative bargaining power of groups, some of them holdovers of the old order.

(a) Capital against labor, men against women, black against white, disabled against abled, and so on.

(b) Consumer against seller (including landlord/tenant, malpractice, and many corporate conflicts between shareholders and financial and management interests).

(c) Environmental protection.

3. A third category has to do with the choice between authoritarian and participatory/therapeutic approaches to the exercise of legitimate authority within whatever framework is established in the above categories.

(a) Force against the body: capital punishment, wife and child abuse, corporal punishment in schools, forced labor, forced sterilization, blood transfusions and caesarian sections, body searches.

(b) Due process rules governing interactions between the government and citizens (when is there a right to a hearing, for example) with equivalent rules for private bureaucracies, such as employment at will, tenancy at will, parental discipline of children, labor participation in management decisions.

(c) Choices between retributive/deterrent and rehabilitative approaches to discipline in all contexts, from schools to business to family law to criminal law.

4. Finally, a fourth set of conflicts involve the rules that define collective decision-making procedures in public and private life. The question is the procedural legitimation of power, rather than the authoritarian or participatory/therapeutic mode of its exercise. The issues may arise on the grand scale of voting rights, federalism, and judicial review; at the level of corporate or union or workplace governance; or at the microlevel of compulsory terms in suburban subdivision association charters, condominium agreements, or family property arrangements.

Liberalism and conservatism

In general political debate, it is common to define liberalism and conservatism as preferences for a larger or a smaller role for "government." This definition isn't very helpful for understanding these ideologies in the appellate courts, because the courts have relatively little to do with many issues of governmental size that dominate in the legislatures, and because the issues they do address evoke a much more complex set of liberal and conservative positions.

American liberalism in the courts might be roughly defined as the project of eliminating status-based inequality, both in formal legal treatment and in private market treatment; promoting cultural pluralism (tolerance); promoting legal rules that increase the relative shares going to workers, other disfavored groups, consumers, and environment lovers, at the expense of the owners of enterprises; promoting a participatory/therapeutic framework for the exercise of legitimate authority; and promoting participatory conceptions of democracy. Conservatism means arguing for preserving the preliberal status distinctions, repressing various kinds of deviance, preserving or increasing the relative shares of enterprise owners in their dealings with workers, consumers, and environmentalists, defending authoritarian means in the exercise of authority, and resisting participatory conceptions of democracy in favor of established institutions.

Both liberalism and conservatism are ideologies because these quite concrete positions in group conflicts are backed up by more or less elaborate universalization projects, which allow advocates to claim that each of the more particular positions is an instance of correct application of general principles. The general theories can be roughly grouped as relying on rights, morality, and social welfare, and what is most striking about liberalism and conservatism is their virtually total agreement on what those principles are. Both sides favor majority rule, individual rights, and the rule of law; both embrace Judeo-Christian moral codes; both favor a regulated market economy with safety nets.

Both ideologies incorporate the same specific sets of standardized arguments in each of these modes but apply them differently. Chapter 6 introduces the legal versions of these "flippable" arguments.

In each substantive area, there are familiar symmetrical tensions within liberal and conservative positions:

1. Liberals favor formal equality of status, while conservatives argue that formal equality ignores real differences; but on racial, gender, and economic issues, liberals argue for "compensatory" status differentiation to promote substantive equality while conservatives focus on formal equality.

2. Liberals abhor paternalist justifications for status inequality and the repression of deviance, but they favor paternalist economic regulation; conservatives do just the opposite, favoring paternalism on social issues but rugged individualism in the market.

3. Liberals tend to favor legalism, technicality, and formality when assessing the actions of strong parties, while favoring paternalism, informality, permissiveness, and in general the participatory/therapeutic approach when dealing with "weak parties"; conservatives tend to do just the opposite, emphasizing the difficulties of the authority's job and the need for strictness for those they see as deviants.

4. Liberals deploy a populist, majoritarian, participatory rhetoric against "entrenched interests" of all kinds, while conservatives defend privilege; but, except in the case of private property, liberals also deploy an antimajoritarian rhetoric of individual rights, while conservatives argue for the "rights of the community" against deviants, except in the case of private property.

There is a kind of pyramid here:

1. At the level of specific conflicts, the two sides are opposed.

2. At an intermediate level, they each deploy arguments for and against equality, paternalism, the participatory/therapeutic approach, and majoritarianism. They cast these arguments for and against in virtually identical form; but on some issues conservatives deploy the pros, the liberals the cons, while on other issues the liberals are the pros and the conservatives the cons.

3. At the most abstract level, liberals and conservatives embrace the same abstract rights, morality, and social welfare premises.

The crucial part of the pyramid is the middle term. In disputes about what rules are best, a surprisingly small set of arguments makes up the whole lexicon, and these arguments get (a) used over and over again in one context after another, and (b) switched back and forth between liberals and conservatives. Of course, each particular rule conflict is different from every other one. An enormous amount of the discourse is concerned with figuring out just how this particularity should change the way the stereotyped argument comes out. But these very specific disputes, themselves interminable, play out within a strikingly stable, simple, large ideological framework.[3]

Epistemes, paradigms, contested concepts, and conceptions

Although it is interminable, I don't think it's helpful to describe the conflict between liberalism and conservatism as "epistemic,"[4] or a matter of "paradigms,"[5] just because so much is shared between the two sides. What is shared is, first, the abstract premises about majority rule, rights, and the rule of law and, second, the vast repertoire of rights, morality, and social welfare arguments about what particular definitions of rules are best. In epistemic conflict (or "paradigm" conflict) people talk past each other because they operate out of different "consciousnesses," each side "experiences a different world," in the strong sense of not having access to the world of the other. It's not just that they don't agree—they aren't "speaking the same language."

In liberal/conservative conflict, there is sometimes an experience of the interlocutor as "other" in a profound way, and the language of episteme, paradigm, and consciousness may be useful in capturing that experience. But it is not to be taken literally because it *is* possible (and it happens all the time) to "enter into" the world of the adversary, to grasp the "logic" of the position, and so on. Indeed, the more common experience is to know "exactly what they'll say" in response to one's own ideological statement, and to know also, one thinks, exactly why they'll say it.

Another problem with this way of looking at ideological dispute is that it puts the overwhelming emphasis on the cognitive dimension of conflict, to the neglect of the experience of collective commitment, group membership, and common purpose, that Sartre tried to get at through the ideas of the project and the "fused group." Liberals and conservatives do "see things differently," but they also "feel" different things and "want" different things. They "identify" with different real and imaginary groups. Although, I hasten to add, I don't mean to suggest that the domains of feeling and wanting and solidarity are different in kind because profoundly arational in a way cognition is not.

Indeed, I think one explanation of the popularity of epistemes and paradigms as accounts of human conflict comes from their promise that we can avoid experiencing the Other as different at the levels of feeling, wanting, and solidarity. Seeing the Other as cognitively different is easier than seeing the Other as different at levels simply beyond reason and even beyond communication through language. If you believe that cognition is potentially rational but everything else is arbitrary, the radically other

Other is terrifying because potentially evil (rather than someone who "just doesn't get it"), and can't be dealt with in case of disagreement except by force.

I don't think liberalism and conservatism are epistemes or paradigms, because they have wanting, feeling, and solidarity dimensions. But these are not outside discourse, and a good deal of ideologized group conflict consists of appeals to wants, feelings, and solidarity on the other side.

We can also capture something of the experience through W. B. Gallie's notion of a "contested concept" and Dworkin's reformulation of it as a "conception" of a concept.[6] The concepts include majority rule, rights, the rule of law, equality of opportunity, Judeo-Christian morality, and a regulated market with a safety net. A large part of the discourse is easy to interpret as conflict over how to interpret these abstractions, rather than over what normative premises to adopt in the first place.

But neither "contested concept" nor "conception" adequately describes ideology in the sense of liberalism and conservatism. First, they leave out the things that are experienced as otherness in the interlocutor—the very things grasped by the notion of an episteme or paradigm. Second, they are no better than episteme or paradigm at grasping the noncognitive dimension of conflict. Indeed, Gallie and her followers, including Dworkin, often seem to be attracted to the notion of the contested concept because it allows us to understand ideological conflict as a philosophical discussion (in the dialogue rather than the bargaining mode) gone wrong, rather than as some other kind of conflict.

Ontology of liberalism and conservatism

The fudged notion of a project may be preferable to the more precise terms paradigm, episteme, and conception, but it has its difficulties. The idea is that a person entering American political life finds it organized, loosely, into ideological intelligentsias, which are self-conscious groups that identify with particular interests, while proclaiming particular normative abstractions, and which have, historically, worked for the adoption of specific positions on issues that supposedly reflect both the interests and the universal norms. An ideological project so conceived is not reducible to any of its components: it is not just the abstract commitments, nor just the positions, nor just the list of people who have at one time or another called themselves liberals or conservatives, nor just the underlying group interests that get universalized.

The reason for refusing these reductions is that as a matter of common observation, and typically of what we commonly mean by ideology, there is neither a tight, compelling logical connection "downward" from the abstract norms to the particular positions and then to the group interests nor a tight, compelling connection "upward" from interests to positions to norms. At the social level, there is no algorithmic definition of what it means, in terms of adherence to principles or positions or in terms of group commitment, to "be" a liberal or a conservative. I will focus here on only one of these aspects, namely, the problem of the coherence of the abstract normative position and of the set of practical positions that supposedly flows from it.

Both the ideologies as systems of discourse, and the people who develop them to meet the endless flow of new issues, are open to critique as internally inconsistent or contradictory. While within each project there is a constant push to reconcile contradictions and develop theories of what makes or should make the ideologies internally coherent, there is no consensus either about how to do this or about whether it has been achieved.

In this situation it makes sense to ask what "determines" the liberal or the conservative position on a new issue, say, on campus hate speech. If each ideology employs the same abstract principles (rights, majority rule, the rule of law, Judeo-Christian morality, regulated market with safety nets), and each switches back and forth between a small set of lower-level arguments (such as those for and against paternalism), then it would appear that it will be an open question how to apply the ideology when a new case arises.

Unfortunately, this understates the difficulty in deciding what liberalism and conservatism "are." Not only do the sides switch back and forth, between, for instance, favoring formal or substantive equality on different issues (bedroom versus boardroom, for example), liberals and conservatives are also each committed to not "going too far" to the left or right.[7] Liberals carry their commitments to substantive economic equality and formal status equality only to a point, and at that point they quite abruptly "flip" and rejoin their adversaries in the name of moderation.

They begin to speak of children, for instance, in a rhetoric that is paternalist and sentimental rather than rights oriented and egalitarian, and of the dangers of "leveling," or "class war," or even mere "redistribution" in economic policy. At this point they sound like conservatives, except that they "draw the line" further to the left. Conservatives are the same on the other side: at some point, when the safety net has been, from the liberal point of view, all but abolished, conservatives draw back from the abyss and adopt the very welfare state rhetoric they have been busily denouncing as crypto-communist.

As a result, two kinds of potential incoherence constantly threaten each camp: there is (a) the problem of reconciling positions in different domains (for conservatives, their antipaternalist economic rhetoric with their paternalist social issue rhetoric), and (b) the problem of explaining, within a given domain, why they draw a particular line rather than "take the position to its logical extreme" (for liberals, why they don't favor the outright redistribution of wealth, for example).

For the observer/theorist (me) who wants to use liberalism and conservatism as interpretive tools in constructing an account of how adjudication works and what effects it has, the vulnerability of the two ideologies to the charge of incoherence poses a classic methodological problem. One of the meanings of mpm is a preference for one type of solution over another.

I doubt that there are "true," coherent versions of liberalism and conservatism for use in analyzing what lies "behind" the "objective" or "impersonal" rhetoric of judges. While it is always possible that liberal and conservative theorists will find (or have already found without my knowing it) abstract formulations that would allow us to speak of the ideologies as "requiring" this or that position on a particular issue, this seems highly improbable to me. So how can I use liberalism and conservatism as elements, as conceptual tools for understanding adjudication, if my own view is that each, when viewed as a "philosophy," is an internally contradictory hodgepodge?

I am equally skeptical about coherent, operational definitions of liberalism and conservatism "from the outside," that is, using external factors, like the supposed objective interests of particular groups or the supposed rational implications of particular (coherent) premises. Such definitions allow the outside observer to categorize motives or actions, for his or her own purposes, as ideological or not, and then as liberal or conservative, without referring to the contested dimension of internal coherence. But an external definition is unlikely to be useful for our purposes because we are interested in the very phenomena of self-consciousness, phenomena like denial, that external definitions try to avoid.

To treat the ideologies as "projects" is to acknowledge or assert the incoherence of their theory components, hoping that we will nonetheless be able to distinguish liberalism and conservatism for our particular purposes because there are factors other than internal coherence that "stabilize" them. By a "stabilizer" I mean something that contributes to our sense that we are talking meaningfully when we say that someone "is" a liberal, or that a position "is" liberal, or that "liberals, but not conservatives, face a hard choice on a particular issue." The basic idea is that the project is an entity stable enough to be useful in analysis because it is more than a theory: it is also a self-conscious group activity with a history and a practical dimension.

Some of the stabilizers that allow us to think we know what we are talking about when we talk about liberalism and conservatism are the following:

1. Self-conscious consensus: it's liberal to come out a particular way on a new issue if liberals say it's liberal, and we are reassured if conservatives say it's liberal too.

2. History: it's a liberal position if people who called themselves liberal thought at some point in the past that it was entailed by liberal premises and incorporated it into their program as such.

3. Structural position vis-à-vis alternatives: it's liberal if it is situated between a well-defined conservative position and equally well defined communist or anarchist positions; it's conservative if it is situated between a well-defined liberal position and fascist or ultra–free market positions.

4. Local coherence: it's liberal if it is so close to a lot of similar, well-defined liberal positions that it would be bizarre to go the other way, given how much is settled in the vicinity.

I hope it's obvious that I'm not claiming anything faintly "scientific" or "objective" about this way of using the terms "ideology," "liberalism," and "conservatism." There will be plenty of room for disagreement, after meticulous application of all the tests I've laid out, about whether any particular person or position is one thing or the other. But I do want to claim that the general notion of a project, and the particular elements I've specified, fit the common usage of the three terms in present-day American political culture.

More important, when members of the liberal and conservative ideological intelligentsias elaborate, to different ends, their common commitment to the rule of law, they routinely contrast "legality," as a motive for decision, with "ideology." When they do so, I think they mean ideology in the sense I've been developing here. In other words, my claim is to have given a kind of anthropologist's description of the typical usage of a culturally significant term.

Finally, I think that liberalism and conservatism, so defined, are sufficiently powerful as analytic tools to make it worthwhile to use them myself in trying to understand how our particular social order works. It's not just a question of the anthropologist learning the way words are used in the local culture. As a participant, as an ideologist, albeit neither a liberal nor a conservative, I orient my practical, programmatic activities on the basis of predictions: the liberals will do this, the conservatives will do that. For purposes of social theory, in this book I think it useful to try to figure out how the institution of adjudication functions on the terrain of ideology thus defined.

Ideological preferences

A liberal or conservative ideological preference is a tendency to choose legal rules associated with liberalism or conservatism. A preference may be obvious or hard to discern, it may be acknowledged or denied, and it may be conscious, unconscious, or half-conscious. A preference, in common usage, is more than a factual pattern (though sometimes economists use it in this very limited sense). When we impute a preference, we suppose we are giving an explanation or an interpretation of patterned action, by attributing it to a psychological disposition of the actor.

When we are inquiring into the existence of a preference in this psychological sense, we consider past choices among what we think were alternative possible legal rules, and we also use the evidence of the judge's choice among available argument-bites or rhetorical tropes that have ideological connotations. As I will argue in Chapter 6, there are legal arguments that directly or analogically translate general political into legal discourse. The rhetoric of self-reliance is conservative; that of sharing, liberal. The rhetoric of self-realization is liberal; that of communal authority, conservative. These are markers from which we infer ideological preferences.

When we believe that a judge has an ideological preference, say, for liberal or conservative rule choices, we often speak of "ideological motives" for and "ideological influence" on particular outcomes. I use these expressions with some misgivings, because they are ambiguous in two ways. First, they indicate that an actor has a preference or predisposition to choose the outcomes that are associated with an ideology, but do not indicate an internal commitment to the ideology as a project. Second, "motive" and "influence" can be established only by interpretive procedures, rather than proved or substantiated through more positive methodologies.

While a pattern of liberal outcomes can be "proven" if we have a sufficiently tight definition of liberalism, the imputed preference or disposition or "sympathy" cannot. But proof is also unnecessary for the purposes of this particular inquiry. People impute "ideological motives" to actors all the time, in the sense of preferences. In fact, a "hermeneutic of suspicion," or search for the hidden ideological motives in judicial opinions that present themselves as technical, deductive, objective, impersonal, or neutral, has been for a hundred years the most important characteristic of American debates about adjudication.

In legal discourse, the evidence for the imputation is almost never a "smoking gun" in the sense of an admission of intent. In judicial opinions, judges *always* "deny," in the common sense of the term, that they are acting out of ideological motives. That is, they explicitly claim that the outcome, their disposition of the stakes of law by choosing one particular resolution of a question of law, of rule definition, rather than another, was reached by following impersonal interpretive procedures that exclude the influence of their personal ideologies. This is obviously a matter of convention and tells us little about what is "really" going on.

In most cases, the only basis for imputing preference, motive, or influence is "interpretive," meaning that the opinion makes more sense if we interpret it as ideologically motivated than it does if we take it at face value. You can't "prove" that it makes more sense; you can only argue your interpretation by showing that the opinion is contradictory or inconclusive when taken on its own terms, but seems at least intelligible if not persuasive when understood in terms of ideological preferences. There is no attempt to show by direct evidence what the judge was thinking. It is a question not of proof but of the plausibility of a "reading."

The other ambiguity in the notion of an ideological motive concerns the degree of commitment implied by the term. I asserted, many years ago, that Sir William Blackstone had an "apologetic motive" in describing the English legal system. Some readers inferred that I was arguing a conspiracy theory of the type that liberal and conservative theorists have often detected in Marxist accounts of capitalist institutions. I was perhaps arguing that legal discourse was a deliberate mystification, cloaking a capitalist ideological agenda in neutral terminology in order to mislead the masses about what was really going on.[8]

But one can identify an ideological preference, or motive, or influence, without asserting that the actor subscribes to the ideology in question as a project, in the sense of having an inner commitment to it as something to further or defend against its opponents. The preference, inferred from the actions that it motivates or influences, is no more than a predisposition in the making of choices in particular cases. A particular actor might be accurately described as much more than predisposed in choice situations— as a true believer, for example, or an "ideologue," or someone who is "politically correct"—but that would require a lot more evidence and of a different kind than just a pattern of outcomes and the use of ideologically identifiable argument-bites.

In Chapter 8 I offer an account of judicial behavior that suggests that the best way to understand ideological preferences in judicial conduct is as half-conscious or in Sartrean "bad faith." Again, I think the idea of a half-conscious disposition—one that is "denied," in Anna Freud's sense, by the judge to him- or herself, rather than either "repressed" outright or consciously conspiratorial—fits the commonsense usage of American political discourse. We speak of a judge's liberal or conservative ideological "bias" in just this sense of half-conscious orientation. And we don't think it necessary to "substantiate" the imputation except through the interpretive technique described above.[9]

Liberalism capitalized

The abstract normative part of Liberalism capitalized, that is, of the larger unit that includes liberalism and conservatism, is made up of the theoretical commitments that liberals and conservatives share, including rights, majority rule, the rule of law, Judeo-Christian morality, and a regulated market economy with safety nets. But the Liberal center also defines itself by semiotic contrast to its "opposite numbers," communism and anarchism on the left and fascism and Manchesterism on the right.

We can and will look at the effects of the institution of adjudication (judicial law making in a condition of contest about the role of ideology in the process) on the political conflict between liberals and conservatives. But the institution, thus contested, also has at least putative effects on the conflict between the liberal/conservative "center," the larger party of Liberalism, the party of "moderation" in the modern West, and the whole spectrum of outlying, more radical, left and right ideologies.

I will not use the term "ideology" to describe Liberalism because I want to reserve it for the more specific universalization projects—liberalism, conservatism, communism, anarchism, fascism, Manchesterism, feminism, and nationalism—that are commonly denoted by the term in American political discourse. I am going to be arguing, first, that the central problem for theories of adjudication in the United States is that of its relationship to ideology in this sense (Part Two) and, second, for a particular response to that problem (Part Three). Referring to Liberalism as an ideology risks confusion of this discussion, both because American political discourse does not treat Liberalism as an ideology (indeed, it is often understood to be the opposite of an ideology), and because the ideological analysis of Liberalism plays such an important part in the very different neo-Marxist theorization I will discuss in Chapter 11.

Is there a critical position "outside ideology"?

Of course not. I approach this study from my own left/mpm ideological point of view, with the blinders that go with that position. That doesn't make it impossible to communicate with people occupying other positions, since as I've been saying ideological conflict has elements of the dialogical, is not epistemic, and doesn't presuppose that one's interlocutor is irremediably the creature of, say, class position.

The stakes of ideological intelligentsias in appellate adjudication

My goal in the rest of this chapter is to distinguish the various kinds of stakes that ideological intelligentsias perceive in adjudication, and to justify their preoccupation with judicial rule making against various kinds of skepticism about its importance.

They care about particular rules both because rules forbid and require conduct that has intrinsic ideological significance, and because rules figure as "rules of the game" in cooperation and conflict over the production and distribution of the good things of life.[10] They also care about the judiciary as a forum in which they pursue their discursive project by trying to persuade judges to be liberals or conservatives, with the hope that to the extent they are successful judges of their persuasion will influence the general public to be more liberal or conservative. I think it is worthwhile to take these distinctions apart into quite small pieces.

Intrinsic versus instrumental ideological interests in the content of legal rules

First, the rules of law—the formal contents of the legal system—affect behavior that is good or bad; right, wrong, or indifferent; and fair or unfair, all according to one's ideological position. Liberals and conservatives view laws about strikes, abortion, government support for the arts, and thousands more issues this way. When the legal stakes in an appellate lawsuit include the choice between definitions of a rule of law, and the rule choice concerns behavior about whose value there is ideological disagreement, then the legal stakes are also ideological stakes. I call these stakes the "intrinsic" interest in the rules.

Second, the rules of law affect behavior in ways that in turn indirectly affect the distribution of the good things of life *other than compliance or noncompliance* with the rule in question, good things of life whose distribution is a matter of ideological dispute. The intelligentsias view rules about, say, the regulation of truck weight on interstate highways as important because of their impact on the relations among different industries, consumers, and taxpayers. We care about these rules less as "norms of conduct" than as "rules of the game" of economic or gender or racial or regional conflict. The rules affect outcomes that ideological intelligentsias care about by changing the balance of power between groups, their ability to get more or less for themselves in their relations of conflict and cooperation in the production of everything from steel to domestic life. I call this set of concerns the "instrumental" interest in the rules.[11]

These two ways of looking at rules are not mutually exclusive. One can analyze the law of strikes from the point of view of the morality or immorality of striking or from the point of view of the effect of legalizing strikes on the distribution of surplus between labor and capital. It has been common to classify rules according to whether they "are" of one or another kind—so that some crimes are malum in se, others malum prohibitum, some rules are based on natural rights, others on what Blackstone called "the convenience of civil society" and what today might be called "policy," some rules aim at compliance for its own sake (criminal and injunctive sanctions), others merely attach legally defined prices to conduct (damages). I am proposing not a classification of rules but a classification of ideological motives for interest in particular rules.

Sometimes it is clear that the actual motive of the rule maker was of one type and not the other. Members of parliament required the eating of fish on Friday to promote the fishing industry, and indirectly Britain's military sea power, rather than because they believed that it was intrinsically wrong to eat meat on that particular day. In the extreme case of rules of a game, the definition of the rules has absolutely no intrinsic moral or rights or utility significance: the height of the hoop in basketball, whether a pawn can take diagonally. At the other extreme, we wouldn't endorse the permission of murder even if it were shown that the murder rate wouldn't change and that there would be a large, desirable increase in the equality of the distribution of wealth.

This distinction between motives does not correspond to that between utilitarianism and rights or morality as normative criteria. One can care about a rule seen as a norm of conduct because one judges it bad according to utilitarian ethics, and one can disapprove of the distributive consequences of a rule seen as a "rule of the game" because, say, it leads to homelessness, which violates people's right to shelter or is otherwise immoral social policy.[12]

When we look at legal rules intrinsically, it is natural to ask questions about compliance and to see norms that achieve high levels as "more successful" than ones that don't. When we look at legal rules as rules of the game or instrumentally, we ask about how this definition of the rule, as opposed to some variant, would affect the distribution of good things not just between victim and violator, but among all the people who will be affected overall by the change in behavior. We ask questions like, how will deregulation affect airline prices and levels of service? The issue of compliance comes up not to measure the success of the rule but as part of the calculus of effects. A littering prohibition that significantly reduces littering—even if it is obvious that people continue to litter all the time and that an individual litterer doesn't see the legal prohibition as likely to ever be applied to him—can be a big success.

Against rule skepticism

Both kinds of interest in rules depend on two important presuppositions. First, we assume that it is possible to know what the rules of law *are,* both in the sense of identifying them and in the sense of understanding how they are supposed to affect behavior when we apply them. Second, we assume that the legal rules do in fact affect behavior, in two ways: by influencing "coercively," that is, by changing the "price" of conduct; and by influencing through "legitimation," that is, by changing people's behavior not through modifying the state-imposed price of conduct but by inducing change in people's valuation of conduct, making them think things are bad or wrong that they previously thought were good or right, and vice versa.

I think both presuppositions are plausibly accurate, and as an observer/activist I use them in my own political assessments. This means that I don't find legal realist rule skepticism convincing, *if* it is (fancifully) interpreted to mean that the meanings of rules are *necessarily* so indeterminate in practice that it isn't possible for actors and observers to predict accurately what they are and how they will be applied in particular cases. Like the other crits who have worked on the internal critique of legal reasoning, I've argued all along that legal rules *can be* easy to identify as "valid" and easy to apply across a vast range of cases.[13] Indeed, we have made from the beginning an even more extravagant claim. It is often possible to predict with at least tolerable accuracy how the choice of one rule over another possibility will affect the behavior and the interests of large numbers of people, including many who will never have the occasion either to obey or disobey it.[14]

It is because they are usually knowable (we can identify which ones are "valid"), because we can usually apply them ourselves in ways that we anticipate will correspond exactly to the way others will apply them, and because we can predict their consequences for various conflicting interests, that we see rules as disposing of the ideological stakes of law. At the same time, the whole point of the critique has been the claim that in many cases in which the ideological stakes are high, legal actors have had a choice between two (or more) interpretations or definitions of a particular rule, and that the choice has had the effect of disposing of the ideological stakes.

For the moment, it is enough to define having a choice to mean that knowledgeable observers attached, *before the fact,* a substantial probability to each of two ideologically opposed alternative rule definitions, or that, though each put a very high probability on one rule winning rather than the other, they disagreed about which that would be. I say "for the moment," because Part Three addresses the subjective or phenomenological aspect of this situation. Because ideological intelligentsias understand the outcomes (rule definitions) as in this limited sense indeterminate, they invest enormous resources in trying to influence them, and it seems worthwhile for people like me to try to figure out how the judges actually decide.

Rules, not rule application

Out of an excess of caution let me reiterate that I am here discussing the choice between rules of law and the effects on ideologized group conflict of such choices. It is easy to confuse the choice between rules of law with the choice between "outcomes" in the conventional sense of "who won" (as between the litigating parties). Liberal and conservative ideological intelligentsias sometimes care about who wins a lawsuit because the lawsuit itself, the final judgment, will dispose significant stakes. For example, a single lawsuit that stops the construction of a nuclear power plant may be important ideologically, even if the basis for stopping construction is so idiosyncratic to the facts of the particular case that it is unlikely that any rule laid down in the case will be important in any future environmental conflict.

But I deal here with ideological interest in the way *rules* affect the interests of *groups*. Who wins a particular lawsuit may be insignificant from this point of view, even if the parties are unquestionably members of the groups in question, and even if the suit disposes important stakes as between the parties. The lawsuit is of interest for my analysis only if it is important beyond the interests of the parties, because in the course of it a judge makes a decision defining a rule in a way that predictably affects ideologized group conflict for the future.

It is often roughly accurate to distinguish between a rule and its application, meaning by "application" the decision whether the factual predicates in the rule that trigger the rule's sanction actually occurred. Did the defendant strike the plaintiff, or was the defendant somewhere else at the time? Where application means fact finding in this straightforward way, application will have ideological significance only where the intelligentsias anticipate that fact finding is a matter of choice, in the sense of being open to ideological "bias." This is especially likely in cases with "mixed questions of law and fact" (was the defendant negligent?). Juries in rape trials may tend over a large number of cases to reason along highly predictable ideological lines in deciding whether there was "force" or "consent."

This book doesn't deal with the disposition of ideological stakes through the application of valid, open textured standards of this kind. It is about the ideologically motivated choice *among* standards, or the ideologically motivated choice to modify an open textured standard like "consent" in order to change outcomes in an ideologized group conflict, by presuming force unless there has been an affirmative indication of consent, for example. In other words, it is about adjudication of questions of law, under the final authority of appellate courts.

When there are a number of possible legal rules that a court might adopt to resolve an uncertainty in the law revealed in a particular case, more than one of these may result in the particular defendant losing. From the defendant's point of view, it makes no difference which of these turns out to be valid law for the future. But from the point of view of the intelligentsias, that choice may be so important that liberals can in one sense "win" even though the litigant who represented their interests loses. For example, the court may define a particular police search as consensual and admit the evidence, while enunciating a standard (say, requiring disclosure of their motive) that is more favorable to defendants than an alternative that might well have been adopted.

Validity and prediction

I am worried that the reader may think that this approach to the ideological stakes of law depends on a controversial definition of "law." I don't think this is so. I would like my theory of ideology in adjudication, presented in Part Three, to be intensely controversial but effective in part because constructed of commonplace plausible elements. To this end, let me reiterate my definition of "validity." What I mean by a "legal rule" is a rule that is "valid" in the *very* limited sense of being agreed by just about everyone to be in force, meaning in force in the *very* limited sense of expected by just about everyone to be applied by the top court in a jurisdiction when lawyers argue it to that court. I am quite sure that there are such rules, as for example that in Massachusetts you can't vote until you are eighteen (an easy case), and that past consideration is generally not effective to make a promise binding (a harder case). This is just "what I mean" by "legal rules," the delimitation of a field of study, rather than an attempt to solve a problem of legal philosophy.

My notion is that if we restrict ourselves to rules that are pretty clearly valid in this sense, we will have a large set with massive consequences, and plenty to do without even considering situations in which it is not clear what rule is valid—until, that is, we try to figure out how new rules get validated ("made") in such situations. When we take up that question, we will abandon prediction theories for the obvious reason that judges don't decide what the rules are by predicting what they will decide the rules are.[15]

The effect of rules on conduct

As to the effect of valid legal rules on conduct, my notion is that it is an empirical question, since it is obvious that a rule can be valid but unenforced, and even that there can exist highly effective (on conduct) rules that flatly contradict the legal rule that purports to cover the situation in question. Nonetheless, it is possible to generalize about how valid legal rules influence what goes on in the world. The choice of a legal rule may influence conduct by fixing in one way or another "costs" or "benefits" as consequences to particular conduct. Social actors seem sometimes to modify their behavior on the basis of a prediction theory of what the courts will do in fact. And they may be "bad men" as well, meaning that they obey rules only to the extent that the anticipated costs and benefits of obeying, in a short-run, individualistic, amoral calculus, exceed the costs and benefits of disobeying.

Normative effects

But social actors also seem to respond to enactment or validity in a quite different way. They undergo "normative effects." First, it seems reasonable to assume that if they believe it to be "the law," some people are more likely to obey a given rule that they disagree with, or that costs them something to comply with, than they would if they believed they were facing identical practical sanctions applied extralegally. Some large number of people believe that one "ought to" obey the law even if it is most definitely not in one's interest to obey and even if one disagrees with the law. I take it that consequently they sometimes do obey against their interests and in spite of disagreement, where they would not obey a norm they believed not to be enacted as law. This is the "obedience effect" of validity.

Second, it seems reasonable to assume that when American judges make law, people tend to conform their normative views to the norm declared by the judges. Some people, at least, believe that if the law requires something, that is in itself an argument for agreeing with the requirement. A valid judicial declaration, in this view, has two quite different political effects: it invokes the norm of obedience to law, and it induces a change in the audience's idea of what it is "right" to do or not do—it has a "conversion effect."

Do these effects exist in fact? Have they been, or could they be, demonstrated empirically? These are open questions, to which I will devote some attention in Chapter 11. But I don't think it is in doubt that the participants in past and present debates take for granted, perhaps mistakenly,[16] that they are, if not real, at least sufficiently plausible so that something more than the predictions of "bad men" is at stake in theoretical discussions of adjudication. Without trying to answer the factual question about the reality of the effects, it may be helpful to flesh out the hypothesis of their existence in order to make it more plausible that they have been a major factor, though only implicitly, in the discussion.

For some part of the audience, according to the common understanding, the effects are independent of whatever is said in justification of the legal result. They come just from reading about the outcome in the paper, without knowing anything at all about how the court justified its declaration of what the law is. A famous historical incident has been taken to instantiate the obedience effect. In the Pullman strike of 1895, the railroad obtained, in an atmosphere of intense polarization and potential violence, a lower-court injunction against virtually all concerted activities the workmen were carrying out. The workmen obeyed the injunction, without the slightest knowledge of its (technically highly questionable) basis in legal reasoning, and, to the astonishment and delight of conservative opinion, simply "went home."

The conversion effect of validity is taken to operate, for part of the audience, in the same "blind" way—that is, people come to believe in the moral or political or social rightness of a norm just because it has been promulgated as law, without regard to the reasons offered. But conversion effects are less "all or nothing" than obedience effects. You either obey or you don't, but you can disobey and still undergo the conversion effect. It may still "work," even though the person in question is clear in his or her mind that the new rule is wrong, by weakening that belief. The effect may weaken belief simply by showing that what seemed obvious is in fact controversial (the Supreme Court disagrees with me), or by making belief more fragile (if the Supreme Court disagrees, maybe I'm wrong), or by opening the way to a future change (now I see what they were driving at), and so on. Note that both obedience and conversion effects, as I've defined them, are independent of what the judges say in explanation of their rule choices.

Summary of rule stakes

Ideological intelligentsias have interests in appellate adjudication because appellate judges define rules in situations where (*a*) their decision is not predictable in advance with certainty on the basis of professional legal knowledge, and (*b*) the choice of a rule will dispose significant ideological stakes. Rules dispose significant ideological stakes either intrinsically or instrumentally. In either case, the nature and size of the stakes are dependent on our hypotheses about the effects of the rule in question on conduct. Rules affect conduct both by affecting prices for bad men working on a prediction theory of law and by normative effects, which induce changes in conduct by inducing blind obedience or blind normative conversion to the rightness of the valid.

Before taking up ideological stakes in appellate adjudication as it functions as a "forum" for ideological conflict, I want to contrast this more positivist part of the theory with the "dispute-resolution" approach to the sociology of law. It seems necessary to justify my focus on appellate adjudication—and I mean justify it rather than apologize for it—because the American tradition in the sociology of law has made it a point of pride to downplay its significance in favor of what trial courts, juries, lawyers, and private parties do as legal actors.[17]

Rule stakes versus dispute resolution

Karl Llewellyn put the argument this way:

> What, then, is this law business about? It is about the fact that our society is honeycombed with disputes. Disputes actual and potential: disputes to be settled and disputes to be prevented; both appealing to law, both making up the business of law. But obviously those which most violently call for attention are the actual disputes, and to these our first attention must be directed. Actual disputes call for somebody to do something about them. First, so that there may be peace, for the disputants; for other persons whose ears and toes disputants are disturbing. And secondly, so that the dispute may really be put at rest, which means, so that a solution may be achieved which, at least in the main, is bearable to the parties and not disgusting to the lookers-on. This doing of something about disputes, this doing of it reasonably, is the business of law. And the people who have the doing in charge, whether they be judges or sheriffs or clerks or jailers or lawyers, are officials of the law. *What these officials do about disputes is, to my mind, the law itself.*[18]

The modest version of the dispute-resolution idea is that "disputes happen" and that the legal system at least sometimes "functions" to resolve them. The modest version adds that if they weren't resolved by something like the legal system, all kinds of bad consequences would follow, like private violence. But the idea is often more reified and abstract than that— it just "is" a social function to resolve disputes and "all societies" have such mechanisms, and dispute resolution just "is" "the" function of a legal system; performing the function is therefore a "good thing," as well as a good explanation of a practice. I will not go into the critique either of sociological functionalism or of the choice of dispute resolution as "the" function of a legal system.[19] All I want to do here is to distinguish this approach from the "distributive" one I will be pursuing.

The sociological approach starts from the fact that society is "honeycombed" with disputes between individuals, hypostasizes the function of resolving them, and asks how it is performed. The distributive approach starts from the fact of ideologized group conflict and asks how it is affected by legal institutions. These approaches seem likely to produce quite different research focuses.

A sociologist interested in how American society performs the universal function of dispute resolution might well decide to ignore the appellate judicial process. Appellate courts, after all, actually consider an infinitesimally small proportion even of disputes that are conceptualized by someone as "legal." When they do consider disputes, it isn't always easy to see how they are "resolving" them in Llewellyn's sense of achieving "peace" that is "bearable" to the parties and "not disgusting to the lookers-on." Certainly there is nothing in the reports of appellate decisions that tells us anything one way or another about whether they lead to peace that was bearable to the disputants and not disgusting to the lookers-on.

It seems plausible that if one eliminated appellate courts altogether, so that all judgments of trial courts were final, there would be neither more nor fewer disputes, in the sociologist's sense, than there are now. It seems implausible to me that there would be a decrease in the abstract value of peace that dispute resolution supposedly preserves, and even more implausible that because the function was "not performed" the society would disintegrate into private violence. If one is interested in the actual performance of the function of dispute resolution, it makes much more sense to do as Sally Merry and Barbara Yngvesson have done,[20] and ask Llewellyn's questions about a local court system, including all its varied personnel, that serves an identifiable community.

My choice to focus on appellate decisions reflects, of course, my own specialization as a teacher of legal doctrine to law students in a law school. But that activity is itself a product of a view about what is socially important about law, rather than being a merely accidental situation. As a person approaching legal dispute resolution institutions with a distributive focus, I find them of interest for two reasons, each of which leads to studying the appellate process. First, legal dispute resolution institutions, at least in common law countries (more on this later), affect ideologized group conflict by producing rules that govern the conduct of people *who do not engage in disputes.*

In other words, these institutions perform a "function" quite different from the one allocated them by sociological theory, the function of producing formal law, mainly through the appellate process. Judge-made formal law is interesting for the same reason that law produced in legislatures or administrative agencies or referendums is interesting. Formal law, it seems reasonable to assume, affects ideologized group conflict through the mechanisms I have described: it disposes of ideological stakes, both intrinsic stakes in the content of norms and instrumental stakes in the distributive effects of rules. But it is interesting for another reason as well: exactly because it differs from legislation in the particular that judges operate under a duty of fidelity to the materials and make law in bad faith (the hypothesis of alienated powers).

The U.S. Supreme Court's decision in Brown v. Board of Education is of interest to a distributivist first of all because it was an attempt to use the federal government to abolish school segregation. Of course, there was a dispute in the case that was "resolved" in some sense. But it is more important that the rule-making activity of a so-called dispute-resolution institution that denies its own political role generated a whole generation's worth of disputes (they still continue) about compliance with the rule change and about what desegregation means. It is still more important that out of this series of disputes there emerged new norms of conduct with respect to "discrimination" and a dramatic series of indirect effects on the distribution of the good things of life between and within racial groups.

Second, dispute-resolution institutions are important because they have part of the responsibility for enforcing formal law—that is, for making sure that the prices law attaches to choices in order to influence the predictions of bad men and thereby influence their conduct will actually have to be paid. The "lower" levels of the system do the actual enforcing, so that the distributive approach suggests an interest in the way they translate formal law into law in action, at the trial-court level and especially at the level of "bargaining in the shadow of the law," in Robert Mnookin and Lewis Kornhauser's phrase.[21] But this is interest in a specific subset of compliance issues: those in which there are ideological stakes.

What counts, if we are interested in dispute-resolution institutions from the distributive point of view, is not whether the institutions successfully or unsuccessfully "cool out" conflicts between particular parties, or whether they "reasonably" settle quarrels, or even whether they do so through ideologically contestable uses of discretion. One thing that does count is the extent to which they generate ideologically patterned noncompliance (particularly by the vast numbers of people who never get involved in lawsuits) that leads to different distributions between groups than would have occurred had there been compliance.[22] We are interested in "nullification" or the "implementation problem." Another is the extent to which ideologically patterned rule application disposes significant stakes not effectively disposed by the choice at the appellate level of a rule to apply (negligence, consent in rape cases).

For example, Marc Galanter's classic study, "Why the 'Haves' Come Out Ahead,"[23] shows how the "valid" procedural rules and informal institutional practices of trial and appellate courts lead to a systematic bias in favor of litigants from some groups (repeat player institutions, the "haves") and against litigants from other, weaker groups (have-nots). The implicit contrast is with a system with the same "substantive" rules about who can do what to whom in civil society but with an enforcement system in which people from different groups have more equal resources. The article convincingly argues that these procedural rules, viewed instrumentally rather than intrinsically, dispose important stakes in ideologized group conflict (conflict between the groups represented generally by liberals and those represented generally by conservatives).

But to understand how lower-level dispute-processing institutions dispose ideological stakes, one needs a good deal of understanding of the appellate level. This morning, for example, the *Boston Globe* carried a front-page story headlined "Female Athletes Gain in Legal Game," with this lead: "After decades of second-class citizenship, women's varsity sports are speeding down the road to equality, propelled by a series of successful lawsuits."[24]

According to the story, schools are currently increasing the resources devoted to women's sports, but athletes and advocates say they will have "to keep the pressure on if they are to achieve full equity, because the government has been ineffective in enforcing the law" (defined as "the requirements of Title IX, the 1972 law that mandates equality in education") "and because there is a growing backlash among male athletes." Before the settlement of a recent suit, a Court of Appeals decision "upheld the government's three part test for equality of participation," and this has "prodded colleges across the nation into action."[25]

To understand how a fraction of the liberal intelligentsia managed here to achieve its objective (cast in the universalizing language of "equity" and opposition to "second-class citizenship") one needs to understand the role of the appellate court in suddenly giving a doubtless ideologically contestable meaning (the three-part test) to the twenty-year-old legislative mandate of "equality" in education. Of course one also needs to understand the roles of lay advocates, lawyers, an administrative agency, and the trial courts.

I am happy to concede that a person with an interest in ideologized group conflict has many reasons to study dispute-resolution institutions other than appellate courts, and that we can't understand the disposition of stakes through formal law without understanding enforcement. But I do think it strange for sociologists of law to assume they can understand the phenomenon of dispute resolution as a whole without some take on how the formal rules of the legal system come into being.

Adjudication as a forum of ideology

Ideological intelligentsias would be "interested" in appellate adjudication even if judges made rules by tossing coins, for the simple reason that these coin tosses would dispose of significant stakes. And they would be interested if the judges made the rules, once someone had identified what *looked like* a gap, conflict, or ambiguity, by applying a method that was "objective" in the sense of demonstrable or algorithmic. But their interest is of a different character. It is based on the commonsense notion that the very ideological positions they represent are actually or potentially present, denied, within the decision process itself. Adjudication is a forum of ideology (rather than "the" forum of principle, as we'll see).

A central idea in what follows is that judicial opinions, and the arguments of lawyers that precede them, are ideological documents, or texts, by virtue of their content, as well as by virtue of the ideological stakes disposed by the rules they make. Liberals and conservatives, among others, care about appellate adjudication because it is one of the places where they pursue their respective projects of converting enough neutrals and enough weakly committed opponents so that they can enact their program as law, and one of the places where they try to make their ideological positions "hegemonic."

"They" are the members of the legal intelligentsia who identify with the general liberal and conservative ideological intelligentsias: lawyers, judges, and legal academics who participate in the organized legal discourse that explains the rules. Judges, advocates, and academics make liberal arguments for liberal rules, and their counterparts make conservative arguments for conservative rules. Neutrals and swing voting judges try to decide between liberal and conservative arguments. Both sides constantly position themselves vis-à-vis the distinction between law and politics, that is, vis-à-vis the discursive convention that their ideological positions as developed in law are not ideological.

Ideological conflict is a long-term, continuous discursive process independent of the disposition of the stakes in any particular conflict, and it has "dialogical" elements. Positions evolve in response to "external" events but also in response to "moves" by the other side. We can ask, and the sides themselves constantly do ask, how they are doing, seen as debating teams, at the task of persuading judges to be, say, judicial liberals and conservatives. We can ask how liberal and conservative judges are doing at persuading the populace at large to be liberal or conservative.

A great deal of ideological dialogue and evolution of this kind in the United States seem to take place in the forum of adjudication, particularly at the state appellate and federal levels, and most obviously in the United States Supreme Court. It seems to have a massive long-term influence on the content of formal law—on the legal rules that judges make—and so to be an important factor in explaining how judges dispose ideological stakes. Through the conversion effect—the ability of judges to validate rules not just in the sense of making them but in that of inducing a change in normative views or sentiments about them—it arguably affects culture more intimately and more pervasively than just by setting rules of the game.

This combination of distributive significance with (denied) ideological discursive content certainly seems more plausible as an explanation of the intense intelligentsia interest in appellate adjudication than either the coin-flip hypothesis or the idea that judges decide hard cases by a method that is objective in the sense of demonstrable or algorithmic. "Taking ideology seriously" in this sense is nonetheless counter, as we saw in the last chapter, to the mainstream of modern American legal theory, one of whose major preoccupations has been to show that judges are not or should not be ideological actors, even though they are unquestionably law makers. The next two chapters offer a historical/political explanation of this preoccupation.

PART TWO

The Problem of Judicial Legislation

4

The Paradox of American Critical Legalism

This chapter has two goals: first, to contribute to the comparative law enterprise of distinguishing what I will call "American critical legalism," an odd combination of utter faith and utter distrust in law, from Western European attitudes; second, to explain the difference by identifying the "viral" strain of ideology-critique in American legal thought, the strain whose relation to the "body" of thought is the theme of this whole book.

In Europe, until recently, the stakes in general ideological conflict have been higher than in the United States. Liberals (social democrats) and conservatives have defended the center against a communist left and a fascist or authoritarian right that have actually held and have continuously threatened to take power. In the United States, neither communist nor fascist positions have been more than marginal to debate. On the other hand, in the United States, the stakes of judicial law making have been much higher than in Europe, because both in private and in constitutional law the courts have played a major role in general political life. Both liberals and conservatives have pursued major law-making projects through the courts. A good part of the total corpus of law has no direct legislative basis, and a good part of this law bears the unmistakable marks of the liberal and conservative agendas.

A first consequence of this American context of centrist politics with judicial importance is that disputes about the rule of law have been somewhat different in the two political cultures. Far more in Europe than in the United States, the rule of law has been an important element in the debate between the liberal/conservative center and the communist and fascist extremes. The center has affirmed the rule of law as the heart of its program, along with human rights and representative democracy based on free elections. It has developed the legislation/adjudication dichotomy, through the politics/law, objective/subjective, and democratic/professional accountability distinctions, as a powerful normative position.

The extreme left and right have tended to endorse the rule of law, and human rights and free elections as well, but only in principle, while blatantly disregarding them in practice. The center has fought the extremes both by celebrating the abstract value of legality and by celebrating its actual, however occasionally compromised, realization in the Western democracies. This way of looking at it is occasionally important in American politics, where the extreme left and right exist as imaginary whipping boys in conflicts within the center. But except for brief moments in the 1890s, 1930s, and late 1960s, the threat to the rule of law (and human rights and majority rule) has been understood to be a threat from abroad.

Internally, the rule of law has figured prominently mainly in the continuous debate generated by alternate liberal and conservative appropriations of the court system as a vehicle for their conflicting projects within the center. The American system of separation of powers has meant that liberals have controlled the legislatures and conservatives the courts for long periods of time, and vice versa. When this divided control happens, legislatively dominant conservatives attack liberal judges for judicial legislation, and liberal jurists defend what they are doing as no more than fidelity to law. When the roles are reversed, liberals critique the conservative courts as sub rosa legislators, and conservatives mount a defense.

Confronted with the American cls critique of the rule of law, Europeans who don't reflexively assimilate it to earlier Marxist critiques tend to explain it by reference to the historical innocence of Americans. Because we haven't experienced either fascism or actually existing socialism, we crits are naively willing to play with fire by questioning a central pillar of humane politics in the modern age of barbarism.[1] This idea isn't absurd, though of course it can't serve as a defense against any particular substantive argument. The securely centrist, first peripheral and then imperial, but continentally isolated American political culture has provided a Galápagos-like enclave for bizarre intellectual mutations.

But the innocence thesis leaves out of account that the mainstream of American legal culture is intensely committed not just to the abstract idea of the rule of law as political icon, but to something that looks to Europeans perilously close to rule by judiciary. It has been common to argue that this American tendency to turn political into legal questions is explained by the absence of either a political or a class culture that makes stability likely.

In other words, Americans have to be judge-centric because if they didn't have a common civic religion of law their heterogeneous society might fly to pieces. Far from being innocents who can afford to play with fire, Americans are bonded to legalism by historical fears that are no less intense, though different from those of Europeans. The left/modernist-postmodernist critique of law seems crazy in the United States, not because it ignores the "historical lesson" that questioning fundamentals leads to communism or fascism, but because it seems to renounce the universal liberal and conservative ambition to rule through, and fear of domestic chaos in the absence of, judicial supremacy.

Though the left/mpm critique is aberrational in this way, it is representative in another. It is an extension of the intense preoccupation of American legal culture with the techniques of critique of substantive legal regimes and of the judicial opinions that rationalize them. Here again the contrast with Europe is stark, and widely accepted as such, but the elements for an explanation are complex. There is no question that critique is taught as the foundation of legal education through the case method and institutionalized in legal academia as an element in any conventionally acceptable scholarly performance.

The question is why Americans see the substance of law and the judicial opinions that explain and justify it as pervasively problematic, in spite of their culturally unshakable commitment to rule not just by law but by judges. Another way to put this is to ask why Dworkin is the emblematic modern American legal theorist. Remember that as with his forebears Cardozo, Llewellyn, Fuller, and Hart and Sacks, the essence of his position is that a judge can be faithful to the rule of law in even the "hardest" case. But even though she won't have to legislate, she can't expect her opinions, even in cases that would be regarded in Europe as routine applications of the method of coherence, to be accepted as objective, demonstrable, or noncontroversial. By contrast with Europe, Dworkin's ideal American judge seems to have infinite power and responsibility but practically no authority at all, if by authority we mean a cultural understanding that the rules she makes are presumptively valid because outside politics.

Civil law versus common law

As to the critical side of this odd combination, a first European reaction tends to be that critique flourishes because substantive law is relatively speaking irrational, that is, substantively incoherent in fact, logically undeveloped, and at the mercy of institutionalized judicial discretion. The simplest European explanation is the naive Continental one that locates these traits in the common law, as contrasted with a Code.

The formal theory of the civil law is that the judge makes law only in the restricted sense of having to formulate a norm for the case, never in the sense of contributing a decision that will be a source of law for future cases. The next judge is supposed to ignore what happened in the prior case, and decide a similar case in the opposite way if his own interpretation of the Code requires it. But he is to have no expectation that his version will be given weight in the future. There is much less possibility of legal conflict than in a common law system, just because there is much less law.

At the same time, there is much more law in the sense that civilians imagine that many more issues than in common law countries have been resolved by the democratically elected sovereign legislature. Furthermore, this law is made through a process that promotes coherent statutory regimes rather than the ad-hocery and incoherent compromise that emerge from both the legislative and the case law processes in the United States.

European legislation, in this naive view, benefits both from the ideological—politically coherent, however "subjective"—basis of the party system and from the high level of European juridical technique. The basic civil codes reflect the ideology of nineteenth-century Liberalism, worked out by brilliant professors rather than by legislative committees.[2] Modern social legislation may be conceptually incompatible with these foundations, but it likewise reflects a coherent social democratic response to classical Liberalism, worked out by only somewhat less distinguished professors of moderate left persuasion.

This means that the judge who has to interpret the law through the method of coherence has a lot of coherence to work with. She may have to do the ideological work of nineteenth-century classical Liberalism on one day and the ideological work of social democracy the next, but except on the rare days when the statutory materials suggest that she has to do both at the same time, she will do the bidding of the law rather than appealing to her personal political philosophy (let alone her personal ideological views).

American comparativists and eccentric Europeans have to my mind quite effectively debunked this fundamentalist understanding of the distinction between the two systems. It doesn't seem worth it to review the work that begins with Rudolph von Ihering,[3] gets an American start with John Dawson,[4] and continues in the work of writers like Sadok Belaid[5] and Mitchel Lasser.[6] For my purposes, it is enough to point out that neither rule by judiciary nor critique is any more popular in England, the Great Cybele of the common law, than it is in France or Germany. Perhaps we can attribute the English positivist notion of the law "running out" to the vagaries of common law, but beyond that English legal culture seems neither judge-centric nor critical, but merely formalist. The distinction between the code and the common law may be the starting point for our comparison, but it certainly can't be the sole explanation of the American paradox.

British law versus American law

Of course, there is an English explanation, smug rather than naive. It is that the arrogation of the power of judicial review "set the American courts afloat on a sea of controversial value judgments, and it became plain that in exercising these wide powers to monitor not only the form and formalities of legislation but also its content, the courts were doing something very different from what conventional legal thought in all countries conceives as the standard judicial function: the impartial application of determinate existing rules of law in the settlement of disputes."[7]

Judicial review generates the American "nightmare" view of adjudication, which is that, either very often or always, the expectation that the judge will be an "objective, impartial, erudite, and experienced declarer of the law" is "doomed to disappointment." The "cynical view," clearly the author's own, is that "if your Constitution has made law of what elsewhere would be politics, it has done so at the risk of politicising your courts."[8] H. L. A. Hart goes on to explain both legal realism and what I have been calling the American version of coherence, in which the judge never has to be a legislator in the strong English sense, as responses to the original sin of the U.S. Supreme Court Justices of "availing themselves of conventional myths about the judicial process to pass off their personal political and economic doctrine of laissez-faire" and then, a couple of generations later, of engaging in liberal "crypto-legislation" like the abortion decision.[9]

Hart took a dim view both of the realist version of the Nightmare and of the countervailing attempt to construct coherence theories that would make it at least imaginable that the judge could avoid being a legislator. I will be defending a modernist/postmodernist version of the nightmare view. It is important to the defense that American critical legalism is the product not just of judicial review but of a variety of other characteristics of American legal culture as well. For this reason, it is hard for American legal theorists to imagine that if only Chief Justice Marshall had been more responsive to "conventional legal thought in all countries," we could have stayed out of trouble. Indeed, the American exceptionalist response to Hart might be that these unusual cultural factors, *along with* the unusual practice of judicial review, led to breakthroughs in legal thought, as well as into the nihilist and romantic dead ends he identifies.[10]

To help explain the American case, we can add to common (as opposed to civil) law the American experience of federalism. Until the rise of the European Community, with its complex program of legal harmonization, only a handful of European comparativists (for example, Rodolfo Sacco[11]) had worried about the existence of conflicting judge-made rules derived in different jurisdictions from identical code provisions. But every American state supreme court will at least cast a glance at solutions from beyond its boundaries, and legal academics who want to write about any private law subject have to be comparativists at least to the extent of "counting the authorities."

A second consequence of federalism was that the federal courts had to decide what role to play when called on to arbitrate state/federal conflicts. It is important to see how shallow Hart's view was: even if the U.S. Supreme Court had declined to strike down federal statutes as violative of the federal constitution, it would have had to decide what to do about its explicit jurisdiction to decide cases in which a state was a party, and about conflicts between state and federal law. This kind of public law jurisdiction, like that of the European Court today, involves questions that are politically charged without there being any question of judges being asked to apply "higher" law against legislative preference.

The sense that conflict and choice are pervasive and inescapable also owes a lot to the historical circumstance that American jurisdictions imported their law from England in the first part of the nineteenth century, in an ideological context that emphasized the broadly "liberal" character of American society, by way of contrast with the relatively "feudal" and "technical" British regime. The experience of reception has been kept alive through the present by the creation of new states, with local judiciaries and no common law, as Europeans settled westward.

Another factor distinguishing the United States from Western Europe (Hart's "all countries") is that beginning early in the nineteenth century the legal profession, including the judiciary, was far more socially and politically heterogeneous than in the Old World. When Alexis de Tocqueville described the lawyers as an aristocracy, he was referring to their status and power, not claiming that they were an "estate" in the European sense, with all that would imply of quasi-hereditary entitlement and powerful internal norms defining what is and what is not legal. American lawyers and judges had a relatively experimental and instrumental attitude toward law in part because many of them were upstarts, whether self-made reactionaries or maverick populists. It was understood from the beginning that it was politically important who got to be a judge.

For Hart, "the most famous decisions of the Supreme Court have at once been so important and so controversial in character and so unlike what ordinary courts do in deciding cases that no serious jurisprudence or philosophy of law could avoid asking with what general conception of the nature of law were such judicial powers compatible."[12] His implicit answer is: with no general conception. But, of course, it is not that the decisions were important and controversial but only that they were "unlike what ordinary courts do" that raised the question. In the contexts of federalism and reception, and the social and political heterogeneity of bench and bar, it was far less clear than it still is in England what counts as ordinary.

Nightmare on Main Street

The simultaneously critical and "believing" character of American legal consciousness, its paradoxical combination of skepticism and faith, owes a lot to the historically contingent juxtaposition of three factors. The ideological stakes of judicial law making have been high, both in constitutional and in common law cases, at both the state and federal levels; the resources of legal tradition have been relatively meager given the novel questions posed; and the political sympathies of judges have shifted dramatically over time, rather than remaining stably conservative. For these reasons, and whether we see it as original sin or as the occasion for insight, the important but legally problematic judicial opinion is everywhere in American legal culture.

High stakes, a thin tradition, and shifting judicial personnel have meant that ideological opponents of particular decisions or trends of decision have had a strong interest in and some hope of discrediting the judicial reasoning that supports the outcomes they find obnoxious. This kind of attack began early in the history of the Republic when federalist Supreme Court judges developed the doctrine of final judicial review itself, along with a law of strong national powers in the federal system, against continuous opposition from Jeffersonian and Jacksonian lawyers. At the end of the period, there was a dramatic reversal of positions, as the pro-slavery forces became advocates of federal power to enforce the Fugitive Slave Law. Then the Supreme Court, in the Dred Scott decision, made a major pro-slavery intervention in national politics by striking down the Missouri Compromise.

After the Civil War, state and federal courts played major roles both in the development of a (relatively) pro-employer common law of labor relations and in setting constitutional limits to social legislation. In the 1930s, the United States Supreme Court invalidated a good part of the first New Deal.

After World War II, the political structure of the situation reversed again, as relatively liberal Supreme Courts confronted more conservative state and federal legislative majorities on a vast range of issues. The Court invalidated some legislation sanctioning members of the American Communist Party, and then attacked the executive practice and statutory law on legislative districting, the rights of criminal defendants, racial segregation, and abortion.

In private law, state supreme courts "revolutionized" tort law in general and landlord/tenant and consumer law in particular, without striking down any appreciable number of statutes, but not without producing a massive reaction of business interests and their legal advocates. When the conservatives began to regain control of the courts in the 1970s and 1980s, the liberals "shamelessly" reversed position once again, becoming enthusiasts for stare decisis and attacking judges like Robert Bork and Antonin Scalia as judicial legislators in the sheep's clothing of strict construction and original intent.

The vast majority of attacks on particular judicial decisions and on courses of decision have been based on the idea that there was a correct legal outcome that favored the political position of the critic. Critics of John Marshall's early commerce-clause opinions argued that the correct interpretation of the constitution required a states' rights outcome. Legal academic critics of Brown v. Board of Education argued that the change in the law could not be justified on the basis of "neutral principles." Since the Court reached a legally incorrect outcome, it was engaged in judicial legislation. This was judicial legislation in the strong sense of imposing its "value judgments," or ideology, on the populace in contravention of what was required by the rule of law.

Of course, each controversial judicial intervention has its supporters as well as its detractors. In the liberal view, Brown v. Board was right not because the judges had no choice but to legislate, so that whatever they decided would be inescapably political in the sense of "raw legislative preference," but because it was the *legally* correct outcome. We remain participants in a familiar morality play in which the question is whether the judges' personal ideology or "partisan politics" will overcome their oaths to interpret the law rather than overthrow it.

Adjudication critique in the context of high stakes

What is most striking about American legal culture is not that court decisions in politically charged cases produce these passionate arguments about what the law "really" requires. It is that the context of controversy has also produced, and here Hart was basically right, a particular, nationally specific form of *internal academic critique* of legal reasoning. Whether liberal or conservative, defenders of particular courses of decision against the charge of judicial legislation have had to respond not just by explaining that the decision was legally correct within the discourse of legality, but also by explaining how adjudication in the abstract, or in the particular case, *can be* different from legislation, even though it is interpretation rather than mere application of legal norms.

At the turn of the century, the United States experienced a long period of conservative judicial and liberal legislative control, one that looked as though it might go on forever. Most liberals simply continued arguing that each specific conservative judicial decision was judicial legislation because there was a right legal answer that the court disregarded in favor of its own subjective ideological preference. But some liberals "couldn't take it anymore" and began to argue that the problem was that there were no correct legal answers to these questions. This was the moment of the American mutation, the "birth of the virus."

These liberals combined the positions of the German and French "free-law" theorists with the English positivist position that judicial legislation is inevitable when the law "runs out." It was particularly likely to run out in the politically controversial cases that judges were then deciding in what looked like blatantly conservative fashion. Whatever they said they were doing, according to this new breed of critic, judges in these cases made choices. Indeed, the general belief that there were correct answers misled the judges themselves, forcing their biases to express themselves "unconsciously."[13]

This book is an attempt to develop and extend this American form of internal critique. To my mind, it is mainly through this project, rather than through philosophy or political theory, that American intellectuals have been participants in the larger, worldwide long-running project of left/mpm critique. American legal theory is one of the quasi-autonomous enclaves, like Western Marxist theory, phenomenology and hermeneutics, and now literary theory, where this project has developed like a Sartrean "worm at the heart of being."

Summary genealogy of the critique of judicial ideology in adjudication

Cls has had the project of resurrecting the critical strands in pre–World War I legal progressive thought and in legal realism, so that we could claim a tradition for our own highly controversial positions in domestic legal academic debate, while at the same time finding a place in the larger development. It is not my goal here to make this past "live again" in its irreducible historical particularity, but I do want to clarify the present situation by identifying a genealogy for particular elements in the modern synthesis. I claim only that writers like Holmes, Wesley Hohfeld, Henry Terry, Arthur Corbin, Walter Wheeler Cook, Felix Cohen, Robert Hale, and Llewellyn invented the basic techniques and ground-level propositions of today's practice.

Their attitudes toward these inventions, the way they fit them into their more general legal and political and cultural postures, were various. None of them seems at all similar, overall, to us, who claim to be their descendants. In particular, none of them seems to have what we would now call a critical project, as opposed to a critical practice. They often invented critical techniques as part of ground-clearing operations for their "reconstructive" efforts, their own ideas about how judges could escape the dilemma of being politically central without a respectably rational judicial method. To this day, their posterity includes the scholar who develops an elaborate critique of earlier attempts to rationalize a field, and then offers his or her own alternative. The alternative sinks like a stone, but the critique not only effectively does in its object but survives as a model for future destructive operations.[14]

There are two parts to the realist heritage: the critique of the coherence of the private law regime of contracts, property, and torts, and the critique of the assumed ideological neutrality of judicial decision making in hard cases. The critique of the coherence of private law doctrine was the outcome of the attempt to rationalize the common law, after the demise of the writ system and in the light of the most sophisticated European thinking. It had two strands, which we might call "nihilist" and "contradictionist." The nihilist was best summed up by Terry, the most brilliant late-nineteenth-century tort theorist, who spent his life trying to figure out the coherence of this new legal field. His last work on the subject was published in 1903, and it provided a motto for all that followed (not to speak of a prefiguration of Henry Hart's famous recession from his third Holmes lecture):

> There is no general rule for determining what legal duties exist, what acts are commanded or forbidden by law. Much labor and ingenuity have been expended in the attempt to find some general criterion of legal right and wrong, some general basis of legal liability. But in vain; there is none. Various acts are commanded or forbidden for various reasons, generally on grounds of expediency; and they are different in different places and periods. In this respect, the law presents itself as having a purely arbitrary or positive character, and the duties that exist in any particular system of law must simply be separately learned.[15]

But the absence of a "general rule" was not the end of the story. The contradictionist side of the critique of doctrinal coherence started with the proposition, implicit in nihilism as I just defined it, that the European theorists of the codes were wrong and their critics were right. Neither European nor American public or private law could be described as individualist (or classically Liberal) in fact. Stronger yet, individualism as applied to law *could not* generate a coherent legal regime. The next move seems never to have taken place in Europe, though this impression may be wrong, and the move may in fact have been made but crushed by resurgent orthodoxy and the political fears I described above.

This move was to assert that there was no way to resolve particular gaps, conflicts, and ambiguities in the existing regime without resorting to "policy," that is, to a choice, in the particular context, between the conflicting ideals of individualism and "interdependence" (or "collectivism," or "altruism") or, within individualism, between the ideal of private autonomy and the ideal of state protection against fraud and coercion. As I will argue at length in Chapter 7, "policy" turns out to be the vehicle for consciously or unconsciously transposed versions of the general ideological debate between, for example, liberalism and conservatism. The much milder position of the first generation of progressives was that the choice between policies was "legislative."

So Terry was wrong when he asserted that "the law presents itself as having a purely arbitrary or positive character, and the duties that exist in any particular system of law must simply be separately learned." One doesn't have to learn the rules separately, because in the contradictionist view they are highly organized rather than purely arbitrary. It is just that they have a dualist rather than a monistic logic. Here is a canonical example:

> The ethical problems involved in the law of contracts result as I see them from four elementary ideas:
>
> (1) *The Tort Idea,* i.e. that one ought to pay for injuries he does to another. As applied to promises this means that one ought to pay for losses which others suffer in reliance on his promises.
>
> (2) *The Bargain Idea,* i.e. that one who gets anything of value by promising to pay an agreed price for it ought to pay the seller the price he agreed.
>
> (3) *The Promissory Idea,* i.e. that promises are binding in their own nature and ought to be kept in all cases.
>
> (4) *The Quasi-Contractual Idea,* i.e. that one who receives anything of value from another ought to pay for it unless it came to him as a voluntary gift.
>
> These ideas, which at first seem trite and wholly harmonious, are in fact profoundly in conflict. The first and fourth proceed from the premise that justice is to be known after the event, and that it is the business of the court to correct whatever consequences of voluntary intercourse between men may be found to have turned out unjustly. The second and third proceed from the premise that justice is to be known before the event in transactions voluntarily entered into, and that it is the parties' business to settle the justice and injustice of the voluntary transactions at the start. The conflict between these two standpoints is perennial; it can be traced throughout the history of the law of contracts and noted in nearly every debatable contract question; there is no reason to think that it can ever be gotten rid of or to suppose that the present compromises of the issue will be any more permanent than the other compromises that have gone before.[16]

Our culturally specific form of ideology-critique of judicial opinions in cases that couldn't be resolved by mere deduction followed from this critique of coherence:

> (*a*) A judge's explanation of his or her choice of an answer to a question of law doesn't work, in the very specific sense of failing to establish that

the rule interpretation was required by the materials, or was the interpretation that fit them best, or whatever.

(b) But it is obvious that the choice between the two rules had a significant effect on the outcome of an ideologized group conflict.

(c) The only rational basis for making a decision seems to be to consider and evaluate those effects on ideologized group conflict, and to choose between the arguments of the two ideological camps present. The decision is "inevitably" a question of "policy."

(d) Because the choice is inadequately explained by the opinion, and because the rational consideration of its effects inevitably involves "policy," and because policy issues are open to ideological controversy, it is plausible that what the judge did in the case was to legislate his or her ideological agenda (not to be confused with agendas that are "personal" in the sense of ice cream tastes or love of blue-shirted litigants).

My view is that there is an actual, dramatic historical moment when this critical strategy was first formulated. It occurred in 1894, when Oliver Wendell Holmes published his article, "Privilege, Malice, and Intent."[17] In discussing recent English and American labor and common law antitrust cases, he wrote this sentence: "The ground of decision really comes down to a proposition of policy of rather a delicate nature concerning the merit of the particular benefit to themselves intended by the defendant, and suggests a doubt whether judges with different economic sympathies might not decide such a case differently when brought face to face with the issue."[18] The rest is history.

Part *a* of this type of critique appeals to "universal" standards of consistency that are supposed to be convincing to anyone and everyone, regardless of context and commitment. It is an internal textual critique of the particular opinion, exposing the chain of reasoning as internally flawed in a way that nullifies its very particular claim of necessity. There is no claim to have identified a "smoking gun" in the text that reveals the judge's "bias." Indeed, the technique works best on opinions that present themselves as utterly outside ideological discourse.

For example, Holmes critiqued opinions that relied on the legal maxim *sic utere tuo ut alienum non laedas* (use your property in such a way as not to injure the property of others) as question begging.[19] The question to be decided was which of two parties would be allowed to injure the other without compensation. Hohfeld criticized a specific set of opinions about labor/capital conflict on the ground that they falsely assumed that one kind of right entailed a quite different one.[20]

In 1935, Felix Cohen summed up the results of two generations of this kind of analysis:

> In every field of law we . . . find peculiar concepts which are not defined either in terms of empirical fact or in terms of ethics but which are used to answer empirical and ethical questions alike, and thus bar the way to intelligent investigation of social fact and social policy. *Corporate entity, property rights, fair value,* and *due process* are such concepts. So too are *title, contract, conspiracy, malice, proximate cause,* and all the rest of the magic "solving words" of traditional jurisprudence. Legal arguments couched in these terms are necessarily circular, since these terms are themselves creations of law, and such arguments add precisely as much to our knowledge as Molière's physician's discovery that opium puts men to sleep because it contains a dormitive principle.[21]

The mocking self-confidence of this passage hides its real weaknesses. As we will see, it is not so easy to distinguish between concepts that meet Cohen's requirement of definition in terms of fact or ethics and those that don't. But what I want to emphasize here is that though general, in the sense of applying across all of law, this critique is in the mode I will call "minimal." It is minimal because it carefully avoids two much stronger but opposite critical claims. (1) It does *not* assert that judicial opinions never convince us that the result was legally compelled, or that law "by its nature" can never determine an outcome, or that because of "social construction" law is "inevitably" an ideological construct, or anything of the sort. (2) Nor, conversely, does it assert that legal reasoning yields a constrained outcome on the side of the question of law that the judge rejected. There is no claim that he or she has violated (whether intentionally or not) the duty of interpretive fidelity.

The second step in the argument is of a different character. It consists of pointing out the distributive stakes in the decision, its impact on ideologized group conflict. In other words, once it is established that the judge has exercised state power without an adequate legal explanation, we inquire, cui bono? The appeal is to common knowledge once a rough empirical analysis has shown what the stakes behind the technicalities really were. Here also there was a breakthrough, summed up in two sentences of Robert Hale:

> The market value of a property or a service is merely a measure of the strength of the bargaining power of the person who owns the one or

renders the other, under the particular legal rights with which the law endows him, and the legal restrictions which it places on others. To hold unequal bargaining power economically justified, merely because each party obtains the market value of what he sells, and no more and no less, is to beg the question.[22]

Hale opened up a whole field of analysis, showing that the most apparently unproblematic background rules of property, contract, and tort were "really" sophisticated regulatory interventions through which the state conditioned the outcomes of economic conflict.[23] Since, according to the hypothesis of contradictionism, this set of rules had no "logic," could not be derived from a coherent theory of economic individualism, the way was opened to choosing among possible interpretations with a view to these distributive consequences. As with Cohen, there was a weakness—the absence of a definition of unequal bargaining power.

The third step is the assertion that the issue in the particular case (not in every case) "is inevitably one of policy." This means that the legal materials and legal reasoning could not resolve the question, could not constrain the judge, in a way that would permit him or her to decide without reference to ideologically contested arguments.

This step is given credence by step *a,* in which it was demonstrated, by appeal to widely or universally shared standards of rationality, that the opinion failed to establish any kind of legal necessity. (It used a false argument.) But the internal critique cannot, of course, establish that it was impossible to write an opinion in the particular case that would indeed have generated a sense of closure or constraint on the side of the actual outcome.

The fourth step is no more than an assertion: Given that the judge offered no convincing legal explanation, and that a rational ground of decision would have had to take account of the impact of the rule on ideologized group conflict, doesn't it make sense to think that ideology played a part? The meaning of ideology in this context might be vulgar and specific—pro-labor judges make pro-labor decisions—or more refined. And the critic might charge the judge with something like having an ideological commitment, or merely with having what I called in the last chapter an ideological "preference," as in Holmes's "economic sympathies," for example.

The turn-of-the-century critics were usually trying to persuade their audience that particular pieces of controversial, conservative, judge-made law were judicial legislation, and that they were wrong. They tended to favor an attitude of judicial deference toward legislative majorities and a frank consideration of the inevitable "legislative" factors by judges doing common law judicial rule making. But they did not, contrary to the current pop academic view of legal realism, equate the legislative with the political. Their analyses of particular cases showed flaws in the reasoning process, and strongly suggested ideological along with other "subjective" influences, but offered some form of "policy analysis" as the alternative. There was no assertion that adjudication was irredeemably ideological.[24] This was true even of such notorious "bad boys" as Jerome Frank,[25] Thurman Arnold,[26] Joseph Hutcheson,[27] and Max Radin,[28] all of whom were mainly debunkers of the "myth of certainty."

This position allowed an alliance with the liberal critics who believed that there were correct—liberal—answers to the hot legal questions of the day but that conservative judges couldn't be expected to reach them. Over the years, some members of both groups of critics supported proposals like abolishing judicial review, codifying large areas of law, creating administrative agencies outside judicial control, electing judges to short terms, and radically easing the constitutional amendment process.

But whether or not such changes occurred, success of the critique of adjudication per se was quickly understood to threaten further consequences. If judge-made law, at least in these controversial cases, is *necessarily* based on legislative considerations, then it is arguably invalid, because it is the legislature that should do legislation under the rules of majority vote and democratic accountability. If many people regarded both the liberal and the conservative law that judges have made in politically important cases as presumptively invalid in this sense, this conclusion might change our political culture.

The American mutation, the emergence of an internal critique of adjudication, is therefore an obviously dangerous fact. Both liberals and conservatives have an interest in legal authority in general, as part of the general liberal/conservative commitment to the rule of law. And they have had divergent particular interests in legal authority as a support for the specific legal agendas they have pursued through adjudication when they controlled the judiciary.

I think it quite common to see the history of American thought about law in the twentieth century as a protracted debate about how to deal with the "viral" tendency of internal critique, with the positions ranging from flat rejection to compromise to flat endorsement. In the course of the debate, the practice of opinion writing, its defense as legitimate law making, and the critique itself, have gone through many transformations and elaborations.

The course of the debate has been powerfully influenced by its situation as a distinct part of the general debate between left and right. The critique has been an evolving part of the general left-wing attack on particular rules and on the power of judges in general, and in itself logically unconnected to leftism.

The first point is historical: the originators and developers of the critique have used it over and over again against particular conservative victories in the courts and generally against rule by judiciary. They have chosen naturally enough to tailor the evolution of the critique, its defense and development, to their left-wing projects. Almost all the classic instances of internal critique, of assertion of the inevitability of "policy," and of imputation of ideology are directed by liberals or radicals against conservative rules and judges.

But there is a whole left-wing legal culture that rejects the strategy represented by the critique, embracing the maximalist position that what is wrong with judges is that they reach the wrong legal results. According to this position, in one case or another the Constitution and statutes and common law gave the victory to the left, but the judges snatched it away through spurious legal argument.[29] There is also a small part of the conservative legal culture that embraces the critique.[30] I don't think this means they have "made a mistake" about the true implications of their general ideological positions (more on this later). For the moment I simply assert that there is nothing intrinsically liberal or conservative about the critique.

There is an extension that we need on the table now. The realists and their cls successors expanded opinion-critique beyond the demonstration that there was a logical flaw. Even a judicial opinion that contains none of the famous errors of formalism may be supremely unconvincing as a demonstration of constraint. In particular, many opinions are unconvincing because although of impeccable internal logic they don't confront obvious responses to their arguments.

In *The Bramble Bush*[31] and in his famous article "Canons on Statutes,"[32] Llewellyn developed this notion through what I would call a "structuralist" formalization of the arguments and counterarguments for broadening and narrowing precedents and statutes. He summed up his theory of precedent in language that applies, mutatis mutandis, following the progress of the virus, to his theory of statutory interpretation and to the cls theory of policy argument:

> What I wish to sink deep into your minds about the doctrine of precedent, therefore, is that it is two-headed. It is Janus-faced. That it is not one doctrine, nor one line of doctrine, but two, and two which, *applied at the same time to the same precedent, are contradictory of each other.* That there is one doctrine for getting rid of precedents deemed troublesome and one doctrine for making use of precedents that seem helpful. That these two doctrines exist side by side. That the same lawyer in the same brief, the same judge in the same opinion, may be using the one doctrine, the technically strict one, to cut down half the older cases that he deals with, and using the other doctrine, the loose one, for building with the other half.[33]

Let me quickly point out that Llewellyn was a contradictionist without being a nihilist (he believed in the Rule of the Singing Reason), and that he did not link the argument-bites he identified in precedential and statutory argument to the liberalism and conservatism of his time. Llewellyn was not a crit. Moreover, I am simply presenting his conclusion, obviously a controversial one, and even more controversial when extended beyond argument from authority to policy argument in general. This extension is the subject of Chapters 6 and 7. My point for the moment is only that when a judicial opinion deploys stereotyped argument-bites without acknowledging that there are equally plausible stereotyped counterbites for each, it fails in a way analogous to that of the logically flawed opinion.

But it is only a matter of analogy. Unlike "pure" internal critique, the claim that opinions are unconvincing because they willfully deny what I will call the "semiotic" character of their own arguments cannot rely on universally or even widely accepted standards of rationality. Whether legal discourse can be said to have this stereotypical organization is open to argument, and for any given opinion there are no clearly agreed standards of "convincingness."

When it is true to the minimalist program, this form of argument eschews any claim that all opinions must necessarily be unconvincing because written in legal prose. Likewise any claim that the judge is a sinner because he or she betrayed interpretive fidelity and reached the "wrong result." The form is: this opinion seems open to a response that nullifies it, not through internal critique but by confronting it with its mirror image on the other side. Given that there is no apparent basis *within law* for choosing between opinion and mirror image, and given that the two opinions represent opposing ideological positions on an issue of group conflict, it seems plausible to suppose that ideology influenced the judge's choice.

The body fights the virus. With respect both to the question of the coherence of particular bodies of law and to the question of judicial method in hard cases, "reconstructive" efforts are constantly under way. The minimalist critical response is to do an internal critique of each reconstruction as it comes along. The goal is to show that this particular account of how judges can be neutral doesn't work. The account has left room for ideology, or it imposes contradictory demands, or whatever. The critical project builds through time both through specific instances that demolish specific reconstructions and by additions to the repertoire of repeatable critical routines. First-year law students today can learn and use Holmes's specific critique of *sic utere tuo* and Hohfeld's critique of the derivation of claims from privileges.

On this basis, there are ongoing ideological disputes between critics and defenders of particular groups of legal rules (labor law, race law, local government law, antitrust, professional responsibility, international law).[34] The critics work to problematize the rules by problematizing the judicial opinions and academic writing that explain them; the defenders try to produce new and better explanations. There is a quite distinct dispute about whether the critiques successfully problematize the very idea of judicial neutrality. Neither side is likely to just "win." As in other ideological battles, the very definition of stakes and outcomes is contested.

There is no extant theory that threatens to end the current ideological conflict about method by compelling a consensus about how judges can and should be neutral. Indeed, the current multiplicity of contradictory theories of neutrality seems a powerful, though of course not conclusive refutation of all of them. I am an admirer of their work of mutual critique. I endorse Dworkin's critique of Richard Posner[35] along with Andrew Altman's critique of Dworkin[36] and Fiss's doubtless forthcoming critique of Altman, and Posner's critique of Fiss (if there is one) and on around the circle. This is not musical chairs but more like a game of "Penelope," in which each writer simultaneously weaves his own and unweaves others' work.[37]

I would summarize the situation as follows. On the one hand, in American legal culture, the gradual accumulation of quite specific critical routines means that opponents can direct a formidable technology of delegitimation at judicial law making in situations of ideologized group conflict.

It is difficult to write a convincing judicial opinion, an opinion that generates the experience of legal constraint, in any case where the opponents of the chosen rule decide to deploy this technology. Judicial law making through adjudication is under heavy suspicion of being disguised ideology.[38]

On the other hand, if the project of legal necessity is a Golden Bowl, no one has found the fatal flaw that would allow us to shatter it with a single blow. Successful critique is "local," even when the locality is a whole theory of judicial neutrality. Even locally, the endless recurrence of determinacy is as much part of our experience as its endless dissolution in critique.

The Continent versus the United States

Continental legal theory is uncannily "other" for an American, perhaps because just about everything in our legal culture is present in theirs, often translated word for word, but nothing seems to have the same meaning. Of course, there is a Continental critical tradition in legal theory. Here is a typology, doubtless seriously distorted because I am much more familiar with Italian thinking than with that of any other European country.

External critiques. An external critique accepts the notion that the law as a whole, or some part of it, is coherent, but criticizes it either because it has a suspect origin or because it has bad effects. The first type shows that coherence derives not from a legitimating external factor, such as the popular will or the abstract concept of justice, but from a delegitimating factor. The two most popular delegitimating outside factors are Liberal individualist ideology and capitalist relations of production. An effects-oriented external critique concedes (or affirms) coherence and then develops an analysis of the bad social consequences that flow in fact from the rules. External critiques can be from either the left or the right. Of course, one can pursue an ideological and a materialist external critique of origins at the same time, and combine both with a critique of effects, as in classical Marxism.[39]

Global internal critique. One can distinguish two types of global internal critique: analytical and sociological. The analytical are critiques of the rule form, perhaps best illustrated by Hans Kelsen's insistence that every rule application is the creation of a new norm, or by the various applications of Wittgenstein, Derrida, and so on, mentioned in the last chapter. The sociological critique is the theory part of the European left program for a regulated market, mixed economy, and welfare state. It is perennially in battle with the "formal" approach to law, supporting antiformal legal reform, an antiformal theory of interpretation, and ultimately an alternative epistemology for legal theory.

The formal versus the social. The formal and the social confront each other at many levels:

The Formal	*The Social*
Private law and the market (property, contract, and tort law, implicitly conservative)	Public law and administrative agencies (labor and regulatory law, implicitly liberal)
Liberty and individual rights	Needs and social rights
Legal rules	Legal standards
Abstraction and deduction (una bella dogmatica)	Context and facts (an excellent empirical study)
A pyramidal logic of norms	A holistic logic of social organization
Strict separation of judicial and legislative powers	The adaptation of powers to situations (e.g., labor courts)
Legal positivism and legal science	Scientific positivism and sociology
Tradition	Modernity
Certainty and stasis	Flexibility and evolution
Etc.	Etc.

Comments: First, the formal and the social are opposed both to fascism and to the Leninist theory of the dictatorship of the proletariat—they share faith in rights, majority rule, and the rule of law. The advocates of the social are no less committed to interpretive fidelity than the advocates of the formal (in Italy, they appeal to the general clauses of the 1948 Constitution affirming human rights and the protective role of the state). Second, each side considers the existence of the other an imperfection— each imagines that the incoherence of modern law, its patchwork combination of formal and social elements, could and should be cured by its triumph over the other. The aspiration is for coherence, even if our fallen state is incoherence. André-Jean Arnaud's wonderful *Les juristes face à la société* is a lament for the suppression of the social in French legal science, rather than a critique of the dichotomy.[40]

Third, as I noted above, the judicial role is unproblematic as long as it is possible to situate each particular question within a subcategory of doctrine that is coherent according to one model or the other. Fourth, with some Italian exceptions the major players in the battle between the formal and the social are the intelligentsias of political parties, which try to impose one vision or the other through legislation (rather than through judge-made law), and legal academics, *but not judges.*

There is a strong resemblance between the Continental social current and American liberal legalism. First, they are politically aligned and can fruitfully borrow one another's doctrinal and institutional innovations. Second, in each case, the practitioners take law seriously, in the sense of aspiring to win their ideological battles by being legally correct. Third, ideas like context and facts and a diffuse confidence that social science favors progress are shared, as in Earl Warren's famous appeal to Kenneth Clark's study of black schoolchildren to refute the idea that separate could be equal.

The most important difference is that the social current is both more and less critical than American liberal legalism. The social current is in a continuing battle not just with conservatism but with a whole conservative way of looking at law, the self-consciously formal. The formal doesn't exist in the United States except as a form of reaction, because legal realism killed it off and promoted a hybrid in which policy argument is included as a supplement to deductive reasoning in both liberal and conservative appellate opinions.

For this reason, European leftists can see the social as antagonistic to the formal at many more levels than the merely doctrinal, whereas American liberals and conservatives mix and match the identical social and formal elements in their legal writing and theory (Warren and his liberal successors resort on a regular basis to civil libertarian formalism). Liberal legalists differ from conservatives only in their preferred outcomes and in their diffuse supralegal "vision of the good society" based more on "compassion," less on "self-reliance," and so forth.

But Continentals don't do the kind of internal critique and hopeful reconstruction of judicial opinions that is the bread and butter of American critical legalism. As a consequence, they haven't developed the particular practices and techniques, transmitted from generation to generation through the case method and the Socratic classroom, that define American legal culture. And so they haven't had to defend against the realist and cls projects of generalizing and radicalizing those techniques in viral form.[41]

The consequence of radicalization has been, about every other generation, a deep challenge to the possibility and even the desirability of the kind of coherence that the Continentals still take for granted *within* the formal and *within* the social. As someone engaged in one of these periodic challenges, the Continental social current sometimes seems to me less critical even than American conservative legalism, because it has never had to confront and adapt to the successes of a native movement of minimalist internal critique. Such a movement would force Continental critical theorists to defend the social not just against the formal and against Marxist external critique, but against an internal critique that might look something like this.

First, each mode is present in the other, so that when an outcome seems to follow from adopting one mode or the other, it is *probably* because someone made the mistake of overestimating that mode's determinacy. The question whether anything follows from putting oneself inside the formal mode as opposed to the social, or vice versa, involves all the complex questions of legal theory that I broached in the discussion above of the realist critique of adjudication.

Second, the conflicting elements of each are present in each of us, so that we are dealing with a contradiction between our own views, rather than an opposition between groups.[42] Advocates of the social, no less than of the formal, worship an Idea of Reason that doesn't work to solve problems in the way they think it does, but that does work to reinforce the social power of its votaries.

I am not at all sure that this is right, or for that matter, that Continental critical legal thought is helpfully analyzed in terms of the formal/social dichotomy.[43] But I am quite confident that the *type* of analysis I've just attempted, combining minimalist internal critique, nihilism, and contradictionism, is typical of American cls and not at all common in Europe.

Britain versus the United States

We are now in a position to ask why the American mainstream, typified by Dworkin, has rejected the English solution of "frank" recognition that the judge is willy-nilly a legislator when the "law runs out." It seems obvious to me that the answer is that, given the viral strand in American legal thought, the admission would threaten to delegitimate "too much" of American law—"too much" in the sense of too many doctrines, given the critique of judicial law making in every field of law. And "too much" in the sense of too important, because judges' decisions in hard cases settle so many ideologized group conflicts in which liberals and conservatives have big stakes. In other words, the stakes in the debate about judicial method, loosely between the realists and their successors and all the generations of American reconstructors, from Cardozo to Llewellyn and Fuller through Hart and Sacks to Dworkin, derive from the stakes of liberals and conservatives in judicial law-making power.

5

Policy and Coherence

*T*his chapter interprets American coherence theories as responses to the problem posed by the widespread and self-conscious use of policy argument in postrealist American legal culture, that is, in lawyers' briefs, judicial opinions, and academic writing. In the first part of the chapter, I try to tease out just what is meant by the term "policy," when it is used in contrast to deduction or, just as commonly, to "law." This is an exercise in the anthropology of legal conceptions, based on my own status as a participant observer, rather than an exploration of what legal theorists think about the issue. I then argue that policy argument, however firmly established as a legitimate legal practice, is commonly understood to be a potential "Trojan horse" for ideology.

In the second part, I describe the asymmetrical stakes that liberal and conservative ideological intelligentsias see in finding a way to represent adjudication as outside ideology, in spite of the presence of policy argument. I argue that liberals, unlike conservatives, confront a dilemma: that of reconciling their historical commitment to antiformalism with their equally historic investment in specific liberal reforms achieved through the judiciary. In the third part I summarize and summarily critique three versions of American coherence theory as responses to this dilemma.

The deductive mode versus the policy mode

American lawyers distinguish two ways to argue a question of law—a deductive mode, sometimes called argument from authority or just "legal" argument, and a policy mode. The traditional view is that even if it decides ideologized group conflicts, adjudication can be nonideological because it is (strong version) objective or (weak version) "not personal." In this view, deduction is clearly nonideological; the contested element is the part that is governed by policy. According to the legal realist version of viral critique, when a case "really comes down to a proposition of policy," that "suggests a doubt whether judges with different economic sympathies" might not decide it differently.[1] The jurisprudential debates about objectivity, and lately about indeterminacy, are both parasitic on the law/policy distinction.

The premise of the deductive mode is that lawyers answer questions of law by determining the meaning of an authoritative or "valid" case or statute, or the meaning of a private expression (contract, deed, articles of incorporation) that is given legal force by a case or statute. In this mode, it is a premise that there is a single applicable norm (the holding of a case or the words of a statute or an expression of legally valid private intent) whose meaning is uncertain. The uncertainty is resolved by the deductive or "logical" or "analytic" or "semantic" process of identifying the definitions of the terms in the norm or the "meaning" of the norm taken as a whole.[2] If it seems at first blush that there is more than one norm, or no norm at all that is applicable, then the logical or analytic or deductive work of the lawyer is to show that in fact only one was applicable, or that a rule that did not at first seem to be applicable was applicable in fact, once we look behind the words to their definitions or meanings.

In the deductive mode, the judge is always moving from the abstract or general to the concrete or particular. The words in the valid norm raise a question of law because they could be interpreted in more than one way in the given case. The answer to the question is the choice of a specification of the meaning of the valid norm that resolves the doubt without in any way challenging the norm's authority. In the case of statutes and case law, a new rule may emerge, one that has never been formulated before, but it is a "subrule" that was always implicit in the valid rule.

The deductive mode excludes the judge's ideology because the subrule the judge chooses is the same as the more abstract valid authoritative rule, except for the logically necessary permutations that come from unpacking the meaning of its terms. Judges may agree or disagree with the valid rule that they interpret deductively, but they can still do the deduction, and others will be able to determine whether they have done it correctly. There is a "right answer" in a strong sense: universally valid or at least widely agreed standards of truth have been applied.[3]

Policy argument is different from deductive argument in three crucial ways. First, it presupposes either *(a)* that deduction from a valid norm doesn't settle the question of law, or *(b)* that the valid norm covering the case requires the judge to consider nondeductive reasons for choosing one subrule or another.

In case *a,* either the law "runs out," so that we have a "case of first impression" or a "hard case," or there is an argument for letting policy argument trump deduction, that is, an argument for overruling a prior case. In case *b,* there are a number of possibilities. (1) The rule of law is that the rule against perpetuities shall be "remorselessly applied," *unless* there are "public policy reasons" for not applying it at all to the particular type of interest in question.[4] (2) A valid rule conditions an outcome on "the equities," whose determination requires policy argument (see, for example, the Restatement of Torts on what the judge is to consider in deciding whether or not to grant an injunction).[5] (3) "Standards" (negligence, good faith, probable cause) require policy argument when we apply them to particular facts or when we choose subrules that give the standard a much more precise meaning for a subclass of cases (violation of a statute is negligence per se).[6]

Second, the content of policy argument—what we do when we are not arguing by deduction from valid rules—is argument about the desirability of a subrule, in terms of some set of social or legal institutional values. The social values are almost always one version or another of utility, extralegal rights, or morality. The legal institutional values are more numerous, but some typical examples are considerations of judicial competence (judicial activism versus judicial passivism), administrability (clear rules versus equitable standards), and federalism (virtues of centralization versus virtues of decentralization). In the language of the realists, the discussion is "legislative," because legislators make these types of arguments to one another when considering whether or not to pass a statute (raising no constitutional issues).

Third, policy argument presupposes a "force field" model of the decision process. The elements of the force field model are:

(a) More than one policy is likely to apply to a question of law, and the policies are perennially (though not *necessarily*) in conflict. In the utilitarian version, we have gains and losses to different parties whose interests conflict; in rights argument, rights conflict; in arguments from morality, there are conflicting moral principles.

(b) Rules (subrules) represent compromises of conflicting policies, "drawing a line" that "gives" more or less to each affected interest, right or principle.

(c) For any given policy question, there will be an indefinitely large number of possible rules, each differing from the others in how much it responds to each policy.

(d) In selecting among the possible rules that would settle the question of law, the judge has to "balance" the conflicting policies.

By contrast, in deductive argument, we presuppose that (a) only one valid rule is applicable rather than a number of conflicting policies, (b) the subrule selected is "the same as" the valid rule rather than the arbitrator of a conflict, (c) it represents not one among a set of possible compromises but the concretization of an abstraction within a pyramidal structure, and (d) the judge defines and infers rather than balances.

Respective roles of deduction and policy

The relation between deductive argument and policy argument seems to follow from their places in the larger Liberal theory of majority rule, rights, and the rule of law. If the applicable norm refers explicitly to policy, or requires a determination of equities, or is in the form of a standard, then the use of policy rather than deduction is required of the judge by his duty of fidelity to law.

If no applicable norm requires policy argument, and there is an interpretation of the legal materials that can be arrived at by deduction from those materials, then it might seem that is the legally correct interpretation. This seems to follow from the notion of deduction as a matter of identities and from the presupposed democratic validity of the legal premises. The hard case would appear to be that in which there is a gap, conflict, or ambiguity in the system of norms, so that there is neither a plausible deductive answer nor an invitation to policy argument built into the materials. In this case, the judge can defer to the legislature (or another democratically legitimate body, such as an administrative agency) if it has decided the question, or do her own policy analysis.

But this is too simple, because in a common law system the judges make rules by interpreting precedents that are in turn based on earlier precedents, with no ultimate foundation in a legislatively enacted code. Judge-made common law is democratically legitimate because the legislature could change it if it wanted to, rather than because it is interpretation of legislative will. This means that there is a perennial conflict between two theories of interpretation.

Under the first, deductions from the holdings of cases are legally valid, and policy is only appropriate when deduction is impossible or the valid rule requires it. Judges can make exceptions to valid holdings or overrule cases altogether only when holdings or cases are contradictory, so that there has to be a mistake somewhere. Under the second, we understand the judges to have made rules all along to arbitrate between conflicting policies, and it is therefore legitimate for them to reject a deductively required outcome in the name of the policies that underlay the original adoption of the rule. In this theory, policy argument can trump deduction in common law cases (although not in statutory interpretation).[7]

There is an implicit lawyers' ontology of legal versus policy questions that operates in both of these theories of precedent, and indeed throughout American legal culture. By an "implicit ontology" I mean the never-articulated presuppositions of a discourse about what exists in the world independently of observers of the world. In this case, the implicit presupposition is that it is possible to typologize legal questions, with some being "by their nature" susceptible both to deductive and to policy resolution, and others being "by their nature," that is, given the state of the legal materials, susceptible to resolution only by appeal to policy.

The application of deduction or policy *should* depend on the nature of the question—on something external to the judge. When a policy question is resolved deductively, someone must have made a mistake, because, given the nature of the question, it just wasn't possible to come up with a deductively correct answer. This is the sense of the phrase "it was inevitably a question of policy." Conversely, when a question that is open both to deductive and to policy resolution is resolved by an appeal to policy, the judge has sinned because he or she should accept the deductive solution, unless he or she can propose a theory of a legitimate nondeductive role for judges (for example, Cardozo's theory that judges should evolve the law to meet changed social circumstances).

Two kinds of deduction

A good part of legal reasoning is deductive, in one or another of two different ways. First, legal reasoning is deductive when a rule states a factual predicate for a legal consequence, and the judge applies the rule by stating that the definitions of the terms in the rule correspond to the facts of the particular case. "If you are convicted of murder, you shall be sentenced to life imprisonment. You have been convicted of murder. Therefore I sentence you to life in prison." Because the fact has been found, the consequences follow.

In Kelsen's sense, the judgment articulates a new norm (you are sentenced to life imprisonment). But no subrule emerges from deductive reasoning starting from the valid rule; it is "merely applied." The case is just an illustration of the "logic" of the rule, rather than the occasion for an "interpretation" of it. This mode of deductive reasoning is pervasive but of little interest for us. Nonetheless, it is reasoning, it is deductive, and it can be extremely complicated.

A classic example is the rule against perpetuities. It is common to produce elaborate reasoning chains from the definitions of the terms in the rule (to be valid, an interest must vest, if at all, within twenty-one years of the expiration of a life in being at the time of the creation of the interest) and the particular facts of an inter vivos trust (from A to B in trust for A's children, living and as yet unborn, to be distributed to each child on attainment of the age of twenty-five). The process of rule application that invalidates the interests of children born after the creation of the trust seems to me well described as deductive.

A second classic example is consideration doctrine, once reduced to a canonical formulation (a promise is not binding unless there is something "bargained for and given in exchange for the promise"). My uncle promises me in writing to give me a sum of money for a trip to Europe, "in consideration of" his "esteem and affection" for me; and unbeknownst to him I buy a suit in preparation; he reneges. I need the doctrine of promissory estoppel because there is no consideration for his promise.

In both of these cases, we understand the process as deductive in a very strong sense: the facts are "data" fed into a system of categories that "produce" an answer. At each step, definitions do the work. There is no need to elaborate a subrule that settles the question of interpretation of how this rule will apply to a class of cases in which its meaning would otherwise be in doubt. We are close to the civil law model of rule application, in which we don't need precedent because the application of the rule is not an interpretation—it involves no choices that are "really" open (the choice to make a logical error is not a choice), and we don't need to preserve it as a precedent because if we have the same case later on we are confident we'll do exactly the same thing even if we have no memory of the first application.

The second form of deductive reasoning is much more important and much more obscure. Lawyers propose two different interpretations of an unquestionably "valid" rule. The two will produce, when mechanically applied to the facts of the particular case, in the manner of perpetuities or consideration doctrine, diametrically opposite outcomes. The interpretations are verbally distinct from the original "valid" rule, they are less abstract, and they will clearly cover a large number of cases, some of which may be hard cases, as well as the present case.

Everyone understands that it is important to record the judge's choice of interpretation, which will become itself a "valid" rule, because otherwise later courts might adopt different interpretations or perhaps misunderstand this one. The interpretation is presented not as an explanation of how the definitions in the authoritative rule apply to the facts of this case, but as a more concrete version of the authoritative but abstract statement, which will in its turn be repeatedly applied to new facts.

The judge decides that one interpretation is right because it is just the restatement of the rule at a lower level of generality, whereas the other interpretation is wrong because it involved a logical error in moving from the general to the particular. A classic example is the idea that a rule of expectation damages follows by deduction from the definition of a contract as the legally enforceable will of the parties. Reliance damages are of course a possible alternative, but to adopt them would be, according to one argument, a logical error.[8]

The choice of the expectancy as the measure of damages is understood to be the rejection of the reliance measure. It is an intermediate step between the definition of contract as the legal protection of the will of the parties and the facts of a particular case. It may well be that the choice between the two rules will be made in a lawsuit, but the question is "one of law" not because judges won't let juries decide it, but because we are dealing with rule definition. Once the judges have chosen the expectancy as the deductively necessary subrule, they apply *it* rather than the more abstract valid rule that contract law protects the will of the parties.

I chose this example because one of the most famous legal realist articles is Lon Fuller and William Perdue, "The Reliance Interest in Contract Damages,"[9] which argues that the deduction of expectation damages is a mistake, an instance of circular reasoning. Instead, according to Fuller and Perdue, the choice of a damage measure is a matter of policy. He proposes that in disputes among family members, inter alia, the reliance measure is better on policy grounds than the expectancy, and there is no "logical" reason not to adopt it.[10]

Because of similar realist critiques of deductive reasoning in many particular fields, and because of realist generalizations like Holmes's famous maxim that "general propositions do not decide concrete cases,"[11] it is common to believe that deduction is "formalism," an invalid, discredited method of decision, and that nowadays we reject it in favor of policy. This seems wrong to me. The judges and treatise writers Fuller and Perdue criticized made a wrong deduction. But this doesn't mean we don't still use their method.

For most modern contract theorists, for example, it follows from adopting the expectation measure that the contract price minus the market price is the correct way to measure the expectancy in a commercial contract on a competitive market. The definition of the expectancy is trying to "put the victim in as good a position as he or she would have been in had the contract been performed." Reliance damages restore the status quo before the contract was made. It seems to be "implicit" in these definitions that contract-minus-market is just another form of the expectancy, whereas restitution plus expenses-in-preparation would not be.

Deduction "guided" by policy

In American judicial opinions and in doctrinal writing, the most common mode is neither deduction nor policy but an intermediate mode, deductive argument supplemented or "guided" by policy argument.[12] The argument has a deductive framework, but the participants understand that nothing like "necessity" or "logical entailment" has been generated by that framework. At each point, the judge or scholar supplements the apparently or weakly or falsely deductive steps in the argument with policy arguments that appeal to rights, morality, utility, or institutional considerations cast nondeductively.

The policy argument itself is presented in loosely or falsely deductive form: *(a)* we all agree that we should reject rules that open the floodgates of litigation; *(b)* this rule does that; *(c)* therefore we should reject this rule. Treatise writers like William Prosser[13] and E. Allen Farnsworth[14] rationalize whole territories of doctrine, making the complex of rules seem soothingly sensible, through this kind of combination. Their "argument-bite" policy arguments have much the same rhetorical effect as the citation of a case but achieve it by simply ignoring the counterbites.

For example, if the question is whether professional degrees or licenses are marital "property" that must be "equitably distributed" under a statute governing divorce, the court will expatiate on the "meaning" or definition of property, while at the same time giving its thoughts on the consequences of one rule or another for "incentives," "trust" between spouses, and the extralegal "rights" of the husband and wife to the rewards of their enterprise. The judges debate the desirability of post-decree adjustments of the valuation of a professional degree in terms of the consequent legal uncertainty, the virtues of equitable flexibility, and so on.[15]

Analogy plays an important role in this kind of argument, in two different ways. Sometimes it buttresses the deductive argument by showing that the meaning proposed for a premise is adopted in other similar cases— for example, that there are many nontransferable interests that are treated as property, so that there is nothing anomalous about treating professional licenses in this way. Sometimes, the role of the analogy is to show that the conflict between policies present in this case has been resolved in other cases similarly to the way it is proposed to resolve it here—alimony decrees, after all, are subject to equitable revision in spite of the problem of uncertainty, so why shouldn't we also allow revision of awards based on the expected value of degrees?[16]

What is formalism?

But if we still use deduction all the time in legal reasoning, what is formalism? Beginning with Ihering's "Heaven of Legal Concepts,"[17] continuing with Roscoe Pound's "Mechanical Jurisprudence,"[18] and culminating with Felix Cohen's "Transcendental Nonsense,"[19] the critics of late-nineteenth-century legal thought characterized it as formalist in two quite distinct ways that are now commonly confused. In one usage, formalism is a "theory of law," though one invented by its adversaries rather than by any known American proponents. Formalism in this sense is the theory that all questions of law can be resolved by deduction, that is, without resort to policy, except for questions arising under rules that explicitly require policy argument.[20]

Their critique of formalism in this sense was that it was possible to maintain the idea that policy was never necessary only by making mistakes. They supported their position by showing in particular cases that a particular analysis, supposed to resolve a legal question deductively, failed. They critiqued not deduction in the abstract but particular deductions, in order to show that formalism as a general theory was wrong. In American legal thought, their critique fit with the pragmatist emphasis on the particular, on practice, on the specificity of the "facts."[21] But, of course, at the lower level, say of the definition of the expectancy, they used deduction just as often and with just as much confidence as the next man.[22]

In the United States, their critique was successful in a very strong sense: until recently, I had never met an American legal theorist or practitioner who called him- or herself a formalist, except in jest.[23] Liberals and conservatives agree that policy is *sometimes* necessary. Yet formalism is anything but a dead issue, and charges of formalism are the bread and butter of legal theoretical and doctrinal dispute. The reason for this is that the charge of formalism has another meaning. In this second sense, it charges an adversary either with making the mistake of thinking that a particular abstract legal norm can generate a particular subrule, or with a general tendency to overestimate the capacity of norms in general to generate subrules by deduction.

In this sense, it makes sense to charge Justice Rehnquist or Justice Scalia with formalism in a particular case or across the board, even though each constantly and explicitly acknowledges that *sometimes* they have to resort to balancing interests, or some other form of policy argument.[24] A friend recently lamented that the briefs before the South African Constitutional Court in the Death Penalty Case were "formalist" because they tried to answer the constitutional question, pro or con, by reference to the words "right to life" in the South African constitution, without reference to the history of apartheid.

The sociological jurisprudes and realists charged late-nineteenth-century legal thought with formalism in this second as well as in the first sense. Their message was that there was a systematic tendency to overestimate the extent to which the most abstract norms of the legal order could generate the more particular norms needed to decide particular cases. They tried to show that the governing abstractions lacked the operative power that formalists attributed to them. They promoted an attitude: "distrust of abstraction." They often argued in constitutional cases that because deduction couldn't settle the question, and it was therefore inevitably a question of policy, the Supreme Court should defer to the legislative judgment. But in private law cases they simply insisted on an overt rather than covert consideration of the legislative question that was "really" at issue.[25]

In short, formalism in the second sense is a derogatory description of your opponent's penchant to overestimate the powers of deduction, either in general or in a particular case. Neither in the first nor the second sense is formalism a *method* distinct from deduction. It can be invalidated as a theory of law, but it can't be invalidated or disproved as a method, because it is a mistaken use of a method that is sometimes valid, rather than a method in itself.

Relativizing the boundary between deductive questions and policy questions

The existence of a practice of charging formalism means that there is often disagreement in particular cases about the boundary between questions that "by their nature" can be resolved only by appeal to policy and questions that can be resolved by deduction. But it is not just that at a given moment some think a given legal issue can be resolved deductively while others think such a claim formalist. Over time, it appears that a whole legal culture can shift its general attitude about the boundaries within the implicit ontology of types of questions, and, of course, different cultures can differ along this dimension.

I mentioned a moment ago that the realists taught "distrust of abstraction." By this I mean that they had a general notion that the more abstract the concepts that went into the definition of a legal norm, the more unlikely that it could be elaborated by deduction to produce a subrule that would resolve a particular case. Thus "contract protects the will of the parties" was less likely to yield a valid, rather than a merely formalist, deduction than "the rule is expectation damages."

One way to look at the history of American legal thought is in terms of shifts over time in the level of abstraction at which it has seemed plausible that legal concepts have the "operative" power to generate deductively valid subrules. Before the Civil War, nondeductive argument was widely deployed to resolve questions that got resolved deductively after that war, and were then again put into the domain of policy by the sociological jurisprudes and realists.[26]

As I've indicated several times already, your ordinary American lawyer is likely to find European solutions to classic legal problems blatantly formalist, in the sense of overestimating the power of deduction, and to find European legal culture in general formalist in the same sense. When Europeans protest that none of them think, or ever did think, that deduction could solve every legal problem, the American lawyer is likely to think they have missed the point, which has to do with an attitude toward abstraction rather than with a theory of law in the jurisprudential sense.

Proponents of historical and comparative study are endlessly optimistic about its capacity to undermine vulgar prejudice. But the modern American sense that the boundary between law and policy is "out there" rather than a cultural artifact, and that as a matter of "fact" policy comes into play as soon as we rise above a low level of abstraction, easily survives historical and comparative exposure. The history of American legal thought has been written overwhelmingly by realists and by their mainstream successors, who have had a passionate commitment to the ideas that there was a misguided Formalist Period and that European legal thought in general is prerealist. The ontology of deductive and policy questions survives unshaken because the views of other times and places look just wrong.

The partial revival of deduction in American judicial opinions and scholarship after World War II might be another source for the idea that what is a policy question and what is a deductive question is not a question of fact. But the neoformalists of our time are, for the most part, either civil libertarians or conservatives. In both cases, they interpret their own practice as simply reestablishing the force of first principles. Because both groups seem blissfully ignorant of the realist critiques that killed off earlier versions of their arguments, they come off as simple-minded rather than as creative reconstructors, in the eyes of the older generation of pragmatists.

In short, the implicit lawyers' ontology of types of questions is alive and well. The critique of formalism (in the sense of overestimation of the power of abstractions) has reinforced it rather than undermined it.

The legal character of policy argument

The notion of policy was introduced into American legal thought during the period of "reception" of English law as one of the two factors that judges could and should use in deciding what rules to adopt, particularly in situations in which there was an English rule that might or might not be appropriate. There was a conventional distinction between "liberal" and "technical" approaches to legal questions. The liberal approach was distinguished by willingness to consider, as legitimate elements in the interpretive process, the purposes of rules, the intent of parties, and the equity of solutions.

Within the liberal mode, policy (convenience, utility) was at first opposed to morality. The legal elite thought of morality in terms of a Protestant Christian ethic of total duties of altruism, sharing, and self-sacrifice. Policy was the countervailing prudential argument for limiting legal duties and legal excuses so as to promote commerce and enterprise generally, and the parallel argument for delegalizing family life.[27] By the end of the nineteenth century, with the general formalization of American law, "policy" came to be used sometimes as the word for all nondeductive factors and sometimes to designate the set of instrumental, as opposed to intrinsic, reasons for a rule choice, whether it involved increasing or decreasing the level of duty. In this usage it is sometimes opposed to "justice," or to morality or to rights. I use it here in its broad sense, which includes all nondeductive factors.

It is crucially important that to this day policy is a standard category in everyday American lawyer-talk. It is not just that all lawyers and judges at least sometimes do policy argument in the course of conventional legal practice. That they do it is a universally recognized and accepted fact. In this respect, the United States seems to be very different from both Britain and the Continent, however true it may be that a functionally equivalent, though unrationalized practice is pervasive there.[28]

In French, it is still an issue how the word "policy" should be translated when it is used in legal texts—"politique" is a neologism unintelligible to most lawyers, because it suggests either politics or *administrative* policy, as in "incomes policy." In England, the idea that "public policy" is an "unruly horse" expresses the notion that it is an exceptional basis for decision, much like unconscionability in American contract law, rather than a word for the routine presence of "legislative" factors in the judicial process.

It is no less important that policy occupies a different place in the American lawyers' conventional understanding from that of argument from authority (deduction).

Policy as mediator and Trojan horse

Policy is firmly within American law, but also firmly less than "law" or deduction or black letter or precedent or statutory authority. It is less because it is understood as situated between the paradigmatically legal appeal to authority and the paradigmatically extra- or nonlegal appeal to "politics" or ideology. It is an intermediate term, partaking of some of the elements of the extremes. Moreover, it is a "fudge word," meaning a word that allows us to evade a problem that would be clear if we said what we meant with more precision.

Because policy argument is unquestionably legal, to make policy arguments is not to ask the judge to violate his role constraint by usurping the legislative function. But it is more than a matter of legal pedigree. Policy arguers present it as different from pure politics, or ideology, because it appeals to universal rather than particular interests.[29] Consequentialist argument appeals to a notion of "social welfare" or "efficiency" or "economic growth." Morality arguments deploy familiar general maxims, like "no man should profit from his own wrong," "do unto others," "be reasonable," and so on. Rights arguments (as we will see in great detail in a later chapter) presuppose the universality as well as the facticity of rights—everyone has a right of free speech, to dispose of property, to protection against fraud or duress, and so on.

Because policy argument deploys the full range of "social values" that are conventionally understood to be relevant to choices among norms, it will allow the judge to resolve any question of rule definition that litigants may put. Policy is therefore a "mediator" of the contradiction in the definition of the judicial role that requires the judge to decide only according to law but also requires her to decide any question over which she has jurisdiction. This means, as we will see, that policy plays the same role in the conventional understanding that coherence plays in modern analytical jurisprudence.

There is nonetheless a serious problem, one that "everyone" in American legal culture is acutely aware of. Although policy argument *formally* excludes ideology, it is "soft" and so operates always under the suspicion of permitting ideology to enter sub rosa. The formal exclusion of ideology means simply that it is "impermissible," it would be a legal "blunder," to phrase a policy argument in explicitly distributive, or explicitly religious, or explicitly "partisan" terms. Everyone has an interest in social welfare, observance of conventional morality, and the protection of rights that everyone possesses. But people are sharply divided about whether it would be desirable to redistribute wealth, to shift social power from men to women and from black to white, to further the growth of the Catholic Church, and so forth.

Even if everyone knows that a particular rights argument will effect some redistribution (say, affirmative action, or the invalidation of a rent-control statute), it is not permissible to give redistribution as the reason for the rule change in question. The distributive consequences must be presented as "side effects" of rights protection, or of a move that will increase efficiency, or of insisting on moral acts by individuals or groups. "Grammatical" policy argument never declares itself as simply "liberal" or "conservative," and a fortiori never declares itself as fascist or communist, because the judge would then appear to be a partisan.

The traditional lay Liberal version of the distinction between adjudication and legislation relied on the notion that there is a sharp distinction between law application and law making. This distinction relied on that between objectively determinable questions, questions of fact or of logic, and "subjective" questions about things like fairness and justice, which have no objectively determinable answers. Something like this opposition gets reproduced in the law/policy distinction. Lawyers see policy as subjective, and policy questions as having uncertain answers. Policy is indispensable, but it is also potentially a Trojan horse for the introduction of ideology into law.

Policy argument as an unrationalized practice

American legal culture offers no widely accepted explanation of why policy differs from ideology. It offers no explanation of how policy can resolve rather than just fudge the contradiction in the definition of the judicial role. Lawyers and law students characterize judges and professors as more or less "policy-oriented," and can be expected to have opinions about whether policy orientation is in general a virtue or a vice. These opinions once tended to align with the liberal/conservative ideological spectrum, with liberals liking policy, up to a point, and conservatives favoring authority, up to a point.[30] It appeared that there was a liberal theory of the role of policy in law analogous to the still-existing European left-wing "social" theory and a conservative theory of "formal" law.

But, as we have seen already, today there are conservative judges and professors of a law and economics persuasion who have reconfigured the debate by adopting a highly deductive form of policy argument from the premise of wealth maximization and who have little or no use for authority. Liberals, by contrast, reject policy argument in favor of deduction across a wide range of issues that they have reconceptualized as involving constitutional rights (free speech, privacy). They prefer the authority of the Bill of Rights, plus a long chain of inferences, to the choice of a rule among many possibilities by balancing conflicting interests on the basis of a contextualized analysis of the facts.

Of course, policy argument itself includes argument-bites that treat the whole idea of policy as suspect (remember the newspaper article that describes the *liberal* Supreme Court justices denouncing their conservative brethren for a "radical" attempt to argue "policy rather than law").[31] The rhetorical goal is to associate policy with the subjective, the political, the ideological, and to extrude it from law, leaving only authority. The counterbites denounce "legalism" or "sterile" or "bloodless" or "rigid" or "mechanical" or "arbitrary" deductive approaches, and emphasize the "inevitability" of policy, as well as its "progressive" and "pragmatic" character. Their goal is to tame deduction, to subordinate it to policy.

Policy in legal theory

The social practice of policy argument in these forms, some of them asserting it as indistinguishable from law and others assimilating it to purely political or ideological argument, is basic to American legal discourse. The rhetorical tropes involved are prior to, rather than responsive to, the jurisprudential debate among American legal theorists about what adjudication "is." No formulation of the nature of adjudication that denies policy argument as a fact, or that asserts that we should get rid of it as a normative matter, can be plausible. The goal of legal theoretical discussion, since the realists, has been to get beyond the mushy, self-contradictory quality of the lawyers' usage to "firmer ground."

For the most part, the realists did not critique the implicit lawyer's ontology of legal versus policy questions. What they tried to show was that the English notion that the judge can reason deductively in most cases but must occasionally act legislatively grossly underestimated the seriousness of the problem. Many, many questions that judges had purported to resolve deductively were in fact policy questions. The failures of deduction occurred not at the margins of the system but throughout. Given the significant rule-making role of the judge, it was not possible to concede the occasional need for legislative judgment and then get on with deduction, because that would leave a great deal of law if not illegitimate at least ungrounded.

Much in the current state of legal theory in the United States is explained by the realists' choice to attempt to reground the rules of law in a combination of fine-grained policy analysis and larger theories of coherence. We can say of this enterprise, first, that it entailed the abandonment of the critical, or viral, strand in their own project and, second, that it was only partially successful.

The realists' critical project was aborted because they never extended their successes in the critique of deduction, precedent, and statutory interpretation to policy argument itself. That, to my mind, has been a contribution of cls. The realists' reconstruction project was only partially successful because it generated, for American legal culture as a whole, the contradictory situation I have been describing. They achieved the legitimation of policy argument but left it in coexistence with deduction without any convincing account of their respective roles, or of its consistency with the asserted nonideological character of adjudication in a Liberal theory of the rule of law.

Since World War II, American legal theorists have been obsessed with completing this reconstructive part of the realist project. In this enterprise, it is important that liberals and conservatives stand in an asymmetrical relationship to the tradition of critique.

The dilemma of liberal legalism

Crudely put, the liberal dilemma is as follows: The main vehicle of liberal reform in the United States since World War II has been the judiciary, and the judiciary, with the exception of a brief period in the mid-1960s, has consistently implemented reform against, rather than in collaboration with, state and federal legislative majorities. It is not surprising that a project of liberal (not Liberal) legal theory is to show that this judicial contribution to the substance of both private and public law is democratically legitimate because it furthers the rule of law, rather than merely legislating judicially.

But, as Gary Peller and William Eskridge have suggested, the liberal critique of conservative legal formalism, from Holmes through legal realism, extended by critical legal studies, has dramatically undermined academic faith in the possibility of judicial neutrality in hard cases.[32] Indeed, the post–World War II liberal project is the lineal descendant of an exactly opposite liberal project: that of showing that the enormous contribution of a conservative judiciary to the shape of the prewar legal system was democratically illegitimate.

The exit from the liberal dilemma has to be a theory of adjudication that avoids the Scylla and Charybidis of formalism, in the sense of excessive reliance on deduction, and nihilism. There are both existential and instrumental political dangers on each side. Antiformalism is a core element in liberal legal identity because it reflects within this technical discipline the general liberal resistance to rigidity, the doctrinaire, and the authoritarian, all identified with nineteenth-century conservative ways of thinking and being. Antiformalism is the taught tradition of liberal legal education and the intellectual basis of the New Deal regulatory regime.

But nihilism about adjudication is no less threatening than formalism. Existentially, liberals with passionate commitments to specific judicial reforms, particularly in the areas of race and gender, have an interest in believing that these decisions were legally as well as politically and morally correct. If the judges "shouldn't have" or "couldn't legitimately" do these things, if the decisions were judicial legislation, then we "should have" gone on with the regime of de jure racial segregation until the gerrymandered state legislatures decided to abolish it in response to majority white sentiment.

At the instrumental level, a successful liberal legalist theory of adjudication must avoid nihilism so as not to cripple the chances for future liberal countermajoritarian reform by undermining the obedience and conversion effects. The federal and state courts at least appear to have been major actors in causing a deep, long-lasting, controversial, compromised, unfinished, but historic transformation of American political culture. It was not obvious that their interventions would have this effect. It seemed throughout the period of intense activism that the judges might change course in the face of organized grass roots and governmental opposition, or that their reforms would be rolled back by later conservative courts appointed by presidents and state governors who ran partly on opposition to what the courts had done.

Those who are skeptical about the obedience and conversion effects have to contend with the facts that large numbers of people obeyed though they disagreed and that judicial interventions seem to have had a massive effect, over the long run, and not just on the substantive views of a majority of white Americans on race and gender and consumer issues. The courts seem to have been important in inducing a diffuse but pervasive, unpredictably militant "rights consciousness" throughout American society that is one of the few effective checks on bureaucratic abuses in both public and private sectors. It has also reduced the legitimacy of all the preliberal, patriarchal, clientelistic, or plain corrupt regimes and arrangements that survived the "modernization" of American state and society in the 1930s and during World War II.

Liberal legal theorists have been at a remove or two from these mass levels. Through World War II, most were judges (Holmes, Louis Brandeis, Cardozo, Learned Hand, Jerome Frank, Felix Frankfurter), law professors, pragmatist philosophers, or institutional economists. Many of them at one time or another played "brain trust" roles in national politics. Since then, they have been mainly law professors in public law fields and jurisprudence professors, writing primarily in specialized legal journals, some with hopes of becoming judges. In the recent past the field of legal theory has emerged outside the curricular categories to provide a common identity.

It is important that the recent participants have been neither conventional political players (by contrast, European political parties often run public law professors for national office), nor "just academics," interested in adjudication in the abstract. They influence judges and elite lawyers, who are also members of the political class, through legal education. Some of them aspire to influence legal development directly through service in liberal Democratic administrations or appointment to the bench. And they suppose that they are part of a loosely articulated general intelligentsia capable of translating technical or theoretical insights into the culture at large through, for example, the *New York Times Book Review,* the *New York Review,* and the *New Republic,* televised Supreme Court confirmation hearings, and the occasional "appearance" on National Public Radio. They think of themselves as players, but only over the long run and indirectly, on the basis of this combination of technical and academic prestige with "access."[33]

It has been obvious to liberal legal theorists, I speculate, that as present and potential rulers through the courts, they have an interest in the ability of the courts to command obedience and induce changes in moral sentiments. Any explanation of why the Warren Court did the right thing that accepts a strong form of the realist and postrealist critique of judicial legislation makes the people seem like dupes of legal mumbo jumbo that is just a mask for the imposition of the liberal ideological agenda. Such an explanation is not a good explanation. It is not good because it delegitimates this form of liberal political power for the future, while unilaterally abandoning the demand for judicial neutrality as a means of keeping today's conservative judges and left-fringe activists in check.

The instrumental stakes in liberal antiformalism are less obvious than those in resisting nihilism. They have to do with this same struggle of liberalism with resurgent conservatism, on one side, and diffuse rights-oriented radicalism (rather than communism) on the other. The polarization of liberal courts against conservative legislatures gradually faded in the 1970s and 1980s, as conservative presidents partially remade the federal judiciary in their own image. There hasn't been another reversal, pitting liberal legislatures against conservative judges in the mode of the long period between about 1870 and 1940. Conservative judges haven't engaged in wholesale countermajoritarian initiatives (there has been no need). But they haven't given up their major role in the management of public life, as exemplified by the U.S. Supreme Court's sustained attack on affirmative action programs.

To this purpose, they continuously redeploy all the formalist (that is, implausibly deductive) legal gambits that they once used to block liberal social legislation. The realist heritage of critique is kept alive in dissenting opinions that carefully reveal the internally contradictory or inconclusive character of the majority's syllogistic reasoning, thereby making way for a liberal policy analysis that comes out the other way (classic examples are Justice Brennan's dissent in the DeShaney[34] case and Justice Blackmun's in Lucas[35]).

At the same time, modern conservative law and economics theorists claim that the goal of efficiency is the sole politically legitimate basis of judicial law making and is sufficiently determinate to indicate a correct answer to almost any question of regulatory law. They urge the judges to adopt that solution, almost always in some sense "freeing" the market to the detriment of economically weaker parties, more or less regardless of what the common law precedents or prior statutory interpretations may say. From the liberal point of view, this approach combines nihilism about adjudication with formalism about economics, and it invites internal critique of the efficiency criterion to make room for "justice" concerns.

While there is no Marxist opposition, there has always been radical pressure on the liberal left flank. A part of this pressure comes from lawyers and legal academics influenced by the history of the critique of adjudication and forever impressed by the success of an earlier generation of liberals in getting the courts to implement their program against legislative majorities. Their strategy is to claim that the Constitution requires, at an abstract level, a regime of rights that corresponds to the radical multicultural program that developed on the left of liberalism in the wake of the civil rights, antiwar, and women's movements.

Left lawyers and academics of this persuasion continuously develop new legal theories designed to mobilize the courts behind programs that have no chance of being adopted by liberal legislative groups, let alone by legislative majorities. Unemployment is an unconstitutional taking of workers' property. The institutionalization of the mentally ill is unconstitutional per se. The courts should guarantee a minimum level of subsistence for welfare recipients, guarantee a right to decent housing, forbid

U.S. intervention in Nicaragua, require the United States to compensate the victims of El Salvador right-wing terror, forbid the implementation of the North American Free Trade Agreement, and so forth.

While any particular liberal is likely to agree with quite a few of the literally hundreds of proposals put before the courts every year, it is obvious that there have to be "some limits." In each case, the external normative system—human rights or some form of socialism—seems convincing and important enough so that the advocate is willing to more or less forget about the idea that judges are supposed to be faithful interpreters of the existing legal materials. This is a genuine solution or response to the problem of the internal critique of adjudication—it accepts the critique and proposes to answer the question of how the judges should behave by offering them a supposedly determinate system external to law that they can just implement.

Like law and economics, this response is formalist as well as nihilist. It treats the Constitution the way the Abolitionists treated the Declaration of Independence, as a sort of higher law charter trumping all positive law, including the case law interpretation of the Constitution, and requiring as a matter of correct popularly sovereign political philosophy that the courts impose a radical restructuring of society. Resistance involves both the defense of legality and the internal critique of left rights rhetoric to make room for "moderate" solutions that "balance" rights in conflict.

Responses to the dilemma

We are now in a position to state the complex conditions of success for what seems to me the core project of liberal legal theory. Liberals need a theory of adjudication that affirms the basic points of their historical critique of ideology in adjudication, as a means of resisting conservative backsliding and radical hijacking, while at the same time affirming the recent history of liberal judicial law making in a way that doesn't undermine the obedience and conversion effects.

The response has been an explosion of alternatives, beginning with the realists' and ranging today from Dworkin's through republican, communitarian, neopragmatist, feminist, and "new public law" theories of the judicial role. In jurisprudence, the questions of the "determinacy" and objectivity of law, along with an influx of humanities graduate students into law schools, have prompted a new literature that applies just about every tendency in ancient and modern philosophy to the problem.

We can identify three generations of American coherence theorists, each responding in different ways to the viral strand in realism. The first is the response of the realists themselves; the second is that of the post–World War II Cold War generation; the third is that of the civil rights and Vietnam (1960s) generation. All three defend policy argument, against the charge that it is necessarily a Trojan horse for ideology, by appeal to metaphors intended to show how to confine it, to keep raw politics out.

In their reconstructive mode, the realists were looking for a method of adjudication that could (a) provide a nonideological modus operandi when deduction was no help, and (b) sometimes justify the judge in rejecting a deductively required result in favor of a more socially progressive solution. In this mode, they proposed a way to deal both with the now open questions that before their critique of deduction had appeared to be susceptible to deductive resolution, *and* with the problem of deductions that were sound given their premises but that seemed to require the judge to play a retrograde role.

The most common realist solution, influenced by the German and French free-law theorists, was the notion of society as an evolving organism with needs and functions. The judicial function was to evolve the rules so as to fulfill the needs. Writers like Cardozo describe this function as the basis of a method alternative to deduction. The judge who did it right was not a partisan, though he had to acknowledge that "subjective" factors conditioned his understanding of progress. The method was to be used not just to answer when deduction "ran out" but also to critique unquestionably deductively correct results, and sometimes to reject them in the name of evolution.[36] The obvious problem lies in the vagueness of the notions of need, function, and evolution, which seem to highlight rather than overcome the Trojan horse danger.

"Process" models of adjudication (Fuller,[37] Hart and Sacks[38]) have the same structure, but this time the image is that of the state as a well-functioning bureaucratic organization based on the division of labor and aiming to "maximize" not profit but "the satisfaction of valid human wants."[39] The idea is that different law-making institutions, including private parties, administrative agencies, and legislatures as well as state and federal courts, have intuitively accessible "jobs" in the overarching scheme. It seems obviously desirable that each institution specialize in the job it does best. Any other solution threatens both organizational chaos and a reduction of the quality of outputs, because institutions will do jobs that would be "better" performed by others.

The judge's job goes far beyond deduction. Process theorists distinguish "kinds" of policy questions, namely, those that are and those that aren't susceptible to "reasoned elaboration" (that is, nonideological resolution through the method of coherence). There are two symmetrical sins in this model: to ignore policy when the judge should consider it ("The Case of the Spoiled Cantaloupes"),[40] and to apply policy analysis to questions that should be resolved "elsewhere" (Brown v. Board of Education, for Herbert Wechsler).[41]

The notion of "institutional competence" within the overall enterprise of pursuing socially legitimate purposes solves the problem of judicial legislation, permitting the judge to deploy policy argument and even to reject deductive solutions on policy grounds, in some cases, while firmly excluding the merely personal or ideological in cases where policy would be a Trojan horse. As I pointed out in Chapter 2, when the question is not one appropriate for "reasoned elaboration," the plaintiff loses for a good legal reason (the coherence of a scheme of separation of powers), rather than through either denial of justice or judicial legislation.

The obvious problems are how to decide which questions have which "natures," and what to do when the image of the division of labor within a well-functioning bureaucracy is obviously unrealistic.[42] The institutional-competence notion worked well in retrospective 1950s liberal analyses of conservative judicial overreaching up to the New Deal. But it proved extremely difficult for its inventors (though not for its current revivalists)[43] to reconcile it with the activist role of liberal state and federal courts after World War II. Writers like Hart and Wechsler, who had begun their careers as liberal opponents of judicial activism,[44] found themselves unexpectedly the intellectual allies of conservative resistance to judicially mandated racial integration.[45]

Dworkin's version of coherence

I will take Ronald Dworkin's work[46] as the paradigm of contemporary responses to the liberal dilemma, but not because his theory is successful and in spite of the fact that very few liberals seem to agree with it.[47] Its virtues lie in that it is canonical, admirably complete, and, to my mind, by far the most sensitive of the lot to the internal tensions the project has to overcome—the most legal realist.

Dworkin's version of coherence explicitly "personifies" the "community" and asks us to imagine that this person is the author of all valid legal materials. Then we are supposed to imagine that this person wants to conform to what Dworkin supposes is an unproblematic norm of personal ethics—that a person should act consistently over time—while trying to achieve the classic policy objectives of fairness, justice, and due process.[48] The judge is supposed to choose a rule that will "fit" the materials imagined as the product of this communal person's project. If the judge tries to act as if he were the communal person, his own potentially ideological convictions about fairness, justice, and due process will be disciplined by the need for consistency with the communal person's earlier decisions.[49]

Dworkin's solution is like Cardozo's and Hart and Sacks's in that it allows the judge to decide "according to law" in every case (no need ever to resort to ideology, as opposed to "political theory"), while at the same time permitting, indeed demanding, nondeductive reasoning. But unlike his 1950s predecessors, Dworkin distinguishes between types of argument, rather than between types of questions. All legal questions have right answers, but these are accessible only if the judge distinguishes rights arguments, defined as the trumps of rights holders vis-à-vis majorities, from the class of what he calls policy arguments. Policy arguments, in his usage, presuppose the legitimacy of sacrificing individual to collective interests—they correspond to the subset I called utilitarian or social welfare policy arguments.[50]

In short, all three theories mediate the apparent contradiction in judicial role constraints by defending the middle term of policy argument (for Dworkin limited to rights argument), as opposed to deduction on one side and ideological argument on the other. They do this by denying that policy (rights, for Dworkin) is inevitably just a mask for subjective or ideological preference. Their question is, How can the judge be neutral? Their answer is that he can be neutral in two ways: by doing deduction when that is appropriate, and by grounding policy argument, when that is appropriate, outside himself in an image—whether of society as an organism, of society as a bureaucracy maximizing through the division of labor, or of an imaginary person who is the author of all laws.

Dworkin left and right

While Dworkin's work (and post-1960s American jurisprudence generally) displays these striking parallels with its predecessors, it also displays far more anxiety about and is far more responsive to critique than Cardozo, Llewellyn, Fuller, or Hart and Sacks. I attribute this to three factors: the need to incorporate into coherence theory some attitude toward the judicial activism of the Warren Court, the critique of American coherence theory by British thinkers like Hart,[51] Raz[52] and MacCormick,[53] and the rebirth of the virus in critical legal studies. What follows is a crit, left/mpm reading of Dworkin as a contemporary.

First, Dworkin makes substantial concessions to the historical critique of adjudication by affirming the political nature of legal interpretation. In his early work, this legitimate political element, sharply contrasted with "personal" or "partisan" politics, always turned out to be belief in rights as opposed to one form or another of utilitarianism. In other words, although the judge couldn't escape having a political theory, that theory was just the opposite of "ideology." The theory constrained him because it was an articulation of connections between general philosophical propositions about the political good and particular instances; the judge who saw himself as a rule utilitarian couldn't switch ad hoc to a rights argument if he didn't like a particular outcome.[54]

In *A Matter of Principle*, Dworkin began to develop his own version of liberalism as a political theory of just this type,[55] contrasted it with conservative political theory, and quite abruptly affirmed that "we should expect to find distinctly liberal or radical or conservative opinions" about constitutional interpretation, and that "this is exactly what we do find."[56] In *Law's Empire*, Dworkin acknowledges the common practice of analyzing constitutional decision making through the lens of current ideology and admits that even his own ideal judge may be well described in these terms (providing we have enough data about his positions).[57] In other words, liberalism and conservatism have crossed the line from the partisan or merely personal into the realm of "theory." The choice among theories, as we saw, may determine the content of judicial law making but can't be justified as noncontroversial, demonstrably correct, or objective.

To this point, it is easy to see how Dworkin can fulfill the requirement that a liberal legal theory provide a basis for attacking both conservative judicial law making and left activist proposals as judicial legislation. Indeed, Dworkin appears as the heir and—in his own attacks on the semantic view of law,[58] on originalism,[59] and on passivism[60]—as the developer of the legal realist tradition. But it is hard to see how he can avoid the English positivist view that the judge is necessarily a legislator in hard cases, and the corollary that the liberal activism of the Warren Court was no more legitimate than the conservative activism it succeeded.

He turns this trick by characterizing his politicized version of adjudication as still very different from legislation. First, as we have seen already, adjudication is properly the interpretation of the relevant legal materials, with a view to understanding what they require if we imagine them to express the views of a single communal person. This distinguishes the judge from the legislator who is free to ignore the solution the materials yield if he thinks he can do better. Dworkin swims with the tide of the 1980s, in which the current of legal theory converged with that of hermeneutics.[61]

But within his version of the interpretive turn, fidelity to the materials is more than a description of the typical judge's attitude that will help us to understand what he does. Fidelity requires a commitment to finding the "right" interpretation in every case, with rightness understood like the judge's personal political theory as possibly controversial and in any case nondemonstrable.[62] The existence of controversial, nondemonstrable right interpretations is attested by our collective practice of looking for them and thinking we've found them. If the judge is committed to finding, and if there always is, a right answer, then the law will never "run out." The judge will never be in the English positivist position of having to legislate no matter how much he would prefer to merely interpret.[63]

Second, in Dworkin's theory of interpretation, the requirement that a solution "fit" with the body of legal materials, the requirement of coherence, will often settle the case without controversy, and the judge will be obviously distinct from the legislator.[64] But where this is not the case, and the judge must choose between competing versions of the coherent solution, the judge can deploy his personal political theory only under two further constraints that don't apply to the legislator. The judge must be able to defend his preferred political theory as offering the most coherent explanation of the materials.[65] And he is supposed to apply it to the case in hand. Together, these three constraints make him principled rather than result-oriented.

The legislator can make law legitimately while disregarding all these requirements. He can choose a rule that is blatantly inconsistent with the larger regime of which it will become a part. He can choose it to further his particular political philosophy even though that philosophy is totally implausible as an explanation of the legal regime as a whole. And he can choose a particular solution in spite of its being inconsistent with the political philosophy he would apply in other similar cases. He can vote in favor of an anomalous "anarchist" addition to a liberal legal regime, even though he himself is a conservative, because his constituents will otherwise vote him out of office, or because his "gut" tells him this is the only fair thing to do.

Third, Dworkin's theory of legal interpretation requires the judge but not the legislator to give a complicated priority in his legal reasoning to rights over other kinds of policies (though in a somewhat different way in common law, statutory, and constitutional adjudication). Final judicial review of legislative action means that when the judges think the statute violates constitutional rights, they strike it down, no matter how important the policies it serves. But in this respect, they differ from legislators only in being above them: legislators shouldn't pass such statutes. The rights/policies distinction distinguishes judges from legislators more clearly in the common law and statutory law making contexts.[66]

Dworkin supposes a general social consensus on the "reality" (not "objectivity") of moral rights, rights that are morally "valid" or "binding" whether or not legally enforceable.[67] To try to identify these, and to work out the consequences of their partial recognition in positive law, is quite different from trying to decide what legal rules best further collective objectives (national security, economic growth). The achievement of policies is measured "in gross," without any requirement that any particular individual receive any particular form of treatment, and Dworkin also thinks that policy is by definition unprincipled because it is not concerned with treating like cases alike.[68]

The function of this distinction in the theory is clear: the moral reality of rights grounds judicial law making through the method of coherence plus political theory. Just as we agree that there can be a right interpretation of a text even though that interpretation is controversial and "can't be proved," so we agree that rights really do "exist" even if their content in a particular case is likewise controversial and nondemonstrable. Or so Dworkin thinks. Adjudication, which is and ought to be focused on right answers to questions about rights, legitimately involves only some of the judge's political theoretical views—his views about rights.

The legislator by contrast is supposed to take rights seriously, but also to have commitments in policy conflicts where this kind of grounding doesn't exist. This allocation of function is appropriate because the legislature is organized to aggregate the collective interests that policies have at stake and to decide the distributive consequences fairly, that is, democratically. The judiciary would be doing the wrong thing if it intruded on this domain, even in common law cases, as well as failing to honor its own historic mission of protecting the individual against majority abuse. Here Dworkin owes more than he has acknowledged to Hart and Sacks.

On the basis of these three claims about adjudication, Dworkin can defend liberal judicial law making as democratically legitimate, not judicial legislation, not even activism, although as he recognizes the defense has to be case by case, or "at retail."

> Activism is a virulent form of legal pragmatism. An activist justice would ignore the Constitution's text, the history of its enactment, prior decisions of the Supreme Court interpreting it, and the long-standing traditions of our political culture. He would ignore all these in order to impose on other branches of government his own view of what justice demands. Law as integrity condemns activism, and any practice of constitutional adjudication close to it . . . The alternative to passivism is not a crude activism harnessed only to a judge's sense of justice, but a more fine-grained and discriminating judgment, case by case, that gives place to many political virtues but, unlike either activism or passivism, gives tyranny to none.[69]

For each case, the question is whether the judges reached the right interpretation of the materials, one that respected the requirement of coherence, was principled rather than result-oriented, and eschewed reliance on the judge's personal views of policy. Even if you agree that the judge's rule making was thus constrained, you may well think the case came out wrong, especially if you don't share the judge's political theory. But you would be naive to expect anything else and foolish to prefer the legislative process for hard cases. What makes law worthy of respect, what makes the obedience and conversion effects tolerable in a democracy, is that adjudication "insures that the most fundamental issues of political morality will finally be set out and debated as issues of principle and not political power alone, a transformation that cannot succeed, at least not fully, within the legislature itself."[70]

A summary critique of Dworkin's response to the dilemma of contemporary liberal legalism

For Dworkin's theory to work as a response to what I called above the "dilemma of liberal legalism," two quite different requirements have to be met. First, Dworkin's assertion that judges should not reason from policy rests on his general theory that judges should conform to the best interpretation of the actual practice of adjudication.[71] So he has to convince us that the exclusion of policy argument in fact fits American judicial practice. Second, he has to convince us that rights argument, sharply distinguished from policy argument, functions to exclude judicial ideology, so that the rules it generates are attributable to "principle and not political power alone."

As to the second point, Dworkin provides surprisingly little in the way of reassurance that rights reasoning is more internally structured, more constraining, than policy argument. In Chapters 12 and 13, I argue at length that, at least to many participants in American legal culture, rights reasoning seems no more plausibly exclusive of ideological influence than more apparently open-ended moral or instrumental argument.

My point in this chapter has been that policy, in Dworkin's sense and also in the broader sense that includes nondeductive balancing of conflicting rights and conflicting moral principles, is pervasive in American judicial practice, and that the question is how to rationalize it. It seems implausible, to say the least, that an interpretation of adjudication that simply excludes consequentialist or social-welfare-oriented policy argument altogether from the repertoire of legitimate judicial behavior can "fit" the practice. I think a reason why many practitioners find Dworkin unconvincing is that as a matter of fact American judges constantly deploy arguments that look exactly like the ones he claims they generally avoid.

Kent Greenawalt made this objection to Dworkin's account of American judicial practice in 1977.[72] Dworkin himself summarized the objection this way:

> Greenawalt takes as his main target my claim that judges in ordinary cases characteristically justify their decisions through what I called arguments of principle rather than arguments of policy . . . He offers, in opposition to [this] descriptive claim, several counter-examples. These are designed to show that American judges at least, often reach decisions in hard cases on the basis of arguments of policy. He fears that I will try to avoid these counter-examples by "ingenious" arguments showing that what are apparently arguments of policy in these cases are really, if properly understood, arguments of principle. But he warns me that if I succeed in this sort of defense I shall do so at the cost of erasing the distinction between the two sorts of arguments, or in some other way making my main claim trivial.[73]

As best I can understand it, Dworkin's response, which defies summary here, falls into the trap against which Greenawalt warned.[74] Indeed, as a student of past and present American judicial opinions, it seems too obvious to merit extended argument that judges constantly evoke, for and against a given rule choice, the whole range of effects the rule will have on people other than the parties, and evaluate those effects in terms of the general goals of the community. Moreover, this practice is explicitly theorized by so many judges with places in the American judicial pantheon that it seems implausible to say the least to redefine it at this late date as treason to the Empire. I offer just one example of my own.

In a famous hard case decided in 1842, Chief Justice Lemuel Shaw of the Massachusetts Supreme Judicial Court held that Farwell, a worker, could not recover damages from his employer to compensate an injury caused by the negligence of a "fellow servant." His opinion clearly states the common understanding of his time as to the role of policy in legal reasoning:

> If we look from considerations of justice to those of policy, they will strongly lead to the same conclusion. In considering the rights and obligations arising out of particular relations, it is competent for courts of justice to regard considerations of policy and general convenience, and to draw from them such rules as will, in their practical application, best promote the safety and security of all parties concerned. This is, in truth, the basis on which implied promises are raised, being duties legally inferred from a consideration of what is best adapted to promote the benefit of all persons concerned, under given circumstances.
>
> . . .We are of opinion that these considerations apply strongly to the case in question. Where several persons are employed in the conduct of one common enterprise or undertaking, and the safety of each depends much on the care and skill with which each other shall perform his appropriate duty, each is an observer of the conduct of the others, can give notice of any misconduct, incapacity or neglect of duty, and leave the service, if the common employer will not take such precautions, and employ such agents as the safety of the whole party may require. By these means, the safety of each will be much more effectually secured, than could be done by a resort to the common employer for indemnity in case of loss by the negligence of each other.[75]

I suppose it is conceivable that what Shaw himself understood to be an argument of policy can be recast as an argument that as a matter of principle Farwell had no right to recover from the railroad for his coworker's negligence. But I agree with Greenawalt that an ingenious transformation of this kind will make the distinction between rights argument and policy argument not exactly "trivial," but rather useless for the purpose of defending liberal judicial reform efforts without falling into either formalism or nihilism.

Of course, Dworkin has had other agendas, indeed many other agendas than that of responding to the dilemma of Warren-Court and Vietnam-era American liberal legalism. Though he might not find the comparison flattering, his early work resembles in many ways the project of Sir William Blackstone, whose *Commentaries* undertook the "Herculean" task of showing that the English common law of the late eighteenth century was best understood as the working out into the details of legality of the rights of Englishmen established in the Glorious Revolution.[76] There is an echo of this still unfulfilled program in Dworkin's gracious response to his mentor Henry Hart's critique of the Noble Dream: "I hope to persuade lawyers to lay the entire [positivist] picture of existing law aside in favour of a theory of law that takes questions about legal rights as special questions about political rights, so that one may think a plaintiff has a certain legal right without supposing that any rule or principle that already 'exists' provides that right."[77]

As with Sir William, the larger Liberal project of reconciling rights, majority rule, and the rule of law takes place in a much more specific political context, for Dworkin the context of liberal/conservative ideological conflict.

Dworkin's Hercules as a left liberal legalist

After explaining why Brown v. Board gave the "right" answer to the question of de jure segregation, but should have demanded far more than "all deliberate speed," and why racial quotas are constitutional, Dworkin asks whether Hercules, his ideal judge, is "too conservative" or "too liberal." He does not answer that Hercules is no more liberal or conservative than he is activist or passivist. He says instead: "You cannot yet say, because your judgment would depend on how closely your convictions matched his across the wide spectrum of different kinds of convictions an interpretation of constitutional practice engages."[78]

This answer makes me laugh. Over the course of his career, Dworkin has endorsed as the legally "right answer" not just Brown without delay and racial quotas, but civil disobedience,[79] nonprosecution of draft card burners,[80] the explicit consideration of distributive consequences rather than reliance on efficiency,[81] judicial review of apportionment decisions,[82] extensive constitutional protection of criminals' rights,[83] the constitutional protection of the right of homosexuals to engage in legislatively prohibited practices,[84] the right to produce and consume pornography,[85] and abortion rights.[86]

Hercules is not just a liberal; he is a systematic defender of liberal judicial activism from Brown to the present. He is actually a left liberal, as close as you can get in terms of outcomes to a radical. As a good liberal should, he has shown that he is capable of drawing the line *somewhere,* but only at defending radical peace activists of the Greenham Common or German antimissile variety,[87] the more extreme demands of freedom of the press,[88] and Catharine MacKinnon's antiliberal critiques of consent in heterosexual sex and of pornography.[89]

Of course, each defense of liberal judicial activism is at retail, on the merits of the particular case, under the constraints of looking for the "right answer" to the interpretive question, of principle, and of the judicial privileging of rights over policies. The same applies to each critique of *conservative* activism and each instance of resistance to overreaching by the left fringe. Hercules

> would not have joined the *Lochner* majority, for example, because he would have rejected the principle of liberty the Supreme Court cited in that case as plainly inconsistent with American practice and anyway wrong and would have refused to reexamine the New York legislature's judgment on the issues of policy that then remained.[90]

Hercules is just doing his job—exercising at every point his "most conscientious judgment," including his "responsibility to decide when he must rely on his own convictions about his nation's character."[91] If you don't agree with these "convictions," that is, with the egalitarian version of liberal ideology that Dworkin has been developing in parallel with his theory of adjudication, console yourself with the thought that when you are a judge, you are invited, indeed enjoined, to impose your version of conservative (but not Marxist, anarchist, or eccentric religious) ideology on pain of condemnation as a "traitor" to law's empire.[92] At that point, you too will be entitled to the obedience and conversion effects, unimpaired, we hope, by nihilism.

I would certainly vote for Dworkin if he were running for the Senate and support his appointment to the bench, supposing in each case that there was no radical alternative. But his (relative) political correctness is only half the story. At the cultural level, he is not a left liberal but a conservative whose goal has been to put a stop to the "eroding" or viral progress of the critical project.

Stopping the virus doesn't mean rolling the clock back to 1900; indeed, it is hard to see how that could possibly work. Dworkin dispenses with some of the dualities that initially both explained and justified the institution of professionally accountable courts specialized in adjudication. Judges make as well as apply law; their law making is political; they aren't validated by objectivity. The tools of reconstruction are the interpretive right answer, the notion of principle, and the distinction between rights and policies. Through them, Dworkin reconstitutes the initial distinctions in a modest mode: not law application but rightness in interpretation; not objectivity but principle; not law versus politics, but rights versus policies.

It is emblematic of American critical legalism that liberal legal theorists attacked each of these attempts at regrounding, trying and to my mind succeeding in showing that none could survive internal critique.[93] It is equally emblematic that they did this, one after another, in pursuance of their own versions of the identical project of reconstruction. Some, for example, take us back to the moderate English version in which legal formalism radically restricts the nonetheless ineradicable moments of judicial legislation; others promise a return to objectivity, albeit in some compromised form; maybe moral reasoning will turn out to have all the qualities legal reasoning has lost; there are pragmatist options that fudge even Dworkin's remaining distinctions.

My goal is to get out of this trap, to see what happens when one takes not rights, and not critique, but their interaction seriously. It is quite wrong to see Dworkin and cls, in the mode of pop jurisprudence, as "opposites"—he thinks there is always a right answer, we think there is never one—since Dworkin takes critique much more seriously than his own critics, and crits love determinacy, in its place, as much as the next person. It is nonetheless a relief to say good-bye, for the time being, to all the reconstructive projects, all so obviously based, at least to my jaundiced eye, on making knowledge with a view to power, and power to serve the holders of that very knowledge.

Some disclaimers. By saying that the liberal legal project has been to defend the legality of the liberal judicial law making of the last fifty years, while remaining true to the liberal critique of judicial legislation, I do not mean to impute bad faith except of the existential type I want to impute to judges as well. Contrast Dworkin's suggestion that some crits "may want . . . to move toward a new mystification in service of undisclosed political goals."[94] Nor am I arguing that the "pure" jurisprudential interest in figuring out the "truth" about adjudication has been irrelevant. Far from it. To say, for example, that Dworkin's theoretical work is incomprehensible without the context of his personal political commitment to the reforms of the Warren Court is not to say that he is dishonest, or not "really" a scholar, or that his conclusions are "suspect" in a way that those of more "disinterested" theorists are not.

Nonetheless, the liberal project inflects and also distorts the jurisprudential inquiry by influencing the choice of hypotheses, the choice between equally plausible interpretations, and, above all, the investment of time and energy in particular problems. In this case, time spent defending rightness, principle, and rights is time not spent on the left/mpm project of unsettling those very ideas.

How does law making by adjudication in an ideologically divided society alter the outcomes from those that would occur under a more transparent process? Suppose that one or another theorist actually managed to successfully answer the question of how a judge can be neutral. It would still remain to be seen whether our actual judges try to be neutral in this way, whether they succeed, and how their adoption of the stance inflects rule making vis-à-vis the outcomes of, say, legislative supremacy.

The liberal legalist investment in Reason sometimes pays off in knowledge that is useful beyond the project, that has as much "truth value" for conservatives or radicals as for its liberal inventors. But the knowledge the liberal legalist project produces is not much help with these questions. We might define the project as a particular strategy for shoring up rightness, principle, and rights so that it will be unnecessary to answer them. In short, the critique of ideologically oriented strategic behavior in judging that I develop in the next three chapters applies to jurisprudence as well.

I propose to put my left/mpm questions, which are peripheral as long as we are mainly concerned to defend the possibility of neutrality, in the center of inquiry, by asking not how judges can be neutral but how they can be ideological.

PART THREE

Ideology in Adjudication

6

Policy and Ideology

The goal of this chapter is to flesh out the intuition that policy is a potential Trojan horse for ideology. I begin by developing a simple model of legal discourse in general, a model based on a sharp distinction between legal norms and the reasons for adopting them. The model is designed not to "explain" legal discourse but to provide a descriptive vocabulary in which to argue three points.

First, legal discourse overlaps with, or interpenetrates, ideological discourse in a way that makes it hard to distinguish an ideological argument from a "neutral" or "objective" or "impersonal" legal argument. Second, over time the pursuit of ideological projects through law has "sedimented" or structured legal discourse in such a way that it "guides" decision makers into framing problems of rule choice in terms of familiar liberal and conservative ideological alternatives. Third, even a judge or lawyer with no ideological project of her own will find that she is willy-nilly an ideological performer, because she has to write her opinions in legal prose. The linguistic units available in legal prose are loaded with ideological meanings.

The methodology through which I explore these asserted phenomena is quite different from that of the last chapter, which purported simply to state explicitly the presuppositions of "standard" American legal discourse or of legal culture. While this chapter resembles the last in relying on no more than "common knowledge" for data, it is "structuralist" in a much more technical sense. It draws on Ferdinand de Saussure,[1] Claude Lévi-Strauss,[2] and Jean Piaget[3] (though in the cannibalizing or "bricolage" mode rather than in that of "application" of their theories) to represent the judge as both liberated and constrained because her job requires her to speak, to argue in, a particular language. Legal discourse is distinctive not just because it is "about law," but also because it is a "langue," or language, in which the judge produces "parole," or speech—namely, a particular argument in favor of a rule choice that will resolve a question of law.

To say that judges argue in the "language" of law is to make the specific claim that this social practice is illuminated by treating it as analogous to the more general phenomenon of language, in the sense of the English language. It is to assert that the familiar structures of English, like the distinction between a syllable, a word, and a sentence, or between syntax and grammar, have analogues within "law talk." Of course, law talk in English is structured by English; the notion here is that law talk has a second structure—it is a language within a language, and the second language has an additional set of structures analogous to those of the English in which it is spoken.[4]

Languages, for example English, have a temporal (diachronic) dimension, as well as a (synchronic) structure at any given moment. We can study the way the vocabulary or lexicon of a language changes through time, undergoes influence from other languages, responds to "material" developments like technological change, or is deliberately changed by speakers who see it as a locale for the playing out of conflicting social projects (Negro, black, or African American? stewardess or flight attendant?). The same is true, if the analogy holds, for legal discourse.

In this chapter, my goal is to identify the aspects of legal discourse that suggest to *informed observers* of adjudication that ideology is a major influence. The premise will be that we have no idea what judges' actual state of consciousness of the issue of neutrality may be. In other words, the claim is that there are aspects of legal discourse that suggest ideological influence even in the absence of any showing of ideological preferences or intentions, conscious or unconscious, in the person doing the argument.

The external point of view of this chapter derives from the modernist/postmodernist theoretical current that emphasizes two things about language. First, there is a discontinuity between speaker and speech, so that opportunistic or strategic use of language is always a possibility. Second, speech is never fully controlled by the speaker (the speaker is in some sense "spoken" by his or her language), so that speech "exceeds" the speaker, propagating meanings independently of "original intent."

The next two chapters appropriate a very different mpm methodology, loosely derived from phenomenology. They attempt to reconstruct judging "from the inside," by imagining what it would be like to be a judge working within role constraints that seem simultaneously to forbid and to require that he bring his ideological commitments to bear in his law making. I don't think there is anything inconsistent about adopting these different approaches one after the other. The idea is to get a handle on a practice, policy argument, in relation to the phenomenon of ideological division. The approaches should cumulate, making it clear how the judge can be an ideological actor by showing, first, what he has to work with and, second, how he does the work.

Rules versus reasons for rules

The first element in my proposed analysis of legal discourse is a sharp distinction between rules of law and reasons for adopting rules of law. By "rules of law," I mean "valid legal norms," or "black letter law," or "doctrine." "To make a contract, there must be an offer, acceptance, and consideration." "Any voluntary physical invasion of another's real property is a trespass to land." Each of these statements is radically incomplete. Depending on what facts you want to apply them to, you have to know many more detailed rules about what counts as an offer, about "defenses" to trespass, and so forth.

With important exceptions to be discussed in a moment, *the rules of law give no reasons for themselves.* They tell us how officials are supposed to respond in different situations. It seems obvious to me that this doesn't make it impossible to follow them, when their meaning is apparent. But it seems equally obvious to me that most of them provide, on their face, no explanation of why they were adopted. They have "authority" behind them— that is, statutory enactment, or declaration as the holding of a case, or an authoritative treatise writer. There are reasons to obey authority. But the reasons for obeying authority are not the same thing as the reasons for adopting a rule in the first place.

I will divide reasons for rules into two categories, corresponding to the notions of deductive and policy arguments developed in the last chapter. A deductive reason for a rule is a claim that there is a more abstract valid legal norm that has the rule in question as a strong or weak deductive consequence. A policy reason for a rule is a claim that the rule is the one among many possibilities that corresponds to an optimal balance between conflicting values (rights, morality, social welfare, and so on) operating in the "force field" model.

The model I am proposing uses the rule-justification distinction as the basis for two structures that together constitute legal discourse. The first of these is the structure of legal rules, or of doctrine. The second is the structure of nondeductive legal justification, or of policy. The structures operate quite differently, and interlock in a complex but also quite intelligible way.

The structure of legal rules or doctrine

The elements of the rule structure, or doctrine, are thousands of statements that have the form, "If these facts are found, the judge should do this." To describe doctrine as structured is to say that it is more than a randomly ordered list. Here are some of the elements of doctrinal structure.

1. Subject-matter structures
   (a) We organize the rules by subject matter. Some subject-matter distinctions are contracts, torts, procedure, the separation of powers, federalism, evidence.
   (b) Within a subject matter, we can speak of the structure of a legal field, the pattern of cases, statutes, and rules in a given area, distinguishing, for example, between fields that are well worked out, full of "settled law," and fields that are chaotic or embryonic.
2. Horizontal structures
   (a) The rule-exception structure. If you took all the rules, you could make thousands of subsystems by arranging them into rule-exception pairs. The logical status of rule and exception is complicated and controversial, but that we tend to organize rules this way is obvious. The "privilege of necessity" seems like an exception to the doctrine of trespass.
   (b) The rule-counterrule structure. This differs from the rule-exception structure because there is no defined hierarchy between the two elements. The First Amendment, where it intersects the doctrine of trespass in shopping-center speech or picketing cases, is a counterrule rather than an exception.
3. Vertical structures
   (a) The rule-instance structure. The point here is that the particular is understood to follow from the general by deduction. If trespass to land is voluntary physical invasion of real property, we are likely to see "going hunting in your neighbor's woods" as just "what we mean" by physical invasion.
   (b) The rule-specification structure. This is different because the particular is much more loosely derived from the general than in the

other case. Specifications are further rules that fill in gaps, conflicts, or ambiguities that may or may not be apparent on the face of the more general rule. Is your invasion of your neighbor's land involuntary if you were ordered onto it at gun point, or only if you were carried onto it? The issue has been decided by adding a subrule to the doctrine of trespass through policy argument.

4. The rule-standard structure. This is a typology of rules distinguishing them according to the extent they use, as triggers for official conduct and definitions of that conduct, relatively particularized, "objective" indicia like, say, age (in determining legal capacity) or vaguer concepts like, say, "maturity" (for the same purpose).[5]

The structure of legal justification

The second structure within legal discourse is that of justification.[6] By this I mean the collection not of rules, or valid legal norms, but of reasons offered to support a choice between rules or between interpretations of a gap, conflict, or ambiguity in a rule. Here the first distinction is the familiar one between deductive and policy reasons. Ironically, deductive justification is done in a more casual and intuitive way, in our legal culture, than policy justification. Since we are concerned with the intuition that policy is a Trojan horse for ideology, we will disregard deductive reasons. But it wouldn't be surprising—indeed, it would be a typical postrealist viral gambit—for someone to develop a structural analysis of the discourse of deduction of subrules from rules, and to show it to be no more immune to ideology than policy discourse.

While it is easy to see the rules as units, and as constituting a structure, it is much harder to see the similar properties of policy discourse. To begin with, the unit of argument is the argument-bite, a brief statement of one of the formulaic reasons for a legal choice. Consider the following four examples of argument-bites.

The proposed rule will be easy to administer;
People have a right to freedom of action of the type guaranteed by this rule;
The proposed solution lacks equitable flexibility;
People have a right to security against the kind of action permitted by this rule.

Suppose the question is whether to adopt a rule that makes it *damnum absque injuria* (injury without a legal wrong, and therefore not actionable) for a person to erect a fence on his or her property even if it blocks a neighbor's light. When we think of the way these argument-bites are likely to be deployed, it is clear that there are structured relationships between them. When the fence builder argues that "the proposed rule will be easy to administer," the neighbor will respond that "the proposed rule lacks equitable flexibility."

1. The first dimension of policy structure is horizontal, and consists of the oppositional organization of argument-bites in matched pairs, as in the example above.[7]

2. The second element is the vertical organization of bites into a primary bite and a support system, by which I mean that there are *conventional* ways to back up the brief content of an argument-bite with further justification. For example, there are utilitarian explanations of why it is a good thing to choose a rule that is easy to administer, and also rights-based reasons ("control of judicial discretion is essential to protection of rights").[8]

3. Subject-matter structures

  (*a*) Argument-bite pairs and their support systems get combined and elaborated into clusters that deal with recurring legal issues. Some examples are legal formalities, compulsory terms, the standard of judicial review, strict liability versus negligence, the choice between rules and standards (these may be internal to a particular rule subject-matter area or crosscut various areas). The clustering of bites means that if the advocate can present the case as involving one of the "typical" rule choices, he or she will have a ready-made argument template for each side.

  (*b*) We can distinguish different cluster structures in different areas. In one area, there will be little development of bite-counterbite pairs or support systems; in another, the arguments pro and con will be so well worked out that they have the quality of a mantra. The arguments for and against formalities, and for and against judicial review, are well worked out; the arguments for and against allowing land-use restrictions that "run with the land" are surprisingly primitive.[9]

4. A fourth element is organization by the kind of value asserted, with my distinction being rights, utility, and morality on one side, and

system values like formal realizability and institutional competence on the other.

Relativizing the distinction between the two structures

Although I think it's useful to distinguish the two structures (rules and reasons for rules), the distinction is not a tight one, as the following cases show. First, some standards and some rights are units in the system of valid legal norms, of doctrine, and yet do provide their own justifications. Second, sometimes we justify the choice of a rule neither by a policy argument nor by deduction from a more abstract rule but by reference to another rule, a rule of interpretation.

There are standards that appeal directly to one of the moral desiderata of our culture, such as "good faith," "reasonableness," "unconscionability," "unfair trade practice." (Other standards refer to general descriptive categories understood to have little meaning until further specified, such as "foreseeability" or "restraint of trade." Unlike the first mentioned, these provide no reasons for their adoption and get explained and interpreted through policy discourse.)

Abstract but clearly legalized rights also violate my distinction between rules and reasons for rules. For example, the constitution prohibits Congress from "making any law abridging the freedom of speech," and refers to the "right of the people to be secure in their houses, papers and effects." Statutes and opinions may also declare rights (the right of privacy has been declared as a matter of constitutional penumbra, as a statutory requirement, and as a common law rule).

There are two different ways in which rights can operate both in the structure of rules and in that of reasons for rules. First, rights authoritatively declared at a high level of abstraction are self-justifying elements in the rule structure, when we treat them as positivized natural rights, even though it is not uncommon to offer non–rights-based reasons for them ("free speech helps the search for truth"). Second, it is standard practice to invoke valid legal norms like the First Amendment as nondeductive policy reasons for deciding cases, as in phrases like "First Amendment concerns weigh heavily here" (as opposed to "the First Amendment requires . . .").[10]

There are rules for the interpretation of rules, such as those of statutory interpretation and those for the determination of the holdings of cases. These are both rules and reasons for rules, and they constitute a "subdiscourse of authority." They are the first resort when there appears to be a gap, conflict, or ambiguity. Like the other rules in the system, they may generate an instant sense of legal obviousness that can be unsettled only by sustained legal work. Thus they can function to eliminate the need to resort to policy, or just defer it.

When we choose among them and interpret them in order to make them applicable to specific questions about "primary" rules, we justify our decisions through policy arguments ("it would cause hopeless confusion to apply the maxim *exclusio unius* in this case"). This second-order policy argument about how to apply rules of interpretation is like the first-order policy argument about what rule to adopt. The units are internally structured, like both primary rules and policy argument-bites. For example, in the famous pieces already mentioned,[11] Llewellyn analyzed the maxims used in statutory interpretation, and in justifying the choices of "broad" and "narrow" holdings for particular cases, into a set of rules and counter-rules, which might just as easily be described as arguments and counter-arguments.

Dynamics of the model: operations

So far, we have a static typology. But the rule structure is dynamic because it contains rules for the generation of new rules, or operations.[12] And the argument structure is a semiotic system, in the sense of a system of signs, a system that people operate to generate new meanings out of a prestructured collection of elements.[13]

The universe of potential rules

The two operations that we perform on the rule structure are "constituting the field" and "broadening and narrowing." Constituting the field means deciding on a particular rule-exception or rule-counterrule structure as the one within which to decide the case in hand. When striking bus drivers lie down in front of the buses, we constitute the field when we decide that "the question" is whether their conduct falls on one side or another of a line dividing "unjustified interference with the owner's property" from "legitimate exercise of free-speech rights."

For a given controversy, there will typically be numerous different ways to constitute the field. The First Amendment is one way to counteract the owner's property right, but another way would be to argue that what the workers were doing was a public nuisance, so that there could be no private action without "special" damage, which the owner failed to show here. Yet another would be to argue that the workers were merely exercising self-activity rights guaranteed by the National Labor Relations Act (NLRA).

My point is not that all these approaches are equally likely to generate the experience of closure in favor of the plaintiffs or defendants. The point is that there is a relatively formalized procedure, an "operation," of thinking up the various kinds of anti-owner or pro-worker rules that could conceivably provide a basis for a pro-worker argument in this case.

Broadening and narrowing are operations we perform by restating a rule-counterrule or a rule-exception structure so that conduct that at first looked as though it was clearly within the scope of a particular rule now appears to be within the scope of an exception or counterrule. Given a side, that is, given a decision to argue for the plaintiff or the defendant, there will be multiple possible rule restatements that will validate the party's position. Here we are not talking about alternative constitutions of the field (the choice between a First Amendment and an NLRA argument) but about the choice between "places to draw the line" within a constituted field. The imagery is of degree, of more or less.

We generate the alternatives in this operation by "disaggregating" the situations covered by a given formulation of rule and exception or rule and counterrule. The imagery is of the rule as a formula composed of a set of abstractions each of which covers a diversity of particular "real life" situations. The goal is to restate so that some of these situations no longer fall within the rule's abstractions (narrowing) or so that they now include situations to which they previously seemed not to apply (broadening).

The operations of field constitution and broadening/narrowing generate a set of alternative rule formulations that will win for either side.

The generation of new arguments

Starting from any given argument-bite supporting a particular rule interpretation, there are a set of relatively formalized procedures for generating a counterbite that will support an alternative rule interpretation. These are *formal* operations, meaning that they produce new bites mechanically, with no guarantee that they will be in any way convincing in the context. An extreme example is the transformation of a sentence by inserting the word "not." Here is a list of operations, starting from "defendant has a right to freedom of action of the type guaranteed by my proposed rule" (for example, a right to lie down in front of the buses).

1. Denial: "There is no such right."
2. Hohfeldian opposition: "Plaintiff has a right to security that would be denied by the proposed rule."
3. Mediation: "On balance, plaintiff's right outweighs defendant's in this situation."
4. Refocusing on defendant's conduct: "Defendant has such a right but has forfeited it by misconduct."
5. Flipping: "Plaintiff's right to the same kind of freedom of action would be denied by this rule."

This list is illustrative. There is no closed catalog of operations; there is no guarantee that any operation will ever produce a convincing argument; it is often hard to decide what operation, if any, has been performed. A structural analysis of this kind provides a basis for an interpretation of, say, a judicial opinion, rather than a theory of "what determined it."

Relationship between rule operations and argument operations

Argument operations are always performed in the context of a choice between two rules. Suppose it looks as though there is a preexisting rule that governs this case and that my client will lose if it is applied. Through the operations of field constitution and broadening/narrowing I come up with an alternative potential rule that would win the case for my side. I then look at the arguments that support the "obvious" rule. *Given* the counter-rule or exception I have chosen, *some* of the transformative operations available will generate plausible arguments for my rule or against the obvious one.

For example, if the obvious rule is in a highly formally realizable form, and my alternative is a standard, I can try the argument-bite "your rule is so rigid that it will produce inequitable results in many particular cases, including this one." If my rule appears to be just as rulelike as yours, however, this bite will not be an appropriate one without some further work to change that initial appearance. If I have chosen a potential rule that is more formally realizable than the obvious one, I will choose the opposite argument-bite: "your rule is so vague that it will generate arbitrary results in cases like this one."

This "fitting" process goes in both directions. As I explore the arguments in favor of my rule, I may modify it to fit the argument I am developing. The work of developing argument-bites and support systems guides rule-generating operations, just as the choice of a rule provides the context for argument-generating operations. The process of mutual adjustment stops when I reach equilibrium, meaning that any change in the rule seems to make it harder to defend, and any change in the argument seems to make the rule less rather than more plausible.

An example

This morning I woke up thinking about how to start this section and read the Sunday newspaper.

Liability Waiver Barred
at N.Y.U. Dental Clinic
by Ronald Sullivan

Waivers that patients of the New York University Dental Center have been required to sign before being treated by students at a reduced cost are "against public policy" and cannot be enforced, an appellate court ruled last week.

The waivers, similar to those used by other university-operated clinics, seek to protect the institution from malpractice claims.

In a unanimous decision, the . . . Court . . . condemned the use of the waivers, which are generally not used by hospitals, medical clinics and private physicians and dentists.

"We find that the exculpatory agreement sought to be enforced between a dental clinic and its patient implicates both the state's interest in the health and welfare of its citizens as well as the special relationship between physician and patient and that it would be against public policy to uphold such an agreement," the court said in its ruling on Thursday.

"It is clear that the state's substantial interest in protecting the welfare of all its citizens, irrespective of economic status, extends to insuring that they be provided with health care in a safe and professional manner," the court said . . .

The patient, Arthur Ash, a retired salesman, was referred to the clinic in 1986 by his dentist, Dr. Charles Lennon, so that he could have about $6,000 worth of dental care done for half the cost. In return for the savings, the center required Mr. Ash to sign away any claim of liability.

According to the court, when Mr. Ash was treated by Dr. Lennon and dental students at the center on Oct. 15, 1986, two gold crowns slipped down his throat and lodged in his right lung and subsequently required surgical removal . . .

The court took note of the services that the dental center provided to poor patients, but said that such services "cannot serve as a basis for excusing such providers from complying with those minimum professional standards of care which the state has seen fit to establish."

Poor patients, the courts said, "cannot be considered to have freely bargained for a sub-standard level of care for a financial savings."

If dental centers were absolved of any liability, the court said, it would create an "invidious" system in which "services received by the less affluent are permitted to be governed by lesser minimal standards of care and skill than that received by other segments of society."

Generally, the courts have upheld agreements in which consumers waive the right to sue for damages, provided that the consumers have sufficient choices; that there is an "arm's length" distance between the parties involved, such as in the case of owners and patrons of parking lots; and provided that the agreements are specific on what they cover.

Howard R. Cohen, the lawyer for the dental center, said the ruling would hurt poor patients by requiring the center to charge more for its services in order to pay for malpractice insurance. He said the center had not decided whether to appeal the ruling or to defend itself against Mr. Ash's suit at trial.[14]

The rule structure is obviously complex. There is the rule (standard) that contract terms "against public policy" are void, and the counterrule that consumers are "generally" free to disclaim liability, with its exceptions, and the very particular rule that parking lot owners can disclaim. "Normal" health care providers do not disclaim, but it is not clear whether this is their voluntary practice or the result of a judge-made or regulatory requirement. (The rule summary in the article is partial and open to challenge in many particulars.)

Once the lawyers and judges had constituted the field within which the case falls as involving these rules, exceptions, and counterrules, they had to come up with formulations of a new specific rule that would decide the case. From what appears, the judges chose a rule to the effect that reduced-price (and also completely free?) services from university teaching clinics are subject to the same regime of liability as regular market health services. This is a relatively narrow choice. We don't know what the other side proposed. But it was probably that reduced-price or free clinics run by universities as part of their educational programs are an exception to the general regime of medical liability.

These decisions involved excluding lots of other possible rules, such as that only nonprofit clinics offering greatly reduced prices or free care *primarily to low-income people* should be able to enforce a waiver, and so on. Did the lawyer for the clinic argue that it should be able to disclaim liability even for gross negligence in the supervision of dental students? These choices reflected a whole array of judgments about the ease with which it would be possible to restate the rules, facts of cases, and policy arguments to fit the candidate interpretation.

Once the field had been constituted and the broadening/narrowing operation performed, the case evoked a whole cluster of formalized policy arguments for and against the two proposed rules. This is the cluster I called "compulsory terms." The arguments for and against compulsory terms that make up the cluster are sufficiently general so that they can be used in, literally, hundreds of different situations.

But since the cluster is a *form,* a set of ritualized thrusts and parries, and since it is *inexhaustible,* it would be wrong to say that the cluster "determined the outcome." What we can say is that the lawyers for the two sides and the judges had, once they had constituted the field and done some narrowing/broadening, an elaborate lexicon of arguments from which to compose their particular defenses of their preferred solutions.

For example, it is a familiar argument for compulsory terms that their purpose is to protect consumers, so the court can justify its rule by appeal to the state's interest in "insuring that they be provided with health care in a safe and professional manner." An absolutely standardized response, for *any* compulsory term, is that the term "will hurt poor [consumers] by requiring [the seller] to charge more for its services in order to pay for . . . insurance." Because argument-bite oppositions within the cluster are so highly standardized, it is often possible to infer from what one party said what the other party almost certainly said to provoke it. Here, the odds are that the statement "poor [consumers] . . . cannot be said to have freely bargained for a sub-standard level of care for a financial savings" was provoked by the other side saying something like "the legally competent consumer has the right, absent force or fraud, to make any agreement he or she wants."

An intriguing aspect of the case as reported in the paper is that the judges twice raised the status issue (the state's duty to protect is "irrespective of status," and it would be bad to create an "invidious" system providing lower-quality services to the "less affluent"). This is a double example of the operation called "flipping," in which an agreed premise is shown to have the reverse of its usual implication.

Within the cluster of compulsory terms arguments, the evil of creating special statuses is typically invoked against compulsory terms, on the ground that to deny a worker or a woman or a poor consumer the right to contract on the same terms as an adult male is to treat them as incompetent. It is supposedly "insulting" as a continuation of the preliberal regime in which they had an "inferior status."[15] The status argument thus flips the conventional argument that the compulsory term will equalize buyers and sellers. Here, the judges flip the flip, deploying the antistatus argument to show that *freedom of contract* would create a special status for poor consumers, since nonpoor consumers are not asked to sign such waivers.

The article restricts itself, appropriately enough, to some of the more striking argument-bites the judges deployed, but doubtless the opinion contains at least rudimentary support systems for those bites. For example, the argument that regulation will hurt the people it is supposed to help gets supported by a standard economic argument, of a complexity tailored to fit the circumstances, to the effect that the poor value the increased protection less than what it will cost them, or they would have demanded and paid for it without legal intervention.

On the other side, the argument that the poor need this kind of protection will get support from the argument that in the absence of liability for negligence, the clinic will have inadequate incentive to take precautions to avoid harm to patients. And so forth. The argument that people of full capacity have the right to make whatever contracts they want to, without paternalistic state supervision, can get support from a disquisition on fundamental human rights, or from one on the economic benefits of consumer sovereignty, or from a single bite like the following: "The consumer is more likely to know what is in his or her best interest than the courts are."

If the opinion is very short, it will probably look more conventionally "legal" than if it is elaborate. If it is short, the judges will restrict themselves to a rudimentary constitution of the field and then assert that the rules apply in a particular way, with only a few more argument-bites than we saw in the article and only the most minimal support systems for those bites. Everything said in the opinion will support the conclusion, and there will be no serious attempt to state, let alone answer, the argument for the loser. The opinion will look legal because it looks as though the judges knew what rule applied and then applied it.

But the short opinion, in a case like this one, will also be unconvincing to anyone skilled in legal argument, because it will provide no answers to the whole complex of arguments that we can generate, without knowing anything much about the details of the case, on the side of the clinic. In the short opinion, the argument-bites that support the court's conclusion are presented as dispositive in a way that we know, given readily available formalized responses, just can't be the end of the story.

A longer, "better" opinion will get into the choices involved in field constitution and narrowing/broadening, so that the reader has a sense of the range of possible rule interpretations. It will also deploy a much fuller repertory of argument-bites and provide a support system for each. The two most familiar forms are the opinion that is like a brief for one side or the other, and the opinion that carefully works out the arguments on each side, and then abruptly resolves in a balancing test.

The interpenetration of legal and ideological discourse

We can identify a variety of aspects of legal discourse, as I've just modeled it, that support the intuition that it is open to or a potential vehicle for ideological preferences. Two of these have to do with its form, and three with its actual modern content.

The form of policy argument

Because it is structured in matched pairs of contradictory argument-bites, legal rhetoric is manipulable at retail, as well as at the wholesale, level of a theory, say, of why judicial activism is bad. Policy argument contains no powerful metatheories that tell us when the virtue of administrability trumps that of flexibility. Because of the "semioticization" of policy discourse, its reduction to a system of contradictory buzzwords that are always available and therefore never persuasive in and of themselves, it is always possible that the judge has "ulterior motives" for his choice of bites.

The "correct" way to get out of this dilemma, according to the realists, is to identify the conflicting policies, rather than pretending that only one is involved, and then "balance" them. The move from a one-sided deduction to balancing saves the "rationality" of the process, but it is understood in American legal culture that this is a weak form of rationality. The image is of a highly objective process (two weights in a scale, suggesting both science and Blind Justice). Ronald Dworkin gives it a pretentious Newtonian spin by referring to the "gravitational force" of conflicting principles.

But as the realists themselves pointed out in the 1950s, when many of them had become judges and had to "balance" First Amendment rights against national security, the process seems obviously open to conscious and unconscious ideological manipulation, at least by comparison with the paradigm of deduction. Indeed, the imagery of balancing, or gravitational force, has an ambiguous meaning. Contradicting its scientistic overtone is the suggestion that the question involved is one of degree, of line drawing. There is a general cultural understanding that the resolution of such questions cannot be "objective" or "necessary" or "independent of the observer or decision maker" in the way that resolution of conceptual or factual questions can be.[16]

Of course, balancing might be highly objective in the sense of producing results widely experienced as necessary, even though nondeductive. The doubt about the ability of balancing to exclude ideology is only partly based on its form; it is also based on the particular content and history of the arguments that American lawyers and judges actually use in policy argument in courts today.

Policy as a translation of ideology

First, the social values—rights, morality, utility—to which policy argument appeals are the very stuff of the universalization projects of ideological intelligentsias. Second, institutional values, like judicial role considerations and federalism, are often understood as stand-ins or surrogates for the ideologized group interests that will benefit from applying the policy in a particular way. Third, there are distinctively legal policy debates that, while not simply "tracking" general ideological debate, appear to be the functional equivalents of those debates within the specialized culture of legality.

An ideological universalization project (liberalism, conservatism) restates the interests of groups as claims on the whole society by casting them in the language of rights, morality, or utility. Particular families of rules and particular arguments about them have histories and ideological pedigrees. Thus liberals have argued to the courts for generations in favor of compulsory terms, from minimum wage and maximum hours laws through workmen's compensation and products liability and the warranty of habitability through today's case about, say, the validity of a disclaimer of liability for malpractice of a not-for-profit university dental clinic. Conservatives have taken the other side for the same number of generations. The policy arguments they deploy are ideological arguments.

The conservative policy arguments are freedom of contract, antipaternalism, the efficiency of free markets, and the tendency of consumer protection to hurt the people it is supposed to help. Typical liberal counterarguments are unequal bargaining power, the substantive inequity of the outcome for the particular person or a class of consumers, their lack of capacity to choose intelligently, and the desirability that producers internalize the social cost of their operations.

Everyday policy argument often presupposes the irrelevance of deduction, provides an elaborate description of what all agree is a "social problem," and then develops all three normative criteria (utility, rights, and morality) and the derivative arguments about, say, freedom of contract and unequal bargaining power, without any pretense that there is an algorithm for combining them, to justify a particular comprehensive legal solution. The judge's opinion doesn't read much differently than a congressional committee report recommending legislation to a chamber divided on partisan lines. (See, for example, Judge Wright's opinion in *Javins*,[17] Judge Traynor's in *Escola*.[18]) The presentation blurs the line between adjudication and legislation.

If we imagine that the judge is asked to choose between two rules strictly on the basis of the ideologically polarized policy arguments that are standard in legal discourse, it is hard to see how her choice can be uninfluenced by ideology. What we mean by "a liberal" is a person who favors compulsory terms on the basis of arguments exactly like the ones in these opinions. Of course, the judge might choose on some basis other than her preference between the liberal and the conservative positions, but if she thinks one or the other is "right," that is, if she is a liberal or a conservative, she is hardly betraying her duty of interpretive fidelity.

The problem goes deeper. The presupposition of policy discourse is the force field model in which no policy argument, liberal or conservative, is ever just "right." In the force field model, policies vary in strength from one fact situation to another, and different rules "draw lines" by balancing—that is, by finding the point of equilibrium. Here again, what we mean by "a liberal" or "a conservative" is a person who balances in test cases in one way or another. The ideologies are not systems of deductions but tendencies defined in terms of one another: a person who draws the line in one place is a liberal just because conservatives draw the line further to the right.

Of course, in the next case the legal representatives of the liberal ideological intelligentsia may "go too far," and the same judge who enthusiastically endorsed their arguments the last time around will switch sides. His opinion will sound conservative, as he cuts back products liability to avoid "abuses" that "drive up prices." But this is just another instance of the standard rhetorical structure of ideological debate in the United States, where liberals and conservatives share identical major premises and switch back and forth, as they draw lines, between identical intermediate-level arguments.

Policy as an instrument of ideology

Institutional arguments, about, say, federalism, or judicial activism versus judicial restraint, are not overtly ideologized in the way the primary arguments are. But they too have histories. Everyone understands that liberals favor federal power, and deploy the whole armory of policy arguments associated with it, when they are stronger at the federal than at the state level, and vice versa. Conservatives favor judicial activism when they control the courts, and they deploy the whole armory of stereotyped arguments for judicial passivism when they lose them but happen to control the legislatures. (But some liberals and conservatives have substantive commitments on institutional issues that are independent of their ideologies, as illustrated by the case of Felix Frankfurter's persistence in judicial passivism after the liberals lost control of the state legislatures after World War II.)

There is nothing "necessary" or "inherent" about the apparent instrumentalization of policy by ideology. It *might* be the case that federalism versus states' rights was the "real" issue, and liberalism versus conservatism just a sideshow. The sense that the parties manipulate the arguments is grounded in the particular history of policy debate in the United States, in events like the shift from conservative to liberal dominance of the federal courts after 1937 or even the temporary reversal of position of abolitionists who became states' rights advocates after the passage of the federal Fugitive Slave Law. And, of course, there is no way to "prove" instrumentalization empirically.

Policy as a parallel ideological development

This third mode of interpenetration of policy and ideology is more complex. There are legal debates that are only "analogous" to general ideological debate, because the subject matter is minor or not salient in the legislative arena but is extensively developed in legal discourse. In "Form and Substance in Private Law Adjudication,"[19] I argued that the endless policy debate about whether to cast norms as rules or as standards, and the subdebate about the virtues and vices of legal formalities (the requirement of a writing in contracts, the requirement of "definiteness," and so on) have this character.

The policy argument consists at one level of paired bites: rules promote certainty, standards flexibility; rules are rigid, standards subjective. But the cursory bites and counterbites are supported by whole systems of more complex argument invoking the opposed cultural ideals of liberalism and conservatism: advocates support rules with arguments that are structurally similar to the arguments for free markets; advocates of standards make arguments that are structurally similar to those for government regulation. At a higher level of abstraction, one finds an ontological and epistemological debate, supporting, for example, standards through organicist and rules through atomist social visions.

Moreover, there is a second debate in private law, not generally theorized but not hard to piece together, between a model of maximum duty and maximum excuse, and a model of minimum duty and minimum excuse (altruism versus individualism). This pair of argument systems displays a strong structural similarity to that of formality versus informality. And like the debate over form, there is a clear affinity between the soft and hard positions and liberalism and conservatism. Yet neither argument is well described as a translation of liberalism and conservatism, because liberals and conservatives habitually instrumentalize these arguments to serve their legislative purposes.

On economic issues, for instance, liberals argue for freedom of action for labor—that is, for minimal duties—but for forcing enterprises to internalize costs to workers, consumers, and the environment; conservatives go the other way. On social issues, liberals generally argue against forcing internalization of the costs of deviance, conservatives the other way; but there are numerous reversals, such as liberal insistence on remedies for wife beating and conservative foot dragging. Each side favors rigid rules to enforce its legislative accomplishments in the face of private or official resistance, but favors standards when they will allow its partisans to undermine or soften a regime reflecting the objectives of the other side.[20]

Though this usage has been much criticized, it still seems appropriate to me to describe these debates as reflecting the internal contradictions of modernist legal consciousness,[21] and the same contradictions seem to me manifest in modern liberalism and conservatism. But for present purposes, my point is only that these structures of policy argument allow endless play for the ideological projects of the legal intelligentsia. Along with the direct translation of ideological into legal debate, and the instrumentalization of federalism and institutional-competence debate, they sustain the characteristic American attitude that policy argument is legal and not-legal at the same time.

The dynamics of ideology in law

Over time, the work of arguing ideologized interests permanently transforms legal discourse, building into it texts (with answers and further development in response to answers) that are cannibalized for reuse in new cases. Thus although legal discourse is in one sense driven by the underlying opposition of ideologized interests, it may also react back on the ideologies and the interests and transform them. The modern legal discourse of civil rights is as much a cause as an effect of civil rights thinking within liberal ideology at large.

Further, the appearance of ideologized group interests in legal discourse is always mediated by the specific intelligentsia interests and the even more specific *legal* intelligentsia interests of the lawyers and judges. Though their input is consistently recognizable as liberal or conservative, it is not a direct transposition but rather a translation, and a compromised one at that, into a very different discursive medium. Nonetheless, the long-run process of ideological conflict about rule definition profoundly affects the way lawyers present and judges decide cases.

Ideological history tells you what kind of case it is

The participants organize new legal conflicts into the existing *legal* schemas or structures that they have used to fight earlier ideological battles. When presented with a new case, they do a kind of mental checklist to see if it fits into any of the well-known types of interest conflict that are ideolo-gized.

If the case does fit in, it is possible to understand it as one of a series of conflicts between two groups or interests, even if the parties don't think of it that way. This will be easiest in the large class of cases that involve resolving a relatively small gap, conflict, or ambiguity in a rule system whose current state is understood to represent the outcome of earlier ideo-logical conflict.

In these cases, the parties are likely to understand the issue as involving the same contending group interests that settled the content of the general rule whose interpretation is at issue here. In that initial dispute, we had to decide whether there would be strict liability or negligence in defective-products cases; the decision for strict liability left open the question whether manufacturers can use an "assumption-of-risk" defense. When that issue comes up, there will be little hesitation in organizing the case so that we have yet another instance of ideological conflict between the same strict liability and negligence forces that were arrayed in the decision of the initial question.

Besides this "nesting" dynamic for "disputes within disputes," prior ideological work provides analogies in cases of first impression. Let's sup-pose that several generations of liberals imagining themselves to be the intelligentsia of oppressed groups have developed a large number of pro-posed compulsory terms in many different situations of alleged economic inequality. Sometimes they have argued them to the legislature and some-times to the courts. Solving a problem with a compulsory term is a familiar liberal economic strategy.

Now suppose that within this general compulsory-terms project there are already fifty cases identified as "about" the validity of seller disclaimers of liability to buyers, in every kind of business from parking lots to legal services, but there has never been a case about any kind of medical service. This case involves a reduced-price university dental teaching clinic that has injured a patient and disclaims liability. Lawyers and judges *may* pick up on the presence of the disclaimer, and organize their arguments by analogy to other compulsory-terms cases, as involving freedom of contract versus the public interest in consumer welfare.

Rules, in short, have histories. If the history is understood by the par-ticipants to be part of a general ideological conflict, then when a case comes along that involves a disclaimer but also lots of other potentially important facts, there is a ready-made, already ideologically organized, compulsory-terms interpretation available. A case that might not be ideologized against a different doctrinal history will be ideologized because the participants have read and worked on lots of other disclaimer cases.

Sometimes it doesn't work this way. No one thinks to fit the case into its possible ideological conflict interpretation, or both sides and the judge as well have reasons for preferring another interpretation and deliberately ignoring this one. But over the long run, legal work supporting the ideological projects creates a body of familiar potential ideological meanings for factual conflicts and for the rules that might govern them. These are available as *forms* into which to pour the interpretation of a case of first impression. This doesn't mean that any case can be poured into any form. It's just that you can see the available forms influencing the interpretations that actually get made.

So far, I have been talking about the way ideological work on the rule structure influences the interpretation of obviously applicable rules and the choice of analogies available in more open situations. But a lawyer who initially experiences a legal situation as clearly governed by a settled rule often manages, nonetheless, through work, to unsettle that initial appearance. Ideological development of particular rules provides materials in this kind of situation. If the liberals have managed to get reform of products liability in the direction of nondisclaimable strict liability, why not try the same thing for tenant injuries from defective premises, in spite of the fact that there are *many* cases in the jurisdiction holding that there is no general duty of care, let alone nondisclaimable strict liability?

Ideological history provides ready-to-wear policy arguments

Once the case is situated in an ideologically contested part of the rule structure, the lawyers apply the set of stereotyped argument-bites and support systems for cases in this cluster. These argument sets are also the product of long-run ideological work. Liberal lawyers and judges have spent years developing justifications for their preferred rule solutions in the languages of rights, welfare, and morality, and so have the conservatives.

Of course, it may be terrible for the interests of a party to cast the case as a choice between rules supported by clusters of argument-bites and support systems with clear ideological histories. That party won't argue it that way. But if it is in the interest of the other party to so cast it, then the first party will have to respond. Both parties may calculate that the best way to do it is to keep the argument-bites and support systems to an absolute minimum and present the case as involving obvious mere rule application. But even then the judges (or their law clerks) often have their own reasons for offering the ideological interpretation the lawyers tried to avoid.

So particular argument-bites and support systems have histories just as rules do, and we can trace them through the sequence of texts. In cases about compulsory terms, we can follow the development of the egalitarian regulatory argument from cases about the eight-hour day, tenement regulation, minimum wages, company stores, products liability, insurance, and so forth, up through today's case about liability of university dental clinics. We can similarly trace the argument that compulsory terms are unconstitutional, economically counterproductive, and not in accord with the common law.

The body of arguments stored in the opinions is available to both sides in every dispute. Remember that the conservatives have been busy developing arguments for statutory rape laws, school locker searches, parental consent to abortion, and so forth, that deploy in the "family values" domain the same paternalist arguments they abhor in the economic context.

The judge is an ideological performer willy-nilly

The work product of liberal and conservative lawyers and judges preserved in briefs and opinions biases or skews the legal work that follows, because it makes it easier to follow some lines of approach and harder to follow others. On the basis of past work, the judge will be able with only minimal new work to develop an interpretation of the facts that places the case in one of the fields of ideological conflict between liberals and conservatives, or between some other pair of opposed, universalized group interests.

If he or she accepts one of these ideological field constitutions, he or she gets along with it a ready-to-wear set of policy arguments on each side. One set of arguments supports rule interpretations that by degrees more fully realize one interest, and the other set supports rule interpretations pushing by degrees in favor of the opposing interest. He or she has only to contextualize the formulas to fit the facts of the particular case. (I don't mean to suggest that this is easy work.)

Because the materials are ideologically organized, the easiest thing for the judge to do is to fit the case into one of the rule-conflict forms, and then develop arguments from the justificatory forms. If he or she prefers a rule that splits the difference between the positions of the two sides, it's easy to justify the aspects of the outcome favorable to plaintiff's group with one set of arguments and those favorable to defendant's group with the other.

If the judge wants to do anything else but this, he or she has to set out to do something to the language, rather than merely speaking it. He or she has to be profoundly creative, somehow find time to make up new arguments, arguments that are outside the organized system. Judges almost never do that. They are much more likely to create by developing the stereotypical argument on one side or the other beyond its earlier state, thereby permanently changing the store of bites, or to create more ephemerally in the work of contextualizing.

The judge who does set out to change the very terms of discussion is likely to find his or her contribution instantly incorporated into the existing system of ideological conflict, but cannibalized by the parties for their own ideologically organized purposes or, quite possibly, just ignored. To be cannibalized is to change the discourse, though not the very terms of discussion (to be ignored is just a warning to those who watched your doomed effort).

The neutral judge is an ideological performer in this sense: he or she develops the solution to a legal problem and then justifies it in a legal language that is also ideological language. The outcome will be understood, not always but often, to have favored a "side" defined ideologically. The explanation offered will become a part of the materials available to the winning and losing "sides" in future ideological conflicts. Attempts to get out of this box sometimes succeed, producing true rupture or reconstitution of the system of ideological oppositions, but more often they are cannibalized or ignored.

7

Ideologically Oriented Legal Work

The question I have been posing is, How can the judge be ideological? How can the judge be ideological, more specifically, if he accepts that he is bound to be a faithful interpreter of the laws, bound to do "law's bidding" if it conflicts with his ideological preference? In the last chapter, I asked why an informed observer might be suspicious of the claim that legal discourse, and particularly legal policy argument, is autonomous from ideological discourse. In this chapter, I attempt to reconstruct the situation of the judge from the inside, so to speak, asking how the judge experiences and responds to the body of legal materials when he has an ideological preference for a particular rule choice.

To pose the question of how judges can be ideological is not to presuppose that all coherence theories are or must be wrong. But it is to take as a point of departure, first, that none of these theories even suggests that all, or most, American judges act according to their precepts and, second, that a judge who accepts a coherence theory will often be uncertain how to apply it. Even if one of the theories is right as a description of how judges do and ought to reason to outcomes in ideologically charged cases, it seems very likely, given the actual state of the bar and bench understanding of law, that judges constantly experience themselves as having to make strategic choices.

In this chapter, the strategic choice involved is in deciding how to deploy their resources for legal research and reasoning. Legal actors, whether advocates or judges, can influence what the law "is" through legal work. In general, legal practitioners don't have and don't feel a need for strong theories of how the law requires one to choose a "direction" for this work. If they are lawyers, they suppose that it is legitimate to deploy their resources to shape law to favor their clients. Strategic behavior in choosing in what direction and how much to work at legal interpretation is an everyday matter; it doesn't violate the duty of fidelity to law because it is constitutive of the law to which one is faithful.

We often speak as though things were altogether different within the process of judicial decision. It seems wrong for the judge to claim that *for her* fidelity to law kicks in only when she has made some law to be faithful to. But, of course, law clerks write opinions that are "result-oriented," in the sense that a rule choice is dictated by the judge, and their job is to produce the best legal case they can in support of it. And judges themselves, when they work in panels, often find themselves in the position of having to produce the best argument they can for a rule choice that differs significantly from the one they regard as most in accord with interpretive fidelity.

Here we will be dealing with what one might call the "core case," in which adjudication is supposed to be nonstrategic—motivated solely by the duty of fidelity—the case in which a single judge decides a question of law. It is a common belief, supported by a not inconsiderable social science literature, that judges, in this situation, often can and do work to make the law correspond to "justice," or to some other "legislative" ideal, and that they direct this work under the influence of their ideological preferences.[1] But it is an equally common belief that this work is constrained by the legal materials. My goal here is to describe this complex phenomenon of strategic freedom constrained by context.[2] In the next chapter, I describe the metastrategy of denial through which, it seems to me, judges maintain their own internal belief, and their audience's belief, that they are fulfilling their duty of interpretive fidelity in spite of the fact that their strategic choices "shape" or "move" the law in one ideological direction or another.

Work in a medium

My theory is quite different from two others—indeed situated in between them. First, we might imagine that the judge is an ideological actor in a very strong sense. Confronted with a question of rule definition, he might always choose the rule he would favor as a legislator, and then he might, if he were a lower-court judge, simply impose that rule, offering a legal justification that was strictly post hoc. If he was an appellate judge, he might approach decision by the panel of judges in the same spirit, looking to get, through the politics of the panel, a rule as close as possible to his preference.

We don't have to assume that such a judge consciously or even unconsciously violates his oath. We might suppose that everyone involved, including the judge himself, experiences what he does as uniquely dictated by correct legal reasoning from the valid legal materials. Yet the duty has no influence over outcomes, because legal materials and legal reasoning are sufficiently plastic that they can offer an acceptable post hoc rationalization of whatever result the judge favors, and judges are habitual rationalizers.

At the other extreme is a model in which there is a method of interpretive fidelity that the judge can pursue in such a way that the result will be the same whatever her ideology, or will at least be uninfluenced by ideology. We don't have to imagine that there is only one determinate correct answer to every question of rule definition in order for the method to exclude ideological influence. The method can be uncertain without being ideological as long as we believe that even in cases where people aren't sure in advance how it will come out, they know that the uncertainty will be resolved without resort to ideology.

In this model, law figures heavily in ideologized group conflict because there are often large stakes that depend on judicial rule choice. But it figures somewhat the way the weather figures in a military campaign. A lot depends for each side on what the weather will turn out to be, because one kind will favor one side and another kind the other. It affects everything, but it doesn't "take sides." We may not be able to predict with certainty what it will be tomorrow, but however it turns out, we don't claim that it was biased against us.

Or take the case of divination in the ancient world. In one model, the diviners are participants in the political events that their interpretations of the flights of birds or of the disposition of entrails strongly influence. They are "pro–Trojan War" or antiwar, even if they and everyone else believes that they are just interpreting the will of the Gods. In another model, they have a "neutral" method of divination that they follow come hell or high water, and the results of divination are the admission of a genuinely external factor into the process by which the Greeks decide whether or not to sail for Troy. From the point of view of the factions, the dispute is decided randomly, in the sense that it is decided outside the complex process of dialogue and bargaining that is ideological decision.

Neither of these models is even slightly plausible as an account of what judges do. I propose instead that we see the judge with an ideological project as "working in a medium," namely law, to bring about the rule choices he or she thinks are just. Sometimes such judges find it impossible to produce a good legal argument for the rule choice they prefer, and they find themselves "constrained," both by the internal force of their oath of fidelity in interpretation and by external pressure, to apply a rule that they would vote against were they legislators. Sometimes they have the experience of being able to work the materials so that they support just the rule they would have voted for. And sometimes they are able to "move" the law so that there is a good argument for a rule that is better than one plausible alternative but worse than the rule they would have voted for as legislators.

Two modes of constraint

There are two situations in which it is plausible to describe judges as bound by law. These correspond to two quite different experiences of judging. The first might be called "unselfconscious rule-following"; the second, "constraint by the text." In unselfconscious rule-following, the judge has facts before her and a single rule in mind. She is focused on the question of what happened, and there are two well-defined contradictory answers. If one version is what "really" happened, then it seems obvious that the defendant has violated the relevant rule; if the other, then the defendant has not violated the rule.

In this situation, no one is thinking about alternative interpretations of the rule. When the facts have been finally determined, the judge unselfconsciously applies it, in the mode of deduction. If we are the audience, we don't advert to the possibility of anything else happening than what does happen, once the judge has decided how to characterize the facts. There is no problem in this situation with what the judge thinks about the rule. She may think it is utterly wrong and that the legislature should change it. But she still, in this situation, just applies it.

A judge who unselfconsciously experiences the legal materials as pointing to just one outcome, as applied to these facts, and then pronounces that outcome in the form of a rule application, is "bound" in a meaningful sense of the term. And it is a constant of everyday life that directives are experienced as having a single obvious meaning. To proceed as though they had a different meaning, or many possible meanings, is bad faith, or disobedience, or evasion. When you ask me to close the door, I don't, typically, see myself as having to make a difficult interpretation. I know what you mean without thinking about it. You don't hesitate to say I haven't closed the door when I close the window.

The polar opposite model of boundness is one in which the facts are known and it is the proper interpretation of the rule that is in question. The judge dislikes the outcome that the obvious interpretation of the rule would produce, does a great deal of work to come up with a good legal argument for a different interpretation, and fails. In the first case, the law operates effortlessly to "guide" the judge's action; in the second, it is "constraint," an obstacle to deciding the case the way you would like to. In the first case, no one is even thinking of law making. In the second, the judge tries as hard as she can to make some "new" (meaning "nonobvious") law, but can't find a way to do it without violating the duty of fidelity to the materials.

External versus internal constraint

The constraint we have been discussing so far is that the judge experiences because he or she is personally committed to interpretive fidelity—to doing "what the law requires." But judges, as an empirical matter, as a matter of plausible social fact, are also constrained by the reactions they anticipate from their audience. In other words, judges, as fallen beings vis-à-vis their oaths, want to *appear* to be "following" rather than "making" law. What a given judge will do in a case depends on what she thinks will "fly" as "good legal argument" in the minds of others, as well as on what she herself thinks about the matter.

The judge operates as a member of an interpretive community, more or less reified in her mind, and this fact is a source of constraint, just as writers like Owen Fiss claim.[3] But it is a peculiar kind of constraint, because the judge is a participant and can affect the community's reaction to the interpretation in question, rather than having simply to register it as an immovable, external fact.

The experience of "internal" constraint presupposes that the judge is looking for a legal argument that looks good to her. "External" constraint presupposes that the judge is looking for a legal argument that looks good to the audience. We shift from investigating the way interpretive work produces the subjective experience of constraint to investigating the way the same work produces the effect of necessity, the experience of legal compulsion, for the audience for the interpretation.

The paradigm case of ideologically directed legal work

I suppose (quite happily, be it noted) that "the law" can be understood to "determine" judicial activity in the two cases of unselfconscious rule-following and constraint by the text. "The law" does this because under the norm of interpretive fidelity judges do things they would not do if they were legislators. And I also affirm that judges are constrained by what they think their audience will think of them.

But there is a limit to how much of legal reality we can understand this way. As I said before, just about everyone now agrees that the naive version of rule-of-law theory doesn't fully explain the role of judges. There are many questions of law of which all or most or some observers and maybe the judges themselves would say that the rule that emerges from the case is a product of the judge's agency in a sense other than willingness to obey. In these cases, the judge's activity, the judge's legal work, affects the outcome, the rule choice, so that it is plausible that a different judge, or group of judges, would have come up with a different rule.

A phenomenological account might look like this. We start from the individual judge with ideological preferences.[4] He is confronted with a question of law posed by the advocates in the case. He has a sense of the stakes for ideologized group conflict that will be disposed by his rule choice. There is an "obvious" rule that seems to apply to the facts as they have been presented at trial and summarized for appeal. What makes it obvious is that some combination of argument from authority and policy arguments seems to constrain him to apply it to these facts. The judges' ideology appears to him to favor a rule other than this one that is "obvious."

The judge understands, as a participant in his legal culture, that he has only a fragmentary knowledge of all the authoritative materials and all the modes of deductive and policy argument that *might* be mustered to resolve the case. I mean, resolve it in a way that would fulfill his duty of interpretive fidelity and his need to generate the effect of necessity for the members of the interpretive community. He also knows that he will have enough time to investigate only a part of this lost continent of possibilities should he decide he wants to do more than just accept and reproduce the "obvious" legal argument for the rule he thinks is unjust. In other words, the judge knows that he is not Dworkin's Hercules, endowed with infinite time and infinite legal skill.

He also feels obliged to do *some* legal work in spite of the apparent obviousness of the binding rule, and he understands the interpretive community to expect this of him. American judges don't see themselves as presiding over a beauty contest between the advocates, as in a moot court. They regularly produce opinions that have only the most tangential relation to the briefs and to the points made in oral argument, using facts from the record not even mentioned by counsel. The judges and their law clerks see themselves as required to do their own work to produce not only the best outcome between the parties but also the best legal argument they can muster in favor of the rule they decide should apply.

I believe that many judges are aware of the possibility, under these circumstances, of undertaking an investigation of the legal universe with the conscious strategic goal of unsettling the obvious solution. They also have the goal of replacing it with a solution in favor of the "just" rule, supported by a legal argument that will appear, at the end of the work process, to be "better" than the one that seemed initially obvious. "Better" means that the new argument for the nonobvious just rule will seem to the judge more consistent with his oath and will be more convincing to the interpretive community.

The judge will also be aware that the undertaking of this strategic search for a compelling legal argument for his ideologically preferred rule choice is problematic from the point of view of the rule of law, and indeed of his oath of interpretive fidelity. The reason for this is that the meaning of strategic search is search that is "result-oriented," understanding this in terms of rule choice rather than in terms of which party wins. It is a strategy because it makes it more likely than would a random search that he will "find" the result he wants, rather than confirmation of the obvious rule he thinks is unjust.

Of course, what he is looking for is "inside" the law, since it is an alternative that is more faithful to the materials than the one it may displace. His search is guided by his prior knowledge of the materials—he doesn't look where he doesn't expect to find. Of course, the search may turn up nothing useful, from the point of view of the judge's ideological preference, and thereby reinforce his initial experience of constraint by the materials in the direction of the unjust rule. In that case, the judge is committed by his oath to apply that rule.

The judge who operates in good faith as an ideologist has also to be open to the possibility that the search process will change his view of what was just in the first place. If that happens, he will have the option of reorienting his work to reinforce the obvious, previously unjust rule by showing that it is good against the counterarguments he himself has been exploring.

Protestations of willingness to submit to the law whatever it may be at the end of the search process, and of openness to the authority of law as a counterweight to one's own ideologized sense of justice, may ease the judge's sense of moral jeopardy. Rule-result-orientation is still problematic.

It is possible to understand the initial experience of certainty about the applicable norm and its interpretation as a communication from "the law" (which just means earlier law makers) to the judge. It is not, I think, possible to understand the work of trying to unsettle that initial certainty as responsive to the materials in that particular way. The materials as they existed in the judge's mind before he began his legal work have had their say. They've said that what the defendant did was illegal. Now the question is whether the worker can cause their meaning to change.

This is merely problematic, rather than "forbidden," only because there is a good argument that he is obliged to engage in a strategic search for a better rule than the obvious one, and a good argument that he cannot do this nonideologically if his sense of justice partakes of his society's ideological divisions. Unfortunately, these arguments are controverted in their turn, leaving him without any clear guide from the interpretive community.

In the next chapter, I will describe typical judicial strategies for dealing with the problem of judicial strategy. The rest of this chapter develops variants of the paradigm case, and relates ideologically motivated strategic search to the ontologies of deductive versus policy questions and of determinacy versus indeterminacy, all in the context of the ideological stakes of rule choice.

Deductive work

We tend to think of a deductive solution to a question of law as the paradigm case of constraint or determinacy or legal necessity, as outside the whole problematic of strategic behavior. This image of legal necessity is grounded in the experience of following a deductive argument, rather than in the experience of critiquing or constructing one. Critiquing is often complex and time consuming, rather than based on immediate knowledge of how the deduction in question was wrong. An initial intuition that critique is *possible* may then require an elaborate attempt to demonstrate that there were alternative premises available, and no explanation of the choice made between them. We have seen already how the realists did this, combining internal critique with the revelation that judges constructed rather than "found" holdings for cases.

Developing an alternative deductive argument to the one that at first seemed obvious involves the same onerous, time-consuming operations in reverse. It involves searching for alternative premises by researching the case law that is even tangentially relevant, looking for a line of cases that will seem like authority in the case at hand only after the holdings have been restated. It involves developing the definitions of the words in holdings so that they have different implications for the facts presented than they seemed to have at first. It involves restating the facts of the case in hand to emphasize elements that would seem irrelevant if the obvious rule applied, and restating the facts of precedents to distinguish some while representing others as on point. In all these respects, deductive work is the same as rather than the opposite of policy work.

Policy work

The paradigm case of policy work occurs when the parties and the judge understand at the beginning that the question of rule definition is one of "first impression," and the legal work they put in does not dispel this sense. When the judge first reads the briefs, knowing that she will have to "strike a balance" by choosing a rule, she may experience herself as fully constrained, as having no choice given her particular understanding of how policy argument is done, her theory of coherence. But she knows that she has the option of *developing* one argument or the other, of working to make it plausible in the circumstances.

Suppose the judge thinks the advocate for the liberal position, the advocate who makes the policy arguments that are part of the liberal project of universalizing consumer interests, say, has done much better than the conservative advocate. On the basis of what has been laid before her, she would have to say that the balance favors a compulsory term in this class of cases. Suppose that she is a conservative, and that her intuition, meaning her informed impression based on her previous work as a judge, is that the liberal legal argument is "actually" much weaker than the conservative one. Suppose that the conservative advocate failed to mention, or to see the relevance, of the argument that this term might make consumers worse rather than better off.

Such a judge is likely to see herself as having a moral obligation to do work on her own to explore the possibilities of developing the conservative legal position, with the thought that when this work is done she may "see her way clear" or "feel obliged" to come out for freedom of contract. The type of work she will do is that which is inherent in the policy mode. First of all, she will have to identify the range of rules that might apply in the circumstances. Then she will have to adapt the policy argument-bites available to the particular facts and the particular rule.

The policy question always exists in a context of "obvious" rules. Ideologically oriented work is not designed to transform the whole legal system. It is work within the system. You have to choose how to define the policy question, what to leave unchallenged and what to challenge. This is a strategy issue of the type discussed below.

Hard cases and easy cases

Lawyers conventionally distinguish hard and easy cases. We can use the distinction to elaborate the paradigm of legal work. First of all, an easy case in the conventional sense is a hard case from the point of view of the ideological strategist. What we mean by "easy" is that there is a rule that obviously applies to the facts, given some explicit or implicit combination of deductive and policy arguments. From the point of view of the person whose ideological preference is for the obvious rule, the case is easy. From the point of view of the person who thinks the rule unjust, this is a hard case in the sense that it will be difficult, it may take a lot of work, and it may be impossible to displace the obvious solution.

It may be enough for the judge to turn an easy but unjust case into a hard case, for which he offers, with much allusion to his internal struggle, the best solution he can manage. But, of course, it would be better to turn it into an easy case for his side, by supporting his preferred rule as both deductively required and optimal as policy.

A hard case in terms of the lawyers' typology is an easy case for the ideological strategist, since in a hard case there are two plausible rule choices, rather than only one obvious one. A hard case is by definition one in which the judge who prefers a particular rule choice won't have to confront an initial probability of failing to make a plausible legal argument for it—what makes it hard is that with minimum work or at first blush it is obvious that there is no obvious answer.

It may be enough for the judge if his work leaves the case a hard one, as long as he can convince himself and his audience that interpretive fidelity favors his preferred outcome and can repel his adversaries' attempts to convince the audience that the case was actually much easier than it looked, and in the wrong direction. Of course, his ideal is to make a hard case look easy, easily resolved on the side of his preferred rule choice.

The economics of legal work

There are several economic dimensions of ideologically oriented legal work. First, the judge has to allocate his time among the cases that presently offer him chances to dispose ideological stakes. He has to calculate the probable payoff in terms of convincing argument and the payoff in terms of ideological significance. It is a hard choice when an apparently hard case (an easy case for ideological work) offers a low payoff in terms of ideological stakes, whereas an apparently easy case that is obviously unjust offers a large payoff but might require a lot of work, with no guarantee of success (in order to overcome the initial sense of being constrained to "do the wrong thing").

A second economy applies within a given case, one dimension being the "distance" the judge can move the law in a given direction, with more distance taking more work, and the other being the payoff, with more distance offering more payoff. An "elegant" legal strategy is one that achieves a rule change that disposes large ideological stakes via a small amount of work that changes the law only a little bit.

The notion of a work strategy implies a third economy. In pursuance of a strategy, you "invest" time in a particular line of inquiry, choosing between deductive and policy solutions, for example, and, as soon as you do so, it will cost you something to change the strategy. This means you may be constrained to continue down a work path, in spite of what has turned out to be a low probable payoff, because it would take so much time to go back to the beginning and start again.

Each of these economies has to do with the internal point of view: the judge is concerned with interpretive fidelity, in relation to work, and has to decide which work strategy for achieving a sense of internal constraint in the preferred ideological direction is best. But there is also an external economy of legal work.

Rhetoricians in general and judges in particular understand that "authorship" is not irrelevant in persuasion, in the simple sense that a particular author, a particular judge, has more or less persuasive power not just on the basis of the particular opinion, but also on the basis of the status or prestige of prior opinions, and on the basis of reputation independent of opinions. We can call this prestige factor the judge's "store" of mana, or charisma, or whatever. The crucial idea is that a store of charisma, once constituted, operates to increase the force of the judge's manipulation of the specific rhetorical devices that we deploy to produce the effect of necessity. In other words, identical opinions written by different judges will have different degrees of convincingness for the audience.

It may be helpful to conceptualize convincingness as the ability to "move" an audience a "distance" from one belief about the correct interpretation of the rule toward another. The "obviousness gap," for example, might be the distance between the interpretation the judge favors and the one that seems obvious to most members of the interpretive community. On this basis, a mechanical but suggestive model of the charismatic economy might look like this.

Judges want to maximize their charismatic store. Charisma is generated by having persuaded people in the past, as well as operating to add persuasive power to arguments in the present. The change in the store caused by a particular performance depends on how much the judge has invested in it, and on the "return" in charisma, which is a function both of the distance the judge has moved the audience and of the importance or salience or visibility of the case.

On the basis of this mechanical model, the judge has to make a calculation in every case along these lines: *(a)* The obviousness gap is x. *(b)* My arguments, from the base line of the zero-charisma judge, will get me $1/2x$ distance. *(c)* Adding my charisma has $y\%$ chance of overcoming the obviousness gap, which would get me q of added charisma. *(d)* But there is a $100 - y\%$, or $z\%$, chance of falling short and losing p of charisma. So the case has a "value" in terms of charisma of $yq - zp$.

Of course, these are continuous functions rather than on/off choices. And not all judges want to maximize their charisma, in the sense of ability to generate the effect of necessity independently of the value of their arguments. But I assert that some economy of this type significantly affects some judges' decisions about how to deploy their legal resources.

Types of field configuration

The legal worker rejects ex ante the conventional ontological distinction between cases that have deductive solutions and cases that don't, though she may endorse the distinction after the fact as an explanation of what happened to her strategy. Before the fact, there are not kinds of questions but kinds of arguments. What looks like a deductive solution that makes the case easy and the rule to apply obvious may, through work, be shown to be a false deduction. The laborious demonstration of a false deduction opens the way to working on an alternative deductive solution, or to a policy argument, or to both. After the fact, if you have trashed the other side's deductive argument without coming up with a convincing one of your own, you conclude that the question was "inevitably" one of policy.

It seems more accurate to characterize a question of rule choice not according to whether or not it "is in its nature" a policy or a deductive question, but in terms of the condition of the "field" of fact situations, precedents, and policies in which it is located. Easy cases occur in an "impacted" field, one in which there are many precedents that are intuitively obviously close in their facts to the case in hand, there is a legal rule that has been deliberately applied repeatedly to a variety of only slightly different fact situations, and the rule represents an obviously plausible compromise between policies, partly because the alternative rules seem wildly immoral, violative of someone's well-established rights, uncertain, rigid, or whatever.

But the field may be "unrationalized" or even "contradictory" instead. In the first instance, there are many decided cases, but perhaps they are based on a discredited mode of deduction (for example, "implied intent") or a policy that is no longer plausible (strengthening the firepower of the militia). Such a field cries out for a "strong" opinion that will generate new holdings for cases, based on new statements of their facts and a new assessment of the policy balance, and a new rule to apply in the case at hand. The contradictory field also cries out for a strong opinion, but because there are many cases that are close on the facts but seem to have been decided in opposite ways, on the basis of two lines of policy argument that ignore one another.[5]

Legal work and the ontology of determinacy and indeterminacy

In both unselfconscious rule application and constraint by the text, it makes sense to say that the law determined the outcome, if we mean that from the point of view of the actor there was no insertion of his or her own desires. But we can't say that whenever the judge describes what happened this way the question of law had a determinate answer. The reason is that it was just an experience and might have been modified by more work differently done.

Because of the "economic" dimension of legal work, the judge doesn't know, when he or she "fails," whether the failure was a product of time, knowledge, bias, skill, strategy, or the "inherent properties" of the legal field. The report that he or she was "bound" can be accepted at face value. But it is not a report about inherent properties directly measured. This question of law had a determinate answer for this judge under these constraints. But it might have had no determinate answer, or a different answer, for another judge, differently endowed and pursuing a different strategy.

The question "does this question of law have a determinate answer?" is therefore meaningless if it is a question about the question of law, rather than a question about the interaction between a particular, situated historical actor and this particular question of law situated in this particular field. Because determinacy is a complex function of work as well as of facts and materials, a function of an interaction, it makes no sense to predicate determinacy or indeterminacy of the question as it exists independently of the particular actor who is trying to answer it.

Of course, one could just *assume* that "in fact" there always is or is not a determinate answer, and treat the judge's work as producing evidence as to which it is. One could ask the judge to keep working until she was "reasonably certain" that she had "the" determinate answer or that there was none. Reasonable certainty might mean that there was a low probability that further work would change the outcome.

I don't doubt that people do in fact sometimes proceed just this way. But that they do is not evidence that a determinate answer exists or doesn't exist independently of the work they put in trying to find it. The assumption that the experiences of determinacy and indeterminacy are "reflections" of an external reality, or truth of the matter, that exists independently of their own efforts isn't made more plausible by the fact that sometimes it doesn't seem to be worth it to invest more time in trying to change the legal situation.

It is common to attribute the phenomenon of legal constraint to things like "interpretive community" or "conventions." This makes sense when we are speaking of the "guidance" of decision in unselfconscious rule-following. It means that sometimes as a matter of fact all the people who are concerned with an interpretation experience it as obvious, and as obvious in the same way.

We all know from experience that if there had been disagreement, and the work of legal argument on both sides, the initial unselfconscious view *might* have ended up seeming "legally wrong." The sense that the rule just "meant" that the plaintiff won might be replaced by a developed sense of constraint, when it turned out that no one could find a way to avoid the argument that a rule interpretation favorable to the defendant was legally correct. That everyone unselfconsciously adopted a view, or no one objected, isn't evidence that the outcome was determinate in any sense we are interested in.[6]

Questions of law sometimes seem obviously controversial, "inherently political," or "by their nature ideological" when first posed. The flag burning case, for example. Sometimes, a judge working on such a question will happily or reluctantly come to the conclusion that the question was not really ideological after all, that the work of legal argument has generated the experience of closure. But when this doesn't happen, and the question still calls out for controversial choice even after the time for work is past, this is not evidence that the question was inherently indeterminate. It might have been that a little more work, or work from the beginning along a different path, would have produced experienced determinacy after all.

If there is warrant neither in the experience of unselfconscious rule application nor in that of constraint by the text for a conclusion that a given question has or doesn't have a determinate answer, we can always look elsewhere. I am not going to argue the proposition that there is no elsewhere. It seems obvious to me. Try the thought experiment of the doctoral candidate in legal sociology setting up his or her empirical study of determinacy. What is the objective index against which to measure judicial reactions—a panel of "control" judges? And what warrants the correctness of *their* answers? And so on.

My approach in what follows neither answers nor rejects, but rather defers or brackets, the question of what, if anything, lies behind ("in" the legal materials) the experiences of openness and closure. I think there is quite a bit we can say about judicial law making without an answer to this more ultimate question. We can explore the "surface," rather than trying to penetrate the depths.

I am proposing to shift the investigation from the questions, "are judges ever 'really' bound? and, if so, how often?" to the question, "what follows from the fact that judges often *experience* themselves as bound?" The inquiry into consequences of adjudication can go on because we can plausibly describe an experience of boundness that affects behavior—by leading the judge to actually do whatever he *felt* he was bound to do, even if he would rather have done something else.

We ask what are the consequences for the political system if judges sometimes experience the accessible surface as structured so as to determine an outcome, and then bring about that outcome, either in the mode of unselfconscious rule-following or in that of constraint. We ask what are the consequences for the political system if judges often experience questions as open, and work to close them in one way or another, but also often experience them as closed and work to open them, sometimes successfully, sometimes not.

How often do legal questions permit ideologically oriented work?

Once we abandon the ontology of determinate and indeterminate questions, we also have to abandon questions like "how much indeterminacy is there in the law?" This question is often seen as crucial to the analysis of ideology in law, along the line that if most questions of law have legally correct answers regardless of who is answering them, then there is little room for the influence of judicial ideology. Conversely, if law is "inherently" or "pervasively" indeterminate, and for reasons that "inhere" in the nature of language or of rules, then it appears that there is lots of room for that influence.

When we conceptualize constraint in terms of work, it seems obvious that we won't be able to answer the question of ideological influence this way. A committed liberal judiciary can change a lot of law that a committed conservative judiciary would leave be, and vice versa. There is no way to say "how much" they can change except after the fact. We can make a list of "factors" that we might expect to help predict "how far" they will go, including personal factors like energy and time and skill and "external" factors like the typical field configurations in ideologically sensitive areas. We can say it's more likely that a committed judge will have success in a contradictory area like regulatory takings law, or promissory estoppel, than in an area that is more "settled," but experience shows that the generalizations will be extremely risky.

And perhaps we can make broad historical and cultural generalizations. There are periods of judicial creativity and periods of no creativity, periods when many or most judges are motivated to do ideological work, and periods when they are not. One legal culture at a given time may be characterized by the widespread judicial experience that there is no room for ideologically oriented work, while another culture with a strikingly similar body of formal law may encourage judges to find opportunity behind every bush. To my mind, this means that the study of ideology in law has to be undertaken at retail, as Dworkin might say, rather than wholesale.

The notion that law restricts the field of ideological conflict

Another common notion is presented by Neil MacCormick:

Stripped down to a claim about the political and/or ideological quality of mainstream legal dogmatics when concerned with fundamental issues of interpretation and of coherence or value in law, the CLS position is a lot less radical, or even anti-mainstream (at least as that would be judged from a British standpoint), than the grander programmatic presentations suggest. The thesis that even the best drawn laws or lines leave some penumbra of doubt, and this calls for an exercise of a partly political discretion to settle the doubt, is not particularly new; it is but the common currency of modern legal positivism . . .

. . . A crucial point, though, is that one ought not to miss or underestimate the significance of line-drawing or *determinatio* as already discussed. The law really does and really can settle issues of priority between principles by fixing rules, and even when problems of interpreting rules arise, these focus on more narrowly defined points than if the matter were still at large as one of pure principle. Fixing rules can be done either by legislation or by precedent; most commonly, in a modern system, by the two in combination. It is one of the gifts of law to civilization that it can subject practical questions to more narrowly focussed forms of argument than those which are available to unrestricted practical reason.[7]

It is of course true that "law" "really does" settle particular "issues of priority" by "fixing" rules. I think this just means that judges choose between alternative rule formulations, supported by different deductive and policy arguments, when they answer questions of law. When the judge makes a rule choice, it becomes, in a common law country, part of the large structure of legal doctrine; it becomes a valid norm from which later judges can reason, subject, of course, to Llewellyn's problematics of precedent. In a developed system, all questions of law arise in a dense pyramidal rule structure of this kind. The judge with an ideological preference has to deal with the structure of authorities as part of the medium in which he works to frame the question of law, of rule choice, and then to produce an argument that will generate the experiences of internal and external constraint on the side he favors.[8]

But it is not at all true that the historical process of successive judicial rule choices has an immanent tendency to reduce over time the possibilities for ideologically oriented legal work. First, there is no tendency for the ideological stakes in judicial rule choice to fall as judges move from "broader" to "narrower" questions of interpretation. Second, there is no tendency for the "forms of argument" to be narrower in "little" cases than in "big" cases disposed on grounds of "pure principle." These points are distinct, and each will take some elaboration.

High stakes for "little" questions

The question "Does the U.S. Constitution mandate federal judicial review of state statutes?" is obviously a "bigger" or more abstract or less narrow question than "Can a federal district court enjoin a state administrative agency from enforcing a schedule of rates for rail shipment of farm products promulgated under a valid state regulatory statute requiring that rates be 'reasonable?' "[9] Both the "initial" decision for judicial review and a long sequence of cases fixing rules for narrower subquestions were obviously "relevant," but they didn't settle in and of themselves this sub-subquestion. Yet the ideological stakes in the little question were understood to be large, certainly greater than those in many a local election, because of the expectation that the state regulatory agency would decide the question of reasonableness very differently than the federal court.

This is an example of high stakes because in long-run ideological conflict, "God is [often] in the details." Sometimes a small question involves high stakes because the size of the wealth or resource transfer that will be settled in the lawsuit is great, even though the question of law, the rule choice, is unlikely ever to be relevant in a later case. The tenant farmers under the "patroon" system of upstate New York litigated a case about whether the form of tenure devised by the owners, which involved an incorporeal hereditament called a "rent," was invalid because a restraint on alienation.[10] When they won, they got a lot of land free and clear. The rule choice had no significance beyond the case at hand, but the ideological stakes were great.

But it is conceding too much if I leave the impression that we are speaking simply of a discontinuity between legal stakes and ideological stakes. What the legal stakes in a case "are" depends on the work of advocates and judges. Legal work, in American history, has often, very often, unsettled rules located way up in the pyramid: see Brown v. Board of Education,[11] Reynolds v. Sims,[12] Miranda v. Arizona,[13] Dred Scott v. Sandford,[14] Lochner v. New York,[15] Escola v. Coca-Cola,[16] Javins v. First National Realty.[17] Once we reject the ontology of determinacy and indeterminacy in favor of the notion of constraint as a function of legal work, it is a question of fact, to be answered only through trial and error, whether the optimal strategy of ideological work in law is to concentrate on little or on big questions. A lawyer who equates the place of a rule in the pyramid of abstraction with its degree of movability through advocacy is incompetent.

Nesting

It might be Law's Gift to Civilization that as judges elaborate the rule structure by working to create and to resolve gaps, conflicts, and ambiguities, they change the "form of argument" through which they resolve sub- and sub-subquestions. As the questions get "smaller," questions might become susceptible to correct legal resolution through narrower and, therefore, less ideologically charged forms of argument. But this is not the case. The questions get narrower and narrower (the ideological stakes may be getting bigger and bigger), but the forms of argument remain astonishingly the same. This is the phenomenon sometimes called "nesting."[18]

I don't want to overstate my case. Suppose that we fix an interpretation of a rule, that is, choose a subrule by nondeductive or only weakly deductive argument. This subrule may well have implications in a later case of sub-subrule choice and may influence the outcome so that it will be different than it would have been if the only relevant authority had been the original rule. The subrule may be a veritable fountain of deductions, whereas the original rule was not. What I want to assert is that it is often the case, and often the case with high ideological stakes, that the subrule does not powerfully constrain the choice of a sub-subrule. The argument will then be no less ideological in form than the one about deriving the subrule from the rule.

Suppose the question is what happens when A kills B in mistaken self-defense, when B was really trying to assist him. If the question of compensation in tort is one of first impression, there is a highly predictable set of policy arguments, referring to rights, morality, and utility, as well as to administrability, that the parties will make to the judge. Suppose the judge allows the defense of mistake, but the question arises whether the defendant's mistake has to be "reasonable" under the objective standard or merely in good faith. The parties will argue this question, using almost exactly the same rights, morality, utility, and administrability argument-bites as on the previous issue.

The plaintiff will say that the defense of mistake should not be allowed: "as between two innocents, he who caused the damage should pay"; we must protect the right of bodily security; we need to deter carelessness; a rule of no defense will be easy to administer. Suppose that the judge decides to allow a defense of mistake. As to whether the defendant's conduct has to be reasonable or merely in good faith, the plaintiff will make the same arguments: an objective standard because "as between two innocents," we must protect the right of bodily security, we need to deter carelessness, an objective standard will be easy to administer. It will often happen that this time the court will come out on the plaintiff's side and impose an objective standard. When it does so, it will reject the defendant's policy arguments, the exact same policy argument-bites that it endorsed when the question was whether there should be a defense of mistake: no liability without fault, the right of self-defense, encourage self-help, solutions should be sensitive to particular facts.

Dworkin pointed out in "The Model of Rules" that principles are not rules because they can be argued successfully in one case, and then rejected in the next, without losing their legal status.[19] Rules, by contrast, are followed or they are not. His principles are among the larger set of policy bites and counterbites. It is not just that they can be accepted as important reasons in one case, and rejected in favor of their opposite numbers in the next, but that the same judge can go down the pyramid, resolving ever "narrower" questions, while switching back and forth between the bites.

Remember that the semiotic structure of argument-bites is related to ideological projects in at least three ways. Sometimes a system of bites, as in compulsory terms, is virtually indistinguishable from the system used on the liberal or conservative side of general legislative debate on the topic. Sometimes the systems of bites are instrumentalized, meaning that they seem to be no more than pretexts that are adopted ad hoc by liberals or conservatives depending on which side they favor in the particular case (judicial role, federalism). Sometimes the legal policy debate is analogous to the general ideological debate but is nonetheless often instrumentalized (individualism versus altruism, rules versus standards).

These ideologized modes of policy argument recur at every level of abstraction. The dispute about whether or not there should be an assumption-of-risk defense to strict products liability turns out to have the same ideological structure as the argument about whether or not to have strict products liability in the first place. A little while later, there will be yet again the same structure to the debate over whether there should be an exception to the doctrine of assumption of risk in products liability cases when the plaintiff's conduct was highly foreseeable by the defendant and might have been prevented by a safety precaution. Policy argument is interminably ideological, and like ideological debate, just plain interminable.

How radical?

Is what I have been expounding no more than "the thesis that even the best drawn laws or lines leave some penumbra of doubt, and this calls for an exercise of a partly political discretion to settle the doubt?" It really doesn't seem that way to me. (Oh my God, am I really just a Hartian?) First, that phrase answers the question "how can the judge be neutral?" The answer is that he can't be, because "even the best drawn lines . . ." My argument is that he can be ideological, not just because "the best drawn lines . . ." but because the legal materials are lying there waiting for his ideologically oriented work. Sometimes his "work in a medium" produces convincing argument for his ideologically preferred outcome when work in the other direction would have produced an ideologically contrary result.

Sometimes he can do much more than "exercise a partly political discretion" in a "penumbra of doubt." Sometimes he can generate a doubt in the core of meaning; sometimes the field configuration invites him to settle not doubt in a penumbra but raving contradiction across a doctrinal domain with high ideological stakes; sometimes the field is unrationalized and he can have the thrill of explaining that its true spirit is libertarianism in offer and acceptance. This is neither the Nightmare (the judge just does ideology) nor the Noble Dream (there is a way to be right), but it is not, I hope, hope, hope, just what the Brits have been saying all along.

If one sees law this way, it looks, *as a whole,* like the ossified record of conflicting work projects. It is not just a list of rules, each with a penumbra within which a little "partly political" discretion can be exercised. The rules themselves have a new meaning—they are not just the command of the sovereign, or what we get when we apply the rule of recognition, but a ragged, contorted boundary trench that marks the outcomes of a thousand sorties and countersorties. (Or maybe the line of scrimmage, just after the snap . . .)

The parole evidence rule of a given jurisdiction looks like the particular working out of the large conflict between a formalist and an antiformalist version, plain meaning versus New Criticism. The next, sub-subquestion about that rule looks like the latest incident in a perennial conflict, and, if God is in the details, one camp or the other may win a major victory even though it lost the last three battles. If God is in the details, the reformulation of what it means for the burden of proof in employment discrimination cases to shift after the making out of the prima facie case may "gut the statute."

I am aware of a formulaic British response, first articulated, I think, with supreme condescension by H. L. A. Hart, who claimed to be able to catch "by a single glance from afar"[20] what had been locally invisible before his overflight. As he summarized the realists,

> What did all this amount to? Seen from afar it appears to many English jurists not to have advanced legal theory far or to have added much to the stock of valuable jurisprudential ideas. But the virtues and beneficent influence of the realist movement lay elsewhere . . . For its main effect was to convince many judges and lawyers, practical and academic, of two things: first, that they should always suspect, although *not* always in the end reject, any claim that existing legal rules or precedents were constraints strong and complete enough to determine what a court's decision should be without other extra-legal considerations; secondly, that judges should not seek to bootleg silently into the law their own conceptions of the law's aims or justice or social policy or other extra-legal elements required for decision, but should openly identify and discuss them.[21]

Cls looks similar to realism in Scottish eyes:

> As a heuristic device, it is, however, certainly good advice to scholars and practitioners that they should always be ready to turn any question upside down and to see whether underplayed principles cannot be played up to create a seriously arguable counter to the view one has initially entertained. The danger of mere dogmatism in legal dogmatics comes from a failure to take seriously the possibility that another view might be argued just as well as one's own initial one (mark you, this can be as true of those who start with a view toward the political left as of those who start from the political right; no party seems to have a monopoly on dogmatism). The uses of this heuristic are demonstrated in many excellent and insightful CLS writings at the level of concrete doctrine rather than general programmatics.[22]

All those modest studies (realist and cls alike) may have been instantiating the liberal humanist virtues of skepticism about claims of authority, candor, and antidogmatism, but they also claimed to be doing something quite different. They also claimed to be showing that the actual outcome of doctrinal debate, that is, the set of rules the judges chose, is much more *intelligible* (insert big German word) if you reject both the Hartian and the American Noble Dream views, and adopt not the Nightmare but suitably chastened ideology-critique.

In short, they were representing the actual content of doctrine as the outcome of an argument between intelligible contending projects, or visions, with big stakes in view, rather than as either a struggle to "work the law pure" or "mere personal preference" exercised in penumbras. The plausibility of this project-to-show-the-projects-at-work does not depend on a global internal critique, like Hart's, of the "inherent" limitations of language. It depends on the plausibility of a minimalist internal critique of the mainstream's attempt to show the coherence of a field, on the plausibility of the restatement of the field as contradictory, and on the plausibility of the formulation of conflicting blocks of implicitly ideological legal argument to account for the cases that came out one way or the other.[23]

The interest, as opposed to the plausibility, of the project depends on an empirical proposition: that as a matter of fact, rather than of necessity, very large ideological stakes have been disposed by the choice of rules in cases in which ideologically oriented work of this kind made a difference. This is the common sense of American lawyers and political commentators with respect to American law/politics.

Perhaps it looks weird to English and Scottish commentators, for whom judges exercise a "partly political discretion" in the "penumbras" that exist in even the "best-drawn" rules, because as a matter of fact British judges have not disposed large ideological stakes through ideologically oriented work. Perhaps it seems positively deranged to Continentals because their judges have disposed even less in the way of stakes than British judges, who have to deal with the pesky indeterminacy of the case method.

I have my doubts. But this is not the place to develop them into theories. The next chapter takes up the metastrategies that American judges adopt to deal with the anxiety of being strategists in a culture of critical legalism.

8

Strategizing Strategic Behavior in Interpretation

*I*n the classic legal realist critique of conservative judicial decisions, the last step was to suggest that, given flaws in the chain of deduction, high stakes for ideologized group conflict, and the inevitability of policy, it was plausible that the judge's ideological "sympathies" influenced the outcome. In the last chapter, I tried to show just how a judge with an ideological preference for an outcome can work to make that outcome law. In this chapter, I suggest three typical postures that judges adopt as workers conscious of the possibility of pursuing ideological strategies. These are the postures of the constrained activist, the difference splitter, and the bipolar judge.

My initial claim is only that informed observers so characterize some judges. I then test the plausibility of this claim against the argument that whatever the observers may think, the categories of liberalism and conservatism are too diffuse to ground plausible explanations of decisions. Having concluded that they will serve, I take up the question of how constrained activist, difference splitting, and bipolar judges square their behavior with the norm that the choice of rules through adjudication should proceed according to a method of legal reasoning that is, if not objective, at least outside the ideological contests of the moment.

My answer is that they, and their informed audience, "deny," in the psychological sense of the word, the influence of ideology. They do so for good reasons, of which the most important is that they would otherwise have to confront the contradictory character of the role constraints under which judges operate. Acknowledging that judges can't coherently be asked to "just say no" to ideology would threaten, in turn, the plausibility of Liberal legalism in general and, in particular, the favorite "legally correct" outcomes of liberals and conservatives alike.

Relativity of the claim about strategic behavior

It was implicit in the discussion in the last chapter that it is always *possible* for the judge to adopt a strategic attitude toward the materials, to try to make them mean something other than what they at first appeared to mean, or to give them a meaning to the exclusion of other initially possible meanings. But it is *never necessary* that he do this, and *never certain* that he will succeed if he tries. Finally, it is *not usually possible* to know whether a particular decision came out differently, as a result of the judge adopting a particular work strategy, than it would have come out if he had adopted some other strategy.

It is always possible to behave strategically in the sense of trying to make a particular rule interpretation look good. There is no definition of the rule of law that could prevent judges from making this effort, and it is plausible that the rule of law requires judges to make it, at least some of the time.

A judge who habitually behaves strategically vis-à-vis the materials may be insensitive to specifically ideological implications or work hard to banish them from her consciousness. She may have an agenda that we would characterize as personal or idiosyncratic rather than ideological. Such a judge has to use the discourse and listen to the arguments while somehow not understanding the situation the way the others do, but things like that happen all the time.

It isn't necessary to behave strategically at all. Many judges seem to approach the materials with the belief that they must mean something, and to have little talent or inclination for legal work. They may experience closure at the end of a process that looks like random search, just grabbing onto the feeling when it hits them. They may repress or never have acquired the ability to strategize.

From our point of view, the input of these judges into judicial rule making is uninteresting (though we might speculate about how their nonstrategic behavior will map in relation to the behavior of judges who are political actors). It is quite important to distinguish this ideologically random behavior both from unselfconscious rule-following and from constraint by the text. It is not unselfconscious rule-following because the judge knows there is a question of law and is trying to find an answer. It is not constraint by the text because constraint means resistance to an attempt to make the materials mean something in particular.

Even if you can always behave strategically, that doesn't mean you can always modify the rule from what you at first thought it would be, or that you can take what looks like an open question and show that the liberal side was clearly right, or whatever. You can always work at manipulation, but you may fail to achieve your objective.

It might be that there are no "real" opportunities for strategic behavior. Maybe judges do as a matter of fact sometimes adopt the strategic *attitude*. But whenever they do so they might be either deluded about what is really going on, because the law guides them behind their backs, constraining them in the end to the right answer, or in bad faith in the strong sense of transgressing the role constraint of interpretive fidelity.

I don't think it possible to refute this possibility except by an appeal to the history of critique and reconstruction. And this history, to my mind, establishes only that it is plausible that ideologically focused work constantly changes the meaning of the materials—that successful instances of strategic behavior are frequent. Judges often produce a convincing meaning for the legal materials different from the convincing meaning a judge with the opposite work agenda would have produced (or did produce in a dissent). In what follows, I try to strengthen this hypothesis through a description of three kinds of agenda that judges pursue strategically. I will introduce my three typical characters first as they might be described by someone interested only in predicting their behavior, someone using the commonsense notion of an ideological "preference" I described in Chapter 3.

The (constrained) activist judge

There are judges lawyers analyze as constrained activists, meaning that they (the lawyers) have a picture of how these judges operate, a picture that they use in predicting what these judges will do. Here's my version of the lawyers' picture. Suppose that the judge, on first exposure to the case, has a clear sense of what the applicable common law rule is and how to interpret it. But suppose that if she were a legislator she would not want this rule applied to cases like this one and would change it (either prospectively or retrospectively) by adding an exception.

Further suppose that if asked to explain her discontent with "the law," and the direction in which she would change it, she would offer a policy critique of the rule and a policy justification of her proposed exception that you would identify with "conservative ideology." Finally, suppose that this judge has a similar conservative policy critique of lots of other rules, and that she never or almost never criticizes the rules in a way that makes her sound like a liberal.

This judge has no intention of disobeying the law. What makes her a constrained activist is that she puts a great deal of time and energy into working out a legal interpretation different from the one that first appeared best. She does this in every case where the law seems "too liberal" to her. Sometimes she is successful and sometimes not. When she fails, she ungrudgingly chooses a rule that differs from her legislative preference. In other words, whichever rule she finally chooses to apply to the case will represent the best legal interpretation she can find for the materials. She writes opinions that are formally "legal" and also reflect her honest belief that the law "requires" the outcome she has reached.

I am calling this judge "activist" because she has an "extrajuridical" motive, namely, the achievement of a just outcome, for preferring one result to another across a wide range of cases, and works to make that result law. Note that this form of activism is oriented to *the legal rules*. The judge has a rule that she prefers to the one she thinks she may have to apply, rather than just a party she wants to win.

In the course of her work, the judge goes back and forth between the case for her new legal interpretation and the best case against it, in the spirit of fidelity to the materials. But she is doing this with a goal: the goal of establishing that her preferred legislative solution is the correct legal solution. In pursuit of this goal, she has been anything but neutral in her use of her resources. She has spent a lot of time inventing a strategy, digging through the books, keeping an eye out all the time for random bits of stuff that might be useful in building her argument.

In developing the best argument against her position, her motive has been defensive. That is, she has tried to think what someone who was as determined to uphold the first impression as she is to upset it would say to her alternative. When she is satisfied that she has a good answer to the objections she can think of, she stops her inquiry and goes on with the affirmative task of buttressing her own position, thinking up another objection to refute.

True, she has undergone in this process a good faith risk of being persuaded to the opposite side. She has really and truly opened herself to the possibility that each argument for her first impression is right, and determined to give in to it if she can't answer it. But it is still the case that she has an identifiable "project," a direction she is going in (to change the unfair rule into a fair one). From her point of view, it will be a defeat if (as often turns out) she just can't find a way around the unfair rule.

Now suppose the activist has a legislative sense of what would be best but anticipates at the beginning of the interpretive process that there is no clearly best answer from the internal perspective of fidelity to the materials. She works away at finding the interpretive strategy that will overcome this first impression by establishing that fidelity requires the conservative outcome she chose on legislative grounds.

If she comes to the conclusion that the law requires the "wrong" interpretation, she will struggle against the conclusion but submit to it if she can't come up with a good legal argument to the contrary. If she ends up with a sense that the arguments for alternative interpretations are evenly enough balanced so that there is an element of choice in deciding between them, she will decide according to her (predictably conservative) sense of what is just in the circumstances and will write an opinion making the best case she can that that result was legally required.

My claims here are, first, that many judges are constrained activists, and they do a lot of important law making through adjudication. Second, the results the conservative constrained activist judges come up with are different from those of the liberals with the same approach. It makes a big difference how you deploy your resources among alternative work strategies in response to your initial reaction to the materials. Liberal judges who work hard and well will find good, even apparently (to them) conclusive reasons for liberal solutions to questions of interpretation. Conservative judges will come out the other way.

Third, if the conservative judge succeeds through work in making the conservative outcome look required, we might say that she has changed the rule of law from what it initially appeared to be. This change was *permitted* by the materials, since otherwise the judge would not, at the end of the process, be operating under the constraint of fidelity in interpretation. But it was not *mandated* or required by them. The law did seem to speak to the judge, in the first instance, generating seemingly of its own force an experience of certainty about what it required. But "it" didn't tell the judge to change it or what to change it into.

The difference-splitting judge

The logic of the Court's precedents suggests that peremptory challenges should be abolished entirely because the right to vote on juries is a fundamental political right. But Justice O'Connor once again tried to split the difference by suggesting in a concurring opinion that defendants and civil litigants, but not prosecutors, should be able to continue to discriminate against jurors on the basis of sex.

Justice O'Connor is a highly intelligent lawyer with sensible political instincts . . . [S]he seems to believe that by rejecting the extreme conservative and liberal position in each case, and by trying to stake out a judicious compromise, she is acting as a voice of principled moderation.[1]

The posture of the difference-splitting judge is, from the point of view of the outside observer, more passive than that of his constrained activist colleague. He has a developed sense of the way groups pursue ideologized conflict through adjudicative rule making. He is oriented to this aspect of adjudication in just the same way as the other participants. But he uses this understanding to work out what the "ideologues," his constrained activist colleagues, would see as the optimal liberal and conservative rule interpretations, and then chooses an interpretation that lies in between. This is possible because the ideological structure of the materials is a thing of continua. The liberal rule and the conservative rule are polar, and in between there are a series of "moderate" positions.

This is not inconsistent with the "either/or," "on/off," or binary character of adjudication. It is true that one party or the other wins, but there will generally be several rule interpretations under which the plaintiff wins and several that produce victory for the defendant. The difference-splitting judge is concerned with the rule structure, rather than with the particular parties. What I mean by "difference splitting" is choosing a rule formulation, an interpretation rather than a party, that is "moderate" from the ideological point of view.

From the point of view of an observer trying to predict his behavior, the difference splitter is *controlled by* ideology, albeit the ideologies of others, even though he eschews any ideological commitment. The reason for this is that what he predictably splits is the difference between other people's ideological positions. He lets the ideologues decide him indirectly by setting up a choice and then refusing it by choosing the middle.

The bipolar judge

The bipolar judge combines traits from the other two. Sometimes, like a constrained activist, he works hard to develop a strong liberal position on an issue. But in the next case, he comes out just as strongly for a conservative position, also like a constrained activist, but of the opposite commitment. The outside observer understands him to have the project of putting together a judicial career that splits the difference, rather than an opinion in the particular case that does so.

His opinion in a given case will be hard to tell from what a constrained activist judge on the same side would produce, except that it will not be looking forward to promoting the liberal or conservative project over a range of cases. (The bipolar judge, however, may well have made up his mind on one side or the other for a whole field of law, and so work with just as much sense of long-term strategy *for that field* as an activist colleague.)

What makes this judge bipolar is that he has a consistent tendency to alternate between the ideologies over time. At the most vulgar level, suppose you are a practicing lawyer appearing before him with an ideologically charged case at a moment when he has come out as a liberal several times in a row. There is a much greater probability that he will go for a conservative rule interpretation in your case than there would be if that very same case had come before him at the end of a string of conservative opinions.

There may be many particular aspects of the case that you can predict will appeal to his particular judicial temperament or his previous pattern of alternation between the sides. But it is also true that his judicial temperament has a general structure independent of these particulars: he is bipolar. He does not in fact belong to an ideological camp. But like the difference splitter, we predict his behavior on the basis of our knowledge of other people's ideological productions. The productions of others define the alternatives between which he fluctuates. Unlike the difference splitter, he "lets himself go" and participates actively in constructing the very ideological positions of which he is at the same time "independent." His liberal opinions influence the evolution of the liberal "side," just as his conservative opinions influence conservatism. But having jumped in, he backs off. Being independent turns out to be another form of compromise.

Interpreting strategic behavior

We might, of course, respond by trying to figure out, in each case where something like this might have happened, what the true interpretation was, as opposed to that which happened to lie along the strategic path adopted by the constrained activist, the difference splitter, or the bipolar judge. We might ask, in other words, how the rule chosen is different from what it would have been had judges "just interpreted" the legal materials.

I argued in the last chapter that it is methodologically incoherent and practically impossible to make the "just interpret" analysis unless one has what we lack: some other criterion of legal correctness than the plausible deployment of the argumentative tools that legal culture makes available to judges trying to generate the effect of legal necessity. Lacking any independent criterion, I don't think it makes sense to ask how these judges' outcomes differ from what they would have been had they "just interpreted" the law.

My plan is to use my three models of the judge as ideological strategizer as elements in a theory of the difference it makes to liberal/conservative conflict that so much of our law is made through an adjudicative process within which liberalism and conservatism are not supposed to play a role. The idea is to contrast the status quo, not with an imagined situation in which judges "just interpret," but with an equally imaginary situation of legislative supremacy.

With this in view, the rest of this chapter takes up two problematic aspects of the description I've given of judicial strategy. The first question is whether the idea of ideology as liberalism or conservatism can work as an explanation of what judges do, and the second question is whether it is possible to account for constrained activist, difference-splitting, and bipolar activity without resorting either to the idea of conscious deceit or to the idea of utter unconsciousness.

The critique of ideology as an explanatory concept

My use of the notion of an ideology in my presentations of the constrained activist, the difference splitter, and the bipolar judge is obviously problematic. The ideological projects of liberal and conservative intelligentsias figure in my discussion as a "behind" that is "revealed" when we discover the plasticity of legal reasoning.[2] But the mere substitution of ideology for legal reasoning as an explanation of outcomes is open to the critique that ideology is no more determinate than what it replaces.

In other words, my approach seems to require us to believe that there is an important difference between understanding legal outcomes as the result of the application of a neutral method of adjudication and understanding them as the result of the pursuit of ideological projects. The strategy seems to be one of exposing the indeterminacy of the surface level of discourse in order to get at the "real" level, which is ideology.

But the ideologies are themselves just "texts" that each individual judge will have to interpret before he or she can decide what is "required" by his or her presupposed political commitment. Saying that the judge is a liberal constrained activist doesn't tell us what liberalism "requires" in any particular case, because of the possibility of strategic behavior within the process of ideological interpretation.

The judge will consult the "principles" and "values" that supposedly underlie or inform liberalism, by contrast with conservatism, and then some list of canonical examples of the principles and values in action. The problem is that both ideologies appear internally inconsistent in two different ways. Each deploys largely identical abstract first principles, and the same set of contradictory intermediate principles, to produce sharply different outcomes across a range of domains. Each is open to the charge of switching back and forth between the contradictory intermediate arguments as we move from domain to domain (bedroom to boardroom) without any coherent larger pattern. And each is open to the charge that within a given domain there is no coherent explanation of why the ideologists don't take their principles to their "logical extreme" (total deregulation of everything versus total socialization of everything).

Judicial policy arguments are complexly related to these general ideological positions, sometimes appearing to be direct translations of the arguments of general political debate, sometimes seeming to be mere instruments for the pursuit of the ideological agendas, and sometimes appearing as a parallel though not identical form. Moreover, there are specifically professional agendas of the legal intelligentsia that can crosscut or contradict the liberal or conservative commitments of the actors.

All of this means that the occasions for strategic behavior in choosing an interpretation of one's own ideology will be at least as numerous as those for choosing an interpretation of the legal materials. Suppose the issue is university regulation of hate speech on campus. There is the liberal commitment to civil liberties and the liberal commitment to racial justice. There are all the particular instances of liberal defense of communist speech, however "hateful," and of liberal advocacy of strong rules against racial and sexual harassment in the workplace.

Suppose that on first examination the liberal constrained activist sees her own liberal ideology as "requiring" invalidation. If she "doesn't like" this result, she can go to work to restate the liberal principles and values, and reconfigure the liberal precedents, so that the outcome changes. Maybe she will be unable to come up with a convincing liberal case against the regulations and will end up feeling "bound" by ideology to a result she doesn't like. But maybe the hard ideological work will lead to a sense that the case can go either way for a liberal, or a sense that any good liberal has to support the regulations.

Of course, we could say that liberal ideology "really" required either one result or the other. A judge might imagine that liberalism required regulation of hate speech, but she would be wrong because liberalism prohibits it. If we had a lot of confidence that the ideologies have this kind of bite when correctly applied, we could use the notion of an ideological project as an explanation of judicial outcomes even though we might have to acknowledge that judges sometimes make mistakes.

The internal critic of this use of the notion of an ideological project may not be able to "prove that it can't be done." But she will point persistently to internal flaws in extant demonstrations of how liberal or conservative principles apply in practice. Then there are all the cases in which supposedly determinate liberal reasoning is unresponsive to alternative versions of liberalism that have apparently equal claim to legitimacy.

Within the ideological "camps" there are diverse groups with different positions, and even different "subideologies." We sometimes see this in terms of the underlying communities on which they draw. Liberal Republicans of the old WASP gentry kind, with their progressivism on civil rights and social issues combined with pro-business, antiregulatory sentiment, are very different from the libertarians, Jewish neoconservatives, white middle-American social-issue fundamentalists, and black conservatives. Feminists, rainbow coalitionists, civil libertarians, liberal union activists, and environmentalists, to name a few, coexist within the liberal camp.

My definition of an ideological project allows for conflict or incoherence among the theoretical premises, and for inconsistency among practices and between theory and practice. It also allows for fluid "membership" in the project, and for disagreement about who is in and who is out. None of this is inconsistent with the experience of closure, but it certainly makes it implausible to claim that liberal or conservative ideology will yield a tighter explanation of outcomes than neutral interpretation of the law.

Indeed, the parallel between ideology and legality suggests an inquiry into how people's false belief in the determinacy of their own ideological positions inflects the course of democratic politics. And then we could go behind ideology to try to find out how judges decide, for example, that they "don't like" being opposed to regulation of campus hate speech, even though it at first appears to them that their own liberalism requires that opposition.

For example, we might follow Jerome Frank[3] and resort to explanation in terms of "judicial temperament." Then we could explain temperament in terms of childhood experience. But each level, from legality to ideology to temperament, requires "the subject" to interpret, and permits interpretive strategy based on the level behind. (Though at each level there are also experiences of closure, of constraint by the text.) At each level, the attempt to persuade us that what happened was caused or required by the text will come up against the objection that the same text could have yielded the opposite outcome had the actor pursued a different interpretive strategy.

It might at first appear that the infinite regress of interpretation simply invalidates each "behind" in turn, so that "explanation is impossible." This doesn't seem right to me. As a matter of fact, the meaning of the ideological projects is sometimes "stabilized" by factors like self-conscious consensus about the political character of a position, the history of a position in ideological conflict, its "semiotic" relationship to opposed positions, and its "local coherence" with closely related liberal or conservative positions. The legal versions of ideological debate are sometimes stabilized in the same way. If the question is whether to impose a protective compulsory term in a labor or consumer contract, there will usually be little difficulty in identifying the opposing legal arguments with ideologies.

For the observer pursuing the critical social theory project, what needs to be explained is *the event* (the judicial choice of a rule), and each level of textuality "behind" the event is helpful. As critical observers, we sometimes feel we "know what is going on," to the extent of explanatory closure, through the process of multiplying the levels available to make sense of the judge's action. As long as we don't expect more of the effort to explain than these experiences of closure, the infinite regress presents opportunities for richer description and more intelligent response, rather than a methodological disaster.[4]

To my mind, this kind of critique is threatening not to explanation in the abstract but to the particular kind of explanation through ideology that leftists have wanted, for leftist reasons, to build into critical social theory. My hypothetical attack on my own use of the concept of ideology is just the latest incident in a continuing modernist/postmodernist attack on this leftist intention. My theory was designed to withstand this attack, in the manner of the last paragraph.

I think, in other words, that the moderation, empowerment, and legitimation effects I describe in the next two chapters can be plausible consequences of adjudication, even if it is conceded that liberalism and conservatism are no more determinate as explanations of outcomes (rule choices) than the rule of law, and even if we won't do any better by going back another level. The *occasional* sense of explanatory closure that this kind of ideological interpretation of adjudication produces seems to me a plausible basis for doing things in pursuance of the left project, even if it will often be the case that liberalism and conservatism are useless for more ambitious explanatory purposes.

A *psychology of strategic behavior*

We could treat my descriptions of typical judges as empirical hypotheses about patterns of outcomes. We might try to verify them using our own "external" definitions of liberal and conservative outcomes, making case-by-case determinations of what we think the constraints imposed by interpretive fidelity "really" were, and then identifying judges as constrained activists, difference splitters, and bipolar judges without any reference at all to their states of mind while judging. It should already be clear why this doesn't seem a plausible course to me. First, external definitions of liberalism and conservatism are hard to come by. Second, I don't think it is possible to determine what the constraints imposed by interpretive fidelity "really" were.

Alternatively, we could see what the judges do as conscious strategy, or as strategy pursued truly unconsciously, as repressed strategy. I think each of these alternatives is sometimes useful. But I have chosen a fourth path. In my descriptions the judges are half-conscious. This is the characteristic posture of mediating a conflict by denial or "bad faith." Such a description seems to me more realistic as a matter of fact than either consciousness or unconsciousness, but there is more at stake in this choice of strategy than the endlessly intriguing question of what they think they're doing.

Another reason for insisting on the psychology of denial or bad faith is that if *judges* are able to operate without confronting openly the problematic character of their role, it is more plausible that no one else confronts it either. The ideological element is a kind of secret, like a family secret— the incestuous relationship between grandfather and mother—that affects all the generations as something that is both known and denied. This is a collective, social psychological phenomenon with political consequences (the moderation, empowerment, and legitimation effects). It could occur even if judges were conscious ideological manipulators deceiving a public that wanted to be deceived, but it would then have the instability of any conspiracy that involves many thousands of people and has to constantly renew itself by recruiting new Grand Inquisitors.

My way of looking at it is to start with the psychology of denial in an individual judge, then suggest mechanisms by which the psychology of the actor in the story gets adopted by the audience for the action. Judges keep the secret, even from themselves, in part because participants in legal culture and in the general political culture want them to. Everyone wants it to be true that it is not only possible but common for judges to judge nonideologically. But everyone is aware of the critique, and everyone knows that the naive theory of the rule of law is a fairy tale, and those in the know fear that the sophisticated versions of contemporary jurisprudence aren't much better.

Denial: not just a river in Egypt

What does it mean to refer to the judge as "denying?" There has to be something more involved than a familiar speech act: when asked whether his performance was influenced by ideology, he responded, "it was not." Denial in the sense that interests us is motivated in a particular way. We impute denial, meaning that we choose a psychological interpretation of the act. As with the initial imputation of an "ideological motive" to a judge, there is no way to "prove" or "verify" that the judge is denying.

This usage originated in psychoanalytic theory, in Sigmund Freud's interpretation of jealousy,[5] for example, but Anna Freud gave it a whole new lease on life,[6] and it has passed into the American popular discourse of daytime talk shows and twelve-step programs ("he's been in denial about his drinking for years"; "she's been in denial about his cheating for years"). My version is adapted from both these sources, and from the related ideas of bad faith and cognitive dissonance, for the particular purpose at hand. This kind of interpretation of judicial psychology has a legal realist genealogy.[7]

We use the word "denial" as an interpretation of a piece of behavior in cases where we agree about what was said or thought and want to figure out what was "behind" it. We feel the need to go "behind" because we (the interpreter and the audience for the interpretation) agree on two things:

1. We agree that what the actor has said is a misrepresentation of his or her own desire, emotion, opinion, or intention, or of important

external facts about his or her situation, but in the special sense of a "refusal to acknowledge," "refusal to recognize," "refusal to admit." The denial requires something like "refusal," because it presupposes that there is evidence for the thing denied, or an assertion of it by someone in argument. When I say that judges "deny" the role of ideology in their decisions, it is implicit that in my view it does play a role in fact—the denier is always wrong.

2. We agree about the misrepresentation that:

(a) It is not merely conventional, as when you ask the terminally ill patient, "how are you?" and he responds, "I'm fine, how are you?" When judges write their opinions in the language of legal necessity, this is just a convention; when we say that they are engaged in denial, we mean that they at least partly believe the convention.

(b) It is not a conscious, deliberate, strategic misrepresentation, not a lie designed to deceive an audience without the speaker having any belief at all in its truth (judges are not consciously trying to deceive us about ideology in adjudication).

(c) It is not a cognitive glitch or random error. For example, we have more data than the statement itself, as in, " 'I am not mad,' he screamed, veins bulging." Or the speaker repeats the misrepresentation after "dismissing" feedback or new data that the audience believes would "normally" cause him to correct it—new data in the form, for example, of a devastating critique of adjudication.

If these conditions are fulfilled, it is common practice to look for a "psychological" explanation, by which I mean an explanation that attributes the persistence of the misrepresentation to the needs or desires of the speaker. The kind of need or desire is both specific and complex. We call it denial when we have the idea that if the speaker recognized the truth about an external fact, or about his own desire, emotion, opinion, or intention, he would experience painful anxiety. The motive for denial is to prevent or get rid of this anxiety.

There is yet another level, another "behind": what causes the anxiety, or would cause it absent denial, is an intrapsychic "conflict," in the sense of a painful choice. It might be conflict between contradictory desires, or between conscience and desire, or between a desire and fear of the consequences of acting on the desire, or just between contradictory versions of reality, where that choice has important implications, and so on.

In common usage, denial is the verbal manifestation of a particular kind of wishful thinking, the wish being that an anxiety-producing conflict, one the audience has decided is "real," should disappear. The speaker resolves the conflict and dispels the anxiety by "falsely" getting rid of one of the two conflicting elements, for example, by denying anger in a situation where one ought not to feel anger, by denying that one feels a compulsion to drink because admitting it would require one to decide whether or not to stop.

The three types of judges as deniers

What follows is an imaginative reconstruction of my three types of judges as deniers. It is an interpretation based on the evidence of opinions read in their historical context, plus a little time spent at judicial conferences. I am not saying that all judges deny the role of ideology, or that those who deny do so all the time, or even that all judges are influenced by ideology. As I said above, some judges are better understood as clueless, or as devoted to agendas that aren't ideological at all in the sense in which I've been using the term; and some judges are best understood as random, or as operating on the basis of truly unconscious motives that are hopelessly complex and also inaccessible. And in many, many cases, judges experience themselves as constrained by the text, so that their liberal or conservative or difference-splitting or bipolar strategic inclinations turn out to be irrelevant to the outcome, at least from their own point of view.

As long as we suppose that a significant number of judges are constrained activists, difference splitters, and bipolar judges, and that they have made a lot of important law that is best accounted for by these ideological postures, the analysis should be interesting. Even if you think that there is always a legal right answer that is the same whatever your "personal" ideological position, it should be interesting if you also think that some judges some of the time behave in the ways described.

The *constrained activist* accepts the constraint of interpretive fidelity. But when she thinks this obligation will require her to reach an unjust result, or when she sees open texture, she works to change the meaning of the materials in the direction of what we have decided is her own ideology. When she writes her opinion, she obeys the convention that requires her to present the outcome as fully determined by the materials and by her reasoning. To the charge that the rule of law means no ideology in judging, her reply is an opinion that denies that ideology had anything to do with it. She offers no account of the role of ideological strategy in her work process.

I've had conversations with three sophisticated constrained activist judges, two liberal and one conservative, in "private," so to speak. The two liberals denied, in the mode of Cardozo, that ideology played any role at all in their decisions, although they heartily agreed that technical reasoning was often indeterminate, that policy was a constant influence, that they were perceived as judicial liberals and often as "partisan," and that liberals but not conservatives had supported their most important judicial initiatives.

They both said that they tried to shape the law "in response to the development of the society." They thought liberal responses to socio-legal problems, such as products liability or landlord/tenant, corresponded better than conservative ones to the "needs" of society, and they therefore chose those responses, with humble recognition that they might well be wrong. This didn't make them ideological actors, in their own minds, because they remained free agents, deciding each policy question on the merits, without any loyalty or inner commitment to the ideology they were implementing over time. The conservative judge was much more "cynical." He saw his liberal brethren as unselfconscious or hypocritical, and gave a sardonic but also uneasy description of his battles with them, emphasizing that his own activism was strictly defensive.

The liberal constrained activists seem to me to be in denial or bad faith because their explanation of how they are independent of ideology is an evasion of rather than a response to the critique. Both liberals and conservatives, like the activist judges, are formally committed to putting into effect the rules that they respectively see as responding to the evolution of society and meeting its needs. What divides them ideologically is that they have sharply different interpretations of "society," "evolution," and "needs." We don't hesitate to call a person a liberal or a conservative with no more basis than that they consistently adopt the interpretation that one or the other camp has evolved, over time, as an application of the shared general principles (rights, majority rule and the rule of law, Judeo-Christian ethics, regulated market economy with safety nets) to each particular question that implicates social need and development.

True, these judges could be ideological in a stronger sense. They might "believe" in liberalism or conservatism as doctrines, and be committed to working both to improve them and to ensure their practical triumph in the world. It is fair for them to deny that they are ideologues or partisans in this stronger sense. But the claim of the critique of adjudication is not that judges are committed but merely that ideology influences adjudication.

If the judge admits that over time she has consistently found liberal solutions to be more just than conservative ones, and consequently has chosen to make them into law, she has admitted enough to validate the critique. The bland persistence in affirming independence when one's vote is highly predictable is a perfect example of bad faith.

There are two kinds of *difference splitters.* One type is an ideological moderate and splits the difference as a constrained (centrist) activist. This judge's legislative preferences correspond to the results he works to bring about through adjudication, and he is a denier and in bad faith to the extent he claims that all he is doing is "calling them as he sees them," without any commitment to a camp. Again, what we mean by ideological influence in adjudication is consistent orientation to a set of results, rather than partisanship or true-believer-ism.

The more interesting type of difference splitter has internalized a strong norm against activist behavior of any type. His idea of his role is that it forbids acting like his colleague who is a "knee-jerk conservative" and also like his colleague who is a knee-jerk centrist. He believes in one of the various theories of his role that excludes an ideological motivation for the work of legal reasoning, even if constrained. He may be a reasoned elaborator of the Hart and Sacks school, or a Dworkinian, or a positivist, or a feminist pragmatist, or he may adhere to the view of the activists that the judge should make law evolve to meet the "needs of society."

His practice does indeed represent a version of neutrality, since his "personal" or legislative politics, which may be liberal or conservative or centrist, don't influence how he comes out. He splits the difference even when he thinks that result monstrous and knows he would never vote for it if he were a legislator. Ideology has no internal, commitment-based influence on his behavior. It influences him only because he allows the ideological positions of others to determine him by setting up the difference that he splits.

But the theory of even the most revisionist advocates of the rule of law is not that judges should consistently choose the path of ideological moderation, against their intuitions of justice when necessary, but that they should be in some sense nonideological. From the point of view of the critique, ideology is no less an influence if it comes in only through the back door, so to speak, by structuring his alternatives.

The bipolar judge, like the difference splitter, comes in two variants. He may be an activist by personal or legislative commitment, first on one side and then on the other. In this case he is, in pop psychological terms, "schizophrenic." He is open to the critique that he is in bad faith on each side of his split personality, because on each side he is an activist. Or he may be best interpreted as acting on an implicit but untenable theory of judicial neutrality, to wit, that as long as he isn't consistently liberal or conservative, he isn't ideological.

Like the other two, he wants to be interpreted as doing just what he is supposed to, that is, calling them as he sees them, without an ideological commitment. He is exempt from the charge of having a commitment to moderation because in any given case he can go all the way with the liberals or the conservatives. The way he decides a particular case is to keep an open mind as long as possible, listening attentively to the arguments on both sides starting from his own understanding of himself as not a liberal nor a conservative nor a moderate, but a "free agent."

This is his problem: He has a commitment to his idea of himself as a free agent, but he would doubt that commitment in himself if he found himself coming out too often on one side or the other. And since he is proud of his independence and thinks others recognize it, he may be in-fluenced not just by his own but by what he thinks his audience's ideas are about what proportion of liberal and conservative decisions you need in order to sustain the free-agent claim.

This type of bipolar judge differs from the constrained activist because he doesn't start out asking whether he would favor the obvious interpre-tation of the rule if he were a legislator. He doesn't see his role that way at all. What he does is to listen to counsel or other judges putting forward their arguments for ideologically organized alternatives and try to figure out which one best "fits" the body of materials. He adopts first one point of view and then the other. Finally, he commits himself. But the commit-ment is ideologically patterned over time so as to keep him independent.

The nonactivist difference splitter as I have described him is an ideo-logical moderate who believes that moderation is not ideology. The non-activist bipolar judge calls them as he sees them, but turns out to see them under the constraint that he must be able to appear to himself, over time, as neither a liberal nor a conservative, no matter how he would react to the merits without that constraint.

They are both classic bad-faith actors, because they deny both to them-selves and to others something that they know perfectly well is going on.

They couldn't possibly accomplish their highly patterned strategic interventions unless *some* part of their minds, some part close to the surface, was constantly picking up the ideological implications of "every move they make." But they have a much trickier, more sophistic response to the charge that they are ideological than the constrained activist has. They point to their difference splitting or long-run bipolar opinions and ask us to believe that they are actually outside ideology.

Psychologizing versus dialogue

We don't get to the point of psychologizing American judges until we have decided that, at least for the moment, there's no sense in continuing our investigation of their views on the merits, because those views are wrong and, indeed, there is no sense in further dialogue with them on their own terms, because, for the moment, it is more interesting to figure out why they say what they say, on the assumption that it's wrong, than to investigate further whether it is wrong. It can be pretty infuriating to be treated this way, if you see your persistence in your view as well founded, indeed as an example of the "reality principle" at work.

But the mere adoption of the psychologizing posture doesn't close off the possibility that there is no misrepresentation, that the view we're about to psychologize is correct. We can keep an open mind on the merits, see what we get when we psychologize, and go back to debate on the merits the next time a judge or a legal theorist produces an account of a decision, or of adjudication in general, that claims to have excluded the ideological. That's where I am now: I don't claim to have shown that it is impossible to exclude the ideological or to have shown that it is always present. But I don't believe the accounts that say either that it always can be or that it is absent. So, for the time being, it seems worthwhile to psychologize.

And, of course, it's easy enough to psychologize in the opposite direction. Radicals have commitments to the presence of ideology in adjudication that it would be hard to give up. From my point of view, the insistence that law is always and everywhere ideological, "socially constructed through and through," and so on, involves as much denial (of the mechanical) as the opposite position. I see myself here as the representative of the reality principle, in the form of my own theory, which is as hostile to global critiques of objectivity in law, whether from the old Marxist or the postmodern angle, as it is to the claim that judges can always be and are in fact usually neutral.

Is denial unconscious?

When you say "I'm not mad," or "my ideology had nothing to do with it," and others think you're denying, rather than being polite, lying, or making a random mistake, it's hard to decide what to call your relationship to the true fact, your true intention, your true emotion.

When we are mistaken about the facts, in a random, unmotivated way, we say that we are "not conscious" of the true facts. In lying, we are "conscious" of the facts. In repression as it figures in Anna Freud, the repressed impulses are really and truly "gone": "But the ego of the child who has solved her conflicts by means of repression, with all its pathological sequels, is at peace."[8] Denial is a much less drastic mode of defense, which takes a less massive investment of energy, and, like the other non-repressive defense mechanisms has "to be brought into operation again whenever there is an accession of instinctual energy."[9] The judge has to deny his ideological role every time someone asserts it, or evidence suggests it; he cannot get rid of it once and for all by a single act of repression.

But it seems odd to apply the adjective "unconscious" to denial as I've defined it. There is a problem in saying you're unconscious of a fact or of an inner state when you muster a lot of energy to "keep from knowing" it. When we say that we are dealing with motivated error or wishful thinking, we are saying that there is some part of the psyche that registers the possibility of the unpleasant truth and then mobilizes to keep from knowing it. The very thing we mean by denial in the psychological sense is that what is involved is more than the mere speech act, and we interpret this "more" as a strategy to deal with an anxiety-producing conflict. This presupposes that the "strategist" in the story knows more than the obtuse performer of the speech act of denial. As Sartre puts it:

> To be sure, the one who practices bad faith is hiding a displeasing truth or presenting as truth a pleasing untruth. Bad faith then has in appearance the structure of falsehood. Only what changes everything is the fact that in bad faith it is from myself that I am hiding the truth. Thus the duality of the deceiver and the deceived does not exist here. Bad faith on the contrary implies in essence the unity of a *single* consciousness.
>
> . . . It follows first that the one to whom the lie is told and the one who lies are one and the same person, which means that I must know in my capacity as deceiver the truth which is hidden from me in my capacity as the one deceived. Better yet I must know the truth very exactly *in order* to conceal it more carefully—and this not at two different moments,

which at a pinch would allow us to re-establish a semblance of duality—
but in the unitary structure of a single project. How then can the lie
subsist if the duality which conditions it is suppressed?

. . . We have here an *evanescent* phenomenon which exists only in and
through its own differentiation. To be sure, these phenomena are frequent
and we shall see that there is in fact an "evanescence" of bad faith, which,
it is evident, vacillates continually between good faith and cynicism:
Even though the existence of bad faith is very precarious, and though it
belongs to the kind of psychic structures which we might call *metastable*,
it presents nonetheless an autonomous and durable form. It can even be
the normal aspect of life for a very great number of people. A person can
live in bad faith, which does not mean that he does not have abrupt
awakenings to cynicism or to good faith, but which implies a constant
and particular style of life. Our embarrassment then appears extreme,
since we can neither reject nor comprehend bad faith.[10]

Sartre's purported way out of the dilemma doesn't seem to me to work.
But for our purposes it seems enough to say that the denier is half-conscious, or conscious and unconscious at the same time, or that the ego
wills its own unconsciousness of something that it must therefore in some
sense know.

Denial as a collective phenomenon

The idea that the legal actors in a given legal culture can engage in collective denial with respect to the true nature of legal institutions is one
with a long pedigree in legal history and sociology. The classic version of
the problem is that of explaining "legal fictions." Here, from Henry
Maine's *Ancient Law,* is a description of the phenomenon of denial in Roman law:

It may be affirmed then of early commonwealths that their citizens considered all the groups in which they claimed membership to be founded
on common lineage. What was obviously true of the Family was believed
to be true first of the House, next of the Tribe, lastly of the State. And
yet we find that along with this belief, or, if we may use the word, this
theory, each community preserved records or traditions which distinctly
showed that the fundamental assumption was false . . . Adverting to
Rome singly, we perceive that the primary group, the Family, was being
constantly adulterated by the practice of adoption, while stories seem to
have been always current respecting the exotic extraction of one of the
original Tribes and concerning a large addition to the houses made by

one of the early kings. The composition of the state, uniformly assumed to be natural, was nevertheless known to be in great measure artificial. This conflict between belief or theory and notorious fact is at first sight extremely perplexing; but what it really illustrates is the efficiency with which Legal Fictions do their work in the infancy of society. The earliest and most extensively employed of legal fictions was that which permitted family relations to be created artificially, and there is none to which I conceive mankind to be more deeply indebted.[11]

A psychological interpretation of denial has two quite distinct parts. The first is the decision to interpret the speech act as a misrepresentation that is not merely conventional, and neither a lie nor a random error. This is Maine's "conflict between belief or theory and notorious fact." The second is to choose a particular conflict or conflicts as the cause of the anxiety that denial gets rid of in the particular case. In the case of adjudication, it is one thing to decide that the denial of the ideological in judging is a misrepresentation of this kind, and quite a different thing to successfully interpret the denial as the product of specific conflicts. Maine, in the quotation above, makes no serious effort at explanation on this second level, appealing instead to the "efficiency" of fictions in the "infancy of society."

The conflicts that plausibly motivate denial in the theorists of Roman society or in judges and their public are not the highly particularized vicissitudes of the instincts that sometimes seem useful in explaining neurotic symptoms or even severe individual pathology. The modern pop psychology of defense mechanisms, however, isn't tied to individual life history in this way. To my mind, what made Anna Freud not merely a competent synthesizer of her father's work but an important innovator as well was, first, her sharp distinction between repression and less drastic defenses; second, the normalization of the defense mechanisms as factors in psychological life; and, third, her insistence on a long list of different kinds of conflict against which we defend.[12]

These three moves make possible our pop psychology of defenses, which has nothing particularly "Freudian" about it. In this version of ego psychology, as in that of Sartre and in cognitive dissonance theory, defense is no longer closely tied to sexuality in general or to the Oedipus complex in particular. Defenses are a technology of self-protection but at the same time the mechanisms through which the subject constructs a "truth." Their use in understanding individual or collective phenomena is perfectly consistent with poststructuralist epistemological and ontological skepticism about a reified unconscious or a "reality principle."[13]

If many judges are denying the role of ideology in their decision processes (and some of them are lying), it seems plausible to look for something common to their situation that produces a conflict, rather than a million idiosyncratic versions of the Oedipus complex.

Denial as a response to role conflict

It is commonly assumed that if judges deny the ideological in their decision processes, when in fact ideology is present, it is because they are violating a role constraint and don't want to admit it. This description fits the behavior of constrained activists, difference splitters, and bipolar judges into the common mold of weakness of will or cheating, things all of us deny all the time.

I don't mean, myself, to deny that judges sometimes experience constraint by the text and then decide against the constraint, violating their oath of fidelity to the legal materials. It is even possible (who knows?) that the main impact of ideology on judicial law making is through this kind of behavior. To the extent that is the case, the study of the impact on our political process of the practice of judicial law making is the study of how judicial deviance, norm violation, plays out in the moderation, empowerment, and legitimation effects I mentioned above.

But it seems obvious to me that there is more to the denial of ideology in adjudication than a cover-up of deviance. It seems obvious that the constrained activist, the difference splitter, and the bipolar judge are responding to a bind. It is true that many, many people condemn them out of hand, on the ground that they should "just say no" to ideology. In this view, the minute they are influenced in their decisions by their legislative preferences (their personal ideologies), they are out of line.

We should condemn them even though they accept the rule of law as a constraint, in the sense that where they find a particular rule interpretation can't be budged by argument, they declare it the law even though they think that as a legislative matter it is wrong. Even when there is open texture, they don't impose the rule interpretation they prefer as a legislative matter unless they can argue in good faith that it is the solution supported by the most plausible legal argument.

This is all very well, but in the conventional view it is not enough: they should categorically exclude their ideological preferences and "stick to the law," or "just interpret the law." The rule of law is not a constraint, in this view, but a source of guidance. The question is whether the judge accepted the guidance, no matter how difficult it may have been to figure out what it was, or, on the contrary, took guidance from something else.

The alternative view, historically associated with British positivism and radicalized in legal realism and cls, is that the judge faces not a conflict between his role and his illegitimate desires but a genuine "role conflict." There is a contradiction between the norms that are supposed to govern his behavior. In this view, the motive for denial is not guilt at deviance but the anxiety produced by the dilemma of not being able to do the right thing no matter how hard you try, because you are being told to do two opposite things at the same time. The denial of the ideological resolves the conflict by making it appear that the role definition is coherent rather than contradictory.

Again, I am not arguing that all judges decide ideologically, and I think it likely that some judges have nothing to deny. These judges don't experience the conflict that my three types experience. My much more limited claim is that it is plausible that constrained activists, difference splitters, and bipolar judges experience role conflict, which motivates denial, as well as or rather than a conflict between their will to ideological power and their roles.

To say they experience role conflict is to say that it would be problematic for them to exclude ideology because there is something in their understanding of the role of the judge that seems to push to include it. I think that in fact judges, and actors in a range of similar positions, do often experience a conflict of this kind—roughly between the overarching general goal or standard proposed to them and the particular rules that supposedly further the goal but sometimes seem to conflict with it. For judges, the goal is "justice under law," and the conflict is between that idea and the categorical exclusion of the "personal," in the sense of the ideological, from the decision process.

For these judges, I imagine, it doesn't seem possible to say that justice under law means no more than law application. First, they are very much aware that their task is to decide "questions of law," meaning questions of rule definition, and that these are questions of interpretation, rather than of application of rules to disputed facts. Second, they are very much aware that "the law" as it appears at the end of the decision process is a function of the work they do on the legal materials, and that different work strategies are likely to produce different law—that is, different legal rules—with no intralegal criteria available to indicate which work strategy is correct.

These judges, I imagine, feel that what they are supposed to do, what their role requires them to do, when the law appears to depend on what work strategy they pursue, is to consult their conception of justice, perhaps concretized as rights, values, or needs. But, I imagine, they also feel that they can't bring the idea of justice to bear on a dispute without allowing ideology to enter the decision process. They don't want it to enter and wish it couldn't; they may even believe that if only they could figure out how, they could exclude it. But as they experience it, the minute you start talking of justice, you have a contested concept, and the contest is the familiar one between liberal and conservative conceptions of just social order—that is, of just legal rules.

These judges are in a bind. Their sense of justice is inescapably an ideological one, in the sense that an outside observer would easily categorize the judge as either a liberal or a conservative on the basis of his or her answer to what justice required in the circumstances. The only alternative to ideological justice, once strategic behavior has become a possibility, seems to be random decision. Random decision violates the role definition of "justice under law" even more seriously, the judge might suppose, than pursuing justice in the shadow of ideology.

In the description I've just given, my goal was to suggest what in fact might motivate judges to deny the ideological in adjudication, rather than "just saying no" and getting rid of it. It may be an accurate description of what some judges experience, even if we conclude that there is in fact a nonideological method for deciding questions of law. If this method exists, judges ought to employ it, but they may be ignorant of it or unable to make it work in particular cases.

In my view, a judge who experiences role conflict is "right," because there really is a conflict built into her role, so that her only alternative to denial is to acknowledge that she can't do her job in the way she is supposed to. The conflict is "real," in my view, because there is no extant theory that plausibly explains how the judge can decide, once she is conscious of the possibility of strategic behavior in interpretation, in a way that excludes ideology, supposing that her sense of justice is congruent with an existing ideology.

Dworkin, for example, says two things to the judge: there are no criteria outside legal argument for determining the rightness of rule choices,[14] and the judge should deploy his own "political philosophy" (which may be liberalism or conservatism),[15] both in the analysis that searches for legal determinacy through fit, and in resolving gaps, conflicts, and ambiguities that persist in spite of that effort.[16] Although he uses the language of "right answers," Dworkin offers no comfort at all for those who propose to resolve the judge's role conflict by having him "just say no" to ideology.

In this light, the judges' denial of the ideological has the very specific content that Sartre identified with bad faith, because the misrepresentation is of oneself as a machine, as interpreting mechanically rather than strategically. Bad faith in this sense exploits the truth (according to Sartre) that human subjectivity is at the same time factoid, just a thing in the world, and transcendent, in motion past its apparent fixity, free. Here, the judge misrepresents himself as factoid, or mechanical, seeming to himself to comply with the role requirement that he be that through and through, in spite of his experience of constraint by the text as a sometime thing, always unpredictably subject to dissolution by legal work.

Motives for the public to deny ideology in judging

So far, we have denial as a way to escape role conflict. But why doesn't the judge respond by saying, "my role has an internal conflict, so it needs to be redesigned"? Why don't academic critics help the judge off the hook by suggesting that we are forcing her into hypocrisy? One way to extend the analysis is to ask what reasons there are for people outside the role to deny the ideological in judging, to act as codependents in the judge's denial. The answer can't be role conflict for these outsiders, since they aren't playing the role.[17] But they can nonetheless have investments in the nonconflictual character of the role, in the possibility of playing it without ideology having a place in the decision process.

Two types of investment in the notion of judging without ideology suggest themselves: *(a)* people may want to believe in it because not believing in it would induce anxieties based on the centrality of judges in the political system, and *(b)* people may want to believe in it because belief fulfills, at a distance, at a social remove, a pleasurable fantasy about the possibilities of being in the world.

Fear of the consequences

There is an apologetic motive for believing in the rule of law as a guide rather than a restraint. If one believes that it is possible to exclude ideology, then even if one is invested in the idea that our system is "basically" a good one (albeit in need of reform), that is, if one is either a liberal or a conservative, it is easy to deal with the idea that judges often allow ideology in rather than just saying no to it. This insight simply requires us to reform the judiciary, to get judges to obey role constraints that "everyone" agrees are valid. Denouncing the tyranny of the judiciary can be a staple of both liberal and conservative politics without threatening "the system" in any way.

But if the critique is correct, this is shadow play, however satisfying as such, because there is no coherent account of how judges whose sense of justice is ideologized can do what their role, defined as keeping ideology out, requires them to do. And since it is hard to imagine how we could exclude people who have this kind of "fallen" sense of justice from the judiciary (especially if we have "fallen" ourselves), "the system" seems flawed in a quite basic way, rather than just subject to the inevitable corruption of judicial deviance.

In short, the viral critique arouses anxiety in part because it is delegitimating. It undermines the broad Liberal consensus not just about how society should be but about how it pretty much, with warts, is organized, namely, in accord with the principles of individual rights, majority rule, and the rule of law. It suggests that, appearances to the contrary notwithstanding, it isn't organized that way in fact, and won't be even after reform of the judiciary. It couldn't be, given the empirical reality of strategic behavior in interpretation and the difficulty of imagining how it could be eliminated.

A second motive, a second kind of investment in the notion of the rule of law as a guide rather than a mere constraint, derives from liberal and conservative commitments to diverse, particular, judge-made legal rules. The liberal stake in the nonideological character of adjudication might be summed up by the question, "Don't you think Brown v. Board of Education was legally as well as ideologically correct?" Liberals and conservatives have many commitments of this kind to the specifically legal correctness of their favorite important judicial decisions. The news that Brown was just a manifestation of liberal ideology, in the sense that it was no more legally, as opposed to morally, correct than Plessy v. Ferguson, is bad news for liberals, and the motive for denying it is obvious.

Yet another reason to deny viral critique is the fear that if it were valid, and if judges fully understood it, they would tyrannize us worse than they do already. This is the notion that belief in the rule of law as a guide, rather than as a mere constraint, is a beneficent illusion, a myth with good social consequences. I think Scott Altman, in his article preaching this fear, is wrong to think that even the judge who fervently believes the myth can unselfconsciously "follow the law," for the reasons already stated. But I don't think the critique can deny that greater judicial sophistication *might* (*a*) increase strategic behavior at the expense of ideologically random behavior, and (*b*) induce some judges to "cheat," by which I mean disregard experienced constraint by the text.[18]

I'm not going to pile speculation on speculation by trying to assess to what extent these imagined dangers of the demystification of judging are realistic. My intuition is that people who want to believe in rights and the rule of law, and liberals who want to believe in the justice of desegregation, will go on believing even if they accept the critique of judging, and that greater sophistication on the part of judges would probably have little effect on the content of judge-made law. But who knows? I assert only that fear of the consequences motivates denial of viral critique.

Overcoming contradiction

From my specific ideological position, that of left-wing modernism/postmodernism, there is a much more cosmic motive for denial, namely, the contradictory character of our impulses and ideas. This notion of the "fundamentality" of the experience of contradiction is one of the defining traits of modernism and its sequelae, something like a premise, as is the longing for coherence as an autonomous force in human life. People want coherence for its own sake, at least some of the time, because it is a pleasure, it is release from a kind of terror. Rather than arguing this position, I'll let it be represented by these two quotations, the first from the first chapter of Sigmund Freud's *General Introduction to Psychoanalysis,* and the second from Anna Freud's *The Ego and the Mechanisms of Defense:*

> It is important to begin in good time to reckon with the fact that mental life is the arena and battle-ground for mutually opposing purposes or, to put it non-dynamically, that it consists of contradictions and pairs of contraries. Proof of the existence of a particular purpose is no argument against the existence of an opposite one: there is room for both. It is only a question of the attitude of these contraries to each other, of what effects are produced by the one and by the other.[19]

> To these three powerful motives for the defense against instinct (superego anxiety, objective anxiety, anxiety due to the strength of the instincts) must be added those which in later life spring from the ego's need for synthesis. The adult ego requires some sort of harmony between

its impulses, and so there arises a series of conflicts of which Alexander has given a full account. They are conflicts between opposite tendencies, such as homosexuality and heterosexuality, passivity and activity, etc.[20]

This idea is familiar at the level of the coherence of desires or impulses: it is unpleasant to want or to want to be two contradictory things at the same time. The intellectual version of this is that it is unpleasant to acknowledge that one believes, or holds to, two contradictory ideals at the same time, and that in particular cases what one does is choose in a non-rational way between them.

We might interpret the social construction of the figure of the Judge as the place where we most clearly develop the collective fantasy of overcoming the endless sense of internal doubleness or contradiction that Sartre presents in the paradoxical language of "being what one is not" and "not being what one is." In "justice under law," justice is transcendence, and so ungraspable, while law is facticity, the dead weight of the past, the compulsion of the text. Most Americans, I suppose, want the Judge to be like Sartre's version of the French café waiter, a person who does his job with a vengeance, rendering himself thinglike or factoid, a mere transmission belt for legal necessity. At the same time, they want to believe that law is justice, the product of the Judge's laser intuition, with no contradiction between the two elements.

At least some real judges, we imagine, want this too, but they have a problem, to which bad faith (theirs and their public's) is the response. They "know" that the facticity of law dissolves (sometimes) to the touch of legal work, *and* that their own sense of justice is less transcendent, less free, less their own, and more factoid, more mechanically ideological, than it "ought" to be. The bad faith consists in simultaneously exaggerating the extent to which they are bound (factoid, thinglike) as law appliers and understating the extent to which they are mere ideologues when they are supposed to be exercising their (transcendent) "independent" judgment. In other words, the denial of the ideological, along with addiction to the drama of inquisition and condemnation for infidelity to law, can be seen as a response to the demand that role incumbents in general "be" their roles, and that judges in particular "be" their roles with a vengeance.[21]

While it seems to me that the judge's role conflict is an instantiation of, or one of the constitutive manifestations of, this particular existential complexity, there is no reason to reduce it to this complexity alone. For example, it may also be useful to see judges as denying, on behalf of their public, the problem that we have no coherent conception of justice, just an aspiration toward something we can't pin down, and that our practice of justice is endlessly contradictory. This is another way of saying that the whole point of the role of the judge is to affirm the possibility of escape from the ideological situation.

Liberals and conservatives share general principles, and find themselves equally contradictory in practice, though in service of different outcomes. The principles are brought to bear on the choice of legal rules through the medium of contradictory argument pairs, deployed by liberals and conservatives in opposite ways over the range of policy domains, with no explanation either of how they pick domains or of how they secure their boundaries against radicalisms of the left and right. The judge, in his own and his public's hopeful fantasy, is like the ideologist in being a votary of justice, but should be unlike her in having an answer that is limited in scope to justice between the parties. And also unlike her, more successful, because outside the "fundamental" situation of contradiction. Denial and bad faith are perhaps (who knows?) the response to the disappointment of this expectation.

Coercive consensus sustains denial

To generate an explanation of denial rooted in role conflict with attendant anxiety, we can add the element of coercive consensus, as a stabilizer of the system. In other words, if most participants are engaged in denial in our psychological sense, then they will have a motive to sanction anyone who brings the bad news that it is merely denial, rather than reality, that adjudication does or could exclude ideology. The motive is to avoid the anxiety that will follow undoing of the defense. (This is a social equivalent of the patient's "resistance" to the undoing of a defense mechanism by a therapist.)

And if people sanction those who try to penetrate the denial, people will be hesitant to try and will lie, or adopt denial themselves, as an alternative to anxiety generated by the conflict between their desire to tell the truth as they see it and the fear of the displeasure that truth telling will bring down on them.

Projection of ideology as a stabilizer of the system of denial

In the pop psychology of defenses, it has become a familiar idea that we sometimes project onto others the impulses or behaviors that we deny in ourselves. Trial judges who fear the anger of losing litigants, and appellate judges who fear the anger of those who disagree with the rules they make, have a motive to displace responsibility onto others, the legislature or prior judges.[22] To the extent they feel guilty about their ideological contributions to law making, they have a motive for the quite distinct operation of projecting ideological intentions onto others.

As I've been arguing, judges find themselves willy-nilly participants in the general cultural conception of judging as a situation of moral jeopardy in which the chief danger is the introduction of ideology into the decision process. It is not, I am supposing, psychologically tenable for judges and their public to respond that there is role conflict here, rather than a moral drama of corruption. They can't acknowledge that the rule of law is only a constraint, and not a guide, and that some of the time, at some very important times, it is a weak constraint, one that doesn't let them off the hook represented by their ideologized, "fallen" conceptions of justice.

In this situation, the stability of the system of denial may get an important support from the projection of symmetrical ideological motives onto one another by ideological opponents, followed by denunciation of those opponents for corruption. This "projective identification" involves a self-reinforcing relationship with the person onto whom one has projected a desire or a characteristic, rather than a mere externalization.[23] The notion seems to me helpful in interpreting the odd persistence in American legal culture of obsessive concern with and equally obsessive denial of the ideological, what I called American critical legalism.

How could one "prove" a proposition like that of the last paragraph? One couldn't. But consider the following letter to the editor of the *Boston Globe* by a liberal participant in the intensely politicized battle over the confirmation of a conservative Harvard Law School professor, Charles Fried, to the Supreme Judicial Court of Massachusetts. Because the letter quotes Fried, as well as denouncing him, it allows a glimpse of the symmetrical character of the projections, and it even contains a denunciation of the very impulse to analyze judges ideologically that it itself perfectly exemplifies.

> Fried has had a distinguished academic career, but I do not believe he is an appropriate choice. He would bring an ideological predisposition and potential divisiveness to a court that has been free of both.
>
> Fried was a committed servant of the so-called "Reagan Revolution," an agenda that had as one of its main goals the dismantling of the legal rights and remedies developed under Republican and Democratic administrations for violations of Title VII of the Civil Rights Act of 1964.

The goal was almost accomplished when Solicitor General Fried helped persuade the Supreme Court to abandon decades of precedent and gut the Civil Rights Act in a series of decisions in 1988 and 1989. The decisions were viewed as so destructive that Congress took the unusual step of overriding them by adopting the Civil Rights Act of 1991, restoring the law to the status it had before Reagan's Justice Department and Fried were so successful in subverting it.

Fried writes in his memoir:

"In many respects the courts themselves had become major bureaucratic actors, enthusiastically, self-consciously enlisting in the movement to substitute the judgments and values of the nonproductive sector of society—lawyers, judges, bureaucrats, politicians—for the self-determination of the entrepreneurs and workers who create wealth. Egged on by aggressive litigators, the legal professoriate, and the liberal press, the courts had become a principal engine for redistributing wealth and shackling the energies of the productive sector."

This jaundiced attitude toward courts and judges should be carefully weighed. Do you want to place on the SJC someone who subscribes to the extremist view that the courts are engaged in a plot to sabotage capitalism and redistribute wealth? Do we want someone who asserts that judges are part of the "nonproductive sector of society" to sit in judgment of other judges? Fried's nomination should be rejected.

Mark S. Brodin
Professor of Law
Boston College Law School[24]

I find it useful, in understanding the way Brodin and Fried manage to do ideological analysis of the "other" while affirming the possibility of neutrality in general and their own neutrality in particular, to refer to Freud's classic analysis of neurotic (as opposed to "normal" and "psychotic") jealousy. Indeed, I think we critics should proudly affirm the analogy between our analysis of the ideological in adjudication and the Freudian tradition of hunting out sexual motives where people are most concerned to conceal them. Here, as elsewhere, the analysis has to be of the chastened variety that eschews pretensions to having found "the" truth of the phenomenon. It is still fun to read Freud on jealousy, substituting "neutrality" for faithfulness, "ideological motivation" for unfaithfulness, and "judging" for marriage.

The jealousy of the second layer, the projected, is derived in both men and women either from their own actual unfaithfulness in real life or from impulses towards it which have succumbed to repression. It is a matter of everyday experience that fidelity, especially that degree of it required in marriage, is only maintained in the face of continual temptation. Anyone who denies this himself will nevertheless be impelled so strongly in the direction of infidelity that he will be glad enough to make use of an unconscious mechanism as an alleviation. This relief—more, absolution by his conscience—he achieves when he projects his own impulses to infidelity on to the partner to whom he owes faith. This weighty motive can then make use of the material at hand (perception-material) by which the unconscious impulses of the partner are likewise betrayed, and the person can justify himself with the reflection that the other is probably not much better than he is himself.[25]

Conclusion

Some judges some of the time pursue ideological strategies vis-à-vis the materials rather than just accepting direction from them. The strategies they choose have an impact on what law gets made in a given case. On the one hand, this impact is not constrained by an electoral process, the way it is when legislators bargain over the wording of legislation. In this sense judges are freer than legislators.

On the other hand, the law constrains them in a way it doesn't constrain legislators because they accept a duty of fidelity to the materials that rules a lot of things out, even if it doesn't determine the choice between liberal and conservative rule interpretations in many cases. In this sense they are less free than legislators.

There is a discursive convention denying that judicial law makers are engaged in an ideological practice. Most members of the intelligentsias (including the judges themselves) believe that there is some truth to the convention, that is, they deny the ideological in adjudication. They consistently exaggerate the difference between what judges do when they decide appellate questions of law in adjudication and what legislatures do when they decide them by deliberating and then voting on statutes.

I am going to argue in the next part that the combination of the law-making power of judges with the bad faith (mis)understanding of adjudication has consequences for ideologized group conflict.

PART FOUR

Consequences of Adjudication

9

The Moderation and Empowerment Effects

Counterfactual legislative supremacy

*I*n most discussions of the rule of law, the implicit question is what would happen if judges were "at large"? The quite different heuristic device employed here is to imagine a different system of governance than the one we now have, one that would eliminate a crucial aspect of adjudication as we currently understand it, and then speculate at length about what consequences would follow for the political system. This method has the advantage of keeping the question of consequences relatively defined while not suppressing the utterly conjectural character of the discussion.

What would happen if, in every case where appellate judges at the highest level decided a question of law, there was an appeal to the legislature, with a strong practice of the legislature considering and deciding the question? There would be no written opinions in the legislature, but there would be debate and legislative history. The legislature might use more or less elaborate fact finding, just as it normally does. "Parties" could submit whatever briefs they wanted to; there would be no rules limiting "standing," once the question was in the legislature.

Imagine the abolition of final judicial review, in the sense that a final adjudication of unconstitutionality of a statute could be appealed like any other question of law to the legislature. Finally, imagine a general understanding that the legislature should approach questions from the courts under decisional norms indistinguishable from those it observes in "ordinary" legislation, including a norm of obedience to the state and federal constitutions.

My claim is that the combination of our current practice of adjudication with current understandings of that practice produces political results that are different from those that would likely occur if we had this different practice and different understanding. It would be a big change. But how big? Your answer will depend on just what you think judges now do, and on how you think people in various publics understand what judges do. It is necessary to distinguish between these two questions because there is so little consensus about the reality of the practice of adjudication. People have widely varying views of the practice, and these affect both their participation in it and their participation in legislation. Since it seems obvious that the views contradict one another, in the sense that they can't all be right, some substantial group seems probably to be misled.

In my hypothetical scenario, by contrast, there is a shared understanding of what is going on (though of course wide disagreement about what should be done in particular cases and perhaps about the new system itself). The question I want to pose is that of the impact on the political system of doing law making through an adjudicative process subject to our particular multiplicity of understandings, including the widespread denial of ideology in adjudication, rather than through a (relatively) transparent legislative process.

Three hypothetical effects of our particular, and particularly misunderstood system of law making through adjudication, contrasted with my counterfactual process, seem worth exploring. The first is the reduction of the power of ideologically organized legislative majorities, and ideologically oriented high-court judges, whether liberal or conservative, to bring about significant change in any subject-matter area heavily governed by law. The second is the empowerment of the legal fractions of intelligentsias to decide the legal outcome of ideological conflict among themselves, with less control by the electoral process than would likely be the case under a regime of legislative decision of appellate questions of law.

The third, which I take up in the next chapter, is a legitimation effect, an increase in the appearance of naturalness, necessity, and relative justice of the status quo, whatever it may be, over what would prevail under legislative revision. All three effects presuppose that our society has a particular main ideological division, liberalism versus conservatism. The moderation and empowerment effects have to do with the fates of liberalism and conservatism under our own versus a different system. The legitimation effect has to do with the question of how other ideologies, for example radical leftism and radical rightism, are affected by the peculiar phenomenon of practically or constitutionally final judicial law making through adjudication.

We can distinguish consequences for common law, statutory interpretation, and judicial review. In the first two categories, the legislature already has the (prospective) power to revise judicial answers to questions of law whenever it wants to. But the current system makes review likely in only a tiny fraction of cases, whereas the alternative makes it available as a matter of course (not as a matter of "right," since such a description would suggest, in our legal culture, the possibility of judicial review of a legislative decision not to review).

There is no reason to think there would be an appeal in every case, any more than there is an appeal every time a trial court decides a question of law. Most judicial rule-following would still fall into the "unselfconscious" category, with the judge and the parties doing business as usual. When the judge was in the position of constraint by the text, feeling that the rule was wrong but unable to come up with a plausible legal argument for her preferred interpretation, the losing party might or might not think it worthwhile to try the legislature.

It would make no sense to appeal where the rule in question was the object of broad consensus, and little sense where the same or a similar issue had just been decided or where a legislative victory would be likely to apply only prospectively. But in cases of ideologized group conflict, there would be political energy and resources available, as well as some prospect of success, and the situation would be very different from what it is now.

The moderation effect

Robert Reich recently wrote,

> There is high drama in the creation of landmark legislation, like the recently enacted Clean Air amendments of 1990. Within such epic struggles, the great issues of a mixed economy get debated. Do we want faster economic growth or a safer and cleaner environment? What are the proper domains of public and private responsibility? . . . At last, in a final teeth-clenching, death-defying act of courage or cowardice (depending on your point of view), the die is cast. The drama is over.
>
> More likely, however, the real drama hasn't even begun, or else it was under way years before the legislators ever got into the act. The practical, day-to-day struggle over government regulation is waged continuously by government bureaucrats and federal judges, as they interpret and reinterpret statutes—some newly enacted, others enacted decades before. The bureaucrats and the judges fill in the legislative blanks, giving mean-

ing to vague statutory language, updating obsolete legislation, applying the law to circumstances that legislators never dreamed of, determining detailed rights and duties that were never specified in the legislation . . .[I]t is here that the real contours of the public and private sectors of the economy are mapped . . .

. . . [Environmental Protection Agency] bureaucrats will claim that they are only implementing the statute; federal judges will say that they are only ensuring that the EPA's implementation is in accord with Congress's intent. But these modest protestations are for the cameras. The bureaucrats and judges, motivated by their own preconceptions of the public interest, as modified by the relentless arguments of parties that can best afford lobbyists and litigators at these lower levels of government, will be making new law . . . [I]n answering these questions, EPA bureaucrats and federal judges will create a complex system with profound implications for American industry and the environment.[1]

One effect of the choice of law making through adjudication, rather than through legislative revision, on the outcomes of ideologized group conflict may be a more "moderate" course, through time, for the whole system of governance. If all the questions of law that affect ideologized group conflict were constantly open to decision or redecision through the legislative process, we would expect the ideologies of the legislators (and of their constituents, to the limited extent the political process functions to reflect voter ideology) to work themselves out as they do on other issues. If there was a clear liberal majority on a given issue, there might be clear liberal outcomes over a whole area of controverted policy.

Our system prevents anything like this from happening because (a) the legislature actually decides only a tiny fraction of ideologized issues, and (b) the judges who do decide them operate under the peculiar system of a duty of interpretive fidelity combined with (denied or misunderstood) freedom to shape the materials. How this might produce moderation is easiest to understand in a case of statutory interpretation like that described by Reich above.

Moderation of legislative regime change

We need to distinguish between law making that is supposed to have far reaching consequences, to *change things significantly,* and law making that is understood by all as elaboration of an existing regime. Both courts and legislatures do both kinds of law making. Courts do regime-altering law making in constitutional law, in statutory interpretation, and in common law, denying it vigorously in all three areas. But they also do vast amounts of mere regime elaboration in all three areas.

Two important aspects of law making in our system are that legislative regime change can't occur without judicial elaboration of the proposed change, and that regime change requires change in all the different interlocking types of law. The system of legal rules is so big, so dense, and so full of gaps, conflicts, and ambiguities, open to conflicting ideological interpretations, that a legislative regime change requires hundreds and hundreds of implementing decisions in many different areas of law.

According to the nesting hypothesis, these decisions replicate the underlying conflict of which the abstract regime change was a resolution. Nesting means that in the elaboration of a legal rule through time, the gaps, conflicts, and ambiguities that emerge with application to new fact situations re-present the ideological conflict the initial formula purported to resolve.[2]

Sometimes the process of resolving gaps, conflicts, and ambiguities can be seen as "merely" routine elaboration of the regime, affecting its "tilt" in a more liberal or more conservative direction but not affecting our understanding of what it "is," what its general purposes and effects were and continue to be. But "God is in the details," which means that we are also familiar with situations in which the implementing decisions end up nullifying the overall purpose. Sometimes the detail work can even turn the scheme into something that in practice has purposes and effects that are the opposite of those intended. Or the initial scheme can be a complicated compromise in which two ideologized group interests are represented, thereby making a legislative majority possible, but the implementation can gradually freeze one interest out.

These possibilities mean that the formal structure of the interpretive process is misleading. We start with a legal rule. It looks as though the gaps, conflicts, and ambiguities are "within" the rule. This makes it seem as though the decision to make the rule is obviously more important than the decisions about how to interpret it. It makes it look as though the interpreter is *implementing* the policy or policies behind the rule. But in fact the implementing resolution of the gap, conflict, or ambiguity may nullify or reverse the policy or policies.

Constrained activist, difference-splitting, and bipolar judges are the crucial actors in this process. To put it crudely, the constrained activist judge might be either ideologically favorable or unfavorable to the regime change. If she favors it, she will do something more than "implement" it; she will work to develop and entrench it, choosing among the possible interpretations those that lead to a real shift in the balance of ideologized group conflict.

If the constrained activist is on the losing ideological side, she will do just the opposite, working to give the statute a minimal meaning, to fit it into the great mass of rules in a way that will deprive it of ideological bite. The difference splitter will position himself between these poles, looking for "moderate" interpretations that can't be tarred with the brush of partisanship. The bipolar judge will flip back and forth between vigorously extending the statute and equally vigorously cutting it back, maintaining balance, but only over the long run.

All of this is happening in the context of constraint. But constraint just means that sometimes each of these judges ends up choosing a rule interpretation that he or she would not vote for as a legislator. Because of constraint, it may well be possible for the legislator to make a regime change and implement it through the judiciary in a way that really does shift the ideological balance. But there is nothing that guarantees that this will happen.

The moderation hypothesis is based on a simple model: suppose that the judges are divided up in a way that roughly reflects the ideological divisions within the intelligentsia or political class, and that the legislature also reflects the same division. It follows that a majority of the judges favor the regime-changing statute and understand it as an ideological victory. But some of them oppose it, and some don't feel strongly one way or another. These underlying *legislative* preferences of the judges will be modified by the role constraint that forbids them to be ideological and drives them into the three postures I've described. In this situation, only the constrained activist judge who likes the statute will do what the majority that enacted it would have done under a system of legislative revision.

The other judges will all, in some measure, work against the more extreme possible meanings of the enactment, even though many of them, as a matter of their "personal" legislative preference, would support those meanings. The constrained activist on the losing side will be systematic about it, doing as much "damage" (from the majority point of view) as is consistent with her sense of constraint by the materials.

But the difference splitter will also systematically moderate the regime change, choosing solutions that are plausibly nonideological because they lie between the "extremes," even when he would have voted, as a legislator, with the activist majority. The bipolar judge will sometimes do just what the ideological majority would have done, and what he himself would have done as a legislator, but sometimes the opposite, behaving like the anti-statute constrained activist in spite of his legislative preference.

The role of constraint in all of this is complicated. At one level, there will almost certainly be a range of possibilities that no judge would see as consistent with interpretive fidelity. But after excluding these, the different judges may have different reactions to particular cases. Conservative judges who favor the regime change will feel constrained, after working hard to extend the statute, to the extension their legal work has produced. Liberal opponents who work equally hard to find narrowing interpretations will feel equally constrained in the other direction.

The result is controversy, with each side claiming in good faith (but more cosmically in bad faith) that the statute "requires" their particular interpretation. The debate about interpretation that would have occurred in an overtly ideologized language under a regime of legislative revision occurs here inside a legal discourse that is also ideologized, but covertly so. This is what Reich means when he says that the protestations about Congress's intent are "for the cameras," and that "judges, motivated by their own preconceptions of the public interest . . . will be making new law."

Five complexities

First, constraint *might* come into play in the opposite way from that just described. A conservative judge might feel more constrained to adopt an "activist," but also self-defeating, interpretation of a liberal regime-changing statute than a liberal. She might see the statute as irrational to start with but think its democratically elected authors entitled to make their own mistakes. The liberal might feel more free to give an apparently conservative, limiting interpretation that would save the liberal statute's effectiveness, by compromising it in a way that would have surprised the enacting majority.

Second, neither side in the judicial implementation process can afford to drop the rhetoric of necessity unless the other side drops it as well. This is the consequence of the (mis)understanding of the judicial role, maintained by judicial and popular knowing and denying, in bad faith, of the shaping power of interpretation. As long as it is judges who are doing the implementing work, each side has available the rhetorical resource of the "rule of law," and each side must use it or lose.

Third, the need to maintain a rhetoric of judicial necessity "for the cameras" masks the similarity between the judicial battle and the legis-lative battle that preceded it. The practical effect of this is to empower the opponents of the regime change in a way that would not occur under legislative revision. In that process, they would appear as "the losers" trying to snatch victory from the details, rather than as ideological neutrals trying to puzzle out someone else's intention.

Fourth, the moderating effect is not a "distortion of the popular will," or of democracy, for three reasons. (1) Under the rule of law as I've defined it, judges who experience interpretive fidelity as compelling a particular result, against their legislative preference, go with the law and against the preference. They must experience their moderating interpretations of the regime change as *permitted* by the legal materials, or they don't adopt them. Given the directed nature of the work process, they will often or perhaps even usually experience them as required.

The moderation effect relies on a notion of constraint but not on any particular or general theory of the "true," "correct," or "neutral" interpre-tation of a particular statute or of statutes in general. The moderation is in contrast with what would happen if the legislative majority could im-plement its own regime change, rather than having to rely on a judiciary that is both internally ideologically divided and motivated by role anxiety not to appear ideological.

(2) It would be wrong to understand the legislative process as producing meanings in isolation from the judicial process that implements those meanings. Sophisticated legislators understand the moderation effect and draft legislation with it in mind. For example, sometimes they draft what *looks like* a regime change, with no expectation that it will be implemented. Sometimes they exaggerate the degree of change in order to overbalance the moderating effect and end up just where they want. The point is not that there has been a distortion but that the medium through which the legislature works has a particular molasses quality, which it might not have under a different system.

(3) The alternative regime of legislative revision would have its own distorting effect on the popular will. There would have to be a large in-crease in the legislature's capacity to consider and enact statutes. However this was organized, it would almost certainly change the balance of polit-ical and bureaucratic power within the system as a whole, creating exten-sive new opportunities for strategic behavior by litigants. And anyway, why treat the existing balance of legislative power as legitimate, given all its familiar distortions and corruptions?[3]

Final point. My assumption at the beginning was that the ideological distribution of judges mirrors that of legislators, which mirrors that of the electorate. As a transition to the discussion of the empowerment effect, it is time to relax this assumption. The judiciary may include ideological perspectives absent from the legislature. Judges pursue these agendas at cross-purposes to the main ideological division of the electorate.

Just as important, difference splitting and bipolar judges construct their nonideological ideological strategies on the basis of *their own* estimates of what the relevant ideological positions are. In other words, if the difference splitter sees the basic conflict as between feminists and diehard gender traditionalists, those are the interests he compromises, even though the diehards in the legislature may be opposed only by gender moderates, with no feminist representation at all.

Both the presence of judges with legislatively excluded agendas, and the tendency of difference splitters and bipolar judges to incorporate unrepresented agendas into their compromises, further dilute the ability of a legislative majority to just carry out a regime change. Indeed, the lawmaking power of judges may work something like the alleged paralyzing effect of proportional representation in a parliamentary regime. The difference is that it is proportional representation not of the electorate but of the ideologized group interests that the legal intelligentsia thinks are important.

Judicial regime change through common and constitutional law

Judicial regime elaboration in common and constitutional law is elaboration of the judges' own regime. The convention of necessity and the denial of ideology mean that judges can't overtly initiate regime changes if they are understood as ideological. Of course they can do regime change if they are willing to disguise it, and they can do regime changes that they themselves perceive as nonideological. Under the empowerment effect, I will consider how these judicial initiatives compare with those that would occur under a regime of legislative revision. Here the point is that however they originate, judges have to implement them.

In other words, majorities of high courts that, under our system, can carry out far-reaching regime change (for example, prohibition of social legislation, desegregation) have to implement their programs through other judges. These other judges will be ideologically divided, and they will work at the gaps, conflicts, and ambiguities of higher-court decisions with the same possibilities that exist for statutory change. The issues will present themselves in the same nested pattern, with the ideological choices supposedly settled at the high-court level re-presented in subsumed decisions that have the potential of undoing the original scheme.

Fractions of the intelligentsia steadily develop programs for transformation of areas of life that are governed by the common law, such as, say, spouse abuse or sexual harassment in the workplace. In the early stages, it is difficult or impossible for them to muster legislative majorities or even interest for their program. The judges may "adjust" earlier, gradually absorbing the new ideas as they work at splitting the difference between what they see as the extant social visions.

Because judges have practically unreviewable law-making power in common law and constitutional adjudication, fractions of the intelligentsia can avoid the legislatures in bringing about policy change. As we will see in the next section, the system operates more flexibly than it would if adjudication were outside ideology in fact. But, at the same time, even judicially initiated ideological change takes place in a muffled, compromised way, rather than in the form of decisive action implemented across the whole relevant range and with all the relevant detail questions resolved in accord with a general plan.

The empowerment effect

The second hypothetical effect of (denied) law making through adjudication cuts in a different direction. In the moderation hypothesis, some judges' commitment to their own neutrality makes them "centrists" within whatever system of ideological oppositions they find themselves. In the empowerment hypothesis, liberal and conservative legal intelligentsias get to settle ideologized group conflicts, through a mystified adjudication process, with less concern for the electoral process than they would feel as legislators.

In statutory interpretation, for example, the moderation effect is quite plainly not the only thing that happens to statutes. Take the development of the law of no-strike clauses and compulsory arbitration after Textile Workers Union v. Lincoln Mills,[4] a major transformation of American labor law, or the development of causes of action under the Civil Rights Act after Jones v. Mayer,[5] or the development of the law of sexual harassment under Title VII.[6] The judicial elaboration of rule 10(b)5 under the Securities Act is another example.

Common law judicial initiatives of a similar type are the development of labor torts around the turn of the century, the reform of the law of business ethics through promissory estoppel and related doctrines, the development of the modern law of consumer protection, the Tort Revolution, the development of the modern law of land use restrictions oriented to protecting subdivision development, the transformation of child custody doctrine, and the abolition of the causes of action (criminal conversation, seduction, and so on) that once gave the marital relation a particular legal structure.

In constitutional law, the epic judicial initiatives have been the attempt to restrict social legislation under the Lochner Court and its successors, and the judicial abolition of de jure racial segregation. But there are lots and lots of less extreme cases, including the reapportionment, police misconduct, and obscenity cases of the Warren Court, the abortion decision, the neutralization of civil rights law during the 1970s and 1980s, and on and on indefinitely. The New Jersey Supreme Court's Mt. Laurel[7] doctrine is based on the clause in the New Jersey constitution to the effect that legislation shall be "in the common interest."

My goal here is to give a political interpretation of this kind of judicial law making through adjudication. The first question is how judicial as opposed to legislative control modifies the outcomes of ideologized group conflict. We need to make the general model a good deal more complicated to make sense of this.

Law as a land mass that can be colonized

Let's look at the mass of legal rules from the perspective of an ideological intelligentsia. Many of the rules are irrelevant to the kinds of group conflict the intelligentsia is interested in. But some of the rules are very important. If a group succeeds, through litigation or legislation, in getting these rules to favor its interest, it moves on to other legal or nonlegal concerns. It has scored a victory and leaves it to the judges, constrained by the language of precedents or statutes, to administer the new regime. Perhaps over time the judges develop this body of law in the direction preferred by the ideological intelligentsia, or perhaps it goes the other way.

A large number of particular rule systems have a history as objects of ideological interest and controversy. Different subsystems, and different particular rules within subsystems, are understood to be favorable or unfavorable to particular interests. But the system as a whole has no single ideological imprint. There isn't even an ideological intelligentsia with a universal law reform plan. There may be a conservative and a liberal position on each issue, but these are uncoordinated, reflecting the activity of all the social subgroups within large constituencies and the divisions within the intelligentsia.

We might say by analogy that ideological intelligentsias, and fractions thereof, colonize the land mass of legal rules. Intelligentsias and fractions have interests in rules and in their development, as well as more abstract interests.

Fractions and constituencies

The liberal and conservative intelligentsias are not self-organized, well-defined groups. As we all know, there is a left-right spectrum, and a structure of coalitions within the liberal and conservative "camps." Moreover, there are well-known differences between the liberal intelligentsia and the mass of liberal voters (pointy-headed intellectuals versus white working-class types), and between conservative voters and elites.

This means that fractions of, say, the liberal intelligentsia passionately hold many positions about public policy that are not shared by other parts of that intelligentsia and may even be abhorrent to liberal "masses." There is a complex process of negotiation between fractions and between the intelligentsia and its constituency, as well as with the opposing intelligentsia and its constituency. Many things that particular fractions want are "just not politically feasible" in the existing legislative process.

A fraction may be able to achieve some of these things through the courts. The judiciary has representation from most of the range of ideological fractions, it being understood that left-wingers and those with styles too openly nontraditional need not apply. All it takes is a few constrained activists from any particular fraction to create a "doctrine." The difference splitters and the bipolar judges then go to work, under their peculiar forms of constraint, to incorporate and develop it.

Once embedded in the great mass of legal rules, the doctrine becomes part of the "property" of the fraction that pushed for it, subject of course to neutralization or reversal through future development. If we had a system of legislative revision, these properties would be in jeopardy all the time from legislative majorities. Under our system, the quasi-finality of judicial decision, along with the denial and misunderstanding of law making through adjudication, make them relatively immune, or "safe." The empowerment effect is the increase in power and sense of possible power that fractions of intelligentsias get, or think they get, through this differential.

The role of judges in creating popular will

This power goes beyond the ability to settle particular rules favorably to one side in an ideologized group conflict. The judge deploys the mana, the charisma, the concentrated authority that derives from our cultural understanding of the Judge. The first, or elementary, importance of this is that it allows the fraction to legitimate rules that favor it through something more than mere state force. The judges who set the rules in their favor also declare that these rules are *required* by "the statute" or "the law," or by "the Constitution." This may make it more likely that people will obey, accept, and eventually approve them.[8]

In so much as putting the charisma of the Judge behind the rule causes people's views on the merits to change, judges form public opinion. They are part of the political system not just as "appliers" of law made by someone else, but also as formers of the sentiments that express themselves in legislation. The most striking recent example of this is the judicial contribution to gradual formation of a legislative consensus in favor of desegregation. But John Marshall's contribution to the current consensus on judicial review itself, and on the nature of federalism, shouldn't be underestimated.

It is simplistic to denounce this process as "undemocratic." There is no "private" sphere in which the will of the people could form without contamination by all the various sources of authority in the society. The persuasive power of judges derives from what we might call the preliberal consciousness of people, their attachment to ideas like God, the King, Father, Doctor. There are numerous sources of authority of this kind. The media filter what authorities say and do, but also amplify and elaborate it, drawing on their own sources of authority. Judges couldn't *not* exercise this kind of mediated authority, unless they deliberately set out to delegitimate themselves. If they did, others would take up what was ceded. Empowerment is the ability of fractions of the ideological intelligentsia to influence, according to their agendas, both the outcomes of conflict and the formation of democratic majorities, by their privileged access to this particular combination of state power, authority, and media.

It is equally simplistic to sanitize this authority through the theory that judges "reflect" changing social ideas and customs. They do indeed reflect them, but in their diversity, and above all in their contradictions. The way the opposing views and habits of the population, their ideological divisions, are represented in the judiciary, and then developed and pursued by judges, affects the direction and speed of change of popular consciousness, the emergence of new consensus. What judges do forms as much as it reflects.

There is no popular will. There is a legislative process, and there is the rule of law. Each is a component of the Liberal theory of democracy. The structure that withdraws so much law making from the legislative process and lodges it in a misunderstood judicial process influences what people in general, and intelligentsias in particular, think about all kinds of policy issues. It is difficult or impossible to know what public opinion expressed through the legislative process would be if we did not entrust so much law-making power to judges, and it is naive to think whatever that was would be somehow purer.

Thus far, I have focused only on the way a shift toward legislative supremacy would threaten the current power of ideological fractions to colonize particular areas of law through sympathetic judges. The balance of power in question is "horizontal": elites and their constituencies fare differently in the judicial system than they would in the legislative. But the empowerment effect empowers only those with access to the judiciary. The next section explores the possibility that the privilege of the intelligentsia in gaining this kind of access helps to explain the phenomenon of denial.

Adjudication as a strategy of intelligentsia class power

Suppose that there is a lot of law making through adjudication, a lot of deeply felt controversy about what the right answers are, and a lot of denial of the extent to which there is leeway for strategic work to give the materials particular ideological meanings. Why doesn't the controversy, along with the endless process of critique of judicial neutrality, eventually undermine the denial?

Of course, one quick answer might be that there is a lot less leeway than I have been asserting, and that the controversy no more disproves the existence of right answers than controversy about "who killed Kennedy" disproves the existence of a killer. In short, the whole denial hypothesis was wrong in the first place. Another quick answer might be that contro-

versy and critique have already thoroughly undermined belief in the possibility of objectivity, and even of constrained interpretive fidelity in adjudication. What is left is no more than a convention, a fig leaf, a
performance "for the cameras."

I tried to respond to these views in the last chapter. Here I am going
to amplify the hypothesis that the intelligentsias of both ideological camps
have a common interest in mystified law making by adjudication. This
interest isn't the obvious one from the point of view of each fraction: the
ability to use the mana or charisma of the judge to enact and enforce their
particular policy preferences. Since the fractions have contradictory preferences, and all have access to the Judge, the accesses cancel one another
out. A common interest means an interest in opposition to a common
danger.

I don't think the intelligentsia has a common material interest, in opposition to the material interests of other social groups, that is strong
enough and dependent enough on access to judicial power to motivate
denial. Intelligentsia class privileges certainly depend on reverence for education, general belief in the power and validity of expertise, and respect
for "intelligence" in the abstract. But I don't think the knowledge classes
see their prosperity as depending particularly on special access to judges,
with accompanying mystic power, in anything like the way, for example,
that late-nineteenth-century big business did.

To make things even more complicated, there is an intelligentsia interest
in believing in law that has little to do with class conflict. Just about
everyone wants to believe in the success of their own ideological universalization project. If they get their interests universalized in law, they
experience them as validated in a way that is not true for legislation. One
of the verses of "We Shall Overcome" that civil rights marchers sang at
the moment of laying their bodies in the way of police violence was, "God
is on our side." Civil libertarians are quite similar:

> Despite these impressive gains, I always tried to remember that the
> strength and influence of the ACLU rests less on numbers than on prin-
> ciples. Thus . . . one is struck again and again by how often ACLU
> policies that seemed visionary or far out at the time they were adopted
> eventually became mainstream and were accepted by courts and legis-
> latures. This record, unmatched by any other organization, is the result
> of our fidelity to the values set forth in the Constitution and Bill of
> Rights. It is also the result of hard work by thousands of people.[9]

Nonetheless, it is at least possible to construct an interest-based theory of why intelligentsia fractions that disagree passionately about what the right answer is, and have long since learned to deploy the whole critical arsenal against any opinion they don't like, should persist in believing that law making through adjudication is different in kind from legislation. Once again, we can make the question concrete by contrasting our current regime with one of legislative revision, this time in the context of constitutional law.

Contrasting legislative revision with final judicial review of constitutional questions

Discussions of the rule of law in statutory interpretation and common law have far less charge than discussions of judicial review of the constitutionality of statutes. One reason for this is that the U.S. Supreme Court plays an important role in our practical politics. But constitutionalism, including final judicial review as a presupposed element, is also an important part of our national political culture.

I am speaking here about a kind of national mythology, rather than about what informed political theorists think. There is a widespread perception that it makes a big difference whether you have constitutionalism with judicial review or not, and that this big difference is one of the things that defines our political society. This is true even though the practice has been the subject of heated debate at several points in our history, with some of the most striking attacks only as old as Learned Hand's lectures on the Bill of Rights.[10]

Here is an alternative. When a statute is challenged, and the court strikes it down, the loser can appeal to the legislature. That body then decides whether its prior work was indeed defective. Constitutionalism, though not judicial review, is still the dominant political ideal, and voters are concerned, as they are now, with the issue. All legislators take an oath of office to uphold the Constitution. In the new order, all or the vast majority of legislators see it as the "governing document" to which all owe allegiance (until amendment).

But imagine that there is no longer a consensus that it is "law" in the Marshallian sense. The courts review statutes as always. But when the question is appealed to the legislature, its members, for the most part, see themselves as having the duty to decide what *they* think about validity, *without* a duty of interpretive fidelity to the whole corpus of relevant constitutional materials. They see themselves as required to form their own judgment as to the rightness or wrongness of prior judicial decisions.

A legislator with training in constitutional law might be quite clear that, if she were a Supreme Court judge under a duty of fidelity to the materials, she would declare the statute unconstitutional. But in the new regime, she might vote to uphold it. The feeling of closure, of determinacy, generated by the total corpus of legally relevant materials is specific to that corpus, which includes far more than the constitutional text. She might have a feeling of closure, of determinacy, with respect to her interpretation as a legislator every bit as strong as the feeling she would have in the opposite direction were she a judge. Fidelity to constitutional law would have required her to do something that fidelity to the Constitution in her legislative role requires her not to do.

Defects of majority rule

The following quotations illustrate what I think is the consensus, "for the cameras," about what would be at stake in a change to a regime like that just described:

> DEFECTS OF MAJORITY RULE. One obvious, oft-cited peril is the tyranny of the majority, which de Tocqueville characterized thus: "If it be admitted that a man possessing absolute power may misuse that power by wronging his adversaries, why should not a majority be liable to the same reproach?" Were majority rule to apply strictly and without constraint, deplorable results would become possible. Brown-eyed people could vote to enslave blue-eyed people; those whose names begin with A through N could vote to confiscate all the property of those whose names begin with O through Z. But in most democracies, the rule of the majority is constrained either by explicitly putting some issues out of bounds— through devices such as the Bill of Rights—or by requiring certain kinds of issues to be approved by more than a majority.[11]

Please note that behind eye color and alphabetization, the two issues are slavery and socialism, race and class. Moreover, the Bill of Rights is a "device." Here is the device idea carried to its logical extreme:

> Pigeons were given a small but immediate food reinforcement for pecking a certain key, and a larger but delayed reinforcement for not pecking. Most of the pigeons tested pecked the key in over 95% of the trials . . .

[So] the experimenters offered the impulsive pigeons the option of peck-ing a different colored key at an earlier time. Those pigeons that pecked the different colored key found, upon waddling into the test chamber, that the temptation of the small, immediate food reinforcement had been removed. They were thereby forced to wait for the larger, delayed re-ward—something that over 95% of them could not bring themselves to do when the temptation was immediately present. Significantly, 30% of those same pigeons learned to peck the earlier key when it operated to foreclose the later temptation. Even pigeons seem capable of learning to bind their own future freedom of action in order to reap the rewards of acting in ways that would elude them under the pressures of the mo-ment.[12]

These quotations are suggestions about the difference it would make if we had just the same constitution we have now, but with the legislature as the "final arbiter" of its meaning.

Judges doing final judicial review are not supposed to "enforce the Con-stitution" against the legislature quite in the way the quotations suggest. The role constraint on judges that is supposed to make their activity anal-ogous to a "device" is interpretive fidelity to the whole corpus of consti-tutional law, including past interpretations. The most we can hope for from final judicial review is that we can use judges to "bind our own freedom of action" according to their assessment of the meaning of the Founders' text plus earlier judicial decisions.

Moreover, the authors of these two quotations do not believe even for a minute in the naive rule-of-law theory. If the defects of majority rule are in every child's commonplace book, every newspaper reader is used to *news stories* (not editorials) that begin like this: "In the past month, the Supreme Court's conservative majority has made clear that it now has the intention and the votes to push criminal law sharply away from its liberal moorings of a generation ago."[13]

Whether judicial review seems preferable to legislative revision should depend on a complex calculus. You might believe that the pigeon idea is powerful not because law is analogous to a machine that withdraws a particular lever from the pigeon, physically preventing an error by the pigeon, but because there are some clear constitutional directives that you agree with, and judges are more likely to follow them than legislators. You might concede that there will be many constitutional questions that don't have clear answers but think that judges are not likely to do much damage, however they decide them, as long as they hew to their task of enforcing the good, clear mandates.

You might not like the text of the Constitution, but like constitutional *law,* seeing the judicial elaborations over the years as a valuable total corpus. You might see the judicial technique of constrained activist fidelity to the total corpus as a more reliable safeguard than the legislature will ever be. And you might believe that even your own ideological camp, in its legislative incarnation, is sorely in need of a safeguard.

But you might see the text as containing good and bad, and see judges as having leeway to give good and bad meanings in accord with ideological agendas you don't like. You might see our form of constitutionalism as sanctifying, "enshrining," bad results and sapping legislative competence and initiative.

People don't resolve themselves on this question behind a veil of ignorance, with no idea of what their particular interests and ideological commitments will be in the regime chosen.[14] We can ask what consequences we might anticipate for ideologized group conflict from switching to the alternative. And there is no reason to think the consequences would be the same regardless of the time at which one made the switch. Switching today wouldn't be the same as never adopting Marbury v. Madison.

Constitutional law today is no more coherent than is the common law. However the textual provisions may have seemed at the start, the process of interpretation has turned them into a hodgepodge, with some built into particular liberal or conservative agendas, others deployed in alternation by liberals and conservatives, depending on which domain of ideological controversy is in question. Some language switches its valence through time, while other words and phrases have never been much use to either side.

Liberals have been devoted to the equal protection clause, and to the religion and speech clauses of the First Amendment, but speech issues are more complex in the era of paranoia about political correctness; conservatives like the just compensation clause of the Fifth Amendment, and the contracts clause. Both sides like due process when it suits their interests (that is, when they get to define liberty and property), and so on. There have been activist liberal and conservative majorities of the U.S. Supreme Court within recent memory, so that the body of materials taken as a whole is quite representative of the ideological possibilities in the general political culture.

I don't think that the commitment of the whole political spectrum to judicial review is explained by the fact that every part of the spectrum has colonized some part of the corpus and wants to protect it against other fractions' legislative coalitions. It seems more plausible that the role of judicial review is to prevent "legislative excess," just as the civics lesson teaches. The denial and misunderstanding of ideology in constitutional adjudication strengthen the ability of the courts to prevent excess.

Of course, one man's excess is another man's good judgment. But the distinguishing fact about American political culture is that, however they define it, both the liberal and the conservative intelligentsias fear it in about equal measure, once it is understood that we are talking about *popular* excess. Liberals fear nationalist, chauvinist, sexist, racist, anti-Semitic, homophobic, majoritarian reactions to political and cultural division. Conservatives fear electoral revolt of the unpropertied many against the rich few, electoral uprising of oppressed minorities that together make a majority. Both sides fear demagogues, Joe McCarthys and Huey Longs, who can get genuine electoral support for departures from the different elements of the status quo the two sides hold dear.[15]

At the same time, neither conservatives nor liberals have a program or even a desire for popular mobilization that would transform the society in a major way. The intelligentsia as a whole is sitting pretty, and sitting on top. The intelligentsia as a whole is genuinely patriotic and genuinely convinced that "for all its defects, many of which are very serious indeed," this terrible system is better than the alternatives.

Given their sense of the tenuousness of their ability to control the dangerous masses, it is doubtful that either liberals or conservatives would take up an opportunity for serious, legislatively based regime change if it were offered on a silver platter. At the same time, both liberal and conservative intelligentsias are worried that the other side *would* change the regime if it could, or at least nudge it along little by little until quantity became quality.

Final judicial review, based on denial or misunderstanding of ideology in law, serves the interest of the intelligentsia as a whole in the stability of the regime, as well as the interest shared by each particular intelligentsia and its constituency in "freedom from" the other side's majoritarian excesses. It does this indiscriminately for right and left because both right and left firmly believe that constitutional law firmly prohibits the popular masses from putting the extreme program of the other side in place through the electoral process. Conservatives think communism is unconstitutional. Liberals think fascism is unconstitutional.

The resulting consensus has a complicated structure. The civics-class rhetoric of constitutionalism, as in my two examples above, points to general dangers of majority rule, dangers that everyone should fear. Then there is what one might call constitutional wishful thinking, the conviction of both liberals and conservatives that the corpus of constitutional law, correctly interpreted, protects them and their constituencies from their enemies and *their* constituencies, while permitting their favorite (moderate) reforms. Finally, there is the pervasive intelligentsia experience of living on top of a disorganized, culturally disparate, ethnic, racial, class, regional, religious stewpot, a stewpot that threatens periodically to boil over into populist, racist, radical, or reactionary intolerance.

In this respect, the American intelligentsia is far more precarious in its authority than the intelligentsias of the nations of Western Europe. Those intelligentsias are by comparison "organic." Their authority is rooted in the cultural and class and ethnic histories of *relatively* homogeneous societies.[16] But their history is also that of the guillotine and fascism and the Holocaust and the gulag.

The American intelligentsia has a naive belief in constitutionalism: the myth of the possibility and the reality of a national life organized in accord with a set of founding principles, along with the myth that the Judge presides "over" politics. But it also has a cynical conviction that it is best for the masses to believe in law, in the Constitution, in the Judge, because without them there is no telling what might happen.

In the absence of hierarchically structured community, which is the (simultaneously secure and stultifying) condition of the Western Europeans, any authority is better than no authority. And our extant constitutional law, whatever its status in the Court of Reason, is, for both sides, a lot better than just "any" authority. Experience formalized as critique drives American liberals and conservatives into bad faith rather than apostasy.

The Western European intelligentsia has no confidence in sacred political texts whose mere interpretation guarantees legitimacy. It believes that "anything can happen," whether or not you have judicial review. Law is not at the center of politics, though I think it plays just as important a role from the periphery, a role that is if possible even more thoroughly mystified than in the United States.

The Legitimation Effect

I call the third effect of law making through adjudication "legitimation," meaning the reenforcement and reproduction of a particular attitude or "sense" about the social world.[1] The attitude is that the universe of possible ways of thinking about society, and particularly about the desirability and possibility of radical change in society, is exhausted by the moderately reactionary, moderately reformist, and status-quo-ist alternatives.

According to the legitimation hypothesis, the particular set of hierarchies that constitute our social arrangements look more natural, more necessary, and more just than they "really" are. One reason for this discrepancy is that alternative ways of understanding are rendered invisible or marginal or seemingly irrational by the practice of withdrawing a large part of the law-making function into a domain governed by the convention of legal correctness and the denial of ideological choice.

What is a legitimation effect?

The connection between denied ideology in adjudication and legitimacy is not "essential" in the sense of deriving from the very "nature" of law or politics. One could imagine "withdrawal" making the political order seem perennially less necessary, natural, and just rather than more. For example, the alienation of social choice into the domain of tradition or religion may have made some societies more vulnerable to disruption by the arrival of modern secular critiques than they would have been had their leaders better understood how social connection was organized, albeit semiconsciously, in the old regime.

Nor is there any reason to think a priori that "delegitimation," by the reincorporation of the domain of judicial law making into politics, would lead to a shift to the left. Nonetheless, the legitimation hypothesis is best understood in its initial context, that of specifically left-wing critique. Here is a schematic model.

The question is, why don't "the masses" rebel against capitalism? The first answer is "tanks." But then there is the problem that so many of the masses believe in capitalism, or believe that there is no better alternative, or that attempts to change it are hopeless. These are like self-fulfilling prophecies. Because people believe them, they don't do things that would in fact destabilize the system (like voting, for example). But they are not prophecies so much as errors.

The legitimation hypothesis starts from the *premise* that the system is less just, natural, and necessary than people think it is, and that their error is one of the things that keeps it in place. The premise might be wrong. Maybe things are just as natural, necessary, and just as people think they are, and the critics are deluded. Or maybe the masses are just as conscious of injustice, constructedness, and contingency as the critics, but have other good reasons for acquiescing in capitalism. To the extent that either or both of these is the case, the rest of the discussion loses interest. It's hard to imagine "proving" the premise.

Accepting the premise, a legitimation hypothesis also presupposes that most people in American society have ideas about why things turn out the way they do. At all levels of the class system, people pick and choose from a common store of conflicting representations of the social order as more or less natural/constructed, necessary/contingent, just/unjust. These beliefs are part of systems or loose structures of belief, in which the parts support or are in tension with one another. What we think about the naturalness or constructedness of economic inequality depends on what we think about lots of other things, even on what we learned in high school about natural science, and on why we think some baseball teams have long histories of success and others don't.

This means that we can't fully explain what a person thinks about the legitimacy of inequality by reference to that person's direct observations and experiences of economic life. Felt legitimacy is a function not just of the processing of data by social actors within a given domain of controversy but also of the way in which one view or another of the justice of the system "fits" into a system of beliefs about just about everything.

The different, but structurally related parts have the quality of a system in equilibrium, meaning that a change in one affects the others. Changing what happens or what we believe in one sector of reality will have (large or small) effects on beliefs in other sectors. The legitimation effect is an asserted structural relationship between beliefs about adjudication, on the one hand, and beliefs about the legitimacy of inequality and the plausibility of proposals for left-wing change, on the other.

The notion is that the practice and (mis)understanding of law making through adjudication influence the way particular people understand their total social situation, making the outcomes of social struggle look more natural, necessary, and just than they would if those people had a better understanding of adjudication. One mistake induces another, or contributes to another. The first mistake is one of the building blocks of the second. Delegitimating adjudication wouldn't "prove" that things are less natural, necessary, and just than at first appeared, or otherwise directly attack the legitimacy of the status quo. But it might induce change in the second mistake by rectifying the first.

We can use the by now familiar device of imagining a system of legislative supremacy, this time in the common law context, to explore just how the legitimation effect might work.

Consequences of legislative supremacy for the common law

Imagine that every time a litigant is displeased with the decision of a question of common law, he or she can appeal to the legislature, and that there is a practice of legislative decision of the question by passing a statute. Let's begin by considering cases where the judges experience themselves as bound by a clear meaning of the common law materials.

The effect of the alternative would be that when the legislature thought this clear common law meaning was a bad one, it would change the rule. Judges would then follow the normal processes of statutory interpretation in deciding how the new statute should be incorporated into the total complex of existing common law and statutory rules.

This already happens all the time, though sporadically. We are talking about a significant increase in the frequency of the practice. Such an increase might (or might not) have a wide variety of effects. There has been a long debate within the Anglo-American tradition about the relative virtues of common law and statutes or codification.[2] An important subtheme of realist and postrealist legal thought has been the debunking of the general conception on which the debate was based. Is the common law more "stable" than statute law? Is it more "rational"? Above all, is there some sense in which common law rules can be understood to be less "political" than statutes?

Stability of law under legislative supremacy

First, why assume that there would be rapid change? The legislature might tend to approve the vast majority of common law rules, and even tend to be more hostile to "reform" than the courts. Of course, the legislature could reconsider whole common law schemes. It could decide that although the common law had been clear, it should be scrapped, or an exception added. There would be no issue of a duty of fidelity to precedent.

But in the debate about the modification or massive replacement of common law regimes, we would expect legislators to put forward all the arguments for stability in the law that we would hear in a discussion of stare decisis. The advocates of change would in turn put forward all the familiar arguments that the "law evolves to meet new social conditions." Legislatures might change common law rules more rapidly than courts have changed them in the recent past, and the process *might* spin out of control. But there isn't a powerful theory that indicates that would happen, so let's suppose it doesn't.

Coherence, consistency, rationality

Why assume less internal consistency? We already have legislative revision, but it is sporadic. If the legislature were engaged in a constant practice of looking at common law rule systems, its changes might become more "rational" rather than less. (In another branch of the debate about judicial versus legislative law making, James Thayer's famous essay on judicial review[3] argued that the legislature is rendered incompetent by constant reliance on the courts.) The technical quality of drafting, concern about preserving the coherence of overall rule systems, and responsiveness to special interests might all be less or more under the new system, depending on the legislature's reaction to its new responsibilities.

There is a European notion (associated with Franz Wieacker)[4] that the codes of the late nineteenth century were internally coherent individualist documents that were then destroyed piecemeal by "socially" oriented legislation. The equivalent American idea is that the common law is an internally coherent body of individualist late-nineteenth-century doctrine, and that it would be destroyed by constant legislative intermeddling.

But the common law never had and certainly does not now have any such internal ideological coherence. As I have argued throughout, it is best understood as the outcome of ideological struggles in which particular rules are compromises. In this kind of structure, it doesn't make sense to speak of preserving ideological coherence because there is nothing there to preserve.

Politicizing the common law

The most interesting claim is that legislative supremacy would "politicize" the common law. What does this mean? It is clearly right in the sense that the following of rules by judges in these cases would be subsumed in a political process. In assessing this change, it is good to keep in mind that the legislature already has power to revise whenever it wants to, and that the judges already have power to overrule cases, though this power is to be exercised in the context of fidelity to the materials—subject to "rules about overruling."

The claim is clearly wrong if it means that the common law rules themselves are not "political" but rather "rational" or "objective" or "neutral," by contrast with the statutes that would replace them. The common law rules are resolutions of issues of ideologized group conflict, even if their authors and appliers do not understand them that way. They are a crucial part of the total political order of the society, as the realists constantly pointed out.

It is possibly right if it means that rules and rule systems that are not now perceived as important collective interventions in ideologized group conflict would come to be seen that way through the process of more frequent legislative consideration. The proposal might increase transparency, in the sense of reducing the illusion of "just thereness," or "naturalness," or "never-thought-about-it-ness" that currently adheres to a large part of the rule system.

The basic idea is that some significant number of participants in our political culture experience the common law part of the legal system as "less political" than it "really" is and, in particular, as less political than the part of the rule system that we understand to be the product of the legislature. Under the alternative, there might be a modification of this misunderstanding of the basis and effects of the rules. The misunderstanding, according to the legitimation hypothesis, reinforces the felt legitimacy of the whole system.

The structure of the distinction between the common law and legislation

Why do people see judge-made common law as less political than statutory law? At an elementary level, we have a cultural belief in the distinctions between law application and law making, between adjudication and legislation, and between judicial resolution of controversial questions of rule interpretation and legislative resolution of equivalent questions.

People have associations with law, and its development through adjudication, that connect to the "natural, necessary, just" pole of the duality, with legislation associated with the traits at the other end. The figure of the Judge is a real one in the imaginations of all classes of people, and it is quite a different figure from that of the Congressman or the Senator.

This belief operates in different ways at different levels of the class and gender and race systems. For example, in popular consciousness, the courts may be strongly associated with the repression of deviance and the settlement of disputes according to widely shared social norms.[5] The legislature is there to take care of problems, to make changes in response to new forms of deviance or to the deterioration of systems. At the other pole, the specifically legal intelligentsias have a clear conception of courts as resolvers of ideologized group conflict according to an often indeterminate method.

For different people, the belief that there is a fundamental distinction goes along with different kinds of critique and cynicism about the judicial role. These views may dovetail only on the proposition that it is not "all politics," though politics has a lot to do with it. The different strata can and do disagree on exactly how or why it is not all politics, without undermining the basic structure, as long as circumstances don't force their (mis)understandings into actual conflict.

In what follows, I am concerned with the way the conservative and liberal intelligentsias, and their specifically legal subparts, (mis)understand the distinction, and with the consequences. In the (mis)understanding of the intelligentsia, there are three structural aspects of the relationship between judge-made common law and legislation that are politically important.

1. The common law is a background, a complete or potentially complete system that is there waiting to dispose of any new case, and does in fact dispose in a routine way of the overwhelming mass of legal business. Legislation is a foreground, a more or less striking intervention that makes things different than they were before, but does this only to a small piece of the total system and does it episodically. Contrast an understanding in which "the Code" is the background on which judges do foreground interpretation, with the legislature occasionally "fine tuning" its own prior work.

2. The common law is, roughly, "commutative," concerned with "righting wrongs" within a well-defined system of individual and collective

rights that is presumptively just. By contrast, legislation is "distributive," concerned to change the balance of success of groups struggling for welfare by changing the ground rules of the struggle.

In legislation, people make arguments based on perceptions of injustice, constructedness, and contingency, both of the rule system and of the outcomes that occur when people play the game within the rules (for example, the NLRA; the Social Security, Unemployment Compensation, and Civil Rights Acts; and environmental statutes). In court, the important question is whether you violated a preexisting norm, or how to interpret a preexisting norm. Distributive arguments are unseemly as well as irrelevant.

3. The common law rules governing economic life are loosely identified with the free market, while legislation is identified with regulation. A free market seems generally to mean freedom of contract and few protections against external effects of property use. The premise is that a judicially administered free market is what we had in the late nineteenth century. For liberals, "legislation has been necessary because there are lots of bad consequences of a free market." For conservatives, populist majorities or rent-seeking coalitions are constantly wounding the goose that lays the golden eggs.

Courts, by contrast, continue to elaborate the free-market regime based on property and contract, except when made to do otherwise by statute. It is clear that there are liberal and conservative positions on common law issues. It is becoming more and more common for conservatives to argue that, in the last twenty years or so, liberal judges have improperly pursued their regulatory agendas through the courts. But only a small minority even of the specifically legal intelligentsia has grasped the legal realist insight that the common law, even that of the late nineteenth century, is no less regulatory, even when the judges pursue free-market agendas, than the statutory regimes that episodically supersede it.

"Withdrawal" as a consequence of misunderstanding

Now let's suppose that the figure/ground relationship between legislation and adjudication is arbitrary. Suppose that the sense that the common law is commutative and legislation distributive is just plain mistaken: the common law operates in fact distributively, and all attempts to construct a coherent methodology for strictly commutative judicial law making are failures.[6] Suppose we accept the critique of the notion that there is a determinate legal structure for a free market, and the common law is that legal structure. The common law is no less regulatory than legislation.[7]

On this basis, we can give a more concrete definition of the notion of the "withdrawal" of a legal domain from politics. Our current understanding "withdraws" the common law from politics in the sense of locating it off the map of institutions that *cause* wealth and poverty, worker or management empowerment, sexual and racial equality or inequality.

The common law, thus understood, is one of the long list of institutions, like the interstate highway system or the steel industry, that have obvious, nonpolitical purposes. Their particular modes of operation are "technical" and derived from those purposes. These background institutions provide the context within which people struggle for welfare and the context within which they pursue ideological agendas in the legislature.

If we imagine a person trying to figure out why some people get more and others less in society, there would be a list of reasons. Some of these would refer to aspects of human nature and social life that we locate in "nature," such as "some people are smarter than others." Others would refer to "necessity," that is, to the existence of painful tradeoffs between conflicting values—"the only way to achieve equality is through a level of day to day coercion that would be unacceptable even to egalitarian fanatics." Other reasons would refer to virtues of inequality—that it rewards different contributions differently and provides incentives for effort.

The "political" reasons for inequality include the unwillingness of the rich to give to the poor, the hope of the poor that they will one day be rich, the ability of the rich to buy the legislative process, the callousness of conservatives (for liberals), or the mush-headed counterproductive policies of liberals (for conservatives). In the domain of the political, the reasons for inequality are the ideologically organized preferences and beliefs of the people in the society, the balance of political power between groups with conflicting views about how bad it is, and the balance between groups debating how much we should sacrifice other values in order to get rid of it.

It would not come immediately to mind that the technical operation of background institutions with clearly nonpolitical purposes is a major cause of inequality. We might want to adjust their practices to fit, say, legislative changes in an egalitarian direction. But this is likely to be an attempt, post hoc, to minimize the "damage" caused by reform.

There is a wide range of views on the question of the relative importance of political and nonpolitical reasons for inequality. At one extreme, one might believe that the whole story is that the people with political power are unwilling to make the small sacrifices necessary to abolish it. At the other, one might believe that no amount of good will and effort and sacrifice could abolish it, because its roots are in human nature and the necessities of social life, and besides there's nothing wrong with it.

With respect to the level of inequality in society as it exists right now, there is a related spectrum of attitudes. The current level might be intolerably and unnaturally and unnecessarily large, or far too small to be consistent with ethics and rationality, or it might be just about right. The argument is that how you see the common law will influence where you stand on this spectrum.

Suppose the choice is between seeing the common law as a nonpolitical background institution whose practices are governed by technical requirements (the interstate highway system) and seeing it as a part of the political system that resolves issues of ideologized group conflict. The claim is that the more you see it as political (in the sense of ideologically disputed choice that increases or lessens inequality), the less likely you are to see the current level of inequality as natural and necessary, and the more complex your argument that it is just. In short, the withdrawal of the common law from politics favors the status quo. Why should this be so?

Political consequences of withdrawal

One way to look at it is in terms of "room for maneuver." If government affects inequality only in a small number of ways, it is less likely that it can have a major impact on it than if it affects it in many ways. If government affects it only in limited ways, then it might be necessary to undertake drastic changes in those ways if we expect to have a big impact on inequality.

But there is a second element to the theory. To the extent the rules made by judges are withdrawn into an area where they have their own peculiar form of justification, then changes in those rules will have to confront reasons for the rules that have nothing to do with inequality. The rules are rationalized by judges and endorsed with judicial charisma. Just because they have entered the domain of consideration as instruments that affect inequality doesn't mean that the political process now has free play to fit them into an instrumental inequality calculus.

Imagine that we begin to develop, as the realists did, a sophisticated "policy science" of the distributive implications of common law rules. When it seems that changing a particular rule would have good (conservative or liberal) consequences, we have to deal with the fact that the rule is located in the common law domain and therefore reenforced by the mana or charisma of the judiciary that established it. To mess with this rule will be understood as messing with one of the set whose derivation is outside the political process but also *in* a domain of authority.

The analogy is to arguing, for example, that bridges should be built differently in order to make it easier for poor people to cross them. Such a proposal comes up against the notion that the authorities "know what they're doing." If the Engineer says it should be built in a particular way, then we ought to do what he says.

But it is not just a matter of floating, prerational charismatic power. Like the Engineer, the Judge has her reasons. There is an apolitical logic of bridge building, based on factors like cost and safety. There is also an apolitical logic to the common law definition of fraud (false statement, made with knowledge of falsity, that reasonably induced reasonable reliance by the addressee, to his or her detriment).

At least it is the burden of the legal opinions that lay down the rules, and of the academic literature that compiles and comments on them, that there is such a logic. This body of texts is "apologetic," in the sense that it argues, under the convention of necessity, that the rules are as they should be, or that the rules should be marginally modified in a conservative or liberal direction. In other words, we withdraw the common law from politics *into* a domain in which there are apolitical ethical and instrumental and purely "technical" justifications for what the judges have done.

The notion that law is apolitical has both a positive and a negative meaning. The positive meaning is that there is a judicial method, that the method is that of fidelity to the materials (to the past, to the previously agreed on), and that the method is, *in some sense, to a large degree,* ideologically "neutral." The negative is the absence, from judicial or academic justifications for rule interpretations, of the kinds of reasons that are culturally identified with the ideological.

These include preference for egalitarian or unequal income distribution, for a particular religious vision, for a controversial version of sexuality, or for the promotion of racial, as opposed to individual or "American," identity. Ideological preferences are present as a matter of fact, as I argued above, built into the universalistic discourse of "policy," and worked out by restrained activist, difference splitting, and bipolar judges. But they are present denied, as the stain of bad faith.

The point is not that the rules thus justified have a liberal or a conservative "tilt." Within the domain of law making by adjudication, the different ideological fractions vigorously pursue their different agendas. Their success varies with time and the process of judicial appointment, subject to the vagaries of the moderation and empowerment effects.

The point is rather that a cost of movement toward greater equality or greater inequality appears to be the "abandonment" of law. It means challenging authority; it means renouncing the security of understanding this part of social order as "necessary" (in the sense that legal outcomes are necessary rather than contingent), in favor of flux. It means finding a way to answer the web of legal argument that asserts the fairness, rightness, usefulness of the judge-made rules, and their transcendence of narrow ideological considerations.

In short, our current understanding, however qualified by cynicism, withdraws these legal rules into a domain in which a whole knowledge industry has worked for generations to justify them, subject again to moderate reformist and reactionary critiques. The legitimation hypothesis is that this limitation of the political imagination is good for the status quo.

Disclaimers

I want to reiterate that the legitimation effect is not based on an assertion about the "nature" of law or legal reasoning. It is far more contextualized than that, indeed specific to American law and politics in this moment. Moreover, the effect is hypothetical. It may or may not be true that law making through adjudication buttresses the status quo in the way I have described. It seems plausible to me, and worth working on, both at a theoretical and at a practical level, but no more. Finally, delegitimating the system through internal critique might be part either of a left- or a right-wing program. I believe that the effect of critique in the specific milieu of the elite legal intelligentsia tends to be consistently left wing, but I may be wrong. Effects in other social milieus are even more conjectural.

An analogy

Imagine a culture that is heavily dependent on agriculture. It is a traditional culture in the sense that, with one exception, it has, from time immemorial, planted, cultivated, harvested, and processed plants in what everyone agrees is "the same way." Agriculture and religion are intertwined. The gods and goddesses are crop gods, weather gods, farmer gods. Every element of the agricultural process has a mythical interpretation, a place in religious beliefs and rituals. There is no science of the consequences of small or large departures from the traditional agricultural techniques. These are understood and explained as responses to commands of the gods, although, of course, the fruits are understood to be necessary to sustain life.

The exception is the system of irrigation. It is understood as an instrumental activity, based on human invention and skill. Its purpose is to maximize the quantity and quality of production. This is fully compatible with religion, and indeed sacralized, but sacralized as pleasing the gods by "aiding their work." There are no specific religious commandments about irrigation, and no part of the ritual system is organized around or depends on any particular irrigation practice.

The idea is that in this society the response to a change in the environment, or to a change in the goals of people with respect to the quantity and quality of food, will focus on irrigation practices. If changing these doesn't work, change may appear impossible, the status quo natural, and the consequent distribution of welfare fair to everyone.

Of course, religious invention and reinterpretation are always possible and may occur in a way that promotes response to environmental or normative change. The religion may have, for participants and observers, qualities of truth, and it may promote values that are highly admirable. It may be wholly "rational" to focus on irrigation in responding to crisis, given the noninstrumental "functions" of religion in the society. But the response is still likely to be different from what it would be if agriculture were an instrumental activity, with religious belief organized around, say, sexuality and reproduction. Our situation is like this, except that the priesthood is in bad faith in its claim of necessity for the rule system it administers.

The practice of delegitimation

The legitimating effect of law making through adjudication, as I've been describing it, differs from the empowerment effect because it reenforces the status quo, whatever that may be. The empowerment effect allows fractions of ideological intelligentsias to exercise power that would be denied them if they had to go through the legislature. The judicially empowered intelligentsia creates a body of doctrine that becomes a naturalized element that helps reproduce the status quo while appearing merely to serve it.

This critique of adjudication has a particular history. It was developed by liberals arguing both against the empowerment of conservative judges and against the legitimation of the conservative status quo. In their delegitimation efforts, the liberals pursued their strategy across a variety of legal domains. But after they gained control of Congress and the executive branch in 1932, and of the federal judiciary over the ensuing years, they stopped doing it. They had become the managers of the post–World War II social settlement rather than critics of a failing laissez-faire state.

It was taken up again in cls, in the aftermath of the 1960s, this time as a radical critique of mainstream liberal legality, rather than as a liberal critique of conservatism. The critique of the common law in relation to legislation, that is, of the separation of powers, offered above is just one of this larger family of liberal and radical critiques. The rest of this chapter appropriates (rather than summarizes or "reads") a variety of critical works to try to show that delegitimating critiques with a similar underlying structure can be operated in many different legal fields.

In each case, what the critic is going after is this phenomenon: there are groups engaged in cooperative but also competitive relations within a legal structure. The activities of the members of the groups are in the foreground, from the point of view of everyone involved, meaning that we attribute the outcomes of competition and cooperation to their actions, to their choices and strategies, and to the distribution of resources among them. The legal rules that structure the competition are in the background. Everyone knows they are there, but they are naturalized, taken for granted, not attributed causal significance in explaining the outcomes of the battles that occur within their framework.

A delegitimating critique of the kind I'm discussing in this chapter is an attempt to operate a background/foreground shift. It attributes causal significance for the outcome to the background rules. The point of the analysis is not transparency, a situation in which all elements of the situation would be continuously before us and nothing would ever be naturalized that wasn't "really" natural. It is rather to perform a specific politically motivated operation of reversing figure and ground.

We assert that something that is background for others is causally important in the hope that if we are right, and we can make people see it, we will make it plausible that there are more ways to change the status quo than previously appeared. We argue against that part of its legitimacy that derived from its appearance of inevitability.[8] The critique was first developed in the context of labor law. I will sketch a version of that effort and then construct six extensions, to the law of federalism, international law, local government law, race law, the law of the First Amendment, and gender law. My presentation becomes more schematic as it goes along and in every case neglects the richness of context and the major differences between the different authors, within as well as among fields.

Labor law

Labor and capital are each organized, with individual workers and unions on one side and capitalist enterprises of different sizes and structures on the other. There are elaborate rules of the game about how the entities can be constituted (bargaining unit definition, union democracy rules, corporate and antitrust law) and about what they can do to each other (covering activities like trespass, picketing, strikes, secondary boycotts, discharge, lockouts, blacklists, and so forth). The outcome of conflict and cooperation is a distribution between the underlying groups behind the legal entities. In the foreground, the outcomes are determined by "bargaining power," a black box that includes the value at the margin of contributions to the productive process, but also strategy, group cohesion, resources, and so forth, of capital and labor.[9]

The first version of labor law delegitimation was that of the progressives up to the passage of the Wagner Act. In the United States the two main movements of opposition to the status quo in the late nineteenth and early twentieth centuries were the agrarian movement and the labor movement. The law of legal personality, especially corporate law, and tort law were focal points. In particular, labor cases put common law judges in the position of deciding issues that were ideologically contested with large stakes. Both labor and capital defined the issue in terms of "unbiased" rules of the game.

The legal representatives of capital developed a version of property rights that conservative judges accepted in many cases.[10] The labor movement developed a symmetrical populist position based on the right of the individual to dispose of his labor and to make agreements with others parallel to those among employers. Outside the milieu of socialism, the demand was for a "fair shake" or for preservation of traditional forms of worker collectivity, rather than for, say, worker control.[11] Labor advocates argued that the conservatives were distorting the true logic of a system of individual rights in order to protect their interests. But their supporters in the progressive intelligentsia had a much more sophisticated notion of what law was and what it could achieve.

The delegitimation strategy was a four-part argument. Later versions in other areas would have the same basic structure.

1. Neither common law precedent nor common law theory, relying on "formalist" reasoning from terms like "property," "coercion," "liberty," and "right," could legally compel the adoption of either a pro-capital or a pro-worker legal regime. Property was just a bundle of rights. There were vast leeways in deciding how to compose the bundle—it was "inevitably a question of policy."

2. The design of the background rules had a much larger effect on outcomes, including not just the distribution of surplus but also the tenor of industrial life and the prospects for economic growth, than you'd think when focusing on the foreground of strikes, collective bargaining, union organizing, and union busting. The rules constituted the bargaining power of the parties, rather than merely providing the site for its exercise.

3. The rules that were in force and that were emerging in the great cases represented a particular choice by a judicially empowered conservative minority. These rules were naturalized through an internally incoherent discourse of legal necessity that claimed they were the logical consequences of having a capitalist system in the first place.

4. We needed to adopt a more "progressive" law of industrial organizations and labor torts, one that would allow the adjustment of the conflict of labor and capital in a way that would not threaten civil order. Under such a regime, the situation of labor would improve gradually, interstitially, by institutional adjustment, toward workplace democracy in a growing economy, rather than through cataclysmic revolutionary strategies. The rights of property and interests of capital could be protected, once we stopped fetishizing absolute rights, without creating a right-wing police state.[12]

The argument that there were no "absolute" property and contract rights, so that social policy was appropriately called on to draw lines, was highly effective, indeed the prototype for legal realist analysis. But as a piece of private law theory it was superseded, indeed it disappeared from consciousness, when the reformers came to power and took the route of a federal statutory reordering of labor relations in the NLRA.

The modern, cls version of a labor law delegitimation project was addressed to this statutory regime and performed on it a remarkably similar set of operations. Karl Klare[13] argued that the moderate liberal judges of the 1940s and 1950s had chosen a particular interpretation of the NLRA, one that was required neither by the principles of statutory interpretation nor by a compelling theory of the background legal context, but rather by a "deradicalizing," moderate liberal ideology. These acts of interpretation by a labor intelligentsia empowered through adjudication created a legal regime that naturalized a particular vision of collective bargaining.

It created a legal context that was systematically hostile to labor militancy, whether at the level of union activity or at that of the rank and file. The promotion of arbitration, enforcement of no-strike clauses, insulation of unions from effective fair-representation suits, constriction of subjects of compulsory bargaining, narrow interpretation of the duty to bargain in good faith, and many other doctrines represented ideologically motivated choices with massive but largely invisible consequences. What came to be regarded by both labor and management intelligentsias as the beneficent logic of the collective-bargaining "system" created by the statute functioned in fact to demobilize workers and then "administer" them.

The obvious difference between the earlier and later critiques is that the first was liberal and the second radical, oriented to worker control, workerist, hostile to what Kathy Stone called "industrial pluralism."[14] Another important difference is that the cls critiques emphasize the reproduction within the antiformalist, policy-driven liberal labor law regime of "social conceptualist" legal reasoning techniques.[15] As we saw in Chapter 5, the realists didn't come close to solving the problem of the coexistence of deductive with policy reasoning, and this made their work vulnerable to a critique analogous to that they had leveled against formalism.

A third equally important difference is that the critical analysis emphasizes the way the labor law regime and its analogues actually constitute the "subjects" they regulate. In addition to distributing surplus by influencing bargaining power, the labor law regime favors the "social construction" of passive workers and then purports to give them what they want through freedom of contract.[16] The progressives tended to take the "subjects" of the conservative regime as given outside the legal analysis, thereby avoiding difficult political questions of "false consciousness" but also underestimating the stakes of law.[17]

Federalism

More or less at the same time that they were critiquing tort law in the labor context, the progressives applied the same tactic to the law of federalism. Liberal/conservative conflict takes place within a public law structure that allocates some powers to the federal and some to the state governments. At any given moment, in the foreground of political conflict, liberals and conservatives compete in elections for control of governments at both levels. The choice of policies with distributive consequences for their constituencies depends on how they do.

But once liberals or conservatives gain power, what they can do at the level they control is conditioned by the rules of federalism. If you control the federal but not the state level, you get only federal powers. If you control at the state but not the federal level, you may be legally blocked by the law of federalism and practically blocked by deregulatory competition among the states.

Again, the progressive motive for critique was conservative judicial interpretation, in this case of the commerce clause and the Tenth Amendment. The federal government had no power to regulate activities whose effects on interstate commerce were merely "indirect"; manufacturing was "not commerce"; the states could not supplement weak federal regulation where Congress had "occupied the field"; the states were prohibited from regulating in some areas even if Congress had not done so.

It is easy to see this doctrinal development in terms of the empowerment effect: conservative political groups achieved results that they might not have been able to achieve through national and state legislatures. The legitimation effect was the "withdrawal" of the issue of the allocation of state and federal power from the political discussion of how to deal with monopolies, child labor, and so forth, because it appeared that federalism was just a neutral framework for the democratic process, rather than a framework shaped by the very interests that were contending within it.

The progressives responded by developing the same force field model for federalism that they had worked out for private law conflict.[18] They attacked all the conservative on/off distinctions as hiding questions of degree that couldn't be decided without reference to policy.

(1) Within the general framework of the Constitution, there are vast leeways in deciding the particular rules of federalism, because terms like "power," "commerce," and "tax" are too vague to preclude setting the rules so as to further the substantive liberal or conservative policies you favor. (2) The choice of a particular specification of the idea of federalism will have large consequences, much larger than appear if you focus on the foreground of state and federal electoral politics. (3) Our specific set of rules is the product of conservative judges empowered through adjudication, legitimated through legal reasoning, and much worse for liberal re-

form than would be an alternative liberal regime. (4) We should change them so that federalism, within the broad limits of the Constitution, favors rather than impedes rational policy making at whatever level of government.

The progressives' analysis was just as successful politically in this area as it was in that of labor law, and it suffered the same fate of intellectual disappearance. At the level of substantive doctrine, when they gained control of the courts during the New Deal, the progressives weakened or abolished the conservative doctrines and promoted national supremacy in fact, if not in name.[19] At a more abstract level, the main accomplishment of the Legal Process school was the working out of a theory of federalism that drew lines between areas of institutional competence through coherence-oriented policy argument, without resort to ideology.[20]

The effect was similar to that of the codification of labor law through the NLRA. The doctrinal entrenchment of federal power was so complete that the sophisticated intellectual routines that had seemed necessary to establish it became irrelevant. When Rehnquist and Scalia began to revive the earlier conservative doctrine in the 1980s, the liberals had all but forgotten the responses that once had seemed second nature. The analysis was, however, one of the building blocks for the critique of local government law discussed below.

Public international law

To my mind, the progressive critique of public international law presupposed a structure analogous to those of labor law and federalism. Competition between groups occurs within the system of states or sovereigns whose relations are ordered by public international law. Ethnic groups may be consolidated within a homogeneous sovereign unit, may dominate many small states, or may be dispersed as minorities within states controlled by other groups. In the foreground, it appears that states compete through war, trade, and diplomacy, with the results determined by their resources, strategy, and so on. But the outcomes for the groups that underlie the state system depend on what a state is, that is, on what sovereignty "is," and on what states can "legally" do to each other in war, trade, and diplomacy.[21]

Progressive "modernists" critiqued this system and tried to revise it through the League of Nations.

(1) Within the general framework of a state system, there are vast lee-

ways in defining sovereignty, which is, like property, best seen as a bundle of rights and powers and which lacks, like property, an internal logic that would make it sensible to oppose any desirable solution for an international problem on the ground that it is "incompatible with sovereignty." (2) The choice of a specification of the concept has much larger consequences than people preoccupied with the foreground of military, diplomatic, and economic conflict within the rules imagine. (3) The pre–World War I rules were put in effect by leaders of a small group of dominant imperialist early modern states and then frozen through legal reasoning as necessary implications of basic concepts. (4) It was urgent to revise the state system by reconfiguring sovereignty and building new institutions, in the interests of the victims, whether those who die in wars, the colonized peoples, or minorities within existing states.[22]

The interwar thinkers, like the progressive critics of labor law and the law of federalism, were successful in the sense that their ideas became a kind of orthodoxy in the era of the United Nations. But as orthodoxy the critique became itself a part of the background, this time for a disintegrated pragmatic policy discourse within the larger structure of Cold War stalemate.

I would cannibalize the work of cls post-Vietnam critics for use in my schema as follows. They hoist the antiformalist liberals on their own petard by pointing out the residual power of a formalist concept of sovereignty within a discourse that claimed to have superseded any such primitive notion. They pointed out the tension between the claim to have superseded formalism and heavy reliance on the notion of expertise to legitimate successive New World Order projects. As had the labor lawyers, they emphasized the subject-constituting effects of legal discourse but included the decision makers themselves as products of their own policy speech. Along with other second- and third-generation crits, they developed a postmodern methodology that had not previously been tried in law. They eschewed programmatic radicalism and replaced analysis in terms of relatively coherent visions with a combination of cultural critique and the kind of semiotic analysis described in Chapter 6.[23]

Local government law

I think there is a good case for describing local government law as defining a field like those above. Rich and poor and black and white compete in markets, which are a foreground for the exercise of bargaining power, against not one but two backgrounds. The first is that of the rules regulating the interactions of labor and capital as bearers of "legal personality," developed in labor and corporate law. But these same groups also pursue their interests within local government law, a "state system" analogous to the international and federal systems.

Groups can homogeneously control their own city, town, or county governments, exist as minorities within them, find themselves "balkanized" or "ghettoized" by the local government system, and so forth. Legal rules govern the formation and dissolution of such governments, and what they can do in competition with one another through their tax, zoning, and voting policies, and legal rules also allocate powers between state and local government. The relative wealth and poverty of groups, as well as their opportunities for consumption of housing and community characteristics like slum conditions and racial segregation, depend on this structure.

There does not seem to have been a progressive critique in this area parallel to those in labor, federalism, and international law. As I read it, the cls version[24] was originally quite close to the early labor law model but built on the realist critique of federalism that was still an important part of the law school curriculum in the late 1950s and early 1960s. Local government law was also one of the locales for the shift to postmodernism. I would appropriate some of its elements for purposes of my schema as follows.

(1) Within the general structure of local government law, neither the public/private distinction nor concepts like plenary state power over municipal corporations and home rule are any more determinate as guides than property, states' rights, or sovereignty. Doctrine develops through opposed rhetorical modes (for example, picturing space as naturally divided or as featureless). There is no reason not to take our substantive views about rich/poor, black/white conflict into account in designing this structure. (2) Its distributive effect—on urban wealth and poverty, for example, or on the national pattern of racial segregation in housing, schools, and jobs—is vastly greater than appears when we focus on the foreground of city budget crises, desegregation decrees, urban riots, or white flight.

(3) The extant rules were frozen in place by nineteenth- and twentieth-century judges with various agendas and naturalized through legal reasoning. They function today to generate outcomes much less favorable to cities, the poor, and people of color than might occur under a different set of rules. (4) We should change the rules to change both distributive out-

comes and subject-creation effects significantly,[25] rather than limiting ourselves to the solutions—tax-and-spend programs and legal strategies based on individual rights, formal equality, and fair procedure—that are typical of modern liberal thinking in the area.

Race law

The legitimation critiques in the areas of race, the First Amendment, and gender law differ from those in the above areas because they do not have progressive forebears. Indeed, First Amendment, and race and gender equal protection law, as developed from the 1930s through the 1970s, represent the main alternative to legal realist policy analysis and interest balancing, namely, the appropriation by liberals of what had been a right-wing rhetoric of individual constitutional rights. In these areas, the liberals were antimajoritarian and therefore concerned to build up, rather than undermine, judicial authority.

As I see it, the analysis in the race area had two stages. Derrick Bell showed how the development of supposedly color-blind, individual legal rights against discrimination in the school desegregation context could have large negative consequences for their supposed beneficiaries.[26] Liberal victories sometimes turned out to undermine black community resources and institutions and to promote the polarization of the black community along class lines. The judiciary, and white elites in general, were at best only ambivalently committed to racial justice. Rather than pushing forward to deal with the unintended consequences of reform, they pulled back from confrontation with the white working and lower-middle classes, and compromised or gutted the set of legal doctrines that had promised to transform the legal structure of black-white relations.[27]

The legitimation critique in the area of race law was of the way in which the prestige of the judiciary, the mana of the Judge, deployed from the 1950s through the early 1970s by liberals against racial oppression, turned against the cause of racial justice when conservatives got control of the courts and switched from the "victim" to the "perpetrator" perspective. Alan Freeman's brilliant analysis[28] was thus parallel in its radical intentions to the critiques of liberal policy analysis in labor law and international law, but he aimed at a different mode of judicial legitimation of the status quo. His work, and some of critical race theory, fits the more general cls schema as follows.

(1) The legal concepts, like equal protection, discrimination, and eq-

uitable remedy, that provide the structure for black-white relations in a racist society that has abandoned de jure segregation are open to contradictory interpretations reflecting opposing ideological orientations to racial justice. (2) The consequences, for the black community, of adopting one or another of these interpretations are large, much larger than appears when we imagine that the legal issue of race has long since been settled by the dismantling of de jure segregation.[29]

(3) The shift from one interpretation of race law to the other was operated by conservative judges exploiting the underlying indeterminacy of the legal concepts and the ideology of color blindness.[30] They naturalized the new rules through the prestige of adjudication, doing their best to make it appear that the massive remaining group inequality is explained in terms of factors like merit and cultural differences between blacks and whites. (4) We should adopt a "race-conscious" approach, and change the rules to fulfill the radical promise of the early desegregation decisions.[31]

The First Amendment

The foreground for political and cultural competition is the "marketplace of ideas" that is said to result from the constitutional guarantee of free speech. Groups compete to dominate in this market, both because having a share of the culture is an end desired for itself and because speech is instrumental in all the other kinds of competition. The background rules here are those that govern what entities get protection (corporate speech, broadcast licensing and regulation), the distinction between speech and action, and the list of what types of speech get protected.

The law of sedition and the rules governing libel, slander, assault, intentional infliction of emotional harm, sexual harassment, fraud, obscenity, and more recently hate speech constitute a speech-tort code analogous to that governing labor/capital conflict. The code influences both the content and the authorship that is in the foreground when we pay attention to discursive conflict.

The critique of free-speech absolutism has no progressive predecessor, though it is a response to the liberal regime that emerged in the 1960s and 1970s from the earlier battles over the proper treatment of issues like labor picketing, communist speech, and civil rights and antiwar protest. The critics have been antipornography feminists,[32] critical race theorists supporting the regulation of hate speech,[33] and crits deploying the realist analysis.[34] I would assimilate it to my schema (not summarize it) as follows.

(1) The regime, constituted by the combination of an individual and a corporate legal right of free speech with a particular legal definition of speech torts, has no more coherence than property, sovereignty, states' rights, or home rule. There are vast leeways in the definition of the regime and no reason to disregard the impact of choices on issues of democracy and subordination. (2) The influence of the background rules defining who is protected, and of the speech-tort code, is far greater than appears when we focus on the foreground in which people speak more or less persuasively to larger or smaller audiences. (3) The rules of the game were put in place by liberal and conservative judges and frozen through legal reasoning. They favor money, entrenched political power, and groups that use speech as a weapon of subordination. (4) We should change them to make them better serve the interests of a mobilized electorate and of the groups whose subordination is perpetuated through various kinds of low-value speech.

The law of gender

It is easy to see how one can mechanically apply my schema to the law of gender.

(1) The regime of legal rules that constitutes men and women and gays and straights as legal subjects, and then structures their competitive and cooperative interactions, has no more coherence than the others described above. (2) Its effects are great, potentially far more important than those of the foreground dramas provided by the prosecution of cases of alleged abuse, the battle over affirmative action for women, or the gender wars beloved of the media. (3) It was put in effect by conservative and liberal judges who thought they could derive it from their (conflicting) ideas about the natures of men and women, gays and straights, and naturalized as background through legal reasoning. (4) We should change it in the direction of radically egalitarian, anti-essentialist gender liberation.

But this is no more than a form. To give it content is to illustrate again that there is no general theorem of the legitimating effect of adjudication, only a series of historically specific examples. In this case, the crucial moves were those that allowed the extension of the labor law model to gender but in the process transformed the schema. The extension was difficult because there are many ways in which we conceive issues of gender law as arising in a context so different from that of labor law that they are irrelevant to one another.

To begin with, labor law is the place where the distributive focus, which frankly asks how law affects the division of the fruits of cooperation between participants, is most developed and has been most developed for the longest time. The law of gender, by contrast, seems mainly preoccupied with two quite different kinds of issues: first, with defining the limits of formal legal inequality between the sexes and, second, with the enforcement of norms thought of as unproblematic, like the prohibition of domestic violence.

In labor law, issues of formal inequality were worked out over the eighteenth and the first half of the nineteenth centuries,[35] so that the preoccupation of theorists of the field, whether Marxist, progressive, or conservative, was how to analyze and respond to the tendencies toward inequality within a regime of formally equally legal rights. The cls critique was, in a sense, third generation, following first the Liberal critique of formal labor hierarchy and, second, the liberal critique of the conservative version of equal rights for labor and capital.

Feminist reformers through the 1970s initially focused on completing the Liberal critique of de jure gender inequality. They had to work out a liberal feminist approach to issues like special treatment for women as child bearers within an only recently established regime of formal equality, and devise new practical remedies for male abuse of women. The radical feminist approaches to legal issues I am about to describe, like the post–civil rights movement race critiques, can be seen as responses to the realization that neither the establishment of formal legal equality, nor its fine tuning, nor supplementing it with affirmative action would "solve" the problem of gender oppression.

The competitive and cooperative relations between men and women occur in a variety of domains, each with its own sociology and its own set of legal background rules. There are the domestic sector, the "street," and the workplace, to name just three. The "stakes" in the domains are different—power over household decisions, the division of housework, and sexual conflict and cooperation differ markedly from competition for jobs and salaries in the marketplace. But power translates or transfers from one domain to another, as when the restriction of employment opportunities reduces women's bargaining power in the home.

The distributive conflicts between men and women are played out between individuals, rather than between legally structured organizations like labor unions, corporations, sovereign states, federal and local governments, and media "speakers." Far more than in economic relations between social classes, we habitually attribute what happens in these face-to-face interactions to "custom" and to the natures, or "identities," of men and women. The role of the state is close to invisible.

To my mind, the crucial moment in the development of feminist legal theory occurred when Catharine MacKinnon[36] and Frances Olsen[37] figured out how to overcome these obstacles to applying the critique of labor law to gender. They found two parallels. First, the distribution of income between labor and capital is mainly rationalized through the notion that distribution results from free bargains between workers who own their labor and capitalists who own the means of production. Likewise, the distribution of a million things between men and women is rationalized through the idea that men and women mutually consent to them on the basis of equal rights to property and bodily security.

Second, like the consent of workers, the consent of women takes place in the context of the relative bargaining resources of men and women, and this is crucially affected by what men and women can do to one another under the regime of tort and crime. The laws governing aggressions by men against women play a crucial role, because their weaknesses—both in legal definition and particularly in enforcement—radically disempower women, inducing them to enter bargains that are much worse than they would be if women were better protected against aggression.

There is a counterintuitive analogy here: law effectively protects the property of capitalists against worker attempts at appropriation, both in the gross sense of constitutionally protecting capitalism and at the micro-level of controlling what unions can do to employers in labor conflicts. The law is far less effective in protecting the bodily integrity of women against male assault, and women are consequently at a vast disadvantage in bargaining compared to what they would have in an alternative more pro-woman regime.

A clear focus on consent as induced in bargaining within these background rules is profoundly delegitimating because, as with the critique of freedom of contract in the labor area, it reveals that coercion is everywhere. It particularly affects the domain of heterosexual relations that Liberal culture celebrates as quintessential examples of human freedom. This is the importance of Andrea Dworkin's critique[38] of marriage and heterosexual intercourse as profoundly conditioned by the realities of rape, prostitution, the abuse of female children, and radical economic inequality. She refuses to treat sex as a domain to which the kind of critique of exploitation we make in the economic realm is irrelevant.

Both the role of bargaining against this background and the background legal regime itself are far less visible than in the labor law area, because of the widespread conceptualization of male-female interaction as "private." Olsen's critique[39] was that this notion has the double consequence of making law more invisible than it ought to be and of rationalizing an antiregulatory attitude on those occasions when the background is noticed and it seems plausible to modify it to favor women.

The trick here is analogous to, and a complex extension of, the way the public/private distinction has functioned in the labor area. First, just as the economy is private in relation to the state, the family is private in relation to the economy. Second, just as the privateness of the economy vis-à-vis the state justifies leaving worker-employer bargains to the outcomes conditioned by the invisible background rules, so the privateness of the family vis-à-vis the market justifies leaving male-female bargaining to the outcomes conditioned by the even less egalitarian background regime of gender law.

On the basis of this figure/ground reversal, combined with the legal realist/institutionalist analysis of the economy, the gender critique developed the notion that the legal regime constitutes the subjects who bargain and consent within it. The regime (along with myriad other cultural practices) creates them as people who will consent to the reproduction of inegalitarian relations that it seems merely to reflect.[40] Just as liberal labor law after the NLRA developed in directions that made workers passive, according to the cls critique, the actual administration of the background rules governing violence against women, and the property regime that keeps them economically weak, has the effect of forming them as characters who will accept and even embrace subordinate status. The rules push them to understand themselves to be heterosexual, monogamous, and maternal beings, as a consequence of the very nature of womanhood.[41]

With some notable exceptions, doctrinal analysis—the demonstration of the incoherence of legal conceptions like marriage, custody, and consent—plays a less important role in this critique than in that of labor law, international law, or First Amendment law.[42] I think it plausible that, as a matter of fact, the (mis)understanding of adjudication and legal correctness, the denial of the ideological in legal work, play less important roles in the reproduction of gender oppression than in other kinds of oppression. It was rather the critique of rights[43] (the subject of the next chapter) and of identity,[44] both important parallels to the critique of adjudication, that developed here with particular clarity, as did the technique of analyzing opinions as texts promoting or instantiating cultural conceptions.[45]

Just as important, by the time the various critical movements in law had extended the initial legitimation schema across all of these fields, it had become something like a critical technology, in the same way that the legal realist critique of conceptualism evolved into a critical technology in the 1930s. It is available for initiatives like Kimberle Crenshaw's "intersectional" analysis of the situation of women of color[46] and for queer legal theory,[47] and will continue to evolve if people continue to find uses for it.

The typical structure of cls-inspired policy proposals

The development of parallel critiques in field after field went along with the development of a large number of concrete proposals for judicial or legislative change in the particular legal rules that made up the structures we were critiquing. We were influenced (although not at all required) by our mode of critique to make policy proposals with a particular kind of structure. I would describe it as follows. Many cls proposals focused on changing the background rules so as to change the distribution of power, as a means to redistributing the good things of life. By contrast, the mainstream liberal emphasis tended to be more on regulating unequal relationships by the two techniques of prohibiting discrimination and requiring particular substantive contents.

Typical "empowering" as opposed to "regulating" solutions are the creation of limited equity cooperative housing,[48] liberalizing the battered woman's right of self-defense[49] and establishing a community-based shelter system,[50] changing labor law rules to promote worker self-organization, worker participation in management decisions, and worker ownership,[51] creating new tort remedies for sexual and racial harassment and hate speech[52] and for employer abuse in the workplace,[53] and modifying home rule to give inner cities a voice in suburban decision making.[54] But the line is not a clear one. In the many cases where the critics favored regulation, it was often, as in the case of the warranty of habitability,[55] with a view to the local, strategic use of new legal tools to pursue distributive ends.

Shifting power balances by changing background rules also fit well with the project, inherited from 1960s radicalism, of equalizing distribution among groups, conceived as crosscutting and intersectional, rather than of, say, guaranteeing equality of opportunity to individuals without regard to their race or class or gender. Typical policy proposals were "race conscious" or "gender conscious," or "class conscious," at the same time that there was a vigorous—ultimately perhaps a little too vigorous—internal debate about the concept of identity and its place in left and mpm theory.

The local focus and the scattered, unsystematic character of the policy proposals were partly the result of a basic difference between the crit networks and their progressive forebears. The post-1960s radicals had no expectation of exercising state power and were skeptical about the possibility of profound transformation of society from the center. Having a program, in the traditional left sense of the term, seemed far less crucial than it had to earlier generations with similar projects.

Cls versus progressive attitudes toward reconstruction

There were many other differences between the cls style of delegitimating critique of liberalism and the progressive-era style directed against conservatism. I've already mentioned the contrast between radical and liberal reformist political motivations, the different methodologies of internal critique, and the emphasis on the social construction of identity through law. Cls has been committed to appropriating whatever is useful in neo-Marxism, particularly its Gramscian strand, and aims to synthesize it with the progressive/realist tradition of legal analysis that had treated the more orthodox Marxism of its time as an "other." The various non-Marxist Continental European intellectual currents that influenced the progressives, from structuralism/poststructuralism through psychoanalysis, had evolved a long way in a generally irrationalist direction by the time the crits tapped into them.

But perhaps more striking than any of these is the contrast between the relatively unified progressive commitment to reconstruction by the application of pragmatism to law and the wild diversity of attitudes toward reconstruction within cls, within critical race theory, and within feminist legal theory. My summaries above suppressed these differences of substance, strategy, and tone. The remaining chapters of this book bring them to the fore.

II

Adjudication in Social Theory

This chapter attempts to clarify the particular critique of adjudication I have been developing by contrasting it with two others close enough to be called cousins. Since the 1960s, various American legal theorists have struggled with the question of how our peculiar national mode of criticizing law might allow us to make a contribution to social theory.[1] The approach I have been describing and those with which I will contrast it are attempts to figure out the consequences of legal realism for the grand tradition of Weber and Marx.

In the grand tradition, both Weber and Marx theorized modern society as an ordering according to intelligible abstract principles worked out in the details of institutional life. This ordering was not a natural development, in the sense of corresponding to natural laws of social life, but rather a complex product of particular ideas with particular dispositions of forces in conflict.

The state played an important role in both theories, in spite of the major difference between them, because it was the vehicle through which the participants in material and ideal clashes turned momentary victories into an enduring regime. Legal regulation, in turn, was an obviously important state function, because through it those who controlled the state could develop principles of public and private order, defined at an abstract level, into particularized norms governing daily interactions, and then make them practically effective through the administration of justice.

The grand tradition looks "formalist" to an American steeped in realism. It treats the bodies of legal rules characteristic of modern societies as possessing a high degree of internal coherence, as developments of the principles of the regime. In this respect, social theory parallels the American jurisprudential coherence theory that viral critics have been challenging since the turn of the century. And the grand tradition imagines legal regulation as institutionally effective in a manner belied by realist skepticism about the correspondence between the law in books and the law in action.

The grand tradition's alleged misappreciation of law seems important because law is such an important element in the tradition. But it is still an open question how the incorporation of one or another version of postrealism might alter the Weberian and Marxist theories. And it is another open question to what extent we can usefully deploy elements from those theories to explain judicial behavior and assess its effects, once judging is seen as underdetermined by logic and incoherent as policy.

The approach I've outlined, looked at as postrealist social theory, has three components: the distributivist analysis of the ideological stakes of formal law making, the notion that adjudication is a forum of ideology, and the theory of denied strategic behavior in legal interpretation. The moderation, empowerment, and legitimation effects of adjudication are supposed to be plausible consequences flowing from the combination of these elements in the context of an ideologically divided society.

What shall I call this theory? Not the "crit" theory, because although I tried in the last chapter to assimilate a large amount of crit work to it (and could have assimilated a lot more in similar fashion), there is no consensus on these issues, as we'll see in this chapter, among people who have identified themselves as crits. It is, likewise, only one among a number of possible left/modernist-postmodernist theories. I'll call it the "Pink Theory," or PT.

The PT developed in the face of and in continuous response to two critiques. The first, the "skeptic's critique," has been that the PT overestimates the social significance of appellate adjudication. The second, the "systematizer's critique," is that the PT underestimates its significance. Both skeptics and systematizers draw on elements from legal realism, empirical and functionalist sociology, neo-Marxism, American populism, critical theory, and other elements too numerous to figure out.

The skeptic's critique is that the Pink Theory overestimates the significance of appellate opinions, because the formal law they produce has little practical importance and their ideological productions have little audience. The systematizer's critique is that the theory underestimates the extent to which the specifics of judge-made formal law can be explained as responsive to and legitimating of either the needs of a market system or the structural requirements of particular stages of capitalist development.

According to the PT, a sophisticated analysis of the distributive effects of legal rules, along with the analysis of hypothetical phenomena like the moderation, empowerment, and legitimation effects of denied ideology in judicial law making, are about what one can hope for from a social theory of adjudication. In this chapter I defend this position against the skeptic's view that this is too much, through a description of the "mandarin materials controversy," and against the systematizer's view that it is too little, through a description of the "rationalism/irrationalism debate" in early critical legal studies.

The mandarin materials controversy

In the 1980s, American legal sociologists who had long since abandoned dispute-resolution functionalism had a biting critique of the cls preoccupation with appellate opinions and other "mandarin materials." This attack came first from older "law and society" mainstreamers, like Lawrence Friedman, and then from the Amherst Seminar, which loosely grouped left "law and society" people, left legal anthropologists, and sociologists working in the European critical tradition.

Both critiques had a strong tone of disciplinary ressentiment (even the sociological mainstreamers seemed emotionally invested in seeing themselves as marginal and disrespected both in legal academia and in academic sociology). The mainstreamers claimed that if you didn't do empirical research, and do it in something more recognizably "the field" than a law library, you certainly weren't a sociologist, or a "real" progressive, and most likely were engaged in reasserting the social power of "law professors" (sneer quotes) through Byzantine doctrinal discussions that we all know have nothing to do with what happens in the real world.

The leftists, by contrast, had neither a scientistic idea of the empirical nor a prejudice against the discursive in general. But they were very much in agreement that the sociology of law should focus on what happens in the field, defined as lower-level, "action-end" dispute resolution institutions. They also agreed with the mainstreamers that, as Susan Silbey put it,

> [s]ome contemporary critical legal scholars reflect this sort of idealism by attending exclusively to doctrinal analysis and ignoring material or behavioral substance in favor of a professional discourse which they treat as the entirety of law. In this way, many critical legal scholars confuse

the rationalizations and argumentation of appellate courts with legal practice . . .

Traditional formalist approaches and contemporary critical legal scholarship takes the law—cases, rules, statutes—as non-problematic, when they are just the opposite. The essence of recent law school trashing, as it is called, is to say, "Hey! You, judges?" (There is no attention to anyone but judges.) "You are not what you claimed to be or what we were taught you are. You are not consistent and inescapably logical. Now, we've got you, you are exposed for being the powerwielders that you are." By the 1980's, this portrait of legal indeterminacy is not a particularly original observation. The limits of doctrine and form were carefully delineated at the beginning of the twentieth century, albeit without the language of ideological hegemony, mystification and reification associated with critical legal studies.

. . . [T]he deconstruction of the rationalist claims of legal ideology has rested upon the discovery of logical incoherence and indeterminacy, encouraging critics to focus upon the minutia of the discourse, without reference or attention to its social construction (social determinacy). This kind of attention to the formal discourse, distinct from action and practice, obscures its connection to external social structures.[2]

A comradely paraphrase might be: *(a)* Legal sociology has demonstrated that the formal rules of law are not a description of the actual regularities of behavior that characterize a society, because there are major discontinuities between the formal rules and the way ground-level legal institutions and private parties apply (or ignore) the rules in practice. *(b)* We have known since the beginning of the twentieth century that the legal reasoning that purports to govern judicial rule making is indeterminate, in the sense of not governing it according to a logic. *(c)* Although legal reasoning does not determine judicial rule making, and formal rules do not determine legal practices, rule making and legal practices are both determined—by social structures external to the appellate adjudicative process. *(d)* Therefore you have been wasting your time studying appellate opinions.[3]

The law in books versus the law in action

My intention is to respond to "books/action" skepticism by confession and avoidance. It is true that the Pink Theory, in its analysis both of the ideological stakes disposed through rule making, and of the moderation, empowerment, and legitimation effects, depends on the notion that appellate adjudication makes a difference in the world beyond the dispute before the court. As I said in Chapter 3, we are interested in appellate adjudication because we see the judges as law makers, in the same way we see legislators and administrative officials as law makers. If it makes no difference (beyond the dispute in question) what law they make or how they explain it, then there are no interesting ideological stakes in the rules, and there is no possibility of legitimation through legal discourse.

I think realist and postrealist American sociologies of law have convincingly and usefully demonstrated that we cannot ever assume, when an appellate court chooses a particular rule interpretation over another, that the various people (not before the court) whose conduct the rule seeks to govern will behave in conformity with it. I would go further: they have also demonstrated that even when the parties conform their behavior to a legal rule, one or both parties often manages to alter some other aspect of the situation so that the rule fails to further the balance of policies the law maker had in mind in choosing it.[4] Thus the rules of constitutional law that judges chose to promote school desegregation have failed in many or most cases to achieve it, because of white flight.

Nevertheless, I don't think the sociologists have intended to suggest that the choice of rules, whether by legislators, administrators, or judges, has no effect on ideologized group conflict. It would be absurd to argue that judicial decisions about school desegregation were simply a dead letter, res nullius, something that might just as well not have happened as far as effects on American society are concerned.

Or take the transformation of American tort law in a strongly pro-plaintiff direction over the last fifty years. It would be wrong to think that judge-made changes in the legal rules have translated in a straightforward way into changes in corporate behavior, as cases like that of the exploding Pintos (not recalled because it was cheaper to pay off the victims) make clear. But it would be just as absurd here as in the school desegregation example to argue, against the evidence of furious corporate lobbying and advertising campaigns for "tort reform," that what the judges did made no difference, disposed no stakes in ideologized group conflict.

So what is going on? It is true that the Pink Theory has been concerned to show (though not empirically) that the rule choices of appellate judges are much more important than people think, and that the sociologists have been concerned to show that the rule choices of appellate judges are much less important than people think. Yet there may be no real conflict of views.

Remember that the Pink Theory is committed to the idea that judges dispose important stakes of ideologized group conflict through choices of interpretation of many different kinds of rules, ranging from the regulation of abortion to the regulation of truck weight on interstate highways. It makes no more sense to ignore them as rule makers, on the ground that particular rules they make don't get enforced, than it would to ignore the legislative process because the same is true of statutes.

The claim that the rules made by appellate courts are more rather than less important than people think is based on the idea that people often fail to advert, in ideological conflicts, to the ways legal rules function as rules of the game, more or less effectively but invisibly altering the outcomes from those that would occur if different rules were in force. The point is not that the rules are more widely effective on conduct than you would think. It is that the legal background rules, to whatever degree they may be effective, are habitually left out of our causal hypotheses about hierarchy and alienation—this is the whole point of the figure/ground reversals I described in the last chapter.

Perhaps the rub is there. If the sociologists were claiming that the rules are so thoroughly ineffective that they cannot be attributed causal force in constituting the relative bargaining power of competing groups, then they would be striking to the heart of the PT. But it turns out on closer examination that they never go that far, though their traditional rhetoric sometimes suggests they'd like to. Here, for example, is a summary of the enormously valuable work of the Wisconsin school on contract law in action:

> [The] focus on business behavior quickly reveals an important insight—that contract law doctrine worked out by appellate courts is insignificant in its impact for many reasons, among them: the sanctions provided by contract law are too weak to deter breach; weak or strong, damage sanctions are usually irrelevant because the value of continuing relationships or of good reputation leads to peaceful adjustment; even when relationships are over, the cost of litigation makes resort to law unlikely; and where significant interests conflict, regulation is almost never left to the common law, but rather administrative regimes are put in place (e.g. labor law or insurance). In sum, appellate contracts cases commonly involve "atypical or freak" transactions and "tag ends of problems nobody cares enough about to regulate in some other way."[5]

As a critique of the content of the typical law school course on contracts, this is pretty devastating. But it is in no way threatening to the PT. To begin with, when "significant interests conflict," that is, where we expect ideologized group conflict and where "administrative regimes are put in place," judges will constantly make decisions about those regimes that dispose ideological stakes. Indeed, I asserted in the last chapter that a major locus of the legitimation effect is the judicial oversight of labor law.

Second, even though "the cost of litigation makes resort to law unlikely," the rules often exert a large enough influence on bargaining, "in their shadow,"[6] so that the judges' choices among the possibilities dispose significant ideological stakes. Likewise, that people in long-term relationships feel intense pressure to settle their conflicts without litigation most definitely does not mean that law is irrelevant to the outcome. The entities that have the long-term relationships and settle disputes within them get their particular form under legal influence, and all the participants make calculations of their alternatives, in deciding what to settle for, about what they will be able to do if settlement proves impossible.[7]

Rather than tending to show that appellate adjudication in general is "insignificant in its impact," this research suggests, and is patently intended to suggest, a quite different but important critical conclusion. From the perspective of the law school contracts classroom, it might appear that contract law requires people to be fair to one another. But many judge-made rules of contract law that purport to give weak parties protections against strong parties turn out to be illusory in practice.[8] The point is not that appellate law is intrinsically ineffective, but that judges have chosen to make rules for weak parties that look better on paper than they do in practice.

Even a savvy student (and a fortiori a cloistered professor) might reach a quite wrong conclusion about how much strong parties can "get away with" in the real world, if he or she relied on appellate opinions. Worse, there are legal reforms that might bring the law in action much closer to the law in books, effectively restructuring power in favor of weaker parties. But the illusion that formal law has already taken care of the problem is a factor contributing to both judicial and legislative inaction.[9] Note that a similar point applies to legislatures, which not uncommonly pass statutes that seem on their face to give one interest or another a lot more than it will receive in practice.[10]

Like legislatures, appellate courts operate under the constraints imposed by the plausible limits of enforcement within the existing system. The New Jersey Supreme Court was no more able to simply impose its "fair-share" requirement for affordable housing in the suburbs than the U.S. Supreme Court was able to abolish the third degree by handing down the

Miranda decision. But, of course, the same is true of legislative regime changes. Looked at this way, the issue is not how important appellate decisions are in the abstract, but what we can say about the practical limits on the pursuit of ideological projects through courts as opposed to legislatures.

It seems to me plausible to pursue this inquiry on the premise that the fixing of the formal rules of the legal system, by courts and legislatures, disposes enormously important ideological stakes, and that adjudication as a forum plays a more diffuse but important role in the production of American ideologies. I do not propose this understanding as an analytic truth, but rather suggest it as an empirically ungrounded empirical generalization about the developed West, and only about the developed West.

My sense that it is right probably owes a lot to the sociological tradition (Marx and Weber) that emphasizes the general importance of the state in imposing a social order that has an intelligible form (not, for us latecomers, a logic). And it owes a lot to Antonio Gramsci's theory of hegemony, which insists that elites generate consent through discourse (the forum idea), as well as imposing it by force. *But* "law is not a one-way projection of authority," as Lon Fuller liked to put it.[11] And Foucault is right that power, including power exercised through law, has meaning only to the extent that there is resistance and gets its practical content from the resistance as well as from "above."[12]

These qualifications are important. A left/mpm program for the transformation of society would have aims that could not be simply imposed by law. First, the ability of the state qua state, the state without "legitimacy," to coerce obedience is obviously limited. Second, much of the behavior a left/mpm program would like to change is so fine-grained, so much involved with "attitudes" and spiritual orientations to action, that it couldn't possibly be mandated in all its detail from above.

If it could, and people just obeyed a totalitarian code, the program would have failed for the reason that the program aims at conversion to a kind of antinomianism, rather than at obedience to correct thought. "The letter killeth . . ." is not an entailment of postmodernism (there are none), but it is a core maxim of left/mpm. A second core maxim is that we study state power to resist it, not to seize it.

Is there an audience in the forum?

Theories of adjudication as a forum of denied ideological conflict have to make it at least plausible that there is some audience for the ideological productions of the participants beyond the parties to the case. This is by no means self-evident, as has been forcefully pointed out in another branch of the skeptic's critique, typified by these quotations from Alan Hyde and from Frank Munger and Carol Seron:

> [O]ne review of the literature on public opinion concluded: "there is supporting evidence for the view that the Supreme Court and its decisions have such low salience as to render improbable popular acceptance of governmental action because of public knowledge that policies have been approved by the justices." Less than half the population can name a single Supreme Court policy or decision they liked or disliked. Less than half the population can select as many as three correct topics from a list of eight possible *areas* in which the Supreme Court might have made a decision. The Supreme Court appears to be the *least* visible institution in the political socialization of American children. Other studies continually show low public awareness of the Supreme Court and even less awareness of the substance of its decisions. The same story could be told about lower courts.[13]

> Underlying [cls] research is an implicit premise: tracing, or mapping, legal decisions will, in and of itself, reveal the ideological role of law, as well as its incoherence. The absence of a serious attempt to examine the relationship between doctrine and other institutions in society insures that this research will fall short of its own goals. Failure to make a creditable case for the ideological role of law in its historical context prevents the Conference from maintaining that law potentially has *any* part to play in transforming society. More important, the Conference cannot creditably rebut assertions made by liberal scholars that it is not class dominated, not repressive, and instead is a rationalizing force (whether or not its doctrine is troubled by logical inconsistency).[14]

Most of the "early" crits claimed only that legal discourse was "effective" for the legal intelligentsia itself, and for the broader educated elite that takes legal discourse seriously.[15] This limited claim seemed plausible to us because we had recently been law students struggling against the puzzlingly seductive influence of the elite understanding. In this respect, we adopted more a Gramscian[16] or Althusserian[17] than a Weberian[18] approach, treating appellate courts as an "ideological state apparatus" that produces one of a plethora of legitimating discourses, such as those of the educational system and the media, each with a different audience and different subject matters.[19]

The Pink Theory can therefore embrace skepticism about the size of the audience for appellate opinions, and agree that for some audiences, for example for people of color, as Kimberle Crenshaw argued,[20] the law may be first and foremost the deployment of state force (empirical studies awaited), while the content of the discourse may be of little or no persuasive importance. This insight doesn't make the moderation effect, for example—the hypothetical reduction of the ability of ideologically organized majorities to bring about significant regime change through the legislative process—less plausible.

The effect depends on the idea that difference splitting, bipolar, and hostile activist judges have enormous interstitial power to "cool out" the legislature's regime-changing abstractions, through interpretation. The effect occurs within the elite group that legislates and judges. It is a consequence of their understandings and arrangements, not of those of the people they govern.

The same is true of the empowerment effect. Denied ideology in judicial law making means that fractions of ideological intelligentsias, and each intelligentsia as a whole, can get things through the judicial process that they imagine they couldn't get through electoral politics. Liberals get Brown v. Board of Education; conservatives get a cutback of affirmative action. If we had both legislative supremacy (no judicial review) and a consistent practice of legislative oversight of judicial rule making, the result, according to the hypothesis, would be outcomes less favorable to the fractions, and perhaps outcomes fulfilling the intelligentsias' symmetrically opposed fears of the masses. The empowerment effect appears to be part of the complex game through which political elites distribute power and vetoes on power among themselves. It can operate regardless of what, if anything, the masses know of appellate opinions.

One might even speculate that in so much as moderation and empowerment effects favor the interests of moderate liberal and conservative elites at the expense of masses, they work better when the masses remain in blissful ignorance of government by judiciary. In this interpretation, the "backgrounding" of judicial law making, its invisibility for the masses, stabilizes the system, as long as the formal law that appellate courts make achieves a modicum of impact on conduct, through criminal enforcement and private civil actions in lower courts and through obedience and conversion effects.

But don't legitimation effects, at least, depend directly on the existence of an audience for appellate opinions outside the legal/political intelligentsia? I defined a legitimation effect as the reinforcement of the status quo by the "withdrawal" of judge-made rules from political consciousness. The consequence is that there seem to be fewer, and more costly, vehicles available for social change than is "really" the case. In the many contexts in which legal rules function as rules of the game of cooperation and conflict between groups (in the contexts of labor and gender, for example), judicial opinions help to naturalize or "background" them. The opinions claim (falsely) to produce the rules through a technical, nonideological method of judicial decision. (The effectiveness of these texts depends on the audience's active participation in the denial of ideology in adjudication, its wishful thinking.)

In both versions of delegitimation—the liberals against the conservatives up to the New Deal, and cls radicals against the liberals in the late 1970s and early 1980s—the point was to bring about a figure/ground reversal. Its elements were the analysis of the distributive effects of the rules and the exposure of the element of denied ideology in the judicial opinions that established them. In each case, the delegitimaters were trying to provide a pragmatic and also an ethical basis for a politics of mobilization. But, in each case, the context was political debate between and within intelligentsias looking to increase their own understanding of their situation and to convert waverers from opposed groups.

We crits didn't claim that judges passivized the masses through appellate opinions. The idea was that the denial of the ideological element in appellate law making, both in general and in many particular fields, led liberals to underestimate the possibilities for changes they claimed to favor or, alternatively, helped them rationalize their unwillingness to do anything that would really upset the status quo. The hope was that the delegitimating analysis might win us some converts from among them and might help in formulating radical strategies. We weren't so dumb as to think that our delegitimating efforts would lead to change in mass consciousness, except, just maybe, in the very long run, through the complex processes by which elite ideas interact with popular ideas in a mass culture.

It is not that law, in the sense of legal rules, has no impact on the masses. All versions of the legitimation thesis assert that the rules have more, not less, distributive impact on real life than people realize. The "advanced" versions of the thesis, whether in labor law, international law, local government law or the law of gender, also assert that the rules have "subject-forming" properties. Workers in the regime of industrial pluralism are made passive by the legally defined structures within which they work (not by appellate legal discourse); women are pushed toward acquiescence in patriarchal roles by the large elements of violence against them tolerated by the legal system. These impacts are independent of legal discourse.[21]

If there is a mass legitimation effect, it might be because the media propagate a popular understanding of judging that denies its ideological content. And perhaps this error makes the status quo seem more natural, less contingent, and more just than it really is. But it seems equally plausible that mass culture steadfastly resists the elite (mis)understanding, even generates its own alternatives, based on real life experience with the criminal justice system or with local courts as local dispute resolvers.[22] This seems to me an interesting empirical question the answer to which won't affect the plausibility of the version of the legitimation effect in the Pink Theory. In that version, the denial of ideology in adjudication mainly affects intelligentsias, and others only through them.

Everybody knows that legal reasoning is indeterminate

We study appellate opinions because appellate judges are major law makers in our society, on a par with legislators. We also study them in particular because, following the hypothesis of alienated powers, their law making is characterized, as that of legislatures is not, by a particular form of denial—the denial that they are legislators.

For Silbey, "the limits of doctrine and form were carefully delineated at the beginning of the twentieth century." For us, on the contrary, it was not at all obvious (and still isn't) how legal discourse manages to produce the "effect of necessity" that allows the denial of ideological content. We ourselves were not sure just how "formalism" was wrong, or that it was dead; we were sure that law was political but not about how it was political. The critical part of the legal realist project seemed aborted, rather than something finished we should move on from. It seemed more important to revive it, and keep at it, than to work at "proving" that the United States is a society in which elite legal materials are relevant to political and popular consciousness.

The problem was and is that the judges' claim of impartiality is partially true, because judges are supposed to, and to a large extent do, behave differently from legislators in choosing what rules should apply to cases. Judges are, to a significant extent, practically "bound" by law and often, often, often declare and apply rules that they would never vote for if they were legislators. Judges sometimes behave in ways well described as "consistent" and "logical," meaning obedient to a role constraint that requires them to apply rather than make law.

For this reason, it is simply fantasy to believe that the limits of doctrine and form were carefully delineated at the beginning of the twentieth century. It proved then and still proves difficult, to say the least, to figure out in just what respect, and with what consequences, any particular instance of judicial rule making is more than mere "reasoned elaboration." The answer proposed in the preceding chapters of this book is no more than an incomplete and often (to my own eye) only loosely plausible account.

The fantasy that someone has, or that one might oneself, figure out once and for all the indeterminacy critique of legal reasoning is shared well beyond the milieu of American sociologists of law who think they understand legal realism. Many cls writers and even more numerous commentators on cls have thought that discovering such a critique was central to the cls project.[23] In the latter days of cls, postmodernist crits sometimes thought they knew, without ever reading a judicial opinion that, "law" just "had to be" indeterminate, because deconstruction had "proved" that all texts are indeterminate.

This is Golden Bowlism, the belief that a given formal discourse will shatter if only one can find *the* crucial pressure point, as a flawed crystal (according to Henry James) will split if dropped in just the right way. Once you've "done" critique, by recognizing the wrongness of legal formalism in one of its manifestations, you've recognized its wrongness in all its manifestations. You should then move on to "constructive" work. I think Tom Heller was closer to the truth of the matter when he argued that structuring and critiquing are interminable activities.[24]

No critique is ever truly global. When someone thinks up a new argument, you need a new answer. Hohfeld's critique of the derivation of rights from privileges exposed a specific "Hohfeldian error" that appeared in some dozens of late-nineteenth-century legal opinions.[25] It was a "motivated error," because it made the choice of right-wing legal rules look like legal logic rather than like legislation. But though Hohfeld's critique is permanently helpful, it does not in itself identify, let alone successfully expose, the errors in Richard Posner's economic rationale for the legal rules that establish private property in the means of production.

In *Knowledge and Politics*,[26] for example, Roberto Unger essays a global critique of judicial neutrality, arguing that once we realize that the meanings of the words that compose legal rules can be determined in practice only through a value-laden interpretive process, we have to abandon the formalist vision. But it seems to me an adequate answer to this that we can and sometimes do formulate rules to minimize the need for value judgments in applying them to facts, and that language can often be made concrete enough so that disagreement will be rare.[27]

There is no single principle or metaprinciple, at least as far as I can see, that links together all the different kinds of argument that we want to call "formalist," except that they all fall to internal critique. And there is no general principle, as far as I can see, that links together all the different strategies of internal critique into a single supercritical unity. So there is no guarantee, as far as I can see, either that there will or won't be a critique available for every assertion of legal necessity.

This means that even if it were true, which it isn't, that the limits of doctrine and form were carefully delineated at the beginning of the twentieth century, that accomplishment would represent nothing more than a model for what critics need to do at the beginning of the twenty-first century. (I believe that this is a rough paraphrase of a passage somewhere in the *Grundrisse* about the critique of political economy, but I just can't seem to find it.)

External determination

Now to the third element in Silbey's critique: external determination. If you think you have discovered that legal reasoning on the basis of a set of legal materials is always indeterminate, it is likely, if you are a social scientist or a political philosopher, that you will also think that "the law" is determined by something else, something "outside" the reasoning process.

If the judges are wrong in their claims that their reasoning process and the preexisting materials determine the rules, you might search for determination "above" or "below" them. If you are going "above," you might be interested in normative or descriptive determination. Many people believe that the law ought to be determined by the prelegal rights of the people it governs, with the judges in the role of translating the external, superior, determinate order of rights into the socially effective medium of legal rules.[28]

The internal indeterminacy of legal reasoning is no cause for concern here, except that it creates opportunities for judges to mislead us about or mistake the external order of rights, and then dress up their false conclusions as required by their illusory procedures. Nor is it cause for concern for those law and economics scholars who think efficiency should be the sole normative criterion in decisions about what legal rules to put in force. Richard Posner can sharply reject the claim that legal reasoning autonomously determines judicial rule making in "hard cases" because he believes that economic reasoning about the efficiency consequences of rules can and should take its place.[29]

The kind of external determination that was popular with the Amherst Seminar at the time Silbey wrote her critique was descriptive rather than normative, and from below. The notion was that while formal legal reasoning is indeterminate, the ensemble of patterns of official behavior that influence the actual patterns of social behavior is not. The key to getting some determinacy at the level of the law in action was to introduce concepts like "culture" and "practice" and, of course, to study what was "really" going on at the "action end" of law.

Austin Sarat has suggested a conceptual framework for this kind of effort:

> Statutes and court decisions are not abstractly stated goals which could ever govern legal or social behavior . . . This does not mean that judicial decisions can't be examined as an influence on, let's say, police arrest activities. Such a study would, however, ask how does one practice influence another rather than why does one depart from the other. Moreover, such an approach allows us to investigate the extent to which the variety of legal practices comprise a coherent whole. Here, the sociology of law may embrace the early concerns of critical legal studies at the same time that it insists on the importance of examining legal practice in the courthouse, the police station and the lawyer's office.[30]

These more proletarian, multi-"voiced," from-the-bottom-up-analyses were supposed to preserve the social theoretical ideal of determination while purging it of "idealism" and concomitant elite focus. In the European context, in the form of the theory of "legal pluralism," they also make possible a challenge to the combination of extreme positivism, formalism, and focus on national state actors that have characterized the civil law tradition.[31] But neither the American nor the European version has yet developed into a general theory that could rival the dominant left mode of arguing descriptive external determination from above.

This mode proposes descriptive external determination from above by the interests of particular social classes, or by the needs or the necessary structure of a market economy or a phase of capitalist economic development. Here the indeterminacy of legal reasoning is remedied by the determinacy of the "big picture," which judges are translating into law all the time they are pretending to be following their autonomous, internally determined reasoning procedures. This approach is the subject of the next section.

The Pink Theory differs from all the variants of external determination that I am aware of in three respects. First, it does *not* assert that "law" "is" globally indeterminate, but only that sometimes judges do legal work on the legal materials in pursuance of strategies that are well understood as ideological projects, and that this work often inflects outcomes in ways that dispose high ideological stakes. Second, the accumulation of such choices over time produces distributive outcomes radically different from those that would have been produced by a different series of judicial choices under conditions of (local) indeterminacy. Third, it seems a plausible hypothesis that the making of this law through adjudication, with concomitant denial of ideological influence, generates moderation, empowerment, and legitimation effects (all mediated by the vagaries of enforcement and the inattentiveness of the audience).

I propose this model in part for political reasons: as a leftist, I am interested in questions of distributive justice between groups. I think the actual distribution is unfair, whereas many think it fair or unfair in ways that can be remedied only by greater unfairness. This analysis is supposed to show that the current unfairness is in part produced through judicial rule making that was neither just "law application" nor a rational response to the needs or structure of the economy. If we changed the rules by making choices different from the ones the judges have made, maybe we could achieve greater distributive justice among groups without the dire consequences that we fear from measures like revolution or gigantic tax-and-spend programs.

Thus the PT emerged both from a critique of legal reasoning *and* from a critique of the notion that there is an external, determinable logic of the economy, its needs or functions or stages, that could plausibly explain judicial rule making once we abandon belief that judges are constrained by the norm of coherence. There are two important points here. In the rationalism/irrationalism debate, we used minimalist internal critique to undermine the systematizer's notion of the logic of the economic base. In doing so, we were trying to use American postrealist legal technique to contribute (albeit destructively) to the grand sociological tradition. At the same time, we adapted from neo-Marxism a much chastened (and, we hoped, much improved) version of the notion that legal reasoning performs legitimating functions, the version presented in the last chapter. The rest of this chapter elaborates this complex relation between the Pink Theory and Marxism.

The rationalism/irrationalism debate

In the "rationalism/irrationalism debate" in cls in the late 1970s and early 1980s, the systematizers argued that we could put the notion of legal indeterminacy to work to buttress systemic analysis of the role of law in capitalism. The "irrationalists" (left/mpm types) countered by deploying the minimalist internal critique of legal reasoning in the "viral" direction, arguing that far from supporting the systemic analysis, it decisively undermined it.[32]

I would put the leftist goals of the critique of adjudication, shared by systemic and left/mpm types, this way: to reveal the large role played by the legal system; to delegitimate the outcomes achieved through the legal system by exposing them as political when they masquerade as neutral; to show that they are in some sense unjust and that their injustice contributes to the larger injustice of the society as a whole; to be, thereby, a radicalizing force on those who read and accept the analysis; and to suggest ways that a radicalizing project should approach the task of making the system less unjust through political action.

The cls "science project" worked to show that really understanding leads in all these directions, within the general framework of the model of alienated powers developed by Feuerbach and Marx. The three parts of that model were to show (a) falseness of the theory that conventionally explains why things are the way they are, (b) sub rosa determination by something else, (c) the need to change to a new mode of determination through human agency according to a correct moral theory.

Systematizers and irrationalists collaborated on the first of these operations through the development and radicalization of legal realism. We attacked the false appearance of necessity by minimalist internal or (to my mind mistaken) global critique. We attempted to show that legal rules played a much larger role than generally supposed in producing the hierarchical, alienated world of our capitalism, and that these legal rules reflected ideological projects, or at least particular, contingent social visions, rather than an inner logic of law.

The second part of the science project involved developing theories of what really happens, and why, that bring to light both human agency and injustice, and showing that they can be causally attributed to "the system."

The notion went something like this: "We have this system as a matter of fact (of science). Having this system necessarily (because of science) requires that you have these conditions that according to our (nonscientific ethical system) are injustices. This knowledge is nonideological."

It was here that disagreement arose. Systematizers argued, plausibly, that the content and evolution of the legal system were in some sense responsive to the content and evolution of "society," so that law could be understood as a dependent variable. They also argued, plausibly, that the legal system performed a "function" in the social system, contributing to its content and evolution as well as reflecting it.

In the late 1970s, there were many extant versions of system among which to choose, including neo-Marxism, Weber's theory of law in capitalism, Parsonian structural/functionalism, and Habermas's theory of communicative action. Perhaps the single most common attitude was "post" in relation to these quite elaborated theories, but influenced by all of them. It seemed obvious that American society had gone through a series of stages, from an agrarian, supposedly individualistic, yeoman society, through industrialization, urbanization, and class stratification, toward a highly "interdependent" welfare capitalism dominated by large corporations and state bureaucracies. It seemed plausible that the legal system had responded to different needs and performed different functions in each period.[33]

The rationalism/irrationalism debate was about whether this intuition could be supported through legal scholarship. It focused on a particular version of system, what I will call the "neo-Marxist theory of law in capitalism," not because the participants were Marxists (a few had been), but because this theory seemed the most coherent and the most leftist. The critique applied a fortiori to the weaker versions of the needs and functions thesis, which I will describe in a moment.

A neo-Marxist social theory of law

A neo-Marxist social theory of law might go something like this. "We have a capitalist economic system. The capitalist system is based on private property in the means of production. If you don't have private property in the means of production, you don't have capitalism. If you have such a system, then it follows that you will have the following kinds of injustice and misery. These things are implicit in the system. They are therefore implicit in private property in the means of production.

"The role of judges is to enforce and interpret the laws that instantiate the general concept of ownership of the means of production. They are part of the system. They are not a 'necessary' part but merely 'superstructural,' because even if there were no state apparatus and no rule of law, the capitalists could maintain control through the use of force within the base, or 'relations of production.' That is, they could coerce workers to accept the system through nonlegal means.

"But if judges did otherwise than interpret and enforce the rules that flow from the general concept of ownership, and got away with it, thereby changing fundamental relations between workers and owners, then we would have something different from capitalism. As long as they enforce these rules, we have capitalism and its attendant injustices.

"The rule of (capitalist) law is supremely *helpful* even if merely superstructural. Along with their administrative work of putting the system in operation at the practical level, judges produce an extensive legitimating discourse that is part of the ideology that pacifies people. Liberal legal theory dovetails with Liberal economic theory in representing the unjust outcomes of economic interaction as the consequence of 'free bargaining' among property owners (workers own their labor) whose factor endowments have different 'natural' values based on their social contributions. Judges form one of the ideological state apparatuses.

"Sure, some measure of marginal reform through the legal system is possible. There may be marginal gaps, conflicts, and ambiguities in the concept of property. And in order to maintain the plausibility of the ideological claim that (capitalist) law is neutral between social classes, judges will follow it against their class interests in some cases. For these two reasons, it is sometimes possible for the working class to win victories through the legal system. The legal system is 'relatively autonomous,' determined by the base only in the 'final instance,' and it is even possible to regard the rule of law as a 'universal human accomplishment.'

"But when it comes to the fundamental rules of the game, which are what guarantee the fundamental interests of the capitalist class, then the law itself is committed to capitalism. To change the basic legal rules of capitalism, the judges would have to go against the 'system' that protects their own class interests. But they would also have to go against the law itself, against their own oaths as judges."

In the fanciest form of this kind of theory, there is legal indeterminacy in the sense of social construction, but only at the abstract level: the commodity form and the legal form are homologous or identical or mutually syntonic. Once we have the legal form (of the commodity), the specific rules of the legal system put capitalism into effect according to a determinate logic of the commodity.[34]

According to the theory, what is wrong with the system (injustice and misery) is a consequence of a basic, pervasive structure of the system, namely, its commitment to private property. Liberal reformism offers mere Band-Aids, overestimating what can be done with its moderate methods, while at the same time understating how bad things are. The positive social theoretical analysis is therefore leftist in the sense that it argues that only "radical" change can get us where "we" want to go. The only way to bring about "real" systemic change would be to have a system based on a different concept, and that requires the rulership of a different class.

The role of indeterminacy in the neo-Marxist theory of law

The critique of legal reasoning, whether in its legal realist or its cls version, at first seems to fit into this project, indeed to contribute mightily to it. It does so by extending the "false-necessity" critique of the "laws of economics" to the rules of the legal system. This extension makes it possible to incorporate a logic of legal change into the story of capitalism. If law is indeterminate *in its details,* as well as at the level of the choice of an abstract form, we can do a political analysis of judging and of the vast private law domain left to judges (on the Continent, left to "legal scientists").

Judicial law making practice can be fitted into the general left political analysis by making judges part of the strategic elite, furthering class interests or working out the logic of the system, rather than merely administering ("applying") capitalist legal concepts. We can interpret this work as that of constantly adjusting the whole corpus of specific legal rules to fit the interests of dominant classes in the successive stages of competitive and monopoly capitalist development. Competitive market capitalism has one set of legal needs, but monopoly capitalism has another. Judges make the needed changes through strategic manipulation of indeterminacy while maintaining the illusion of legal compulsion.

There is no necessary tension between the more "instrumental" and the more "structural" theories. Each stage (structure) might produce and be produced by a capitalist class whose instrumental interests correspond to that stage's development. The class will then appoint judges who choose, among the possible meanings of an indeterminate legal corpus, those meanings (rules) that will promote the development of the stage and its dominant class.

De-Marxifying the analysis

This flexible version of capitalist economic development brought the neo-Marxist theory into surprising convergence with the liberal mainstream. Indeed, an analysis structurally similar to this one underlay just about all of the sociology of law, as it developed after World War II, at least to the extent that it was influenced by legal realism and had social theoretical ambitions (as opposed to strictly positivist, empirical, behaviorist, or number-crunching ones).

There was an apologetic version, which had the same stages but no notion that capitalism was defined by "relation to the means of production." This version employed the logic of economic growth, rather than of capital accumulation; it was steered by democratically chosen policy makers who were more or less wise about the public interest, rather than by the ruling class. The outcome was a prosperous open society with some serious problems, rather than exploitation.[35]

In between, came the progressive historians' version, derived from Charles and Mary Beard and Vernon Parrington, with a soupçon of Marxism and a large dose of legal realist nihilism. In this version, law had exactly the same functions and served exactly the same needs as in the other two theories, but there was much more emphasis on the way elites manipulated the process to serve their own interests than in the apologetic version, and much less interest in the analytic systematicity of the process than in the neo-Marxist version.[36]

The role of the critique of adjudication in all of these approaches is strictly limited: it is to loosen law up just enough so that it can be the instrument of a developing rather than a static capitalist system. It is made pliable, or internally contradictory, or fluid, but only just enough for something outside it to give it new shapes through time.

The initial form of cls (as opposed to legal realist) internal critique, the mode of "contradiction," fit this role particularly well, though it is important that those of us who developed it were hostile[37] or ambivalent[38] toward the base/superstructure analysis of the neo-Marxists. We showed that there were two "models" or "visions" or "forms of consciousness" that could be teased out of the mass of legal materials in a given doctrinal area.[39] This innovation lent itself to cls theoretical developments with only analogical ties to the neo-Marxist analysis.

There were different versions of the internal structure of doctrine in different fields, but the point was that fields had internal structure. One use of the conflicting elements was as building blocks to which you could hook up antagonistic class interests, in the neo-Marxist theory or in some softer version. But there were other axes of conflict, as well, race and gender conflict, for example, and other types of theory, theories of patriarchy or of racial domination, for example, to which they might be hitched.[40] At the same time, one could interpret doctrinal development at a much lower level of abstraction as the playing out of conflict between specific groups within the elites, or between conflicting normative orientations much more specific or more "philosophical" than that between capitalism and socialism.[41]

This was easy to understand as left analysis. On the model of traditional ideology-critique, determination by law's autonomous force or by democratic legislative will—or the derivation of law from a few universally accepted ideals or natural rights—is revealed as mystification. Determination by something at once more human and less savory is revealed. And there is an explicit or implicit appeal to "people" to take advantage of this revelation of freedom and oppression to change things for the better.

The irrationalist critique

The rationalism/irrationalism debate in critical legal studies was about whether the exposure, first, of law's powerful distributive effect and, second, of the simultaneously structured and plastic character of legal reasoning, could be put to the uses of left theory at a more ambitious level. The issue was *not* whether the discourse was structured and influential; that was common ground. It was not whether it was useful in understanding doctrinal change to see it as the working out of conflicting political, economic, social, and purely ideal ethical projects; that was common ground. And it was not whether the judges and doctrinal writers who "froze" these projects into positive law, understood to have a nonideological origin, had the political effect of bolstering the status quo.[42] That too was common ground, though with disagreement over how important the legitimating effects really were.[43]

The disagreement was over whether there was a higher level of abstraction at which one could understand all of this in terms of the system, its "logic," its stages, its structure (as opposed to the lower-level structures of doctrine), its needs, and "the" function of law within it. The issue was the "actual" (as opposed to mystified) link between law and economy, the second step in traditional ideology-critique. The stakes concerned whether an internally structured, but plastic, legal regime was determined in some sense by the economy, or some other social system, such as patriarchy or racial supremacy. For these purposes, progressive historians, post-neo-Marxists, some critical race theorists, and some feminist theorists of patriarchy constituted a coalition of systematizers.

The irrationalists simply abandoned—walked away from—the claim that the models or visions or forms of consciousness that coexist or succeed each other in legal thought are linked to changes in the economy or the society in any readily intelligible way.[44] The internal structures of the models and their sequencing were asserted to be good descriptions of reality, but only of the reality of textual structure. The link with extant stage theories was problematized, and no new theory was proposed in their place. The historical drama became that of the "death of reason," or the loss of faith, first in law's autonomous rationality, and second in the economy's autonomous rationality, played out in the arena of group conflict with local stakes, rather than the drama of capitalist development.[45]

There were three different critiques of the systematizers' left project that justified the abandonment of the stronger claim. Note that two of these are classic examples of minimalist internal critique, applied now not to legal reasoning but to the notion of a logic of the relations of production. The third was analogous to the "incompleteness" mode of legal critique: "I can write an opinion on the losing side that is just as plausible as yours for the majority."

The first internal critique was of the base/superstructure distinction. The definition of the economic formation that supposedly determined the "legal needs of capitalism" that the judges fulfilled through manipulation included the very legal terms (property, labor, contract, commodity, wage) that the judges were interpreting in the course of making new legal rules. Each alternative legal definition of property, contract, commodity, and so forth, therefore meant a different definition of the base. It would be reasoning in a circle to define the base in terms of the legal rules that supposedly met its needs.[46]

This idea of law as "constitutive"[47] was, mutatis mutandis, just as threatening to progressive functionalist accounts as to the neo-Marxist ones, although none of the former would have been caught dead making a base/superstructure distinction. The needs and functions they attributed to society and to law, respectively, were hopelessly vague rather than hopelessly specific. If one took the needs and functions seriously, it appeared that there were many legal regimes that might have done the job. These regimes would have produced wildly different distributive outcomes and indeed wildly different economies.[48]

The second internal critique was of the distinction between capitalist and socialist law. Once it is acknowledged that legal rules define the "base," we can ask about the "logic" of these rules. (1) Hohfeld's analysis shows that "property is just a bundle of rights," with no "core"; there are an infinite variety of particular private law regimes each of which will produce a different allocation of resources and distribution of income, all fully consistent with any coherent definition of private property.[49] (2) Socialism, in the form of collectivist, altruist, egalitarian values, is already present in the capitalist legal system, and just as much within the supposedly Liberal individualist core of private law doctrine as in the social democratic regulatory add-ons.[50]

(3) Modern mixed capitalist legal regimes have no overall system logic: each is an internally inconsistent hodgepodge of "social" and "individual" elements with conflicting valences.[51] This was also true of communist regimes, which couldn't operate the vague abstraction "state ownership of the means of production" without elaborating internal rules of decentralization that functioned the way the law of the commodity functions in capitalism.[52] (4) Rather than a distinction between reform and revolution, there is a mushy continuum between collectivism and anarchism, hierarchy and equality. There aren't even any privileges among places to struggle ("bourgeois dinner parties are sites of resistance," and so on).[53]

The third critical move was to argue that the proponents of a (rationalist) left legal theory, whether in the neo-Marxist or the progressive historical mode, couldn't produce a logic of economic development that was any more than an ex post description of the consequences of particular ruling-class legal strategies. Is there a way of using the insight that different possible legal rules lead to different economic outcomes, to show that a given legal regime promotes capital accumulation (economic growth, production), or some set of class interests?

Since the systematizers didn't have much in the way of an actual theory of the logic of capital, or the needs of monopoly capital, or whatever (I say this respectfully—after all, we irrationalists didn't have one either), a good part of the debate took place in the critique of efficiency theory, a closely analogous but right-wing form. The critical line was that efficiency, as defined by economists, just doesn't produce clear answers to the question what rules will maximize consumer welfare, let alone a dynamic theory of welfare over time.[54]

It followed that the left-wingers couldn't employ the concept of a "subsidy" through legal rules to organize a theory about how a "dominant class" can use the legal system to promote its interests, or economic growth, or capital accumulation. The problem was the absence of a neutral economic baseline (which would replace a now impossible neutral legal baseline). There was no point from which to measure the subsidy.

It might be true that the actual legal actors involved all *believed* that a particular rule or rule change was necessary (or just desirable) to protect class interest or the accumulation process. And it was often possible to show plausibly and concretely how particular interests might gain or lose from a particular rule choice.[55] But the extant attempts to demonstrate the connection between legal and economic variables at the much more abstract level of "capitalism" or economic growth were either no good internally (see the critique of cost-benefit analysis), ignored counterinstances (where the wrong class adopted the legal program in question, or the right class adopted the wrong legal program), or were open to the formulation of an equally plausible but ignored counterstory (in which the economic effects of legal change were plausibly predicted to be just the reverse of those asserted).[56] All the systematizers could show was ruling-class strategies, adopted under conditions of practical and analytic uncertainty, justified by phony appeals to economics, and then critiqued by the left using equally phony but politically opposite appeals to economics.

As in the critique of legal reasoning, the strictly internal critique was different from the "incompleteness" critique that showed that you could construct alternative, equally plausible arguments for opposite results. "Yeah, but that rule change might have *hurt* the ruling class; that rule might have *impeded* capital formation, indeed probably actually did hurt and impede, for all you can show, given this alternative version of the facts."

This kind of argument, as we saw in Chapter 4, is less logically tight than strictly internal critique. It leaves the field open to determined showings that in fact the effects were indeed x or y, and to endless attempts to qualify the systematizers' claim just enough to meet the critique without losing all scientific power (see the debate about "tilt" as a substitute for the "logic of capital").[57] There's no way to prove that someone won't soon come up with a totalizing theory that works.

But until someone does comes up with one, the Pink Theory rejects (walks away from, "parks") the whole model of an internally indeterminate legal discourse determined by external facts or structures (the needs or stages of the economy). This is one of the postmodern elements in the PT, though it's odd to call it that, because it was present before any of us had heard of postmodernism.

Be it noted that giving up on the idea of a base whose structure determines legal rules does not mean giving up on establishing a connection between legal rules and their social, economic, and political context. When we find that the discourse of legal justification is internally contradictory in ways that *sometimes* render it plastic, open to ideologically oriented legal work, we try to increase our understanding by "going deeper" (just as the systematizers do), by appealing to ideology, in the vulgar sense of liberalism and conservatism. Isn't this the same old model of outside determination? No, it is not, for reasons already elaborately canvassed:

(a) Liberalism and conservatism, understood as discursive systems, as ideologies, are inside rather than outside legal discourse itself; legal and political versions of liberalism and conservatism are mutually constitutive.

(b) When judges choose, "for ideological reasons," which way to move within their contradictory discourse, the liberalism or conservatism that motivates them is not only internal to law but also no more (and no less) determinate or internally coherent than the formal discourse they inflect.

(c) Within the opposing sides in the legal argument there are opposing sides in an ideological argument, and within them antagonistic character types and within them opposed cultural styles and within them . . . opposed modes of legal discourse. There is a circle or an infinite regress, in which there is never a determining outside discourse or fact but a series of never final unveilings. If we're lucky, we get knowledge with enough bite so that we want it before we have to decide how to act, though not enough bite to tell us how to act.

(d) Although "outside" factors influence adjudication, they do not impose on it an outside "logic." The first reason for this is, as just stated, that they do not determine the rules judges make, in any ordinary sense of the word "determine." The second reason is, as we irrationalists argued against the systematizers, that neither the economic base nor patriarchy nor racial supremacy has any more internal coherence, any more "logic," than the process of legal reasoning from the extant materials.

Contrast with neo-Marxist theories of ideology

After the theory of "determination in the final instance," the second most important element in the neo-Marxist theory of law is the theory of legitimation through ideology. This is an important element in the "output" side of the theory, the part about how law affects society (external determination being the "input" side). As I mentioned above, the Pink Theory is a variant, a chastened version of this theory.

Writers in the Marxist tradition, such as Georg Lukacs,[58] Gramsci,[59] and Althusser,[60] and also Jürgen Habermas,[61] have used the term "ideology" to describe what I have been calling "Liberalism" (belief in majority rule, rights, the rule of law, and some version of a regulated market economy with safety nets).[62] In the classic analyses, it is ideology in this sense that legitimates. This usage is closely linked to the notion of a logic of the economic formation and is quite different from the use of the term in the Pink Theory.

To identify ideology with American liberalism and conservatism is to adopt a different definition of the word, and a weaker theory, than Marxists have typically wanted to develop and deploy in their accounts of capitalism. A strong version of ideology, which I will call "Ideology" (capitalized), has four characteristics.

(a) Ideology is an interpretation of reality that is either consciously or unconsciously shared across the whole social and political spectrum; specifically, it is something "deeper" than the "surface" disagreements that mainly preoccupy actors in those areas. Thus a common belief in God underlies religious sectarian conflict, which looks to the participants to be a matter of salvation and damnation. Thus a common belief in the naturalness, justice, and efficiency of private property in the means of production underlies political conflicts between liberals and conservatives that seem to them to involve basic questions of social justice.

(b) There is something behind Ideology, something that is not itself Ideology, that causes or explains it, and thereby indirectly causes or explains Ideology's effects. The something is the forces and relations of production, or the needs of capitalism at a particular stage, "the base." The play of intense surface conflicts within Ideology reflects divisions in the base. While there may be feedback from the ideological to the material domain, a strong version of Ideology privileges the material. "In the final instance," the base trumps the superstructure, or the theory is not a strong one.

(*c*) Ideology legitimates the structure of forces and relations of production that causes or explains it. To legitimate, in this context, means to persuade people to accept the overall social order founded on the underlying economic structure, rather than to persuade people that particular actions are right or wrong. Legitimation is Ideology's function in the social order seen as an integrated totality, or at any rate its effect. The legitimating effect of Ideology is more important than the various effects that flow from the disagreements within it that seem so important to the participants.

(*d*) Ideology is demonstrably false. That is, we can appeal to widely agreed on criteria of truth and falsity to show that it doesn't work as an interpretation of reality. Both the arguments for the existence of God and those for the natural justice of capitalism are tissues of contradiction. By contrast, the theory of the structure of capitalist society, and of the laws of its development, are "scientific" in a quite strong sense.[63]

Note that in this type of theory, Ideology, a singular noun, is the product of the underlying structure of economic forces and relations, which it legitimates, whereas in the common parlance of American political culture, there are many ideologies linked to a variety of economic interests. For the reasons discussed in Chapter 3, I've chosen this usage of the word, rather than the Marxist one.[64]

Liberalism and conservatism are not Ideology in the Marxist sense.

(*a*) Neither is shared across the society, and indeed the conflict between them is just the kind of surface phenomenon that the classical theory tries to get beyond.

(*b*) There is nothing more substantial behind them than an ideological intelligentsia with more or less definite ties to a "community" with some definition of its own "interests," at the same time that the intelligentsia has interests of its own that diverge from those of the represented groups. The interests are as much a function of the ideologies as vice versa.

(*c*) Liberalism and conservatism are "universalization projects" of intelligentsias that claim to represent particular group interests, rather than "the" legitimation mechanism for a particular type of society.

(*d*) Each is contested, both by its semiotically defined opposite number and by Marxism, anarchism, fascism, and Manchesterism, but there seems little prospect that either will be "proved false" in any definitive way. In my scheme, there is no "scientific" alternative to life as an ideologist.

But what about Liberalism (capitalized)? The Liberal conception of the rule of law, and the denial of the ideological in adjudication, are widely shared across the political spectrum, like Ideology in the Marxist analysis. Moreover, I have been arguing that attempts to establish the coherence of the Liberal conception, to show that adjudication is or plausibly could be nonideological, have failed. The denial of ideology in adjudication is a response to the incoherence, so that we are dealing with something closely resembling "false consciousness."

In the Pink Theory, adjudication disposes of the stakes of ideologized group conflict by defining the rules of the game, and the presence of ideological motives in adjudication is mystified by its representation as neutral, impersonal, or objective, so that judges and their audience are in bad faith (rather than simply deluded). Contrasting this kind of regime with the counterfactual situation of effective legislative control of all law making generates the moderation, empowerment, and legitimation effects. For this reason, the Pink Theory belongs to the same family as the classic Feuerbach/Marx theory of alienated powers, as well as to the larger family of Marxist ideology theories.

Moderation and empowerment effects have to do with the evolution of liberal/conservative conflict within a regime where there is a lot of mystified judicial law making. This part of the analysis uses the non-Marxist notion of ideology, in the sense of liberal and conservative universalization projects, and suggests how the Ideology of Liberal legalism affects their fates as political movements.

In the legitimation effect, the mystified discourse of judge-made law in general, and numerous specific discourses explaining particular legal regimes, contribute to the naturalization of existing social relations of domination (hierarchy, inequality, alienation). Both the general and the more particular discourses contribute to naturalization by making it appear that background rules that are "really" the product of judicial ideological strategy flow instead from merely technical reasoning.

Naturalization is an Ideological effect because proposals for change that are outside the liberal/conservative "mainstream," as it defines itself in relation to the "extremes," seem, to the participants in political culture, less plausible than they would in a more transparent system. (By "transparent" I mean less mystified by the denial of the ideological in adjudication.) In other words, these nonmainstream alternatives are "cognitively"[65] excluded from consideration as impractical, rather than excluded on the basis of consideration on the merits. (By "on the merits" I mean without the mystifying effects of bad faith and denial.)

The Pink Theory differs from the Marxist analysis in the following respects.

Law's influence on society: What is legitimated is the status quo, rather than capitalism or the relations of production understood as a structure. The status quo is an incoherent hodgepodge of heterogeneous elements, without a system logic. Whatever it may be at any given moment, that's what gets naturalized by the denial of the ideological element in judicial law making. In this respect, the analysis is closer to populism than to Marxism. It points to the distortion of the results that would occur under a more transparent law-making process, rather than to necessary functions of the legal order in a particular kind of regime.

Society's influence on law: Neither liberalism and conservatism, nor Liberal legalism (the rule of law with denial of the ideological in adjudication), is caused or explained by the deep structure of capitalism. To repeat, the PT denies that any such deep structure has been plausibly demonstrated. Liberal legalism serves the status quo, not a deep structure, but is derived from it only in this sense: I allege that liberal and conservative judges and legal theorists share an apologetic motive that influences their descriptions of adjudication in general and of legal regimes in particular.

That motive is to defend the status quo against the extremes. Denial and bad faith with respect to the ideological in adjudication are *in part* a half-conscious strategy designed to represent judicial institutions and particular legal regimes as internally coherent and also just, when they are better understood as the opposite (from my heavily ideological, "extreme" perspective, of course).

In the article on Blackstone's *Commentaries* that I mentioned in Chapter 3, I characterized Blackstone's proto-Liberal project as apologetic in this sense but also as "utopian." I would say the same about modern Liberal legalism. The notion of utopian aspiration is implicit in what I have been calling the "abstract normative element" in liberalism and conservatism, that is, in their commitment to social transformation in the direction indicated, however ambiguously, by the body of Liberal principles and texts (rights, majority rule, the rule of law, a regulated market with safety nets, Judeo-Christian morality).

The idea of apology is the dark side of the idea that the ideologists are committed to the interests of the groups they represent. An ideology, seen as the universalization project of an intelligentsia, "mediates" between the utopian (abstract normative) element and the apologetic (interest-based) element. To say that Liberal legalism is apologetic is to say that as a matter of fact, rather than of analytic necessity, the liberal/conservative center has been concerned to present the status quo as better than what the extremes have to offer, in part because liberals and conservatives benefit from the status quo by comparison with the extremes.

But it is to say more than that—that the apologetic motive or intent has inflected Liberal representations of legal institutions and regimes, falsifying or distorting the analyses. The particular form of distortion, or motivated error, is the denial of the ideological in adjudication and of the contradictory nature of the legal regimes produced by judicial law making. I mean to attribute a disreputable motive, albeit a half-conscious one, for this distortion.

The PT as "chastened" left theory

What this perhaps overly intricate theoretical model adds up to is an account of adjudication as the locus of liberal and conservative ideological projects with distributive effects, and an account of Liberal legalism as denial and bad faith with utopian and apologetic motives and legitimating effects. If it is convincing, it establishes, in Alan Hunt's words, a "connection between doctrine and its historical context" of the type that "critical theory promises."[66]

But it is a much weaker, more contingent connection between two much less coherent entities (a deconstructed status quo and a deconstructed legal regime) than the Marxist analysts originally hoped for. A theory of this kind may delegitimate the existing order in terms of its own theory of itself, and it may suggest ways in which the institution of adjudication plays a stabilizing role in our particular kind of capitalism. But it actually reduces our ability to "understand" the system in the traditional leftist sense of reducing its operation to laws or grand tendencies. Indeed, the critique of law, in the mode I am proposing, has the effect of making it implausible that we will be able to establish a relatively parsimonious explanatory paradigm to undergird the leftist project.

It seems to me unlikely that the left will succeed in finding a strong alternative to a weak version of this general type. I think the best we can or should hope for is the kind of chastened theory contained in this book. But it is worth noting that the rationalism/irrationalism debate within cls, which seemed at the time to be grappling with issues that were basic to Marxist, Weberian, Parsonian, and Habermasian social theory, has had virtually no resonance beyond the narrow confines of the left legal academy.

The "hypercritical" character of irrationalism

The irrationalist attack on the systematizers' left theory doubled the use of the minimalist internal critique of legal reasoning: law is plastic in the sense that it could have been shaped in two or more ways; but the theories that are supposed to give definition to a plastic legal body fall to the very same internal critique that had loosened law up in the first place. The internal critique gets applied, directly when the theory includes legal concepts, and by analogy when it doesn't, to the implicit or explicit theories of the logic of capital that were supposed to explain law. Internal critique becomes a colonizing force in its own right, rather than a condition permitting colonization of legal by economic theory.

This kind of viral progression is something we will see happening over and over again in the evolution of the theory debate. Right from the start, it produced a political critique: indeterminacy theory was "going too far" if it deprived us of our ability to produce not just "covering laws" but any meaningful generalizations at all. Internal critique would become a demobilizing force if its argument was that history was just one damn thing after another. Moreover, it tended to support interest-group pluralism, in which groups have strategies that they pursue within a "process" framework, with no overall logic of the system. Interest-group pluralism was associated with legitimation of the status quo by "rules of the game" and was therefore clearly a bad thing.

The issue didn't go away and still hasn't. The code words are: "What we need is a general theory. You can't beat something with nothing. It's easy to critique—the hard part is to create a theory. The critical project is finished; now it's time for reconstruction." The danger of sliding into liberalism or pluralism, the loss of the sense that theory can orient practice, and the fear of the demobilizing effect of indeterminacy, contextualism, complexity, and contradiction, are still major themes of discussion. So is the idea that the critique "proved too much" and couldn't be right, because it would make *all* knowledge impossible (see Chapter 14).

Critics of cls from the right have exulted in the "lack of" or "failure to develop" a general cls theory,[67] for much the same reason that some cls people themselves have lamented it. "Outsiders" (not American legal academics) who want to be sympathetic sometimes say they would be able to be sympathetic if only there were a general theory. Among us middle-aged white males, there are only a few participants in the debate (I'm one of them, most of the time) who don't feel ambivalence, or at least nostalgia, in regard to the "abandonment of totalizing theory." The situation in the later white male generations, and among white feminists and critical race theorists is more complicated.

In retrospect, the rationalist/irrationalist debate appears to have been the beginning of the legal version of the general intelligentsia's debate about whether postmodernism is "inherently" or "tendentially" conservative, and maybe psychotic to boot. It began in cls before most of us had heard of postmodernism, and it ran out of steam not because one side or the other won, but because, as in any narrative, "something happened." What happened was the "rights debate," to which we now turn.

PART FIVE

Post Rights

12

Rights in American Legal Consciousness

Up to now, the critique of adjudication has been designed to make way for one kind of reconstructive project or another. If legal reasoning is frequently indeterminate, and when determinate represents nothing more than earlier answers to open questions by those who happened to have the rule-making power, then extralegal normative commitments are inevitably part of law. So we can argue for "correct" normative commitments.

This is the third part of the Marx/Feuerbach model of ideology-critique. The revelation of political bias behind a mystifying facade is a prelude to putting in judges who will "do the right thing." Doing the right thing means having normative projects that are better than those currently embedded in the law and better than those of current judges.

Until World War II, there were two main left reconstructive projects in the United States. One was socialism, meaning public ownership of the means of production, or the more or less complete abolition of the markets for labor and products. The other was the "reform" program of reconstructing the market and also influencing it, by a combination of structural changes (empowering labor unions), fiscal policy (progressive taxation), welfare programs, and regulation of just about everything.

Both of these groups might have found ultimate justification in ideas like freedom or human rights, but they were strongly predisposed to understand outcomes for unfortunate people as the consequence of a *failure of planning*. That is, of a failure to properly understand the social totality and intervene to shape it from the center to make outcomes correspond to what *the collective* wanted, whether the collective was "the working class" or "the American people." (There were exceptions: the rights of labor versus the rights of capital rhetoric in labor disputes at the turn of the century, women's rights). The counterprogram of the American right was usually

cast in terms of the defense of individual rights against the collectivity
(exceptions being protofascists, the Catholic right).

That is no longer the situation. This chapter describes the rise of a liberal
rights-based version of reconstruction, the role of rights in American legal
consciousness now that they are the basis of both liberal and conservative
ideological projects, and the left/mpm phenomenon of loss of faith in
rights.

The role of rights in left legal thought, circa 1975–1985

There are three liberal subdiscourses of rights that overlap in legal reasoning but do not reduce to legal reasoning. These are liberal constitutionalism, fancy reconstructive rights projects in legal philosophy, and the
popular political language of rights that flow naturally or automatically
from the assertion of "identity." The three discourses are partially autonomous, because each corresponds to a fraction of the liberal intelligentsia.

Liberal constitutionalism is part of the ideology of the milieu of activist
liberal law professors, judges, and public interest lawyers mainly oriented
to legal reform through the courts. Public interest lawyers include the
American Civil Liberties Union, the Legal Defense Fund, and the dozens
of newer institutions that have sprung up to litigate on behalf of women,
Latinos, the environment, gays, and so on. This group also includes the
post-1960s National Lawyers Guild and the Legal Services Corporation of
the same era. A recent addition to this family is international human rights
activism.

Constitutional rights discourse is argument in briefs (and supporting
law review articles) for the legal recognition, development, or defense of
liberal legal positions. The advocates argue that these positions are "required" by the correct interpretation of the constitutional law materials,
particularly the provisions guaranteeing citizen rights.

Fancy theory (that, for example, of Ronald Dworkin, Bruce Ackerman,
Frank Michelman, Martha Minow, Margaret Radin, Dru Cornell, and Patricia Williams) is the project of the milieu of elite legal academic intellectuals self-consciously concerned with universalizing the interests of various oppressed or disadvantaged groups. They support specific liberal
positions that have gotten legal recognition, and are therefore already "represented" in legal discourse in (maybe only dissenting) judicial opinions,
by linking them to the liberal political philosophy of the day (that of John
Rawls, Richard Rorty, Carol Gilligan, Habermas, Derrida, and others). In

the 1980s, they were joined by Central European theorists of "limited revolution" under the banner of human rights. All show that philosophy, something at once higher than, more intellectually sophisticated than, and also more determinate than postrealist legal reasoning, supports legalizing liberal rights claims.

The popular discourse of rights pervades not only the formal political culture but also just about every milieu where people argue about who should do what, including, for example, the family, the school, and the entertainment industry. The identity/rights rhetoric in particular is that of organizers, advocates, and spokespeople of subordinated groups (blacks, women, gays, the handicapped). They argue the existence of an identity, that given the identity there are rights, and that these rights should be recognized by the legal system.

Within legal academia, but virtually nowhere else either in the world of law or beyond it, there is a left/mpm critique, loosely identified with cls, of these three versions of the liberal project.

The effacement of radicalism

The left intelligentsia has not always been organized this way. Although the current liberal project has its "origin" in the fifties, during the 1960s the left intelligentsia grew exponentially and then split sharply and repeatedly over such questions as direct action versus legal strategies, revolutionary communism versus liberalism, black nationalism versus integrationism, separatist feminism versus "sleeping with the enemy." In each of these splits, one subelement was different attitudes toward rights and rights rhetoric, associated with different degrees of "radicalism," as we defined it then, meaning different beliefs about how great and possibly even violent the changes would have to be before anything was "really" different.

The political radicals' critique of rights had little to do with the kind of internal critique of legal reasoning I have been describing. Indeed, they leaned toward external, economy-based, race-based, or gender-based theory (consider Shulamith Firestone and Eldridge Cleaver). The political radicals also failed or were defeated or self-destructed, however you want to look at it. In the 1970s and 1980s, the left intelligentsia was much as it had been in the early 1960s, with a small radical fringe and a giant liberal mainstream always about to be devoured by neoconservatism, yuppieism, and lots of other things.

Perhaps the biggest change from the 1950s and early 1960s was that the white male working class no longer played a significant role in left thinking. White male left liberals and radicals saw themselves as deserted or betrayed by that class, had lost their faith in it, or had never identified with it. For most left political activists, the straight white male working class was, at worst, the core of the enemy camp and, at best, the necessary object of conversion.

From class politics to identity politics

The hopeful version of the situation of the new New Left is neatly put by Cornel West, who asserts the existence of an "inchoate, scattered yet gathering progressive movement that is emerging across the American landscape. This gathering now lacks both the vital moral vocabulary and the focused leadership that can constitute and sustain it. Yet it will be rooted ultimately in current activities by people of color, by labor and ecological groups, by women, by homosexuals."[1]

The different levels of the left intelligentsia relevant to us here—namely, fancy legal theorists, law reform litigators and organizers—reorganized around or persisted in rights discourse and successfully *reinterpreted* what had happened in the 1960s. They remembered it as a triumph, in the civil rights, women's and antiwar movements, of constitutional rights, representing the best instincts and true ideals of the American people, over an earlier regime representing a reactionary or morally torpid version of those instincts and ideals.

What had happened, according to them, was the triumph of universalizing intellectuals (Martin Luther King, Gandhi), allied with civil rights lawyers and legal services lawyers, allied with community organizers. Together, they asserted, litigated, and then justified rights guaranteed in the Constitution, against legislative and administrative regimes that denied those rights.

The rights were usually defined in terms of equality, but equality in a special sense. They did not involve the demand for equality in the distribution of income or wealth between social classes, regions, or communities, but rather "equal protection" for individual members of previously subordinated social groups. The rhetorical emphasis on identity and antidiscrimination was a complex new synthesis of the "nationalist" and "integrationist" strands in 1960s black and women's protest movements.[2]

By the 1970s and 1980s, there were no longer "popular movements" aggressively raising rights claims, there were no longer federal courts willing to invalidate legislation and regulations in the interests of oppressed groups, and there was no longer the sense of the undeniable moral/philosophical correctness and ineluctable coherence of left constitutional theory. From different places within the left intelligentsia, the causal links between these three failures looked different.

There were some advantages to the new situation, as well as obvious disadvantages. The remaining left intelligentsia was rid of the radicals who had made their lives miserable throughout the 1960s and freed of the worrisome problem of the white male working class. The left liberals were now *the left*. They could, sometimes, institutionalize themselves and develop all kinds of more or less oppositional or collaborative attitudes toward the mainstream, without worrying about the horrible dialectic of "taking up the gun" or "selling out." And the left intelligentsia did survive, with a good deal more in the way of numbers and resources and ideas than had been around in the 1950s and early 1960s.

New recruits, post-1960s children, continued to trickle in, particularly women and minority recruits to the law reform and theory intelligentsia fragments. For many of them, the 1960s seemed a Golden Age. They had personal memories of that time, often of formative events in their own lives. But their memories were filtered through childish consciousness, and there was little in them that might conflict with the rights-oriented reinterpretation of what had happened. Its nostalgic emphasis on the importance of popular movements, but suppression of intraleft division, seemed far more plausible than the mainstream story of the 1960s as the Dark Ages.

It is easy in retrospect to see the weaknesses of this project. But in 1980, say, the year before Ronald Reagan took office, it was plausible, even if the times were hard for the left. I think a lot of its strength—as an intelligentsia project—derived from the combination of political correctness (struggles of oppressed groups), legal correctness (the Constitution was law and authoritatively demanded massive liberal reform), and philosophical correctness (the fanciest moral philosophy supported left liberal law reform on behalf of oppressed groups). Wow.

The cls critique of rights

Against this background, the cls critique of rights (Mark Tushnet,[3] Peter Gabel,[4] Frances Olsen,[5] me[6]) was *perverse*. But it was *not* perverse for the reason asserted by the first-stage critics of cls, who saw only one of its originary strands—namely, Marx's critique of rights as individualist rather than communist, and specifically the Marcusian critique of "repressive tolerance." There is an undeniable genealogical connection between this critical strand and the communist practice of denying any legal enforcement of rights against the state, in the name of the revolutionary truth that "bourgeois civil liberties" were a reactionary or counterrevolutionary mystification.

The initial critics of cls on this front were veterans of the wars in the forties and fifties and then again in the late sixties and early seventies between the communists (and other orthodox Marxists and third world Marxist-Leninist revolutionary types) and the liberals. For these anti-Marxists (Louis Schwartz),[7] anti–New Leftists (Phil Johnson,[8] the *New Republic*), and post- or ex-Marxists (Straughton Lynd,[9] Edward Sparer,[10] Michael Tigar[11]) *any* critique of rights automatically smacked of Stalinism.

But the crits were not the radical activists of 1965 to 1972 reemerging as Marxist academics to pursue the old war on a new front. Though they preserved the radicals' animus against mainstream liberalism, their critique was perverse not because it was Stalinist but because it was *modernist.* It developed, with many hesitations and false steps, exactly the kind of minimalist internal critique, leading to loss of faith, that the crits had applied to legal reasoning.

Feminists[12] and critical race theorists,[13] who took up the critique of the critique after the anti- and post-Marxists, saw this clearly. They objected not on the ground of totalitarian tendency, but on the ground that rights really did or should exist, or on the ground that it was demobilizing to criticize them. This response was plausible because rights played more or less exactly the same role in their post-1960s political thinking that they played in American political thought in general.

Rights in American political discourse

Rights play a central role in the American mode of political discourse. The role is only intelligible as part of the general structure of that particular discourse. It is a presupposition of the discourse that there is a crucial distinction between "value judgments," which are a matter of preference, subjectivity, the arbitrary, the "philosophical," and "factual judgments," or scientific, objective, or empirical judgments.

Rights mediate between factual and value judgments

Values are supposedly subjective, facts objective. It follows that the status of all kinds of normative assertion, including moral or utilitarian assertion, is uneasy. Claims that something is "right" or "wrong," or that a rule will "promote the general welfare" are *conventionally* understood to be on the subjective side of the divide, so much a matter of value judgment that they have to be arbitrary and are best settled by majority vote.

While there are many ways to account for or understand the nature of rights, it seems to me that in American political discourse they all presuppose a basic distinction between rights argument and other kinds of normative argument. The point of an appeal to a right, the reason for making it, is that it *can't be reduced* to a mere "value judgment" that one outcome is better than another. Yet it is possible to make rights arguments about matters that fall outside the domain commonly understood as factual, that is, about political or policy questions of how the government ought to act. In other words, rights are mediators between the domain of pure value judgments and the domain of factual judgments.

The word "mediation" here means that reasoning from the right is understood to have properties from both sides of the divide: "value" as in value judgment, but "reasoning" as in "logic," with the possibility of correctness. Rights reasoning, in short, allows you to be right about your value judgments, rather than just stating "preferences," as in "I prefer chocolate to vanilla ice cream." The mediation is possible because rights are understood to have two crucial properties.

First, they are "universal" in the sense that they derive from needs or values or preferences that every person shares or ought to share. For this reason, everyone does or ought to agree that they are desirable. This is the first aspect of rights as mediators: they follow from values but are neither arbitrary nor subjective because they are universal.

Second, they are "factoid," in the sense that "once you acknowledge the existence of the right, then you have to agree that its observance *requires x, y,* and *z.*" For example, everyone recognizes that the statement "be good" is too vague to help resolve concrete conflicts, even though it is universal. But once we have derived a *right* from universal needs or values, it is understood to be possible to have a relatively objective, rational, determinate discussion of how it ought to be instantiated in social or legal rules.

The two parts are equally important. It is no good to be a believer in universal human rights if you have to acknowledge that their application or definition in practice is no more a matter of "reason" as opposed to "values" than, say, the belief in Motherhood and Apple Pie. They have to be both universal and factoid, or they leave you in the domain of subjectivity.

The project of identifying and then working out the implications of rights is thus a part of the general project of social rationality. As such, the rights project is part of the same family as the project of identifying and working out in practice a judicial method based on interpretive fidelity, rather than mere legislative preference. Moreover, since rights are conventionally understood to be entities in law and legal reasoning, as well as in popular discourse and political philosophy, the two projects are intermingled. But they are not the *same* project. We might think that extant theories of legal reasoning fail to avoid the pitfall of mere preference, but that rights theories don't, and vice versa. This possibility is real because American political discourse presupposes that rights exist outside as well as inside the legal system.

Inside and outside rights

I pointed out in Chapter 6, in the discussion of the structure of legal discourse, that rights occupy an ambiguous status with respect to the distinction between rules and reasons for rules. "Congress shall make no law abridging the freedom of speech" is an enacted rule of the legal system, but "protecting freedom of speech" is a reason for adopting a rule, or for choosing one interpretation of a rule over another. In this second usage, the right is understood to be something that is outside and preexists legal reasoning.

The outside right is something that a person has even if the legal order doesn't recognize it and even if "exercising" it is illegal. "I have the right to engage in homosexual intercourse, even if it is forbidden by the sodomy statutes of every government in the universe." Or "slavery denies the right to personal freedom, which exists in spite of and above the law of slave states."

The Constitution, and state and federal statutes, legalize some highly abstract outside rights, such as the right of free speech in the First Amendment or of property in the Fourteenth. Positive law also legalizes less abstract rights that are understood to derive from more abstract, but not enacted, outside rights. For example, in the nineteenth century, the Supreme Court interpreted the constitutional prohibition on state impairment of the obligation of contracts as legal protection of one species of the more general, but unenacted, category of vested rights.

American courts have also, on occasion, argued that the Constitution protects outside rights even when it does not explicitly enact them as law. At various points in the nineteenth century, courts did this quite boldly, claiming that the protection of unenumerated outside rights was to be inferred from the "nature of free governments." In the twentieth century, the Supreme Court has seen itself as protecting an unenumerated outside right of privacy whose constitutional (legal) status the Court infers from a variety of more specific provisions (for example, the Fourth Amendment protection against unreasonable searches and seizures).

In classic Liberal political theory, there was an easy way to understand all of this: there were "natural rights," and We the People enacted them into law. After they were enacted, they had two existences: they were still natural, existing independently of any legal regime, but they were also legal. The job of the judiciary could be understood as the job of translation: translating the preexisting natural entity or concept into particular legal rules by examining its implications in practice.

While the language of natural rights is out of fashion, it is still true that Liberal theory understands *some part* of the system of legal rules as performing the function of protecting outside rights, rights whose "existence" does not depend on legal enactment, against invasion by private and public violence. We don't need, for the moment, to go into the various ways in which lay people or specialists understand the mode of existence of these exta-legal or outside rights. The important point is that judicial (or, for that matter, legislative or administrative) translation of the outside into the legal materials is still a crucial element in Liberal understanding of a good political order.

Thus we can distinguish three kinds of rights argument: the strictly outside argument about what the existence of some right or rights requires the government (or a private person) to do or not do; the strictly inside argument about what the duty of interpretive fidelity requires judges to do with a body of materials that includes rights understood as positively enacted rules of the legal system; and the form characteristic of constitutional law (and of some private law argument as well), in which the arguer is engaged at the boundary between inside and outside, interpreting an existing outside right that has already been translated into positive law.

Constitutional rights *straddle.* They are both legal rights embedded in and formed by legal argumentative practice (legal rules) and entities that "exist" prior to and outside the constitution. For this reason, an argument from constitutional rights mediates not just between factual judgments and value judgments, but also between legal argument (under a duty of interpretive fidelity) and legislative argument (appealing to the political values of the community). Once again, the word "mediation" means that this form of argument participates in the characteristics of both sides of the dichotomy.

On one side, the argument from constitutional rights is legal, because it is based on one of the enacted rules of the legal system (the First Amendment, say); on the other, it is normative or political, because it is in the form of an assertion about how an outside right should be translated into law. The advocates and judges doing constitutional rights argument exploit *both* the notion that adjudication proceeds according to a highly determinate, specifically legal method of interpretive fidelity, and the notion that the outside right is a universal, factoid entity from whose existence we can make powerful inferences. Their goal is to make the apparent objectivity of rights theory dovetail perfectly with the apparent objectivity of judicial method.[14]

Rights in the universalization projects of ideological intelligentsias

Rights are a key element in the universalization projects of ideological intelligentsias of all stripes. A universalization project takes an interpretation of the interests of some group, less than the whole polity, and argues that it corresponds to the interests or to the ideals of the whole. Rights arguments do this: they restate the interests of the group as characteristics of all people. A gay person's interest in the legalization of homosexual intercourse is restated as the right to sexual autonomy, say. The right here mediates between the interests of the group and the interests of the whole.

When groups are in the process of formation, coming to see themselves as having something in common that is a positive rather than a negative identity, the language of rights provides a flexible vehicle for formulating interests and demands. There is an available paradigm: a group based on an identity, from which we infer a right to do identity-defining things, a right to government support on the same basis as other identity groups, and protection from various kinds of adverse public and private action (a right against discrimination). New groups can enter the discourse of American politics with the expectation that they will at least be understood, if they can fit themselves to this template.[15]

Once the interests of the group have been assimilated to the interests of the whole polity by recasting them as rights, the factoid character of rights allows the group to make its claims as claims of reason, rather than mere preference. Since you do or at least ought to agree that everyone has this universal right, and that reasoning from it leads ineluctably to these particular rights, it follows that you are a knave or a fool if you don't go along. To deny these particular rights makes you *wrong,* rather than just selfish and powerful.

This general Liberal idea is available to all. In other words, both liberal and conservative intelligentsias argue that the group interests they represent should be recognized in law by asserting that the recognition would be an instantiation of some set of outside rights. The proposed legal rules are not "partisan" but rather represent political beliefs and commitments that transcend the left/right divide. Rent control is unconstitutional. Likewise, the liberal intelligentsia argues that its program is just the vindication of outside rights, enacted in the Constitution, against their mistranslation in wrong legislative, administrative, and judicial decisions.

I argued above that only since the 1970s has the left in general come to rely on rights as the principal basis for universalizing its positions. Before the 1970s, there had always been a live controversy between Marxists hostile to the whole rights formulation, social democratic progressive planners with a universalization project based on savings from eliminating wasteful and chaotic markets, and civil libertarians.

For the conservative ideological intelligentsia, the alternative to rights is efficiency. An efficiency claim has many of the same mediating properties as a rights claim: it is a value judgment that is universal (who can be opposed to making everyone better off according to their own understanding of better-offness?) and factoid (efficiency arguments are nothing if not technical and they are supposedly empirically based). But while these alternatives exist, rights now bear the main burden of universalization for both camps.

The parallel investments of ideological intelligentsias in legal reasoning and rights discourse

In the discussion of the empowerment effect, I tried to figure out the basis for intelligentsia investment in the idea of a judicial method in general and judicial review in particular. I argued, first, that people really like to believe that whatever they believe in is validated by the mana of the Judge. Then I argued that legal correctness is a weapon equally of the left and the right, so that neither side should see it as "in its favor," and that the privileges of the intelligentsias do not seem to depend in any profound way on belief in the nonpolitical character of judicial method.

Having thus cleared the ground, I argued that American political intelligentsias of left and right experienced empowerment vis-à-vis legislative majorities through constitutional wishful thinking—the belief that correct judicial interpretations of the Constitution would make illegal their opponents' programs, permit the moderate version of their own programs, and check the dangerous tendencies of the masses.

There is a clear parallel between the role of judicial method and the role of rights. The double mediating effect of rights, between fact and value and between law and politics, allows both camps to feel that they are correct in their rights arguments, just as they are correct in their technical legal arguments. Both claim a whole history of triumph over the other side under the banner of rights. Each has colonized a part of the legal corpus and believes that its colonized area represents correct decision according to outside rights. Each recognizes that the other holds some territory, but interprets this as manipulation of legal reasoning, or wrong legal reasoning, to conclusions that violate outside rights.

For both sides, rights are crucial to countermajoritarian security as well as to countermajoritarian reform. The general societal belief in rights, like the parallel belief in legal reasoning, empowers intelligentsias that no longer believe (or never believed) that they represent the "will of the people." For the left in particular, the move to rights rhetoric meant abandoning any claim to represent an overwhelming (white male) working-class majority against a "bourgeoisie" that was by definition a tiny minority and getting smaller all the time.

A final parallel is that rights talk, like legal reasoning, is a discourse—a way of talking about what to do that includes a vocabulary and a whole set of presuppositions about reality, some of which I have been trying to tease out. Both presuppose about themselves that they are discourses of necessity, of reason as against mere preference. And it is therefore possible to participate in each cynically or in bad faith.

Cynicism means using rights talk as no more than a way to formulate demands. They may be "righteous" demands, in the sense that one believes strongly that they "ought" to be granted, but the cynic has no belief that the specific language of rights adds something to the language of morality or utility. When one attributes the success of an argument couched in rights language to the other person's good-faith belief in the presuppositions of the discourse, one sees the other as mistaken, as having agreed for a bad reason, however much one rejoices in the success of a good claim.

Bad faith, as in the case of legal reasoning, means simultaneously affirming and denying *to oneself* the presupposed rationality of the discourse, and of the particular demand cast in its terms. It means being conscious of the critique of the whole enterprise, sensing the shiftiness of the sand beneath one's feet, but plowing on "as if" everything were fine. Bad faith can be a stable condition, as I argued at length above for the case of legal reasoning. Or it can turn out to be unstable, resolving into loss of faith or into renewed good faith.

Loss of faith in rights

Beginning with legal realism, the left-wing critical project has gotten its impetus from the need to delegitimate particular instances of legal reasoning, right-wing instances, and to delegitimate the general claim of judicial neutrality in order to bolster the power of "the people" (actually, in the United States, liberal legislative majorities). In Chapter 4, I distinguished three versions of critique—the minimalist, which asserts no more than that critique (internal and by parallel construction) invalidates extant claims, that of the maximalists who think they can prove the indeterminacy of judicial method, and that of the maximalists who think the judicial method *should have* reached a particular outcome and use critique tactically to demolish the case for the other side.

At this point, the critical project moves in a different direction according to how one interprets the actual experience of the indeterminacy of legal reasoning. People who adopt the minimalist position, by contrast with the other two, tend to interpret indeterminacy as a cause of or occasion for *loss of faith* in judicial reason. One group of maximalists interprets it as a demonstration of the power of critical reason, not a loss of faith but the demolition of an error. The other maximalist group interprets it as the occasion to subject indeterminate legal reason to an "outside" normative reason, namely, rights reasoning.

To lose your faith in judicial reason means to experience legal argument as "mere rhetoric" (but neither "wrong" nor "meaningless"). The experience of manipulability is pervasive, and it seems obvious that whatever it is that decides the outcome, it is not the correct application of legal reasoning under a duty of interpretive fidelity to the materials. This doesn't mean that legal reasoning never produces closure. It may, but when it does, that experienced fact doesn't establish, for a person who has lost faith, that closure was based on something "out there" to which the reasoning corresponded. It was just an experience and might have been otherwise (had one followed another work path, for example).

As for attempts to demonstrate abstractly that legal reasoning does or could produce closure, the extant examples within law look open either to internal critique or to the critique of partiality by ignoring equally good arguments on the other side. The post-faith minimalist critic finds not that "it can't be done," but only that "it doesn't seem to have been done yet, and I'm not holding my breath."

Loss of faith is a loss, an absence: "Once I believed that the materials and the procedure produced the outcome, but now I experience the procedure as something *I do to* the materials to produce the outcome I want. Sometimes it works and sometimes it doesn't, meaning that sometimes I get the outcome I want and sometimes I don't." Loss of faith is one possible resolution of the tension or cognitive dissonance represented by bad faith. One abandons the strategy of denial of the ideological, or subjective, or political, or just random element in legal reasoning. One lets go of the convention that outcomes are the consequences of "mere" observance of the duty of interpretive fidelity.

The loss of faith in legal reasoning is the across-the-board generalization of a process that has gone on continuously with respect to elements within legal thought at least since Jeremy Bentham's critique of Blackstone. Two examples are the gradual loss of faith in the forms of action and in the characteristic eighteenth- and nineteenth-century legal operation of "implication." When faith is gone, people say things like Holmes's remark: "You can always imply a condition. The question is why do you do it?"[16] Or they write, "Much labor and ingenuity have been expended in the attempt to find some general criterion of legal right and wrong, some general basis of legal liability. But in vain; there is none."[17]

Loss of faith in legal reasoning bears a close analogy to one of the many kinds of experience of loss of faith in God. The atheist who believes that he or she, or "science," has disproved the existence of God is analogous to the maximalist who believes that postmodern critical theory has proved the indeterminacy of legal reasoning. The other kind of maximalist is like the Catholic who becomes a Protestant, rejecting authority while continuing to hold a theology. Loss of faith, by contrast, is not a theory and is not the consequence of a theory.

I think of my own initial faith in legal reasoning as like the religion of eighteenth-century intellectuals who believed that there were good rational reasons to think there was a God, that the existence of a God justified all kinds of hopeful views about the world, and that popular belief in God had greatly beneficial social consequences. But they also had confirmatory religious experiences that were phenomenologically distinct from the experience of rational demonstration.

They engaged in the work of critiquing extant rational demonstrations and in that of constructing new ones, without any sense that their faith was in jeopardy. And they had occasional experiences of doubt without any loss of interest in and commitment to the enterprise of rational demonstration. (This is me in the first year of law school.) Loss of faith meant that they woke up one morning in the nineteenth century and realized that they had "stopped believing."

It wasn't that someone had proved to them that God did not exist. They didn't find any extant rational demonstration of this proposition convincing. Nor had they decided that it was impossible to prove that God exists. It was just that they didn't find any extant proof convincing. They might even continue to have experiences like those they had once interpreted as intimations of the divine. But somehow the combination—the processes of critique and reconstruction of rational demonstrations, along with the process of doubt and reaffirmation—had "ended badly."

It no longer mattered that more work might settle the question rationally, that the idea of a world without God was profoundly depressing, that they might lose their jobs in the clergy if anyone found out what they really felt, or that a generalized loss of belief in God threatened all kinds of terrible social consequences. It didn't even matter that people much smarter than themselves were pushing rational demonstrations that they hadn't refuted and perhaps wouldn't be able to refute when they tried.

They were in a new position. It was neither a position of certainty nor one of uncertainty. It wasn't certainty because no certainty-inducing rational demonstrations had worked. It wasn't uncertainty because the only possibility left was a surprise: someone might come along and prove that God did or did not exist, and everyone would have to come to grips with that development. In the meantime, there was no subjective state of wondering, no interrogation of the world. The question was "over," or "parked." They were post-God.

I said earlier that loss of faith is neither a theory nor the outcome of a theory. It is an event that may or may not follow critique. For example, in the spring of my first year in law school, I was working on a law review case note. At lunch with a second-year student editor, I waxed eloquent on the doctrinal implications of a paragraph in Chief Justice Warren's majority opinion that indicated, I thought, an important change in the Court's First Amendment theory. The editor looked at me with concern and said, "I think you may be taking the language a little too seriously." I blushed. It was (unexpectedly, suddenly) obvious to me that the language I had been interrogating was more casual, more a rhetorical turn, less "for real" than I had been thinking. No judicial opinion since has looked the way some opinions looked before this experience.

Working for a law firm during the summer of my second year, I prepared a brief arguing that a threatened hostile takeover of our client would violate the antitrust laws. I was a fervent trust buster and "believed" my argument. The lawyers on the case let me tag along when they visited the Justice Department to urge the Antitrust Division to intervene. Back in New York, in the elevator going up to the office, we ran into another lawyer who told us that a new offer had persuaded our client to go along with the takeover. The lead lawyer said to me: "You know the argument so well, it should be easy to turn it around." Something in my face shifted him from jocular to pensive. "On second thought, we'll get someone else to do it," he said, and patted my arm. Ah, youth!

Nothing was "proved" in either incident, and in each case the person who jolted me was trying, nicely, to induct me into bad faith, not no faith. It would have happened some other time if it hadn't happened then, and so forth.

Though it is arational, a "leap" in reverse, rather than a "consequence" of critique, loss of faith is nothing like a fully random event. It is a familiar notion that critique may "undermine" or "weaken" faith, preparing without determining the moment at which it is lost. And loss sometimes proceeds by a process like metaphor (or is it metonymy?) in poetry. For example, in the rationalism/irrationalism debate, loss of faith seemed to "spread" like a disease, or "jump" like a forest fire, from legal reasoning to totalizing theories of law and economy.

In the next chapter, I describe the structural relationship between the critique of legal reasoning and the critique of rights. The idea is not to explain but rather to describe the context within which occurred the migration of loss of faith from one domain to the other.

13

The Critique of Rights

*T*his chapter describes a series of contexts for the loss of faith in rights, arranged as a kind of route for the progression of the virus. I begin with the role of rights "inside" legal reasoning, that is, with the way judges argue about the definition and elaboration of rights that are clearly established by positive law. Doubts about this process suggest doubts about the constitutional rights that "straddle" the inside and the outside. And these lead in turn to doubts about popular rights discourse and fancy rights reconstruction projects in political philosophy. I close with an attempt to dispel some common misunderstandings of the nature and implications of rights critique.

From the critique of legal reasoning to the critique of constitutional rights

The point of closest contact between legal reasoning and rights talk occurs when lawyers reason about inside rights. This practice is important for rights talk because through it outside rights are "translated" into the legal order. As we saw in the last chapter, this translation is a crucial part of the Liberal program for a good society. Failure in the process of translation— say, a loss of faith in the possibility of doing it while maintaining the double mediation between factual and value judgments, and between legal and political discourse—would be a failure for Liberal theory.

But it would pose (has already posed) another danger as well: doubt about the coherence of legal rights reasoning at the business end, so to speak, of the rights continuum threatens to spread "back" to constitutional rights, which "straddle," and thence to fully outside rights. It is just such a progression that I will suggest here.

Legal rights in legal reasoning

The critique of legal reasoning operates on inside rights argument in the same way it operates in general. It does not deny that it is "meaningful" to speak of legal rights. For the judge under a duty of interpretive fidelity, legal rules stated in the language of rights are part of the body of materials that "bind" him, or that he transforms through legal work. Appeals to legal rights, whether constitutional or just mundane common law rights, influence the course of decision, as do appeals to legal rules that are not stated as rights (such as rules about interstate relations), and to precedents or policies (for example, security of transaction). The appeal to a rule cast in the form of a right, or to a value understood to be represented by a right, may produce the experience of closure: given this legalized right, you can't think of a good reason why the plaintiff shouldn't lose the case.

Participants in ideologized group conflict formulate their demands in rights language and then try to get particular rights legalized (enacted by a legislature, promulgated by an administrative agency, incorporated into judge-made law), both at the particular level (*Miranda* rights) and at the more abstract level (the Equal Rights Amendment). If they succeed, "there is a right to a lawyer during police interrogation," meaning that there is a legal rule requiring a lawyer, one that influences real world practices as do other rules in the system. In drafting a charter for a limited equity co-op, it makes sense to provide for the "rights" of the cooperators, of the community land trust, and so on.

While rights arguments have meaning and effect in legal discourse, it is clear that they are open to the same analysis of open texture or indeterminacy as legal argument in general. The crucial point about the critique of legal rights is that in the process of pursuing the general left-wing project of showing the manipulability of legal reasoning, critique flattened the distinction between rights argument and policy argument in general. It did this in two distinct ways. First, when the asserted right deployed in argument is seen as a legal rule, a positive prescription to be interpreted (right to counsel during police interrogation), then we interpret it using the whole range of policy argument. Whatever the right "is," is a function of the open-ended general procedure of legal argument.

Second, when the arguer appeals to a right as a reason for adopting a rule (protect free speech, secure the owner's property rights), minimalist internal critique reduces legal rights reasoning to policy reasoning by showing that it is necessary to balance one side's asserted right against the other side's (protect the right to a nonabusive workplace, tenants' rights).

According to the critique, what determines the balance is not a chain of reasoning from a right or even from two rights, but a *third* procedure, one that in fact involves considering obviously open-textured arguments from morality, social welfare, expectations, and institutional competence and administrability. None of this precludes the phenomenon of closure or apparent objectivity of the rule interpretation. It merely undermines its rational basis.

Legal argument about rights that are legal rules reduces to policy argument

Judges making legal arguments about interpretive fidelity in common law adjudication and statutory interpretation typically convey that they are dealing with a dense network of rules that have to be followed regardless of their sources and regardless of what the judges think about their rightness or wrongness. The correct interpretation of the materials is a very different question from the question what would be the best thing to do under the circumstances (the "legislative" question), and from the "philosophical" question of what political morality, or protection of natural rights, say, requires under the circumstances.

In the context of common law or statutory interpretation, rights and rights reasoning are submerged in the argumentative mass that includes precedent, canons of statutory interpretation, institutional competence and administrability arguments, general moral arguments for or against the conduct of parties, utilitarian arguments about how different rule choices will affect the conduct of private parties beyond the parties to the case, and arguments about the welfare consequences of those changes. Since the word "right" is generally used synonymously with "a rule legally protecting an interest of a party," there is nothing even slightly odd about casting a judicial opinion in the form: "We hold that the plaintiff has a right to *x,* and the reason is that this will honor precedent, correspond to legislative intent, keep us within our institutional competence, reward morality and punish vice, be easy to administer, and maximize consumer welfare."

The critique of this kind of legal rights reasoning is aimed at the ability of judges to produce convincing, closure-inducing, doubt-eliminating chains of reasoning about particular legal outcomes in the context of interpretive fidelity. The rights are just legal rules, more or less abstract, more or less formally realizable, that we are trying to interpret along with all the other legal materials to justify outcomes.

Loss of faith in this discourse is loss of faith in the judge/legislator distinction, or in the idea of the objectivity of adjudication. It is the development and extension of the critical project that I described in Chapter 4. Of course, it might mean loss of faith in *law,* or in legal authority, as well. But the rights—that is, the legal rules that don't produce closure—might come from anywhere. They might be morally admirable or monstrous; they might be grounded in majority rule, or natural law, or custom, or whatever. In other words, no matter how threatening to *legality,* the critique and loss of faith in legal rights reasoning does not necessarily imply a loss of faith in *normativity* in general, or in the use of rights and rights reasoning to decide what we leftists think the law should be.

Nonetheless, it is one part of the context of loss of faith.

Rights argument within legal reasoning reduces to balancing and therefore to policy

I have been arguing that the rights system, like the rule system as a whole, turns out to be open to strategic work designed to exploit or to generate gaps, conflicts, and ambiguities in particular cases, with the goal of making legal rules that will favorably dispose ideological stakes. Within the mass of argumentative strategies (deduction, precedent, policy) that apply across the range of legal questions, there is a subset of rights arguments that are virtually identical to those used in political philosophical rights discourse. These are the "operations" that one uses to move from rights generally stated ("everyone has a right to privacy") to specific outcomes. For example, a right holder can lose because she waived the right asserted (versus, say, a claim of duress) or forfeited it by misconduct (versus, say, a claim of inevitable accident).

For the purposes of critique, the most important of these techniques are those for generating a right that supports what your side wants to do or what your side wants to stop the other side from doing. As Hohfeld showed for property rights, the right your opponent is asserting will often be defined in such a way that you can appeal to the very same right on the other side.[1]

You can also work at constructing a new right by recasting what you want to do as an instance of a more general interest, and then as an instance of an already existing legal right that protects that interest. For example, it was not until the 1930s that labor picketing was reconceptualized as free speech.[2] Or the advocate can claim that a set of precedents previously viewed as protecting several different rights actually protect a single interest, which should be legally protected as a new right. The classic example is the generation of the right to privacy, first by Louis Brandeis in the private law context,[3] then by W. O. Douglas in constitutional law.[4]

Another part of the mundane legal practice of rights argument is the critique of your opponent's rights claims. The most basic technique is the internal undoing of a rights argument by showing that it relied on a false deduction, typically on a conceptualist overstatement of what was entailed in the definition of the right. The right to contractual performance does not entail the right to expectation damages.[5]

The upshot, when both sides are well represented, is that the advocates confront the judge with two plausible but contradictory chains of rights reasoning, one proceeding from the plaintiff's right and the other from the defendant's. Yes, the employer has property rights, but the picketers have free-speech rights. Yes, the harasser has free-speech rights, but the harassed has a right to be free of sex discrimination in the workplace. Yes, the landowner has the right to do whatever he wants on his land, but his neighbor has a right to be free from unreasonable interference. And each chain is open to an internal critique.

Sometimes the judge more or less arbitrarily endorses one side over the other; sometimes she throws in the towel and balances. The lesson of practice for the doubter is that the question involved cannot be resolved without resort to policy, which in turn makes the resolution open to ideological influence. The critique of legal rights reasoning becomes just a special case of the general critique of policy argument: once it is shown that the case requires a balancing of conflicting rights claims, it is implausible that it is the rights themselves, rather than the "subjective" or "political" commitments of the judges, that are deciding the outcome.

Once again, the prevalent experience, first, of the manipulability of legal rights reasoning and then of its reduction to balancing tests, doesn't preclude instances in which rights reasoning produces the opposite experience of closure. Nor does it show that outside rights don't exist. It is just another context for loss of faith.

Rights mediate between law and policy

The application of the critique to legal reasoning about inside rights reveals yet a third mediating function of rights in political culture. *Within legal discourse,* rights arguments are situated midway between merely "technical" or deductive arguments about rule application, appealing to ideas like the plain meaning of words, legislative intent, stare decisis or the "will of the parties," and "pure" policy argument. Remember that policy arguments are understood to be inevitably present within legal argument, but they are disfavored and marginal in status, compared to arguments that appear more consonant with the supposedly objective character of adjudication.

Rights arguments involve something more than the logic of the valid, because they explain and justify rules, rather than merely apply them, but they are less "subjective" than pure policy arguments, because of their "factoid," half-fact/half-value character. Loss of faith, or the failure of mediation, occurs when we begin to see the techniques of "manipulative" rights argument as potent enough to reduce "every," or at least any particular, rights argument to a question of balancing.

The proliferation of balancing tests reduces constitutional rights questions to policy questions

The second context for loss of faith in rights is the specific history of balancing, or of conflict between rights, in constitutional law. I think the attitude of political lawyers in the United States toward rights has been profoundly influenced by this nationally specific history. As I see it, it has four parts.

1. The legal realist attack on the rights reasoning by which conservatives had embedded a particular understanding of property rights in constitutional law. The realists argued that because the conservative constitutional rights case against reform statutes necessarily involved mere policy argument, the courts had no specifically legal basis for overruling legislative judgments.

2. The moderate and conservative attack on the liberal attempt, in the 1950s, to embed a particular understanding of freedom of speech and equal protection in constitutional law. Moderates and conservatives argued that because all the courts could do was balance rights against powers, or rights against rights, they had no specifically legal basis for overruling legislative judgments.

3. The liberal success, in the 1950s, 1960s, and early 1970s, in getting the liberal conception of equal protection and identity rights embedded in constitutional law (the victim perspective), followed by

an equally successful conservative counterattack, in the 1970s and 1980s, that embedded a contradictory understanding of rights in constitutional law (the perpetrator perspective).

4. The emergence, in the 1970s and 1980s, of contradictory rights claims within the liberal coalition, based on different conceptions of identity.

Before I briefly describe each of these contexts, I want to reemphasize that none of them compelled loss of faith. Loss of faith is an event that occurs for some people in one context, and for others in another. Some people lost their faith in constitutional rights reasoning in the 1930s. Others lost their faith in the late 1980s. Many lost faith and then regained it, or lost faith in one kind of rights reasoning but not in another, and so on.

What the contexts have in common is that they each presented the problem of how to make abstract rights (property rights, free-speech rights, equality rights, reproductive rights, privacy rights) concrete at the level of rule choice within the legal system. The initial question was, "Given that we all agree there is a right of free speech, can a city restrict leafleting on downtown streets?" Or, "Given that we all agree that there is a right of privacy, can a woman decide without the consent of the father to abort her fetus in the first trimester of pregnancy?"

The second thing the contexts have in common is that the inquiry into how to concretize the abstract right occurs in the presence of a countervailing right, or of a power of the legislature presumed to derive from majority will, or from the legislature's duty to protect the rights of parties other than the claimants. This means that there are two opposing concretization projects going on, one from the plaintiff's side and the other from the defendant's. It is always possible that the judge or observer will see these two projects as producing a "draw" or a "stalemate" or a "clash of absolutes."

The third thing the contexts have in common is that the opposing sides in the dispute attacked each other's concretization projects as unsuccessful, on their own terms, in linking the preferred rule to the abstract right. Each side then accused the other of motivated error, that is, of having consciously or unconsciously masked an ideological—a deeply contested—claim about what the law ought to be in a false claim about interpretive fidelity to the body of extant legal materials.

The liberal legal realist origin of the critique of rights

The historiography of balancing in American legal thought is in its infancy.[6] But the idea has well-known legal realist origins. Holmes (not, of course, a liberal, just a hero to liberals) is a convenient starting point. In numerous private law and constitutional decisions, he emphasized that the recognition of rights was a matter of degree, of quantity not quality.[7] No one got recognition of his or her right to the full extent that might be justified by consideration of its definition in the abstract. Where the right of one party ended and that of the other began had to be determined by looking at the consequences of drawing the line in one place rather than another. The mere recognition and definitional statement of the right (free speech, property) was inadequate because it would seem to justify more for the claiming party than was consistent with equally well established rights claims of the other side.

This kind of formulation fit the scientistic, antimetaphysical, relativist, pragmatist biases of realism. But it was given a kind of bite that survives the biases by Hohfeld's insight that the word "right" sometimes means a privilege to hurt someone without having to pay and sometimes means a claim to be compensated when hurt. When we talk about property, in particular, we are referring to a collection of rules some of which authorize injury and others of which forbid it. Whenever there is a gap, conflict, or ambiguity in property law, one side can invoke all the rules in the "bundle" that suggest protection, and the other the rules in the bundle that suggest freedom of action.[8]

Learned Hand, who saw himself as a devoted follower of Holmes and Hohfeld, proposed balancing tests in a series of contexts, including the law of unfair competition,[9] antitrust,[10] the definition of negligence,[11] and the definition of free-speech rights threatening to national security.[12] For Hand, as for Holmes and Hohfeld, the move to balancing was initially part of the liberal critical project, because he saw overt judicial balancing as formal acknowledgment that judges decide questions of policy without any methodology that distinguishes them from legislators.

If that is what judges do, there is less basis than there would otherwise be for judges to overrule legislatures. Indeed, if judges can't decide constitutional questions without balancing, one can ask why their balance, their views of policy, should prevail over those of the elected representatives of the people. If balancing means looking in detail at the consequences of drawing the line in one place rather than another, then it would seem that judges are less "institutionally competent" to the task than legislators.[13]

The realist position was that interpretive fidelity just "runs out" in many (not all) cases, because they involve conflicts for which there is no other resolution than balancing. In other words, the emergence of balancing was an extension of point two of the basic minimalist critical routine: given the internal critique of extant attempts at determinative legal reasoning, many questions of law can be resolved only by looking at them as questions of policy that will evoke differing responses according to one's ideology.

This extension of the critique did not necessarily produce loss of faith in constitutional rights. The emergence of balancing occurred in an odd and complex context. Balancing was initially liberal because, in private law (right against right), it undermined the claim of judicial objectivity and, in public law (right against power), it undermined the legitimacy of the Supreme Court's protection of property rights against progressive legislation. As such, it was not antirights but only anti–property rights. At the same time that the liberal Court was drawing most clearly the conclusion that questions of economic regulation were so "legislative" that it was inappropriate to interfere, the liberals were gearing up for the defense of human rights, through the *Carolene Products* footnote[14] Powell v. Alabama,[15] "picketing as free speech,"[16] and the flag salute cases.[17]

Balancing and the conservative critique of liberal rights claims

When the Democrats gained control of the Supreme Court in the New Deal, their legal realist appointees developed a new body of constitutional law doctrine that glorified legislative power. The Supreme Court exploited the gaps, conflicts, and ambiguities of legal rights doctrine, plus the power to overrule its own decisions, to make legal reasoning a principal support of legislative supremacy.[18] The realist critique of adjudication—that it often involves policy choices, which amount to value judgments that are ideologically contested—was an important element in the argument for this turn.

But once the liberals were in control, and fascism and Stalinism emerged as the threat, the realists abandoned the project of internal critique, in favor of the more pressing task of managing the new liberal, regulatory, interventionist state. As post-1945 legislatures turned conservative, while liberals retained control of the judiciary, the left intelligentsia went for the adjudicatory empowerment effect. That is, it adopted the position that the federal Constitution enacted a wide range of liberal policy preferences and flatly prohibited a wide range of conservative policy preferences.

It is important to see that this project had two parts. One was to develop the kind of reasoning from individual constitutional rights that liberals had allowed a marginal survival during the period of their attack on constitutionalized property rights. Faced with McCarthyism, police brutality, and conservative gerrymandering, and positively committed to racial justice, the left liberals attacked the jurisprudence of legislative supremacy they themselves had constructed, and became civil libertarians with a vengeance.

The second part was to reconstruct the theory of the judicial role, repairing the damage that their parents and grandparents, or they themselves, had done to the mana of the Judge in the process of storming the robing room. Though some, like W. O. Douglas, weren't able to do it with a straight face, the liberal intelligentsia in general followed Herbert Wechsler (neutral principles)[19] or Hugo Black (absolutes),[20] according to taste, in reaffirming the possibility of judicial neutrality and the distinction between law and politics. Here again, balancing was the key.

The initial battle was over the criminalization of the Communist Party. Moderates and conservatives argued that because it was necessary to balance communist free-speech rights against the legislative power to protect national security, and because the balancing process was nothing more than the redoing of the (ideologically charged) policy decision that the legislature had made in passing the statute, the judges should "defer" to the legislature.[21] In short, they used the liberal legal realist critique of judicial activism against the left.

The left liberals answered that the First Amendment was an "absolute," thereby both firmly tying their position to the vindication of individual rights against the state and establishing a basis for nonideological judicial enforcement through adjudication.[22] The conflict played out in a long series of cases. Though the liberals won many of these cases, "absolutism" did not survive the realist critique.[23] Balancing became a paradigm for constitutional decision in one area after another.

In the second round, the moderates and conservatives critiqued judicial activism in the civil rights areas, producing counterrights that had to be balanced against left liberal claims. Wechsler, in his famous article, pointed out that white segregationists were asserting their right of free association with just as much subjective sense of entitlement as the blacks demanding integration. Since there was no "neutral principle" by which to decide between the two demands, the judges should have deferred to the legislature.[24] In other words, to assert that the Court should straightforwardly balance in favor of blacks would have been a usurpation of legislative power.

The moderates and conservatives also developed a second strand of pre–World War II progressive argumentation, that which had favored federal deference to state government regulatory initiatives. Hart and Wechsler's famous casebook, *The Federal Courts in the Federal System,*[25] provided a theory not of states' rights per se but of common interests in the viability of decentralized government. These interests had to be balanced against the rights-based demands of the civil rights movement for intervention against racist Southern government officials and private parties. Once again, the inherently ideological nature of the choice, the necessity of balancing, argued for federal judicial (though not necessarily congressional) deference to state power.

Neither these balancing disputes, nor those in the area of apportionment (right to vote versus states' rights) or regulation of police conduct (suspect's rights versus right of the community to protection from crime), *necessarily* led to loss of faith. Indeed, since the left was usually arguing for a recognized individual constitutional right against a proxy (national security, states' rights, police power) for "rights of the community," it was possible to see each conflict as "good" rights of the individual against "evil" powers of the majority.

Nonetheless, there was something "weakening" or "undermining" about the fact that the liberals were using exactly the rhetoric they had denounced before World War II, about the failure to come up with any alternative to balancing as a methodology for protecting rights, about the very facility they began to feel at inventing new rights (privacy being the most striking case), and about the parallel facility of their opponents at inventing counterrights of one kind or another.[26]

Revalidated constitutional rights reasoning switches sides in the 1970s

The violent Southern racist reaction to the civil rights movement, combined with the triumph of the liberals on the Court of the 1960s, had an impact on the critique of rights quite similar to the impact of fascism, Stalinism, and the Roosevelt Court on the realist critique of adjudication. In short, there are no atheists in foxholes.

As I mentioned above, there was a persistent radical 1960s critique of the judiciary as a tool of the Establishment, a critique that fed on every hesitation, compromise, or betrayal by the liberal Supreme Court. It was also grounded in the experiences of local activists, movement lawyers, and legal services lawyers with the arbitrariness or just plain conservatism of local courts of all kinds. But for the liberal ideological intelligentsia, and particularly the legal part of it, these were minor themes compared to the major theme of empowerment through adjudication based on rights claims.

Faith in rights within law fed on the explosion of different popular movements in the 1960s and into the 1970s. The "corrosive" effects of the realist critique of conservative property rights, and of the conservative critique of 1950s personal rights, were internal to the legal intelligentsia. Faith flooded in from outside, at just the moment when liberal lawyers found that their rights arguments had an almost magical effect on the liberal judges with whom they shared the agenda of adjudicatory empowerment.

The dramatic reversal brought about, over fifteen years, by the Burger and Rehnquist courts changed all this. Conservative judges deployed a new version of rights rhetoric and drew on a new version of conservative white, male, straight, working- and middle-class popular rights culture. The familiar arguments, which had come to seem "correct" in part just because they worked to mobilize the mana of the Judge, stopped persuading. The rights of "victims" gave way to the rights of "perpetrators," perhaps most dramatically in *Bakke*,[27] and then across the board. Balancing was everywhere—the left had no alternative—and was everywhere patently an invitation to conservative ideological intervention.

The left in the 1980s was in the position of the right of the 1940s, which had relied for several generations on a rhetoric of property rights that made no careful distinction between natural rights arguments and arguments based on the Fourteenth Amendment. The right had achieved massive victories in getting the Supreme Court to strike down all kinds of social legislation. In the process, it had woven the natural right to property more and more tightly together with the constitutional right to property, until the legal part of the position was much more developed, more coherent, and more convincing than the "external" part. The left of the 1960s had performed a similar operation with the equal protection clause.

The right in the late 1970s and the 1980s exploited the gaps, conflicts, and ambiguities in the system of rules, the open texture of the doctrine of stare decisis, and the semiotic, formulaic, pro/con character of policy argument to cut back and dismantle the liberal victories much as the liberals had done with the conservative victories forty years earlier. Of course, it was possible to interpret this trend, yet again, as no more than the triumph of vice over virtue. But the demonstration, yet again, of the manipulability of rights arguments back and forth across the political spectrum provided a third context for loss of faith.

The internal disintegration of left rights rhetoric

In the late 1970s and the 1980s, at the same time that the left legal intelligentsia was constructing its version of the sixties as a constitutional rights revolution, organizers, activist lawyers, and theorists all began to come up against a kind of rights-overkill problem. Rights for gays, old people, the mentally retarded, Native Americans, children, mental patients, animals, prison inmates, endangered species, the handicapped, prostitutes, crime victims, people with AIDS, all made sense, if what one meant by each of them was a specific program of law reform in favor of the group in question. But remember that the whole point of adopting rights rhetoric was to get beyond or outside the posture of the mere ideological or interest group demanding something on policy grounds.

Left thinking evolved in reaction to internal debates about the content of these "proliferating" rights claims, whether phrased in terms of equality within the legal order or in terms of substantive rights to freedom of action. The most striking of the equality debates addressed "equal treatment versus special treatment" within the feminist legal community. A series of efforts to use the notion of a right to equal treatment as the basis for a program of law reform ran up against the classic problem of deciding between formal and substantive equality as the content of the right. In so much as the debate had an outcome, it seemed to be that rights definition should proceed ad hoc, through something very like balancing.[28]

The equivalent within the black community was the dispute about whether equal protection meant affirmative action in the form of integration or in the form of development of black institutions. In such contexts as schools and housing projects it seemed that the price of integration would be subjection to unending white racial hostility, acceptance of white social norms, and loss of black power and opportunity within the integrated settings.[29] At the same time, a black conservative movement began to challenge affirmative action in general, arguing for a definition of the right to equal protection as formal equality.[30]

The substantive branch of identity/rights doctrine has to do with a newly formed identity-based group demanding its rights. The group typically demands lifting of restrictions on its characteristic, identity-defining activities, affirmative governmental support for the group's interests, and the imposition of restrictions on other individuals or groups that are attempting to suppress the newly asserted identity. Thus the left supports the pregnant woman's right to abortion over the right to life of the fetus, and the right to engage in consensual adult homosexual intercourse over the community's right to prohibit what it views as evil conduct.

But then there are splits about whether the woman's right to abort excludes any rights at all for the father, about whether the state should suppress Nazi or Klan neighborhood marches, pornography, and racist and sexist speech on campus. Leftists who combine antistate libertarian commitments with cultural pluralist commitments find themselves constantly balancing freedom-of-action rights against security rights.[31]

Finally, there is the problem of "intersectionality": rights that supposedly flow from a particular group identity may be oppression for subgroups that have a crosscutting allegiance. For example, black feminists face the nationalist assertion of a black male right to "discipline" black women and of a black community right to freedom from majority or state interference with this practice.[32]

In white feminism, first came the argument that Equal Rights Amendment advocates were denying or attempting to suppress more "traditional" forms of female identity, then that white feminists had defined female identity in essentially white terms, and then that cultural feminists in the antipornography movement were abridging the rights of pro-sex or sex-radical women to read and write erotica. These quarrels were totalized by postmodern feminists under the banner of anti-essentialism and given added bite when gay men began to challenge the monolithic cultural feminist construction of male identity.[33]

For some, the project of identifying identities and then defining rights to protect them, in their freedom to engage in defining practices, in claims on public resources, and in protection against discrimination, began to seem a pipe dream. One might lose faith in it as a project, without losing enthusiasm for cultural pluralism or for one's particular list of law reform proposals, just because the process of deciding what the rights were was no different from general policy analysis. The project of identity rights looks uncomfortably like the nineteenth-century project of guaranteeing "everyone's right of freedom of action as long as they don't interfere with the security rights of others," or *sic utere tuo ut alienum non laedas.*

But, once again, there is nothing inevitable about this interpretation.

While I have no theory of loss of faith, I would hazard the hypothesis that in the legal context "erosion," "undermining," "unraveling," and "contagion" are likely to be precipitated by the spectacle of reversal: the anti-rights arguments of the old left used by the new right, the left occupying the exact position of an earlier right. This kind of flip by the two opposing camps undermines belief in the technique in question in a way that criticizing something that is simply analytically incoherent and politically incorrect doesn't. I wonder how abolitionist litigators dealt with their own dramatic shift, from nationalists to states' rights advocates, after the Fugitive Slave Law put the federal government on the side of the South against resisting Northern state governments.

A second hypothesis is that it is undermining to experience the unexpected disintegration of an apparently robust rights discourse within one's own camp. In both the 1950s and the 1980s, a discourse understood unproblematically as a righteous weapon against the wrong thought of enemies suddenly foundered on the inability to convince one's supposed allies that a particular right was good rather than bad.

From the critique of constitutional rights to the critique of outside rights

Does the flattening of constitutional rights argument into policy argument have any relevance to the outside rights that are supposedly "behind" or translated by legal enactment? The loss of faith in reasoning about legal rights raises the question of whether one can still have faith in the normative rights project carried on outside legal discourse. If the inside discourse, the translation, is "mere rhetoric," under constant suspicion of ideological partisanship, then isn't that likely to be the case for the "outside," "original" text as well?

The critique shows only that there is often no difference between an argument that you have a constitutional right to *x, y,* or *z,* and an argument that on general moral, political, utilitarian, competence grounds it would be better overall for the legal system to intervene on your side. It does not show that there is no valid procedure for reasoning from rights as prelegal entities to conclusions about what law should be. This was the mode of reasoning of those abolitionists who saw the Constitution as a pro-slavery, hence immoral, document. They were antilegalists but in no sense critical of rights.

Moreover, it is still possible to believe that one chooses one's intralegal rhetorical posture by reference to the extra- or prelegal element in constitutional rights discourse. Advocates making constitutional rights arguments can go on believing that the part that is outside, existing prior to the legalization of the right in the Constitution, has a kind of reality quite different from the reality of the right understood as incorporated into positive law, and subject to all the mechanisms of legal interpretation.

If you can be correct about the outside right, it isn't so bad to have to give up the objectivity of legal rights reasoning. You can be extremely "legal realist," or even "nihilistic," about law but still believe that correct reasoning from rights solves ethical problems. The point, then, is just to get judges who will manipulate the plastic substance of legal reason to achieve the results that are correct in terms of outside rights.

Or you can believe in the correctness of the outside rights judgments but believe that these judgments are "in the abstract." They may have to be modified "in practice" by the kinds of nonrights considerations typically raised in legal reasoning—utilitarian or institutional competence constraints, for example.[34]

But if the inside/outside divide is breached, and the critical spirit gets applied to the outside rights, there *may* be trouble. Given the content of the critique of constitutional rights, there is little reason to hope that either fancy theory or lay rights discourse will be able to sustain their extralegal normative claims.

Critique of the lay discourse of rights

In lay discourse, the word "right" is used in all the ways it is used in constitutional discourse. There is, to begin, a strictly legal positive usage: "women have no rights in Iran," "there was no right of free speech in Stalin's Russia." Rights just mean rules in force to protect particular interests. But the word is also used in lay legal argument about what the U.S. courts should do about particular statutes or executive actions. The speaker assumes the existence of a "straddling" constitutional right, and reasons from it to a conclusion, deploying some version of the standard legal interpretive techniques, including precedent (consistency) and moral, utilitarian, institutional competence and administrability arguments.

Lay discourse also uses rights in self-consciously legislative argument, with the issue no longer interpretive fidelity but rather what people with law-"making" (as opposed to law-interpreting) authority ought to do. Here is an example:

> Civil libertarians shriek about the right to privacy of those infected with AIDS. To me, Kimberly Bergalis had more a right to live than her dentist had to privacy. In the balancing act, there is no contest. But it is important to protect those who test positive with strong antidiscrimination laws.
>
> Those opposed to mandatory testing argue that the risk of patients contracting AIDS from workers is very low, that workers are more likely to contract AIDS from patients. So why not test all patients who are to undergo "invasive" procedures, while at the same time testing health care workers who perform such procedures? Protect everyone, rather than no one.[35]

In this passage, the writer treats rights argument very much as would a lawyer disabused of the sense that "rights are trumps." Rights conflict; they are quantitatively rather than qualitatively powerful; they have to be balanced; how we do the balance depends on the practical context and on nonrights arguments about things like the degree of harm that will flow from different resolutions of the conflict.

The same presuppositions may underlie statements like "there is a conflict between privacy rights and free-speech rights," "the statute gives inadequate recognition to the right of free speech," "the statute should have recognized a free-speech right," "we should recognize a right of privacy," "our society has a consensus in favor of a right of privacy," "this is an attempt to cut back the right of privacy," "we have to find a way to reconcile landlord's rights with tenant's rights."

The justifying role of rights here is ambiguous. The speaker might go on to explain that the reason the statute gave inadequate recognition to free speech was that free speech is an interest more important than the interest in, say, national security, that there were other ways to achieve the national security objective, that the resolution gives courts too much power, and so on. Rights then function as no more than interests (perhaps with an exclamation point). Because the discourse treats rights arguments as no more than policy arguments, they perform no mediating function, produce no transcendence of the fact/value or law/politics divides, as those are commonly presupposed in the discourse.

The same is true of explanations like "we should establish a right of privacy in order to safeguard people from unreasonable searches. . ." or "to assure a woman control over her reproductive life." Here, the idea is to change a legal rule by inserting a right-concept, but the reason given is to change a state of affairs defined otherwise than in terms of violation of the right. If you have lost your faith in the mediating power of legal rights discourse, having come to experience it as no more than a form of ideologically permeable policy talk, then you are not likely to see these forms of lay discourse as any different.

Sometimes lay people appeal to fully outside rights without employing either positivist legal reasoning or legislative policy argument. The rights claim is intended to be something more than just a claim about what is politically and morally best. The speaker seems to presuppose that it is more "objective" or "absolute" or "conclusive," that it is possible to "be right" about it, to make a "correct" argument, in a way that differentiates it from other kinds of claims: "Banning abortion is wrong because it denies a woman's right to control over her own body," "rent control is wrong because it denies the landlord's right to private property."[36]

When challenged, the speaker may quickly turn to defense of the right in the normal legislative way, offering all kinds of arguments as to why a legal decision maker should agree. (Institutional competence—it should be up to the woman rather than the court to decide; social welfare—back-alley abortions will increase and are an unacceptable cost.) When this happens, it reemerges that the right is a "value judgment," supported by a rhetoric, perhaps a rhetoric one finds utterly convincing, but without the mediating power promised in the initial formulation.

When the speaker sticks to unadulterated rights talk, the problem is that the assertion is conclusory. The speaker seems unaware that *there is a counterright* that can be asserted in the same tone of voice and that cancels out the first right. I may be missing the existence of a lay rights discourse that avoids this pitfall without slipping into mere balancing. But my own experience has been that the critique of constitutional rights reasoning has spread corrosively from legal to lay discourse.

It is not, not at all, that someone has proved that rights "do not exist," or that they are "nonsense on stilts." It is not a question of proof. It is a question of mediation—of whether one gets any more from rights talk than from social welfare or morality or administrability talk.

From the critique of constitutional rights to reconstructive projects in political theory

That we don't find convincing rights talk in popular discourse doesn't mean it can't be done convincingly somewhere else. The whole function of fancy theory is to show that it is possible to construct rights arguments, using the most sophisticated philosophical apparatus, that will validate left-wing popular assertions of rights. Here the problem is not that the discourse is conclusory but that it has the same sophisticated indeterminate quality as legal reasoning, at a less complex and interesting level.

There are an infinite variety of possible nonlegal, purely rights-oriented defenses of statements like "a woman has a right to reproductive freedom and therefore a right to abort her fetus." Without ever straying into obviously contestable utilitarian or institutional competence or "mere value judgment" arguments for the asserted right, fancy theorists can try an indefinite number of strategies to achieve closure or, if not closure, something a lot better than mere political rhetoric.

I would say about this enterprise what I have said already about the closely analogous, indeed overlapping enterprise of showing how judges can decide cases according to an adjudicative method that is not mere policy. On the one hand, as a minimalist, I don't believe it has been shown that it is impossible to do a successful argument from outside rights or even to reconstruct the discourse. On the other hand, the last time I looked into it, it seemed as though critics of each particular rights argument from fancy theory are still managing to show, for one contender after another, that it doesn't quite work on its own terms.[37]

At some point, one just loses the energy to do another internal critique. *You can't prove it can't be done.* Conceded. Therefore it is possible that the most recent contender is successful. But you don't believe anyone has done it in the past, and don't believe anyone is likely to do it in the future, and it seems like a waste of time to take up each new challenge in turn. In short, the project of reconstructing outside rights through political philosophy is another context for loss of faith.

Things the critique of rights is not

People sometimes say, "A critique of rights? But if you got rid of rights, then the state could do anything it wanted to you! What about the right of privacy? We wouldn't have any way to object to state intrusion!" They are just missing the point!

In the Western democracies, rights "exist" in the sense that there are legal rules limiting what people can do to one another and limiting the executive and the legislature. The critique of rights recognizes the reality of rule-making, rule-following, and rule-enforcing behavior. It is about faith in the rational procedures through which legislators, adjudicators, or enforcers elaborate gaps, conflicts, and ambiguities in the "text" of inside or outside rights.

There is nothing in the critique that might suggest a reduction in the rights of citizens vis-à-vis their governments. Having lost one's faith in rights discourse is perfectly consistent with, indeed often associated with, a passionate belief in radical expansion of citizen rights against the state. Moreover, loss of faith is consistent with advocacy of greatly increased tenant rights in dealings with landlords, as well as with the reverse, just as it is consistent with favoring more or less government control over abortion decisions. It is not about the question of how we ought to define rights but rather about how we should *feel about the discourse in which we claim them.*

When people want to claim things from the legal system, they put their demands into rights language, as they once put them in religious language.[38] But rights are more than just a language—or we might say that, like any language, rights talk does more and less than translate a clear and constant meaning from one medium into another. Rights talk was the language of the group—the white male bourgeoisie—that cracked open and reconstituted the feudal and then mercantilist orders of Western Europe, and did it in the name of Reason. The mediating power of the language, based on the presupposition of fact/value and law/politics distinctions, and on the universal and factoid character of rights, was a part of the armory of this group, along with the street barricade, the newspaper, and the new model family.

Since the bourgeois revolutions, one group after another has defined its struggle for inclusion in the social, economic, and political order as a rational demand for enjoyment of the same rights of freedom and equality that belong to a postulated "normal," "abstract" citizen in a bourgeois democracy. An important part of the struggle between liberals and conservatives within these societies has been over how far to go in incorporating those not included in the initial Liberal formulation of the Rights of Man into the order the revolutions established for a select few.

There has been a connection between rights language and the acquisition by these oppressed groups of an identity in the subjective sense. Rights talk has been connected to daring to claim things on a basis that might previously have been disqualifying, to claiming things "for" blacks, women, gays, or Hispanics, when the feeling before might have been that "because" one was one of these things one was disentitled to make claims. (I think it is as easy to exaggerate as to underplay the role of rights talk—

as opposed to religious or moral or just rebellious or even acquisitive discourse—in popular rebellions against oppressive circumstances. And it is not at all clear to me that oppressed groups needed rights talk to know that they were oppressed.)

The critique is not an assertion that these demands for inclusion, for acceptance as equals by the dominant groups in these societies, are wrong or misguided. It is certainly not an assertion that they should chasten their rights rhetoric, when it operates effectively, to suit the evolution of belief within a fraction of the white left intelligentsia. But, in its minimalist form, it "applies" to excluded groups, as they have defined themselves on the left since the 1960s, as much as it applied to the white male working class of the nineteenth century, to which Marx originally addressed it.

Marx's critique of rights

The Marxist origin of the critique of rights lies in the project of showing that the inclusion of the proletariat in the regime of the Liberal Rights of Man did not end illegitimate domination of that class. Its first point was that if you had, under capitalism, all the revolutionary freedoms, and strictly equal civil and political rights, you would also have, through the very economic mechanism defined and protected by those rights—the "free market"—exploitation even to the point of death.[39]

Its second point was that rights were by their very structure, their definition as "trumps" against the claims of others, immoral, because they were based on the idea that the invoker of the right can disregard the wishes, over some subject-matter domain, of the people under the duty corresponding to the right. This was Marx's utopian communist critique of Lasallean "equal rights" socialism, quite distinct from the positive analysis of how the property and contract system necessarily worked under capitalist conditions. It was an argument about how to conceptualize a good society. Specifically, it was an antiformalist assertion of the priority of consensus, sharing, and sacrifice over *any* assertion (group or individual) of the legitimacy of ignoring a person affected by one's actions.[40]

Though they are important origins, neither the first nor the second point is implicit in the minimalist internal critique of rights. Marx's necessitarian model of the evolution of capitalism was a "rationalist" construction. It has been, I argued above, a victim of minimalist critique rather than an extension of it. As to the second point, the minimalist internal critique and the posture of loss of faith do not suggest an alternative faith that, because human nature is intrinsically "good," we can do without coercion. If the critique suggests anything, it is the constant possibility of undermining or "corroding" *any* faith in the derivation of a utopian scheme from a theory of human nature.

It is an expression of loss of faith in the possibility of conclusively formulating or even of initially deciding on substantive demands through a "logic" or an "analytic" or a "reasoned elaboration" of rights. It is an attack on the claim that rights mediate between fact and value, the rational and the subjective, the political and the legal, law and policy. It is a posture of distance from a particular attitude of some people, some of the time, when they are demanding things from within the liberal order, *and* when they are demanding inclusion from a position of exclusion and oppression. The distance comes from loss of faith in the presupposed rational character of the project of rights definition.

There was a third element in Marx's critique. The Liberal constitutional regimes that emerged from the bourgeois revolutions fostered, he argued, a particular kind of false consciousness. He saw Liberalism as based on the fantasy that, by the exercise of universally valid political rights (voting, speech), we participate in a benign collective process of guaranteeing our universally valid private rights (property and contract). It is these rights that define the capitalist mode of production, and their enforcement, their entrenchment in the Liberal constitutions, guarantees that real life in "civil society" will operate according to principles of selfishness and exploitation that are the exact opposite of those proclaimed in political theory.[41]

I have been arguing throughout that there is no more a legal logic to Liberal rights than there is an economic logic to capitalism. For this reason, Marx's presentation of the selfishness and exploitation of civil society as necessary consequences of abstract property and contract rights seems seriously wrong. But his psychological analysis, of the public/private distinction and of rights consciousness, is the prototype for the kind of alienated-powers theory I've been developing throughout this book. His notion was that the belief in universal political rights functioned, together with the belief in universal private rights, as a fantasy resolution of our contradictory experience of being, at once, altruistic collective and selfish individual selves. At the same time, the fantasy performed, for the beneficiaries of capitalism, the apologetic function of explaining why they were entitled to the profits they derived from exploiting the propertyless.

I don't think it plausible that rights consciousness, in and of itself, plays either an intrinsically progressive or an intrinsically conservative role in our current politics. But, from my post-rights perspective, and with deference to believers, I do think the view of rights as universal and factoid, and so outside or above politics, involves denial of the kind Marx analyzed. As with the denial of the ideological in adjudication, there are many ways to theorize the conflicts that give rise to this particular form of (what seems to me) wishful thinking.[42] And, as with adjudication, psychologizing denial involves suspending dialogue with those for whom the reality of rights is close to tangible.

Why do it?

In part for these reasons, leftists engaged in the rights debate, myself included, often feel that it is dangerous. I don't mean now to critique an argument but to describe an emotion. The discussants may be willing to confront the critique and take in good faith the risk of loss of faith. But isn't it an experience we should all wish to avoid if that were only possible? One part of this question I have already discussed in the analogous contexts of legal reasoning and rationalism versus irrationalism. It is the sense that if "we" lose our belief in rights, we will be disarmed in dealing with our opponents. The notion is that rights rhetoric is or at least once was effective, and we would be giving that up by losing faith in rights.

Of course, it is not an argument in favor of rights that rights rhetoric "works." The critique is not about effectiveness, though possibly useful in understanding that subject.[43] One can lose one's faith in an utterly effective rhetoric and keep it in a rhetoric that practically no one seems to find plausible. And it is not a response to the critique of rights rhetoric that everyone uses it, or that our heroes or our parents used it, any more than it is a critique of rights that conservatives used or use them to great effect.

But to explain the sense of danger, one might respond that if "we" lose our faith in rights rhetoric but "they" don't, then they will gain an advantage over us. This is plausible to the extent that the "we" in question derives some measure of power, in confrontation with "them," from the sense of righteousness, of mediation, that rights have historically provided. "Giving up" rights would be like a professional athlete giving up steroids when all her competitors were still wedded to them.

If you have *already* lost your faith in rights, the argument has the sound of that in favor of religious faith for the masses, no matter how delusive, on the ground of its beneficial consequences. It is the same kind of idea of beneficent error that Scott Altman propounds for judges. Yet if we are really talking about effectiveness, it seems merely conjectural.

My own experience has been that some people who lose faith in rights become more politically committed, some become less, and some stay the same. Some switch sides, and some gain rhetorical astuteness in dealing with the good-faith, bad-faith, or cynical rights arguments of opponents, becoming more powerful rather than less. Many committed leftists, including most of those in the anarcho-Marxist, or Western Marxist, or neo-Marxist anti-Stalinist tradition, today and yesterday, never had faith in rights to begin with. If we are speaking of actual, empirical effects, I think it's hard to make the case one way or another.

Rights are not the "core" or "centerpiece" or "heart" of Liberal legalism, either as an ideology or as a social formation generating a complex mix of happiness and unhappiness, legitimacy and oppression. The prevailing consciousness doesn't have, to my mind, a heart or a core. It is an enormously plastic, loose congeries of ideas, each of which appears from moment to moment to have the force of many army divisions and then no force at all—from Gramscian hegemony to Roseanne Rosannadanna's "Never mind." The critique of rights, even when totally convincing, is a good deal less "effective" than it seems from the position of threatened faith.

But there is an aspect of the sense of danger that I want to acknowledge as rationally grounded. Undermining faith in rights threatens to undermine the unity of the left and its sense of inclusion in "American citizenship." If some on the left have lost faith in rights, and others have not, then those who have will face a constant dilemma, forced to choose between arguing with those who haven't, keeping silent, or engaging in cynical or bad-faith manipulation of the discourse within the movement.

Given that the critique is not a solution to any problem of the left, not a panacea or a program, given that the consequences for militancy and commitment are at best uncertain and at worst disastrous, then why do it?

14

Conclusion: Landscapes along the Highway
of Infinite Regress

Why do it? This chapter sketches a justification for the critique of adjudication in general and rights in particular. It is a two-part argument. First, both critiques are part of the mpm factional version of the left project. Second, they are related, obliquely but I think closely, to the left/mpm project of politicizing professional/managerial workplaces in late-capitalist societies.

The mpm version of leftism is quite different from common or garden American radicalism, and it is very much a minority strand. It chooses the ethos of post-ness, doubleness, yearning, irony and the aesthetic, the element of self-conscious formal manipulation in the name of unknowable primal underforces and dangerous supplements, cut by the critiques of the subject and of representation.[1] It chooses them over the traditional course of leftist righteousness (whether in the mode of post-Marxist "systemacity" or of identity politics) and, with equal intensity, over the compromises of left liberalism. I will try to convey how the critique of adjudication looks from within such a project, contrasting the picture sharply with the way it looks from more familiar left vantage points.

In the specific circumstances of the American left today, the critique of adjudication seems, at least, to have a second kind of importance. It is one element in the argument that leftists should buck against, fly in the face of, or subvert the pervasive demand that managers and professionals deny the political element in their workplace practice.

Taking it as a given that statecraft is not for us, that we are not and will not become either judges or legislators, what is the significance of the insight that judges engage in strategized strategic behavior in interpretation, both with regard to legal reasoning and with regard to rights discourse? My answer is that judges are like the rest of us. In our various

339

positions within the bureaucratic institutions of our system, we do the same. Like them, we have to confront the question of bad faith, and, like them, we might gain from critique a margin for boldness.

I claim no *intrinsic* political spin for this or any other form of critique. It is always possible that a given critical practice, by undermining or inducing loss of faith in a particular mode of rightness, will sap the will to resist. As I said at the end of the last chapter, this seems to me an empirical question. Moreover, the mpm impulse within leftism, the impulse to "trash," demystify, and undermine the modes of bourgeois self-certainty, whether liberal or leftist, has an autonomous psychological and social dynamic, which I will try to describe honestly. This dynamic has nothing specifically leftist about it. The point of the left/mpm project is to keep it in tenuous but exciting balance with the equally autonomous impulse to fight the status quo from the left.

A person who experiences self-certainty, rightness, or righteousness, who finds himself or herself possessed of the truth about what's wrong and what to do about it, is unlikely to see anything good in left/mpm, aside from the occasional instance of local internal critique that can serve a particular tactical purpose. Likewise, the characterologically quite distinct difference splitter within the left, who wants to be progressive but also well loved by his or her more moderate colleagues, to be "effective." For both types, it is self-evident that reconstruction should ideally always follow critique, and that the critical impulse should be carefully, protectively channeled away from those elements in the left analysis that have instrumental political value in the larger project. I don't think I can prove that such an attitude is wrong. My strategy aims only to undermine and entice.

Why do it?

Leftism is aimed at transformation of existing social structures on the basis of a critique of their injustice, and specifically at the injustices of racist, capitalist patriarchy. The goal is to replace the system, piece by piece or in medium- or large-sized blocs, with a better system. Mpm is a critique of the characteristic forms of rightness of this same culture and aims at liberation from inner and outer experiences of constraint by reason, in the name, not of justice and a new system, but of the dialectic of system and antisystem, mediated by transgressive artifacts that paradoxically reaffirm the "higher" forms of the values they seem to traduce.

Critique is always motivated. The practitioners of the critiques of adjudication and of rights have often had mixed motives of the kind I am describing here. One motive is leftist and the other is mpm. Suppose for the moment that one didn't have to worry about the leftist implications, what would be mpm motives for critique? The answer is that legal correctness and rights are important parts of the overall project of bourgeois rightness, or reason, or the production of texts that will compel impersonally. An important strand, a defining strand in the mpm project, is a particular attitude toward rightness.

This is the attitude that the demand for agreement and commitment on the basis of representations with the pretension to objectivity is an enemy. The specific enemies have been the central ethical/theoretical concepts of bourgeois culture, including the autonomous individual choosing self, conventional morality, the family, manhood and womanhood, the nation state, humanity. But the central ethical/theoretical concepts of the left have also been targets, including the proletariat, class solidarity, party discipline and socialist realism, and, more recently, sexual and racial identity.

The mpm impulse is to counter or oppose the producers of these artifacts with others. The transgressive artifacts are supposed to put in question the claims of rightness and, at the same time, induce a set of emotions—irony, despair, ecstasy, and so on—that are crushed or blocked when we experience the text or representation as "right."

If we define the left project as the struggle for a more egalitarian and communitarian society, it is not intrinsically connected to rightness in any particular form. But within the left project it has always been true that rightness has played a central role. Leftism has been a bourgeois cultural project within which many leaders and many followers have believed that they were not just left but also right, in the strong sense of possessing coherent and complete ("totalizing") descriptive and prescriptive analyses of the social order.

Of course, critique has been crucial to the dominant "rightness" faction of leftism—that is, critique as ground clearing for the erection of new edifices of rightness. In the Marxist tradition, the slogan of the "scientificity" of Marxism was the repository of the impulse to be right. For the non-Marxist left, the slogans of "planning," "rational social policy," and "the public interest" played the same role. But in the United States, by the end of the 1970s, with the rise of identity politics, left discourse merged with liberal discourse, and the two ideas of the rights of the oppressed and the constitutional validity of their legal claims superseded all earlier versions of rightness.

Moreover, in the diffuse general culture of the bourgeoisie, the rule of law and rights seem to function as crucial paradigms of rightness for everyone. There has been a kind of concentration of experiences of rightness into the two contrasts of law versus politics and rights versus mere preferences. Finally, in the specialized legal academic culture of the United States, legal discourse in general, and rights discourse in particular, underwent an aborted, or perhaps just a compromised, modernist revolution in the legal realist period. Some 1950s postrealist scholars adopted a detached, superior, ironic, nostalgic posture toward law and lawyers and their fellow law professors, a kind of dandified modernism (particularly associated with international law, naturally, since American modernists have always been fascinated by Europe and North Africa). But legal culture as a whole seemed to slide backward into a combination of resurgent formalism with a reified version of policy analysis.

Remember that we are assuming, just for the moment, that it is possible to pursue the mpm project without hurting the left project of change in an egalitarian and communitarian direction. A person with mpm aspirations would "naturally" choose adjudication and rights as targets, and try to counter or oppose the demand of leftists for agreement and commitment based on correct legal reasoning or on the existence of rights. And such a project would have a larger mpm appeal to the extent that the rule of law and rights have become prime vehicles of rightness for the whole society, and for legal discourse in particular.

The mpm counter to rights and the rule of law looks, at first, like the more traditional mode of left theory, based, say, on the model of alienated powers. It deploys internal critique to loosen the sense of closure or necessity that legal and rights analyses try to generate. But rather than putting a new theory in place, it looks to induce, through the artifactual construction of the critique, the modernist emotions associated with the death of reason—ecstasy, irony, depression, and so forth.

There are two familiar ways to misunderstand this kind of mpm project—as proposing "authenticity" as an alternative to classical form, and as proposing a theoretical demonstration of the impossibility of objectivity.

The transgressive artifact

Mpm is the search for intense experience in the interstices of a disrupted rational grid. The characteristic vehicle is a transgressive artifact or performance that "shatters" the forms of "proper" expression in order to express something that those forms suppressed. This kind of definition, which is supposed to get at the characteristic intention of the modernist-postmodernist "auteur," is different from a definition in terms of the specific styles of modernist and postmodernist art, the styles of avant-garde twentieth-century painting, music, dance, fiction, poetry. It is also different from a definition in terms of the specific styles of twentieth-century theorizing in the neo-Marxist, poststructuralist, psychoanalytic, and literary critical traditions.

To escape the oppressive force of the different reified modes of bourgeois representation, one must go through something more than a critique. It is the artifact, not the analysis, that dissolves the reified concept. But the experience mpm proposes as solvent, as a way of living through the concept out onto the other side of it, is always in danger of being captured along the way in forms of expression that will deprive it of that solvent power. Formal innovation is an attack on our will to normalize experience, an attack on our impulse to make experience consistent with, a mere instantiation of, the reified concepts.

The mpm auteur produces an artifact or a performance that is supposed to have this disruptive, potentially ecstatic effect on its audience, but the auteur doesn't imagine that he or she is beyond or outside form—quite the contrary. A basic mpm goal is to create a style at the same time that you destroy a style. Once the style is there in the artifacts or performances, other people can adopt and adapt it to their purposes. Le Corbusier can be a model for the dreary skyscraper style of the 1950s through the 1970s, until postmodern architects innovate again and create a new style that will soon be old and dead.

So we have to distinguish between the disruptive intention that the artifact did or did not realize, and the style that the artifact did or did not launch. By analogy, the intention behind a critique of rights in a particular moment—our own—is a particular kind of disruption. The critique might succeed as disruption in its context and then get reproduced as a theoretical routine, as a piece of critical "normal science," performed over and over again without either disruptive effect or disruptive intention. First-year law teachers teach that *sic utere tuo* is a bad reason for an outcome, without the slightest sense that they are being bad in the way Holmes was being bad when he first formulated the critique.

In short, the whole idea of the transgressive artifact or performance is that it does something, the disruption, that can't be fully accounted for by looking at its content outside its context of belief. And if the artifact succeeds in disrupting its context, it destroys the basis on which it produced its effect, surviving its context as a mere object of admiration or imitation and, of course, as a potential element in a new message.

The left-wing activity of ideology-critique is not part of the modernist/postmodernist project when it aims at clearing the ground for a new construction that would perform the same function as that which is destroyed. But internal critique is part of the project when it is aimed at the pleasure of shedding Reason's dead skin. Mpm internal critique can be leftist in two senses: *(a)* when it is carried out by people who see themselves as doing to leftism what mpm artists see themselves as doing to "art," that is, moving it along by attacking its presuppositions and opening it to what it wants to deny; *(b)* when it proposes that the left should confront those with whom it is ideologically engaged through transgressive artifacts, as well as (or instead of) rational analysis.

Mpm is not about "authenticity"

I might describe the "origin" of the left/mpm attack on adjudication and rights in terms of a respectable left aspiration to make the left more effective by getting rid of some analytic errors that made it hard to link theory and practice. But this would be to betray what is mpm about mpm critique. It would be better to say that by the late 1970s there were, scattered around, people ("diverse" people) who wanted to be leftists, in the sense of wanting to struggle in whatever way for more equality and community, but who experienced the discourse of the left—not just that of its spokespeople—as at the same time self-righteous and simpleminded. Left discourse had moved from its "rational social policy" phase through a brief, late-sixties Marxist phase, in the direction of the Liberal rule of law and rights discourse of the general political culture. But it seemed as reified, indeed as premodern, as ever, in the eyes of people whose allegiances were to modernist and postmodernist sensibility, as well as to leftism.

The question was whether it was possible to challenge this quality of the discourse. The challenge seemed to be working when we identified adjudication and rights as things to critique, and then self-consciously stopped affirming that the trouble with law was that it had a right-wing bias, and that what we needed was to recognize the rights of the oppressed. We began to listen to both plain and fancy legal and political discourse with an ear for the flaws developed by internal critique, and to find them everywhere, and immediately.

In the first, intoxicated phase, you don't expect the rights argument to work any more. You even stop wishing or hoping that it will work. Most of the time it seems all right, indeed even preferable to be "grappling with the real issues," at least when one compares one's situation to that of people who still spend a lot of time generating and believing in rights arguments that seem transparently circular, ambiguous, or incomplete. Grappling with the "real issues" can produce frustration or despair but also wild moments of breakthrough insight and intense moments of emotional involvement with others who are also grappling, perhaps with you—in short, it can produce intersubjective zap.

You purge the conclusory or otherwise "incorrect" use of rights discourse from your own vocabulary, though you find yourself occasionally spontaneously producing it. Then you have to wonder, as you work at the internal critique of your own utterance, whether to interpret it as "just a hangover, a bad habit," in which "the language is speaking me rather than me speaking the language," or as "a trace of a true discourse that I have subordinated by a mere act of power." After working at this conundrum for a bit, you give it up, just the way you gave up trying to prove, first, that legal reasoning, second, that "scientific" social theoretical discourse, and, third, that rights rhetoric "can never work." It *might* be a trace of a true discourse—there's no way to be sure it's not.

On the other side of this experience is the anxiety that is often expressed and often responded to in both the legal and the literary theory versions of the debate, that if you can do this to rights discourse, you can do it to any other discourse as well. In the legal version, both Jeremy Paul[2] and Jack Balkin[3] have interpreted my own work as presupposing that critique made room for "authentic" discourse and as failing to see that there is no possibility of authenticity, given the critique of the subject as situated within discourse and, Balkin adds,[4] the "social construction" of everyone's subjectivity.

"Authenticity" is the last thing people like me meant to appeal to as the "behind" that we might liberate through the critiques of adjudication and of rights. It would be more accurate to say we were trying to liberate "contradiction," "alienation," "desire," "irony," "doubleness," "despair," "ecstasy," and "yearning." Of course, maybe we wanted to liberate them because we thought that they were authentic and that the conventional forms of legal discourse were not. But it seems, at least in hindsight, more accurate to say that we wanted to liberate them because we felt them, and felt their exclusion as a wound.

The crucial difference is between, on the one hand, having a theory of authenticity that might be opposed to a practice of conventional deadness and, on the other hand, feeling contradiction, irony, alienation, despair, and so on, and wanting to get them in play, into the discourse. You don't have to believe that they are authentic in some premodern, perhaps romantic sense in order to feel them, their exclusion, and the potential excitement of their inclusion. You might even say that the whole point of these hallmark modernist experiences is that they deny pretensions of authenticity. It's true that the worst thing in the world, from my 1950s viewpoint, was to be "phony," but the best thing was to be "cool," and then to be "blown away."

Critique, even of adjudication and rights, sometimes delivers (not produces, or causes, but just drives up to the door in a big square truck with) these hallmark experiences. We found ourselves alienated both from still-believing rights speakers and from ourselves, as occasional, inadvertent rights speakers. It was ironic to realize the boundless yet meaningless possibilities of rights discourse, to become its masters, at the price of being able to speak it any way "we" wanted to. Irony was also a way to say to someone else that, although we agreed with what they were advocating, we thought their left legalist assertions were nonsense.

And it was ironic to find oneself saying in rights outbursts just what one thought one didn't think. There was doubleness, both in the experience of having to communicate with believers without believing, and within oneself. Ecstasy came when, after rights talk, one found oneself passionately planning—buzzed out by confrontation but still desirously connected—something to do with others of like mind. Loss, nostalgia, yearning, depression, despair, all describe the way it feels to be zapless in a rightsless world.

Modernism and postmodernism in mpm

In art, postmodern style follows the cultural modernist style I've been talking about, whereas postmodern "theory" follows not that, but another modernism—the rationalist modernism of "the Enlightenment." These usages give rise to a lot of confusion. The mpm I'm referring to has cultural modernism, the avant-garde of the period from the 1890s through the 1950s, as its referent for "m." It has both postmodern style in architecture and painting and postmodern theory, in the sense of Foucault, Derrida, Jane Gallop, and Judith Butler, as its referent for "pm."

This makes mpm an odd duck. I have been emphasizing the "unity" of mpm by defining it in terms of formal innovation, disrupted rational grids, primal underforces, and dangerous supplements. Just now, I tried to draw them together in the critique of rightness, whether in the sense of representational objectivity in art or descriptive and normative objectivity in theory. But one might critique this formulation by emphasizing the differences between artistic and theoretical practices, or the ways in which both aesthetic and theoretical postmodernism have a critique of aesthetic modernism, as well as a critique of the Enlightenment.

Aesthetic modernism as I've been reading it is revolt against the Enlightenment fetishes of rationality and objectivity, and the bourgeois fetish of conventional morality, but it is open to the postmodern critique that it glorifies the auteur. In modernism, the moment of critique and the moments of alienation, doubleness, irony, ecstasy, and despair, especially as condensed in the artist's moment of transgressive artifact creation, all can still be totalized or theorized as an aesthetics and an ethic, even a heroic ethic.

Moreover, the auteurs insisted on theorizing their practice—the creation of transgressive artifacts—in just this way. Wassily Kandinsky wrote about painting, Ezra Pound about poetry, Henry James about the novel, Le Corbusier about architecture, François Truffaut about cinema, Arnold Schoenberg and Ornette Coleman about music. Ernest Hemingway propagated his own mystique.

Postmodernism generalizes the critical element, turning it against modernism as aesthetics, as ideology, as ethic, as system, as mystique, accusing the avant-gardists of mythologizing the subject as the locus or site of the dissolution of everything that was not the subject. Postmodern art endlessly critiques the auteur—flaunting eclecticism, copying, the mundane, and the mechanical, in the face of our hope for Prometheus. Postmodern theorists argue their hypercool ethic against Prometheanism through the critique of the subject/auteur as the product rather than the creator of culture. But here again there is a case for the continuity of the project.

The postmodern critique applies far better to the writings of modernists about modernism than to the artifacts they created. The artifacts seem no less "critical of the subject" than those of postmodernism. The Promethean auteurs were premodern as critics; they slid back into mere rationalism or romanticism the minute they began to theorize their transgressive artifacts. By contrast, the postmodern critics are modernist performers. Derrida and Jane Gallop and Judith Butler are stylistically Promethean, and their writings have power as transgressive artifacts, power that the critic/auteur hopes goes beyond the analytic value of the theory of performance that is ostensibly the thing being performed.

One way to see mpm is as the bleeding together of surrealism with the structuralist critique of the scientism and humanism of both Liberalism and Marxism, under the sign of Friedrich Nietzsche, perhaps. But as long as it's convincing that there is something in mpm that can be talked about, it doesn't seem important to get the genealogy just right.

Critique of critical maximalism

The easiest of all the ways to misread mpm is as a global internal critique, an impossibility theorem that invalidates or refutes the possibility of objectivity, rationality, subjectivity, or representation, or all of them at one blow. In law, for example, the moment of loss of faith has been, since the beginning of the realist critique, often formulated in Holmes's general proposition that "general propositions do not decide concrete cases." In the first attempts to appropriate postmodernism for the use of cls (after the rationalism/irrationalism debate but before the rights debate), it was common to read Jacques Derrida in particular as proposing a general impossibility theorem about representation that could be applied to all claims of determinacy in law.[5] A recent pragmatist version of critical maximalism is the following from Frank Michelman and Margaret Radin:

> Universality implies transcendence of difference, a reach for consensus. So it requires that an order's fundamental premises of right be cast at very high levels of abstraction. But from highly abstract principles of right, convincingly neutral and consistent treatments of concrete cases cannot be derived.[6]

But what we mean by deciding a case by applying a rule is that the abstractions of the rule produce, deductively, an outcome. Whenever we apply a rule, an abstract proposition decides a concrete case. And we apply rules all the time. I see two possibilities: Perhaps every time we apply a rule we are making a mistake and have only the illusion that we have achieved a "convincingly neutral and consistent treatment." Or, perhaps the problem is not with all abstractions, which would include all concepts in the critique, but only with abstractions that are "highly" abstract.

Against the first possibility, I would argue, as I did in Part Three, that we endlessly do experience abstractions as deciding concrete cases, and we fail in our attempts to disrupt the experience of closure. It may be true "in theory" that it is always possible to operate this disruption, but to assert that as truth is to substitute a metaphysics of absence for one of presence, a substitution that doesn't seem like an improvement to me. Minimalist internal critique asserts simply that often, very often, we do succeed, using a socially constructed and transmitted repertoire of critical techniques, in opening closure. But even when we succeed, we have no warrant in the success that what we did was an accurate representation of the "true" openness of the question, as opposed to a mere effect of our critical operations on it.

As to the second possible interpretation, it doesn't seem plausible to distinguish "highly" from otherwise abstract propositions, except in the sense that if the argument from the abstraction succumbed to critique, we know, ex post, that it was "too" abstract. Sometimes abstractions that seem highly abstract are used to decide quite concrete cases—"Thou shalt not kill" may be quite enough to produce closure in a particular case. And sometimes propositions that don't seem abstract at all produce a lot of controversy—"No vehicles in the park," for example.

Minimalist internal critique asserts simply that we often escape the sense of being impersonally compelled to agreement or commitment, with attendant modernist emotions, through an attack on the application of the abstraction. Of course, we unhesitatingly resort to abstractions ourselves in the next moment. Recall the critique of formalism as overestimating the power of particular abstractions (as opposed to the critique of formalism as the theory that all cases can be resolved deductively).

This debate within legal theory has a close parallel in the general culture, where "deconstruction" is sometimes interpreted as a theory that "you can always deconstruct" a claim to objectivity or rationality or representational truth. I think it much more plausible to interpret deconstruction as a practice of minimalist internal critique, as an operation that you can always try on a text, but without any guarantee that it will work in any particular case. When it doesn't work, it doesn't follow either that the text was "in fact" objectively true or rational or that you were a failure at a game someone else could have played successfully.

A deconstruction is better understood as an artifact that "works" in relation to another artifact (the deconstructed text), by dissolving the second artifact's "effect" of impersonal compulsion, always in the name of an unrepresented something (the dangerous supplement, the primal underforce). A deconstruction that works, works like a piece of abstract art that plays off expectations of representation, denying those expectations yet somehow managing to induce new versions of the emotions that we thought we could have only as responses to representation.

In this interpretation, deconstruction doesn't invalidate or refute claims to representational or normative objectivity, except case by case. Postmodernism doesn't show that the subject is "just an intersection in language," or is socially constructed in a way that refutes free will, or even authenticity or spontaneity, except in particular cases. Postmodernism can't refute your personal claim to be the voice of universal reason, when you opine on, say, the decline of academic standards, until it brings its critical technology to bear on that claim; and when it does, who knows, your claim may survive the assault.

I want to be careful not to fall aporetically into the interpretation I'm rejecting here. I'm not sure that it's impossible to show—maybe someone can show—that objectivity, rationality, the subject, and representation are all impossible. I just don't think anyone has shown it so far, but I could be wrong. I've lost faith in the enterprise of trying to show it, as I have in the idea of a perpetual motion machine, in spite of the fact that I have neither a good grasp of the third law of thermodynamics nor a theory of why it's impossible to show that objectivity is impossible.

I can't resist adding a bit of left/modernist critique of postmodernist internal critique. From the Promethean modernist point of view, the postmodern commitment to internal critique seems associated with a psychological commitment to being right in the critique of rightness, and to avoiding either submission to or production of commitment, at any cost. For this reason, it is both funny and satisfying when Derrida, the master of double-invaginated critiques of representation, reveals himself, in *Spectres of Marx,* as a Social Democrat (and one without much in the way of a cultural politics).[7]

Psychologizing the mpm project

I have been describing a series of contexts for loss of faith. In each context, the precipitating factor is critique, and then critique "spreads" to a new context. But critique, when it has an mpm motive, doesn't spread of its own accord, and it is "no accident" when it produces loss of faith. Here are two explanatory frameworks in which one might understand what is happening as something that people do to themselves and to others. The point is that mpm as a critical practice is very much "socially constructed," and the point is also "so what if it's socially constructed?"

First, we might understand critique as a deliberate act of destruction aimed at the experience of rightness in all its forms. It succeeds, as aggression, when the sense of rightness is destroyed in oneself or in others. There is an element of sadism when we direct critique at the beliefs of others, and of internal self-wounding when we direct it at ourselves. We could interpret it as hostility, and in a Freudian way as Oedipal, with rightness figuring as the Father and the superego. The sense of loss and the depression may be consequences of doing in the symbolic father and having no one left to be mad at but oneself.

Second, we might see mpm psychology as exhibitionism, by which I mean the desire to take one's clothes off in public and find oneself applauded rather than punished. Outrageous display that demands approval is the extreme version of the mpm commitment to the artifact, the intermediate term between "official" art and the mundane, between theory and practice, between thought and event. The idea is to turn daily objects into art objects, and daily living patterns into theater or dance, in a way that disrupts both poles, rather than affirming their harmonious distinct existences, and still to please.

Seeing mpm as aggression and exhibitionism is an antidote to seeing it as nothing more than the characteristic style of a cultural moment. A defining element of the cultural moment has been the existence of networks self-consciously pursuing the project of changing "traditional" into mpm culture, understood as a culture of "permanent revolution." It seems to be an open question whether this is the first time in history that such networks have existed (how do they compare with early Buddhist or Christian communities?). The point is that mpm is not just the project of changing one style into another, of bringing about a particular innovation, but also the project of originality, of innovation for its own sake, the "cult" of innovation.

Sanford Levinson and Jack Balkin[8] describe the cultural moment as one in which even the people who are most hostile to modernism and postmodernism, that is, self-conscious "traditionalists," are themselves modernists and postmodernists willy-nilly. They are caught in the same contradictions, deal with the same issues, and use the same vocabulary as the "avant-gardist" networks. They can be traditionalists only in the mode of antiquarianism or political reaction, because the unselfconscious character of the premodern moment can never be restored. But it is only from a peculiar position—either far above the fray, or very frightened of engagement—that the relationship between action and reaction, between aggression and victimization, between exhibitionist and audience, is so utterly effaced.

Closer to the ground, it is obvious that the aggression and exhibitionism are directed not mainly at reactionaries but rather toward the unselfconscious. The project has always been situated within capitalism, with its complex relationship between intelligentsias, middle classes, and masses. It arose and thrives on cultural heterogeneity, but not just any heterogeneity. It is directed at the vital, or at least still breathing, traditions of the bourgeoisie and at the bourgeois project of assimilating peasants, and then workers, into a particular version of "Western" culture.

It has also always drawn on, without merging with, "subjugated knowledges," from African art and African American jazz and rock and roll to "the feminine," "the sexually perverse," and the addicted.[9] In other words, we have to put it in the same frame with leftism, an alternative oppositional/utopian project, but aiming at bourgeois cultural hegemony rather than at bourgeois ownership of the means of production. This is not to say that the image from physics of action and reaction saves us from confusion. The modernist action that "produces" reaction is itself produced just a little earlier (though not *necessarily* in the family romance). Further, the exhibitionist strand in the modernist project makes it dependent on the proffered attention of an audience, an attention that structures the provocateurs.

Mpm as a socially scripted project

This leads us to another perspective on mpm as opposition and innovation. We do it as a culturally scripted project, as the acting out of a part made available, in Western culture, for relating to authority, headed, through the predetermined activity of internal critique, to the predetermined epiphany of loss of faith, toward the predetermined attitudes and artifacts that follow it. The mpm "experience" of giving up and acting out, of dissolution, is not something that just happens; because it is ideologized, it is "one way to go," it gets you allies and texts to read, and these exert normative pressure in the direction of letting go and acting out. Postmodernist, no less than modernist, subjectivity is a norm of culture, a choice that is preformed before "you" adopt it as one of the postmodernist lonely crowd.

It happens to the same person over and over again, and to thousands of different people, in very similar ways. A congeries of literatures instruct us in how to do (simulate) critique, how to recognize (induce) our own loss of faith, how to describe (invent) the appropriate post-loss emotions. If one does it with others, they discipline one if one diverges from the norm. Within the project, there are scripted variations and deviations (rebellion against the project, time serving, entrepreneurship . . .). One can succeed or fail within mpm, become addicted to its sequences, "do it" cynically or in bad faith, just as one can "do" belief in rightness. The mpm progression is long since normalized, become an institution.

At the *same time,* it seems (at least some of the time) like an act of choice, within a constraining context, by a subject unsure if he or she is a subject at all. Mpm is a project, but it is not the only one. People are coerced and seduced into the project, as well as into other ones, but they sometimes experience vertiginous moments of undetermination, though it may always be an illusion.

After choosing to work a bit at this conundrum (am I a chooser, or what?) as it applies to my own case, and then choosing to work at the general problem (free will, or what?) for a—in my case, very short—bit, I find myself adopting the attitude that I can't see any prospect of solution but can't prove it can't be done; attention flagging, I move on, Oedipally, according to script, to something else. (Then there is the scripted character of the Oedipus complex, the chosen character of that script—and so on around the circle, until, "Frankly, my dear, I don't give a damn.")

Mpm as an elite project

Mpm is undeniably an elite project—as a matter of fact—in three quite different senses. First, it is a development within bourgeois, and usually upper-middle-class bourgeois, culture, dependent on particular forms of elite education to provide the rational grids that it disrupts. It is intelligible as disruption only to people who have mastered the various formal languages it targets. This doesn't have to be so, and there are analogous forms of resistance within popular culture. But as long as it is so, it suffers from all kinds of class blindness.

But mpm as already mentioned has always been a project full of people from oppressed, marginalized, and victimized groups, and mpm types have identified, however hypocritically in the eyes of their critics, with "outlaws." This makes it elite in a second sense, in the sense of being a society of self-conscious "illuminati," who reject conventional ideas and indicia of status in favor of the superior ethics, taste, and style of mpm, seen as a project of opposition to the bourgeoisie. It is important to understand that mpm types from nonelite backgrounds often come to it through experiences of rejection or marginalization in their own oppressed communities. Their presence confirms the sense of secret society, both for them and for those from privileged backgrounds.

In this second sense, mpm networks tend to be elitist as well as elite. By this I mean that, just as they are driven by aggression, exhibitionism, and the desire to successfully enact a particular script, they are driven by the pleasures and fears that are associated with belonging to a group that sees itself as "better than," more sophisticated than, ahead of, those it habitually opposes.

There is an analogy to the way liberals in the United States have tended to regard conservatives—that is, as in some sense primitives, people who "just don't get it," as behind the curve cognitively as well as politically. But mpm elitism is neither that of the left in regard to the right, nor that of the "cultural elite" in regard to the "masses." My sense is that it is best grasped by the notion of the "revenge of the nerds," meaning specifically the revenge of the alienated fringe of the intelligentsia against the middle-brow establishments of bourgeois culture, on the one hand, and against the bourgeois leadership of committed leftist groups, on the other.

Finally, mpm is elite, and open to the charge of elitism, because it is organized around performance (the production of transgressive artifacts rather than political "actions") that is supposed to produce reaction. Mpm takes the premodern cultural Other as object (audience), whether that Other is conceived as premodern through and through or as an only partially realized mpm person like the artist herself. It aims to *épater les bourgeois* (rather than to nationalize their property), in the modes of aggression and exhibitionism described above. It presupposes the superiority of mpm, the "right" of mpm performers to hurt the audience, as well as to induce ecstasy and depression, in the name of higher values accessible to the artist/performer and "good for" the audience (while commonly denying—defensively and hypocritically—that it cares at all about audience reaction).

Tit for tat

Elitism is a very bad thing in American popular culture, and particularly in the culture of the American left. But the popular and left critiques of mpm elitism are open to an mpm response. Yes, it is true that mpm vices are elitism, snobbism, condescension, and cultural arrogance. But the anti-elitism of popular and left culture goes well beyond condemnation of these bad attitudes. It looks, from the mpm perspective, like a demand for conformity, a demand for agreement and commitment within culture, that flows from a combination of philistinism with class anxiety. American popular culture insists hysterically on anti-elitism because the dirty secret of the society is intense stratification, and elites pay the price for owning and running absolutely everything in the cheap coin of ordinary-guy-ism.

Within the left, those who are most offended by mpm elitism are the representatives of oppressed masses, whether workers or blacks or women, who are themselves overwhelmingly highly educated, upwardly mobile middle-class people who see themselves as acting for those less well off than themselves. Their anti-elitism represents an implicit deal with those they imagine to be their constituencies (who often include their own parents), a deal that has the same structure as that of the class bargain. Anti-elitism is the price they pay for their roles as leaders.

The mpm strand in leftism rejects these implicit deals, for reasons that vary from person to person. The part of left/mpm elitism that is defensible is the attitude of finding secret allies, sharing various kinds of shame and hopelessness, but affirming the reverse superiority of the outcast group, including its genealogy of transgressive artifacts and performances that signify that we have always been a force in the larger culture on whose rejection we feed.

This kind of elitism is associated with the refusal even to want to be a leader, if the cost includes denying doubleness and claiming a place of the kind that liberal, systematizing, and identity political leftists seem willing to claim. It is elitism with a stoic quality—it can be validated only through despair that is not denied or sublimated into a sense of entitlement, whether the entitlement operates through reason, rights, or victimized identity.

The elitism of left/mpm is in part a fight with the elites of the society over the definition of the obligations of privilege, and in part a fight both against the pretensions of left elites to speak for their constituencies and against the compromises those elites are willing to make on the cultural level to sustain what they imagine are more serious political projects.

Left critique of mpm

It is common for anti-mpm leftists to respond simply that what they mean by leftism is a set of goals, and a set of methods for achieving them, that are incompatible with mpm, so that mpm leftism is an oxymoron. It is also common for them to respond that if we regard mpm not as an (erroneous) theory, but as a set of attitudes or a cultural style, then it is an unattractive, obnoxious style that is inferior to the style of the rest of the left. And it is common to argue that if mpm is to be regarded as one of the theories available for use by leftists, then leftists should be wary of its "tendency," which is to demobilize, to sap the will to fight.

The basic left/mpm response here is not to claim that there is a superior definition of leftism that would allow us to be included as leftists, let alone to show that we are the only "true" leftists. A project, as I defined it in Chapter 1, is an amalgam of a social organization with a textual tradition, and (outside the world of party-building groups) there is no mechanism to settle disputes about inclusion and exclusion other than long-term social/intellectual conflict within the milieus and the discourse of the project. In short, we left/mpm people engage in ideological struggle with others who define themselves as leftists, hoping to convert them if possible, to win particular battles, and to acquiesce with good humor when we lose, and the dialogic moment gives way to the moment when people have to take action of various kinds without full agreement.

This section responds to two versions of mainstream left critique of left/mpm: first, that it trashes objectivity, rationality, representation, subjectivity, legal correctness, rights, and identity, just at the moment when previously oppressed and marginalized groups have, at last, a chance to deploy them against the dominant discourse; and, second, that mpm critique *(a)* destroys our ability to decide what to do, and *(b)* leads to totalitarianism.

First, however, let me list some genealogies of left/mpm, for no other reason than to suggest that we have been present within the left for a long time. Victor Serge and Rodchenko and Stepanova; the early Wilhelm Reich, Jean-Paul Sartre, and Herbert Marcuse; Ralph Ellickson, James Baldwin, Harold Cruse, and Michelle Wallace; surrealism, situationism, and Michel Foucault; Virginia Woolf, W. H. Auden, and Jean Rhys; the Dos Passos of *U.S.A.,* Alan Ginsberg, and the yippies.

Taking the marbles and going home

One way to respond to a new player is to fold the game. Isn't it "odd" that just when women and minorities are getting some rights, the left/mpm types (or is it "white males" in general?) decide that rights are meaningless? Just when third-world peoples overcome colonialism, these same "allies" produce a supposedly devastating critique of sovereignty. And so it goes.

The people doing the trashing have seen themselves as, in some sense, "free" to do it, because they have not been contending for state power or for mass acceptance of their ideas. Initially, it didn't seem sensible to ask questions like, "what will happen to the women's movement if people lose faith in rights?" But, over the last fifteen years, identity politics has revived the academic left. The newly arrived white women and minority academic activists see themselves as having both an audience in the educated non-academic left and some voice in the national policy debates organized by the media. They have revived the question of the political consequences of different rhetorical choices.

In the last chapter, I argued that it is an empirical issue whether loss of faith increases or decreases activism, and that the argument "but they use steroids" embraces bad faith without, to my mind, making a case that there really is a nasty trade-off between honesty and effectiveness. Moreover, liberals have trashed Marxist grand theory, Marxists have trashed rights theory, and left/mpm types have trashed both, for generations, since long before the civil rights movement or the second wave of feminism. All this trashing may have been wrong from the start, but mpm types have engaged in it for a long time as a strategic activity, and not only as a response to the (limited) empowerment of oppressed groups.

The left/mpm position *is* critical of the middle-class intellectual leaders of the new social movements, to the extent that they assimilate themselves to the dominant discourses of legality, rights, and identity, whether they do so out of faith or as an effective maneuver. It is not a "demand" that they stop doing so, nor a claim that there is a more effective alternative way, but merely a comradely expression of disagreement, in the form of a transgressive artifact or two.

A variant is that it is easy enough for upper-middle-class white males to trash legal correctness, rights, and identity because they don't need them, being immune through white skin privilege and maleness to the oppressions visited on Others. The discourses of legal correctness and rights are, I argued at length in Parts Four and Five, powerful stabilizing elements in the American political system. If one can imagine a left academic critique that "destroyed" them, then I suppose one can imagine a political free-for-all, in which conservatism would have a good chance of doing in liberalism and moving the system as a whole to the right in a way far more profound than the Gingrich Revolution. The principal victims of such a shift to the right would be the poor, white women, and minorities.

So, as I said in the last chapter, I am all in favor of deploying these discourses for strategic reasons, whether before courts or in general political debate, as long as the deployer has in mind the element of bad faith in his or her performance. And I agree that there is an element of "luxury" in the identity position of the academic who renounces the struggle for state power, so as to be "true" to the truth-telling impulse, even while denying the possibility of truth. The left in left/mpm supports spending some time looking for ways to intervene in policy debates that seem likely to be good for the oppressed, without betraying mpm. And, as I will argue at the end of this chapter, it also supports, without requiring one to choose, the alternative of left workplace politics, localism without national resonance.

One presupposition of left/mpm is that the system is stable over the long term, in spite of the endless Marxist and post-Marxist production of crisis theories and in spite of real crises all the time in particular places. A second is that developments in academic theory have virtually no consequences for national politics (other than to provide, in the titles of PMLA panels, material for right-wing parody).[10]

This may be wrong, and it may be that academic leftists should spend *all* of their time developing rhetorically effective interventions in national political debate and no time helping the virus on its course. I think this makes some sense for left liberals and for white women and minorities in general. But I don't think it makes sense for the very small group of academics, male and female, white and of color, whose post-Marxist or left/mpm sentiments make it difficult to imagine masquerading effectively as mainstreamers. And I don't believe the reason I think this is that I personally have less to lose from, say, the erosion of civil liberties than my colleagues whose backgrounds are less privileged than my own.

It was once plausible to make the much stronger response that mpm was intrinsic to leftism, because loss of faith represented the recovery of alienated powers. In other words, internal critique showed us the ways in which we allowed our understanding to be controlled by reified entities, forms of necessity invented and projected out onto nature or society (God, the market, the law, Marxism). And the projections could be seen as em-

powering experts, the owners of the technical discourses of religion or law
or economics or Marxism, to pursue their conscious or unconscious political projects through the manipulation of the supposedly objective and
rational "sciences" of understanding society.

In this model, mpm critique is leftist per se, because it is a necessary
part of the egalitarian and communitarian project. It returns to "ordinary
people," or to "mobilized masses," powers that they had delegated to experts under the illusion that the experts possessed knowledge not accessible
to them. Left/mpm would then represent the antinomian or anarchist
strand within leftism, with at least a claim to be the true (antifaith) faith.
We might even add that leftism is just as essential to mpm as mpm is to
leftism, because the various forms of hierarchy and alienated community
block or frustrate the production of mpm. This sometimes seems true to
me, but more often it seems impossible to fuse leftism and mpm this way.

First, there is nothing to guarantee that the disempowerment of experts
through de-reification would lead to egalitarian or communitarian decisions by ordinary or mobilized people. Second, what you get from de-
alienation is not authenticity, as I argued above. There is no end to the
layers of reification, or even a meaningful sense in which one could function
without reification. Third, mpm sometimes thrives on repressive structures
and withers in their absence. In order to believe in an organic connection
between critique and the egalitarian and communitarian impulses, one has
to go beyond left/mpm and believe in reconstruction.

Against reconstruction

It was once the case that the answer to left/mpm was a theory, whether
Marxism or Liberalism. That is no longer the case, at least in the academic
left. The answer to left/mpm is rather a charge, the charge of "nihilism,"
a critique of the bad consequences of nihilism, and a project—reconstruction.

Sometimes the author has a specific reconstruction in mind and presents
it full blown as the next step after critique,[11] as something to replace what
has been critiqued. When this is the case, the only fair response is to
critique it in its turn, subscribe to it, or just ignore it. More often, the
author proposes the project of reconstruction, rather than any particular
reconstruction. One favors the project not because one has a proposal but
because one believes that we ought to do it, or at least try it, that bad
consequences will follow if we fail, and that there are at least some inter-

esting possibilities, some hopeful avenues, some useful bits and pieces available for the task.

A striking aspect of calls for reconstruction is that the author not uncommonly treats critiques as decisive refutations of previous theories. An important trope is the suggestion that critique is easy, while reconstruction is hard, that it is self-indulgently pleasant to go on trashing one thing after another, since we all know how to do it, but morally bracing to roll up our sleeves and get down to the less fashionable but in the long run more constructive task of reconstructing.

A second striking aspect is that the same reconstructionist who asserts the validity of prior critiques, and claims that they are easy to do, is likely to explicitly or implicitly call for reconstructions that will perform just the same function that was performed by the critiqued entities. This is the function of representing social order in a way that would allow us to have some assurance that we are right to be left, and right to pursue particular strategies in favor of equality and community. Here is an example, from the very end of an article about international legal scholarship:

> Ultimately, by following modernism to its logical conclusion, the New Stream purists—those arguing from within the limits of critical epistemology—produced what can be understood as the last modernist text of international law . . . The next wave of international legal literature must find a way to overcome what seems a fundamental tension between objectivism and criticism. From the modernist perspective, international law cannot transcend its *problematic.* If international law discourse stands a chance to live up to the role created for it in the fight for world justice, we must conceive of an ethical foundation for international social life beyond modernism.[12]

This style of reconstructionism can be seen as the disinherited scion of the classical project of recuperating alienated powers. The idea is that internal critique dissolves the reified entities that we project onto nature or society in order to explain the necessity and justice of the way things are. But it does this only as ground clearing for a new theory, one that locates agency in human beings, discrediting the way things are while simultaneously indicating how to make them better. The survivors of the shipwreck of grand theory have always believed in internal critique, for example in Marx's critique of bourgeois political economy, or in a pragmatist critique of the way individualism corrupts social policy, and they have never believed in rights or identity in their modern forms. But they still believe in the "systematicity" of social order and in the possibility of an ethical foundation.

This form of endorsement of critique doesn't problematize the category of theory. Quite the contrary, critique is in the service of ultimate rightness, and the call for reconstruction is an affirmation of faith in theory as way to rightness. The project of reconstruction (as opposed to any particular proposal) looks, from a left/mpm point of view, like the reification or fetishism of theory, in a mode parallel to the fetishism of God, the market, class, law, and rights. Left/mpm, by contrast, is caught up for better or worse in the "viral" progress of critique, and in so much as there is a lesson from the progress of the virus, it would seem to be to anticipate loss of faith in theory in general and general theory in particular. But I hasten to add once again that losing faith in theory doesn't mean giving up doing theory—it just means giving up the expectation of rightness in the doing.

It will come as no surprise that I don't think I can demonstrate that reconstruction is impossible. But, as usual, I do think something can be said about the rational side of faith. Here, as elsewhere, as in the case of God, legal correctness, and rights, reconstructionists urge us to believe in and strive for reconstruction because there would be many bad consequences of its failure or impossibility, such as that we wouldn't have any assurances either in our leftism or in our particular leftist strategies, that we would become totalitarians, and so forth. Although I don't think these are the real issues, I'll address them as best I can.

Nihilism

Mpm critique, the induction of loss of faith, and characteristic associated emotions, seen as a project, negate a particular experience, that of rightness, in favor of another experience. When it comes to "deciding" whether or not to be a leftist, this project has nothing to offer. Because of these commitments, to critique and loss of faith, without commitment to providing other forms of rightness in the place of what is dissolved, it is common to describe it as nihilist. And it is well known that nihilism is both wrong and of evil tendency.

As Michael Fischl has pointed out,[13] there is something odd about this argument. It seems to presuppose that we prefer error to enlightenment, when enlightenment is at the cost of beliefs that seemed useful when we still believed in them. Why wouldn't we welcome the critique, no matter how left/mpm its ulterior motive, as long as after hearing it we were no longer convinced of the truth of our previous view?

Critique doesn't leave us with "nothing," in the sense of making it impossible to decide what to do, say, whether or not to be a leftist, or of making it impossible to figure out enough about how the social order works to choose a strategy of left action within it. Those of us who are not moral realists (believers in the objective truth of moral propositions) are used to committing ourselves to projects, and deciding on strategies, on the basis of a balancing of conflicting ethical and practical considerations. In the end, we make the leap into commitment or action. That we don't believe we can demonstrate the correctness of our choices doesn't make us nihilists, at least not in our own eyes.

We misunderstand internal critique if we imagine that it might lead to a situation in which we had lost faith in "everything," so that we just wouldn't know what to believe in or do. Critique changes our attitude toward a particular theory (whichever we successfully critique) that generated a particular sentiment of rightness. It leaves us whatever we had before critique, in the way of tools for working out our commitments and our concrete plans for the future. It seems odd to me to suppose that we could ever, conceivably, be without resources of this kind, even if each of us was a veritable Hercules of critical destruction.

Of course, a person might be committed to egalitarianism only because of belief in rights, and in particular rights. The loss of faith in rights in general might lead such a person to abandon egalitarianism, in favor of another attitude, say, belief in natural inequality, that seemed more plausible when not countered by a particular belief in rights now undermined by critique. But the causal chain might move in the other direction as well: loss of faith in property rights might permit previously thwarted egalitarian sentiments to flower.

It might be possible to make convincing generalizations about the causal tendency of the left/mpm project of critique, loss of faith, and attendant emotions. After the proposal that the tendency is demoralization, the most popular may be that left/mpm leads to Hitler and Stalin. As I understand this argument, it goes something like this. Stalinism and Nazism represent the powerful, irreducible force of evil in human nature. But they inflicted previously unimaginable suffering, degradation, and destruction, far beyond the normal. They were able to do this because they were nihilist, meaning that they denied the validity of fundamental human rights. Nietzsche's cult of the Superman and the moral relativism of Weimar are responsible.

The mirror image: Stalinism and Nazism represent the powerful, irreducible force of evil in human nature. But they inflicted previously unimaginable suffering, degradation, and destruction, far beyond the normal.

They were able to do this because they were totalitarian, meaning that they proclaimed the absolute truth of their theories. Therefore, skepticism is the true antidote to the repetition of the Holocaust and the gulag. Hegel's cult of Absolute Reason and blind obedience to authority are responsible.

It may be possible to combine the theory that the evil of the twentieth century is caused by the denial of reason (nihilism) with the theory that it is caused by excessive commitment to reason (totalitarianism). Perhaps on a higher level true believers are nihilists and vice versa. Or perhaps one should be a true believer in fundamental human rights and a nihilist about racist and Marxist theories.

But from the point of view of loss of faith in reason (which is not an impossibility theory about reason), it seems unlikely that either believing or disbelieving in reason in general, or in any particular rational construction, has this kind of causal power. It seems more likely that belief and denial of reason can each have many different meanings and combine in an infinite number of ways with idiosyncratic or socially constructed attitudes, sentiments, and dispositions. Belief and denial more likely were constitutive but not controlling elements in many forms of collaboration with and opposition to Nazism and Stalinism, rather than elements with a single intrinsic or inherent tendency.

Left/mpm as an intersectional project

Left/mpm artifacts are at the intersection of two projects, one leftist and the other mpm. These are designed to play two dramas on this single stage. One idea is to modernize or postmodernize the leftist project, and the other is to move the world leftward by doing in right-wing forms of rightness. What this means is that there is strategic behavior within the intersection. The mpm part of left/mpm aims to move the left project along rather than to destroy it—allegiance to mpm is no more "absolute" than allegiance to leftism. In ideological struggle/dialogue with the right, we choose our themes/targets with an eye to converting waverers, and avoid themes/targets that can be predicted to demoralize other leftists (would that we were so powerful) when the left/mpm payoff is small or nonexistent.

In other words, the left, as I am using the term, is a "site" for particular, outward- and inward-looking ideological encounters and coalitions, rather than a set of principles or a program.[14] It is, for me, a "position" as well, by which I mean that I much prefer to hang with liberals, identity politicians, and post-Marxists, rather than with the varieties of right-wing or centrist/mpm types. But it is no more conceivable, to me, to be left through and through than to be mpm through and through.

The social construction of rightness

I think the protective impulse toward one's own sense of rightness is socially constructed, by which I mean that we learn rightness as a way to deal with despair, depression, and internal contradiction, and also learn it as a script that promises social power to those who master it. I don't mean to propose a theory of human nature, an anthropology that would explain or be right about the origins of rightness. The following Foucaldian account of legal education is meant to suggest that there are investments in rightness that one might give up without threatening one's selfhood, rather than to show what rightness "is."

I want also to urge a social theoretical claim about modern Western society: that legal discourse and legal education are sites for the production, through discipline, of the modern subject's commitment to rightness. Rightness may be a defense mechanism—armory through reified texts against fears and longings—or it may be the superego, but it is also a structural element in a disciplinary society. Law and legal education are among the producers of the attitude of the professional who operates disciplinary mechanisms from the location of a disciplinarian self constituted by discipline.

Rightness and legal education

Novels, movies, and television shows about elite legal education and law practice are staples of American popular culture. The portrait they offer makes the first year of law school look strikingly like the institutions Foucault describes in *Discipline and Punish.*[15] He was preoccupied with disciplines that transformed bodily capacities and constituted desires, as in monastic, hygienic, sexual, and military discipline. Legal education is focused on a different complex: the capacity to be right about the exercise of state power, and the desire to put that capacity to someone else's use. But the parallels are numerous.

Legal education uses the techniques of "normalization," that is, of oral examination, written examination, the compiling of dossiers, and the production of résumés that allow us to understand each person involved by placing him or her in relation to others on measurement scales. It does this much more intensely than other American educational institutions, with the exception of medical school, which is the object of a similar pop cultural fascination.[16]

The centerpiece of legal education, as of all the Foucaldian disciplinary institutions, is the "examination" (the military review, confession, hospital "visitation"), in the form of the Socratic method. As in Bentham's panopticon, the teacher observes from the front of the class. He or she can at any time require any student to produce legal discourse in response to a question, and then offer small pellets of praise or punishment according to the performance.

The goal is to induce "thinking like a lawyer," that is, to constitute the student as a subject who can perform according to the disciplinary plan as a matter of internal commitment, rather having to be controlled from the outside by threats and promises specific to each situation. The extraordinary exposure of the Socratic method is designed to change the student, so that this very kind of supervisory technique will be unnecessary when the student becomes a lawyer. As with the other forms of discipline, the idea is to produce an "automaton," to shape the will rather than to break it, to give it new, particular capacities (thinking like a lawyer) that go with a new, particular submission to authority (the client and the judge).

From the beginning, the teacher conveys that there are right and wrong, or at least better and worse, answers to her questions, but there is no formula offered by which the student can "compute" these, no verifiability, and the teacher, in the pure version, never gives an answer herself. The sequence of questions is supposed to lead the student and the class to recognize that the student's formulation of a rule or of a reason for a rule (a "principle") is wrong because inconsistent with what the student and the class already know but hadn't seen as relevant.

The teacher requires students to speak as if they knew they were right about the legal question before the class, and then to take the consequences if they turn out to be wrong. (The most important consequences have to do with fear of failure and loss of face.) The teacher rejects—treats as wrong—responses in the form of a question, an expression of ambivalence, a request for more information, a distanced comment on the situation ("isn't it interesting that. . ."), and especially a lay normative evaluation ("it doesn't seem fair that. . ."). The only way to be right is to perform in the role of law speaker. But the teacher does not explain why an answer offered in role was wrong, except by demonstrating that it leads to a contradiction with the answer to another hypothetical. To be right is simply not to be shown wrong.

In this situation, students hunt (often desperately) for a mode of response that will be effective in the setting. What they find is that they get by the first hurdle only by speech that presupposes that there is a correct legal answer to the question, and that the speaker knows it and is offering it. In other words, at this first level, they can't participate unless they accept the self-understanding of the profession that its discourse is autonomous from the general political (ideological) discourse of the time. Students learn to produce the mode of law speech appropriate to the institution of adjudication (as opposed to legislation) by trial and error, looking for whatever the teacher will accept. They discover, not in a book, but in themselves and in their fellow students, the voice of the neutral law speaker, willing to commit to a particular solution, and it works.

When it comes to the way to be right once one has learned to speak (not think) like a lawyer, the situation is much more complicated. In gross terms, conservatives teach students to be right by deduction and liberals teach them to be right by policy argument. But there are the reversals of (deductive) conservative economic policy argument and (deductive) liberal rights argument.

The well-prepared elite law student learns to adjust the response to the type of rightness the teacher is looking for, learns the variety of discourses of rightness that prevail in the academy, as models of the variety of necessitarian discourses that judges will accept. Here again, students know they are doing well only because in fact their production of necessitarian discourse works with the particular teacher, inducing a good grade in response to the teacher's induction of their new lawyer subjectivity.

The quite surprising, even shocking, power of all this as transformative experience has to do with the following paradox. The student learns, first, to distinguish a meaningful contribution to the process of decision from the various evasions that we endlessly engage in, through the classroom experience of the rejection of all statements that don't focus on what the law is or should be. Second, the student learns that there is a limited set of discourses of necessity, and that they work.

But the student learns no metadiscourse that permits necessitarian choice between necessitarian discourses. Indeed, the overwhelming suggestion is that there is no such discourse available in the setting. The only thing that works is to figure out what side you are on (later, what side the client is on) and then argue according to the predilections of the decision maker (here the teacher, later the judge). The self that emerges from this experience will be committed to the kind of bad faith I described in Chapter 8. Strategic behavior is everywhere. But the student and the lawyer learn that they must always suppress it, submerge it in a necessitarian discourse that everyone knows is only part of the story.

Rightness is a complex technique one has mastered—something other people can't do, something that has effects in the world (first grades, then appellate decisions)—and simultaneously "just a rhetoric." On the surface, the law speaker says that he is right because the materials and good legal reasoning in the particular situation compel the outcome (whether a jury verdict or a rule choice) impersonally. Below the surface, we scramble to psyche out the client and judge as anything but impersonally motivated, with predictions of effectiveness the only basis of choice about what to do.

It is, I think, easy to see how one develops a deep investment in rightness thus understood. For the lawyer and the judge, though in different ways, rightness is simultaneously power and safety: power because it works, safety because it protects against the charge of moral nihilism for the lawyer and against the charge of arbitrary violence for the judge who wields state power. But it also delivers these with a safety valve: legal rightness is not totalitarian, because "everyone" understands that, at the same time that it empowers and protects in fact, one doesn't have to take it altogether seriously.

This may explain its iconic status in popular culture. The lawyer and the judge are hardly omnipresent in everyday life. But the attitude they represent, the bad faith, inside-outside, strategized production of the discourse of rightness, is omnipresent. In both the corporate world and in that of public administration, actors constantly assert that they are just following the rules, doing their jobs by the book, without responsibility for the "political" consequences. They plead compulsion by correct interpretation to do things they would never do, they claim, if they were themselves the legislator (board of directors).

The objects of administration, both in the private corporate sphere and in the public one, are more and more likely to be themselves administrators in another context. We know, from our lives as administrators, that when those who are administering us speak the language of rightness in the interpretation of their bureaucratic mandates, they are as likely as we are in our jobs to be strategizing for or against, rather than merely "applying the regs." And we know there is real drama in their decisions, because we know that sometimes we ourselves are "really" bound, that we allocate our time according to ideological projects that may be no more than prejudices, but may be also what we believe in most deeply, and that in the allocation we make endless economic choices about credibility and plausibility with our interpretive communities.

Legal discourse as an instance of managerial discourse in general

I have written at length elsewhere on left/mpm strategies for changing legal education to reduce its complicity in constituting the particular subjectivity I have been describing.[17] This section pushes the argument in a different direction. As I pointed out in the last paragraph, many institutions operate through discourses that have the same bad-faith quality as legal discourse. There are two levels to the parallel.

First, most large organizations that employ professionals, technicians, and managers have "missions" that define them: private corporations are supposed to maximize profits while "serving" their customers, hospitals and schools and universities have health and education missions, government bureaucracies have statutorily defined goals under the general rubric of the public interest. These roles are partial from the point of view of ideological conflict: the organizations are part of a system of division of labor, of role specialization. The theory is that each should "do its job" rather than either the jobs of other institutions or the "political" job of looking out for its impact on the system as a whole.

The role of looking out for the system as a whole is supposedly *(a)* located in the legislative branches of local, state, and federal governments (themselves geographically and jurisdictionally specialized) and *(b)* "political" in just the sense that the specialized subroles of businesses, nonprofit organizations, and government agencies are not. Liberalism and conservatism, and all the other types of politics as well, are supposed to be present there, but not in the organizations of "civil society." In this respect, the relationship of the judiciary to the legislature is a special case of the very general mode of organizational role specialization of the advanced mixed-capitalist societies.

The second element in the parallel is that the people who participate in collective decision making within these bureaucracies know that their decisions have big effects on the distributional conflicts that are organized through the ideas of liberalism and conservatism. Moreover, these big effects are not clearly determined by the initial definitions of organizational roles. What the corporation does will, for example, sometimes have a massive effect on the economic life of the community where it is located. But profit maximizing is far too vague to specify how to direct that effect. Internally, everyone knows that different workplaces have radically different "corporate cultures," ranging, for example, from the relatively hierarchical and formal through the relatively egalitarian and informal. Management consultants develop typologies on the assumption that corporate culture is not uniquely determined by mission.

Like judges making legal rules with distributive effects, managers cast decisions about what these organizations should do, externally and internally, in the manipulable rhetorics of institutional mission, profit making, health, education, and public interest, all referring back to the explicit mandates of corporate organizational documents or statutes. The strategy chosen, within the general role specification, is like a judge-made rule, in that it may have massive distributive effects without being compelled by the discourse that legitimates it. This seems equally true for corporations, hospitals, schools, universities, and government agencies.

The people who run institutions operate in bad faith in the same way judges do. On the one hand, they often experience their missions as sufficiently defined, given the practical circumstances, so that they are compelled to adopt particular strategies and reject others. To do anything else would be "unprofessional," a "breach of trust," "suicidal from the point of view of the bottom line," or whatever. On the other hand, they also manipulate the discourse of necessity to present all kinds of strategic choices that are not thus compelled as necessary and right. They constantly deploy their resources, they constantly work, just as judges do, to shape and reshape the necessity that they are supposedly merely submitting to. Competent "players" know this to be true, although there will often be disagreement about when and where there is "really" discretion. But the public discourse, as opposed to the back-room discourse of the organization, resolutely denies it.

Like legal discourse, the discourses of management seem remarkably stable, by which I mean that, for most participants, most of the time, there seems to be no alternative to casting decision making in their terms and little danger that the widely perceived element of indeterminacy will lead to erratic or even unpredictable organizational behavior. To some extent, this stability reflects the prevalence of the experience of being bound or constrained by widely accepted mission definitions. Organizations do what they do because that's what they were organized to do. But given the indeterminacy, given the possibility of strategically directed work, the stability has to have other sources.

One such source is the common perception of liberal and conservative managers that, while it is permissible to manipulate "at the margins" in a liberal or conservative way, it is important not to "go too far" in trying to achieve extradiscursive political objectives. The exercise of discretion shouldn't upset the general balance that exists, at any given moment, among overtly or implicitly organized internal factions. This "metarule" of moderation gets much of its force from an implicit theory: If you take your liberal or conservative views about how to handle the distributively significant leeways within the mission statement too far, you risk "politicizing" the institution, and you will be seen as "disloyal."

Politicization and disloyalty

The idea of politicization is complex. It refers, on one level, to the content of debate about what decisions to make and, on another, to its quality as a reflection of the life of the institutional community in question. At the level of content, we say the debate is politicized when participants have "agendas" that go beyond the implicit or explicit definition of the mission of the institution *and* push those agendas beyond the leeways that everyone understands to be inevitable. The cardinal sin is to abandon the convention that the discourse is one of necessity, openly acknowledge its manipulability, and appeal beyond it to general political right and wrong.

But politicization also connotes a "slide" into immoral behaviors that go beyond interpretive infidelity. There is the Madisonian idea of faction, often the referent of the word "partisan." Loyalty to a faction can take precedence over loyalty to the institution. People support their friends even when they know they are in the wrong, and submit blindly to clique discipline, forfeiting their ability to exercise independent, principled judgment without regard to persons. Another reference is to corruption, to actual cheating, lying, or stealing in order to increase one's share of money or power or prestige, without regard to the common interest.

Paradoxically reinforcing this idea of the triumph of the merely personal is the idea that the politicizer has been seized by ideology in the bad sense, in which it indicates fanaticism, willingness to let the end justify immoral means out of a misplaced excess of righteousness. The ideological politicizer demonizes enemies, treating his own side as all good and the other as all bad, guided not just by the spirit of faction, but also by a deluded sense that his own side has a correct theory that shows that the other side is evil. The ideologue is a character, unable to compromise, a polarizer or splitter, the enemy of collective good feeling.

This diffuse combination of connotations, including faction, corruption, and the fanaticism of the "true believer," puts the ideologue outside the tenuous, intermediate position of bad faith. In bad faith, one honors both the idea that the discourse of decision is a neutral one, within which the parties are searching for a right answer, and the idea that we all know that there is an element of manipulability to that same discourse. Staying in bad faith is tricky work. You push your agenda through the discourse, never indicating the slightest doubt about its necessitarian presuppositions, while honoring the implicit rules about what would be going too far.

Politicizing is disloyal almost by definition. First, it endangers the organization's ability to perform its mission. Second, it endangers everyone's investment in institutional life, including the investment in a particular set of "private" patterns of interaction and the investment in the prestige of the institution in the world it serves.

Loyalty is partly a contractual idea and partly a notion of solidarity based on the concrete history of group life. When you join the institution, you implicitly sign on to the set of arrangements, styles of interaction, collective conceptions of role, and so on, that define it. When you work with people every day, depending on them in many ways that aren't codified, and don't have anything to do with large political issues, you need an ethic of mutual forbearance, of compromise and boundary observance, or everyone will be miserable. Avoiding this misery is more than a matter of self-interest—there is an ethic of collegiality that is independent of interest, just as it is independent of politics.

Loyalty is a "spirit" that you can have more or less of and that you can also just plain lack. Then you are disloyal, which is positively to be bad, rather than ranked low on a common scale. Groups reward people according to loyalty, but they sanction them for disloyalty. Moreover, loyalty issues invoke the *raison d'état* aspect of administration. Usually, you aren't fired for it, or formally sanctioned in any way. But once your bosses, perhaps tuned in to coworker gossip, clearly identify you in their own minds as in this category, then everyone expects them to exercise all their different kinds of low-level discretion to make sure, for the good of the organization, that you don't get promoted or otherwise rise to power.

Everyone understands that gossiping groups, administrators, and clique leaders operate on a kind of benefit-of-the-doubt system with regard to loyalty. We know that we can't see into the soul directly, and that the concept is sufficiently fluid as to allow many situations in which equally loyal people have different interpretations of what loyalty requires. But it is also true that disloyalty is something a person would want to hide, both because it is intrinsically shameful, and because if it is found out, there will be terrible sanctions.

So suspicions or doubts about disloyalty can exist, which are quite different from disagreements about what loyalty is or about how much of the virtue of loyalty people have. As a negative quality of the soul, people can let it slip or betray themselves as betrayers in unthinking moments. Violating a rule that everyone had agreed was necessarily implicit in the idea of loyalty is one of the few ways a person can make his or her disloyalty positively known. And, from time to time, people quite blatantly behave this way, because they have to honor their other commitments, or because they are a little crazy, or because they can't help bearing witness to their vices.

In this context, to be loyal is to be committed to preserving the integrity of the bad-faith discourse, first, by never openly challenging its necessitarian conventions and, second, by not pressing its leeways so far that the fragile structure of denial threatens to collapse into politicization. I think there are many participants in institutional politics, in our system, for whom it goes without saying that there is a real trade-off here: they believe that the institution should play a different, more left-wing role than it does, but they fear that to push for this role would risk politicization and would be perceived as disloyal.

The notion that this is the real choice gets strength from real experiences, in which people, at whatever institutional level, get embroiled in destructive conflicts, cast in terms of rightness, that bring out the monster and the lunatic in all concerned. And sometimes people who, to the observer, seem merely naive or stubborn or idealistic or literal-minded, rather than vicious, get tagged as disloyal, never manage to shake the tag, and suffer career disaster.

Disloyalty as loss of faith

Loyalty to the institution, in this complex sense of the will to preserve its bad-faith discourse, so as to preserve its external and internal equilibrium, can be the faith of bad faith. By this I mean that loyalty can be deeply felt, even though it can also be feigned; it can be wholehearted even though it can also be coerced. Loss of faith in loyalty as something to strive for can be like loss of faith in God or legal correctness. Sometimes one feels loyalty as a fact, as one feels legal constraint as a fact. But one loses any sense that it is better to be loyal than disloyal, that the constraint when one feels it is the reflection or emanation of something behind, that is "intrinsically" right, and so forth.

Disloyalty of this kind is a characteristic left/mpm attitude. It starts from the idea that you are wherever you are, so that "if you don't like it here, go back to Russia, where you belong" isn't an alternative. The contractual idea lacks force, because we middle-class, highly educated types grow up in a world in which the question is which large organization to work for. They all have missions that are partial and ethics of loyalty that you will be expected to sign on to. But they are also compromised or complicit in the larger order.

From a left point of view, there are a few public interest organizations that have explicit progressive goals such that loyalty to the organization does not require even a pro forma renunciation of the idea that political and private life can be integrated. If, for one reason or another (including, perhaps, lack of moral fiber, mpm intolerance, or student loans), you are not going to work for one of these, you have to decide what attitude to take toward the particular mission definition and demand for loyalty imposed by an ostensibly apolitical organization.

A typical attitude is to recognize the left critique of the organization, and to hope, first, that it won't be as bad as its bad rap and, second, that the leeways of the bad-faith discourse will permit moving it in a progressive direction, once one has done one's time and acquired some power. Liberal recruiters subtly or blatantly encourage this understanding. But often, often, it turns out that the leeways are narrow, and the implicit metadiscourse of avoiding politicization and demonstrating loyalty effectively closes down any possibility of left workplace politics.

Then you will find yourself not believing in what they say you have to believe in if you are to be a "true" member of the community. If you declare this, you will be ostracized. So you play the game, but without giving up your reservations. You find yourself endlessly speaking a language of rightness, while internally denying its presuppositions. You resign yourself, but feel complicit in the retrograde aspects of the organization's performance and guilty about not using your institutionally granted powers for the good of the oppressed.

In a short time, the cognitive dissonance between what you said to yourself you were doing (boring from within) and your actual situation (bored with your job) becomes intolerable, and you find yourself unthinkingly reproducing the implicit stabilizing consensus, rather than resisting it. You develop a variety of mentor-mentee and coworker relationships that provide depoliticized forms of personal happiness. The contract now has a new form. First, leaving becomes more costly with each passing year. Second, internal strategies that might disrupt the bad-faith discourse will jeopardize relationships that make daily life tolerable.

Disloyalty can be a vice. But, in this situation, it is more matter-of-fact. You just aren't loyal, though you might, you can see, looking down the road, become loyal (like "them"). That might be a bad outcome. If you think so, disloyalty is refusal of allegiance rather than a vocation of betrayal.

In defense of politicization and passivity

For people who have lost (or never had) faith in bad faith, who have lost the capacity to believe and not believe at the same time, so that they experience the discourse sometimes as brute (desacralized) constraint and sometimes as merely instrumental, the demand for loyalty to avoid politicization is completely understandable, however unmeetable. Indeed, one reason for keeping up bad faith is the belief that if one loses faith in it, one has to choose between politicization and hypocrisy or time serving. What about the left/mpm project? If there's nothing else to do, I'm all in favor of abandoning it.

But it can't be that there is *never* anything else to do. If there are any possibilities at all, I'm proposing not a solution but an attitude, taking hope from Holmes's aphorism that every idea is an incitement. Sometimes it makes sense to strategize, not the best result within the discourse that will leave the discourse and its implicit metanorm of moderation intact, but the politicization of the setting. Sometimes it doesn't make sense, in which case passivity by all means. Alternating between politicizing and passivity might be a better attitude than alternating between bad faith and passivity. Better a contradiction than a defense mechanism.

Politicizing the environment doesn't mean setting out to destroy it, and in the mpm version of leftism, it obviously doesn't mean believing fanatically in one's truth. It does mean trying to set up a political identity to the left of liberal bad faith, without being or seeming to be a wrecker.

Sometimes, politicizing means using the resources of the bad-faith discourse to push its contradictions to the point where everyone feels, though still within the discourse, that something fundamental is at stake, that the discourse has been changed by the revelation of deeper levels of disagreement than had previously been allowed access to consciousness. Sometimes it means challenging the presuppositions, in the name of left/mpm anti-truth—coming out of the closet, or being "off the wall."

The politicizer must respond to the objection, not that he is urging civil disobedience, but that he is urging disobedience to two less formal norms. The first is that because the system as a whole has specialized political mechanisms for dealing with oppression, and your institution has a different, nonpolitical role, you must leave the big issues for others. The second is that by joining the institution, you signed on to the general understanding of its nonpolitical nature and to the antipolitical norm of collegiality, so that politicizing the setting is betraying it.

It is common, in discussions of civil disobedience, to argue that if the regime as a whole is sufficiently evil or unjust, an institutional actor has a moral obligation to disregard role constraints—to disobey the law or to refuse to participate in applying it. It is common to see lying or other kinds of disloyal behavior as fully justified and appropriate if, for example, the society in question is Nazi Germany or Stalin's Russia. In this all-or-nothing context, it is often implicit that if one can't condemn the regime the way, in our society, we wholeheartedly condemn Nazi Germany or Stalin's Russia, then the role constraints of obedience to law, or faithful application of it (if a judge), are assumed to apply. Likewise, the role constraint of institutional loyalty in the general universe of management.

I don't think the limiting cases of Nazi Germany and Stalin's Russia illuminate the left/mpm actor's situation. Much more relevant is Joseph Raz's question "whether only degenerate societies fail to be decent societies, or at least approximately decent ones." He continues,

> If, as some would argue, most human societies to date fail this test, if most of them are such that their members (ought to) feel shame in their societies and guilt by association for their character and actions, then there is little we can learn about the law in general from the notion of an approximately decent society.[18]

If, as a leftist, one feels shame in one's society and guilt by association for its character and actions, then the dilemma posed by the alternatives of politicizing, of bad-faith strategic behavior in interpretation, and of passivity is a real one, even though this is neither Nazi Germany nor Stalin's Russia.

The left/mpm actor who politicizes insists that it is not enough, in defending a particular course of institutional conduct, external or internal, to appeal to the general understanding that the organization has a specialized, nonpolitical role in the social division of labor. If in the particular context there is enough shame and guilt by association, then there needs to be some further discussion of whether it isn't possible to exploit gaps, conflicts, and ambiguities or frankly to reject the norm of role specialization given the circumstances. Of course, the left/mpm actor won't propose a general theory of how far we can go in bending the mission statement before we break it, or of when we ought to break it.

Politicization has its attendant costs, including the risk of defeat, the deterioration of the quality of group life that comes from finding the political everywhere when it had been elsewhere, and the risks to one's own career and to the careers of friends and allies that are present the minute one goes against this particular grain. Sometimes these costs are worth paying. I am talking about a balance, not politicization at all costs, above all not "principled" politicization, which to my mind is just another way to be right.

Rather, opportunist politicization that recognizes four maxims: find a friend/collaborator, live to fight another day, extremism in the defense of liberty is indeed a vice, the personal is political. When these maxims suggest that, in the particular circumstances, oppositionism is the wrong thing to do, then quit or go back to passivity—another form of disloyalty—rather than denial. In other words, doubleness, in the mode of W. E. B. Du Bois's doubled consciousness of people of color, vis-à-vis the very institutions that nurture us and make it possible for us to fight against their complicity, our complicity, in group oppression.

NOTES

INDEX

NOTES

1. INTRODUCTION

1. Jean-Paul Sartre, *Being and Nothingness: An Essay on Phenomenological Ontology,* trans. Hazel Barnes (New York: Citadel Press, 1965); Jean-Paul Sartre, *Critique of Dialectical Reason,* trans. Alan Sheridan (London: Verso, 1990).

2. Herbert Marcuse, *Reason and Revolution: Hegel and the Rise of Social Theory* (Boston: Beacon Press, 1968); Herbert Marcuse, *One Dimensional Man: Studies in the Ideology of Advanced Industrial Society,* 2d ed. (London: Routledge, 1991).

3. Michel Foucault, *Discipline and Punish: The Birth of the Prison,* trans. Alan Sheridan (New York: Vintage, 1979); Michel Foucault, *Power/Knowledge: Selected Interviews and Other Writings, 1972–1977,* ed. and trans. Colin Gordon (New York: Pantheon Books, 1980); Michel Foucault, *The History of Sexuality,* 3 vols., trans. Robert Hurley (New York: Vintage, 1988–1990).

4. See Duncan Kennedy, "Psycho-Social CLS: A Comment on the Cardozo Symposium," 6 *Cardozo L. Rev.* 1013 (1985); Gerard Clark, "A Conversation with Duncan Kennedy," *The Advocate; The Suffolk University Law School Journal,* 24 (no. 2, Spring 1994), 56; Duncan Kennedy, "Note sur l'histoire de cls aux états-unis," in *Dictionnaire encyclopédique de théorie et de sociologie du droit,* 2d ed., ed. André-Jean Arnaud (Paris: L.G.D.J., 1993).

5. Guy Debord, *The Society of the Spectacle,* trans. Donald Nicholson-Smith (New York: Zone Books, 1994).

6. Paul D. Carrington, "Of Law and the River," 34 *J. Leg. Ed.* 222 (1984).

7. Ludwig Feuerbach, *The Essence of Christianity,* trans. G. Eliot (New York: Prometheus Books, 1989).

8. Karl Marx, "On the Jewish Question," in *Writings of the Young Marx on Philosophy and Society,* ed. and trans. Loyd Easton and Kurt Guddat (Garden City, N.Y.: Anchor, 1967), p. 216; Karl Marx, "The Fetishism of Commodities and Its Secret," in *Capital: A Critique of Political Economy,* vol. 1, trans. Ben Fowkes (New York: Vintage, 1977), p. 163. See Chapters 11 and 13 and, on the fetishism of commodities, Duncan Kennedy, "The Role of Law in Economic Thought: Essays on the Fetishism of Commodities," 34 *Am. Univ. L. Rev.* 939, 968 (1985).

2. THE DISTINCTION BETWEEN ADJUDICATION AND LEGISLATION

1. Norberto Bobbio, *Stato, governo, societa: Per una teoria generale della politica* (Turin: Einaudi, 1980).

2. See Jules L. Coleman and Brian Leiter, "Determinacy, Objectivity, and Authority," 142 *U. Pa. L. Rev.* 549 (1993); Heidi L. Feldman, "Objectivity in Legal Judgment," 92 *Mich. L. Rev.* 551 (1994).

3. Stanley Fish, "Working on the Chain Gang: Interpretation in Law and Literature," 60 *Texas L. Rev.* 551 (1982).

4. David L. Shapiro, "Courts, Legislatures, and Paternalism," 74 *Va. L. Rev.* 519, 556–557 (1988)(emphasis mine).

5. Jeffrey Rosen, "Breyer Restraint," *New Republic,* June 11, 1994, p. 20.

6. I don't mean to be taking sides in any extant debate here. Even Ronald Dworkin agrees that judges make law in the minimal sense indicated in the text. Ronald Dworkin, *Law's Empire* (Cambridge, Mass.: Harvard University Press, 1986), p. 6.

7. Linda Greenhouse, "Fierce Combat on Fewer Battlefields," *New York Times,* July 3, 1994, s. 4, p. 1.

8. Anthony Flint, "Breyer Set for Senate Hearings," *Boston Globe,* July 10, 1994, s. 1, pp. 1, 16.

9. John Noonan, "Master of Restraint," *New York Times Book Review,* May 1, 1994, p. 7.

10. Vincent Blasi, "Judge Him Unpredictable," *New York Times Book Review,* June 19, 1994, p. 3.

11. Adam Levine, letter to the editor, "Unpredictable Justice Powell," *New York Times Book Review,* July 10, 1994, p. 31.

12. H. L. A. Hart, *The Concept of Law,* 2d ed. (Oxford: Clarendon Press, 1994).

13. Hart's attitude toward this question is perhaps well represented by this statement: "At this point [where the law runs out] judges may again make a choice that is neither arbitrary nor mechanical; and here often display characteristic judicial virtues, the special appropriateness of which to legal decision explains why some feel reluctant to call such judicial activity 'legislative.' These virtues are: impartiality and neutrality in surveying the alternatives; consideration for the interest of all who will be affected; and a concern to display some acceptable general principle as a reasoned basis for decision." Ibid., p. 200.

14. Hans Kelsen, *Introduction to the Problems of Legal Theory,* trans. B. Litschewski Paulson and S. L. Paulson (Oxford: Clarendon Press, 1992), s. 36. For an interesting collection of essays on Kelsen's theory of interpretation, see *Cognition and Interpretation of Law,* ed. Letizia Gianformaggio and Stanley Paulson (Turin: G. Giapichelli, 1995).

15. Roberto M. Unger, *Knowledge and Politics* (New York: Free Press, 1975), p. 88.

16. Mark V. Tushnet, *Red, White, and Blue: A Critical Analysis of Constitutional Law* (Cambridge, Mass.: Harvard University Press, 1988), pp. 52–57.

17. Gary Peller, "The Metaphysics of American Law," 73 *Cal. L. Rev.* 1151, 1181 (1985).

18. James Boyle, "The Politics of Reason: Critical Legal Theory and Local Social Thought," 133 *U. Pa. L. Rev.* 685, 710–711 (1985).

19. Owen Fiss, "Objectivity and Interpretation," 34 *Stan. L. Rev.* 739 (1982).

20. Paul Brest, "Interpretation and Interest," 34 *Stan. L. Rev.* 765 (1982).

21. Duncan Kennedy, "Legal Formality," 2 *J. Legal Studies* 351, 364, nn. 21, 22 (1973); Duncan Kennedy, "Form and Substance in Private Law Adjudication," 89 *Harv. L. Rev.* 1685, 1687–1688 (1976).

22. Southern Pacific v. Jensen, 244 U.S. 205, 221 (1917)(Holmes, J., dissenting). See Thomas C. Grey, "Molecular Motions: The Holmesian Judge in Theory and Practice," 37 *Wm. & Mary L. Rev.* 19 (1995).

23. Felix Frankfurter, "The Supreme Court of the United States," in *Law and Politics: Occasional Papers of Felix Frankfurter,* ed. Archibald Macleish and E. F. Pritchard, Jr. (New York: Harcourt, Brace, 1939), p. 21.

24. Joseph Raz, *The Authority of Law: Essays on Law and Morality* (Oxford: Clarendon Press, 1979), ch. 10.

25. See Lon Fuller, "Positivism and Fidelity to Law—A Reply to Professor Hart," 71 *Harv. L. Rev.* 630, 666 (1958).

26. Benjamin Cardozo, *The Nature of the Judicial Process* (New Haven: Yale University Press, 1957).

27. Karl Llewellyn, *The Common Law Tradition: Deciding Appeals* (Boston: Little, Brown, 1960).

28. Lon Fuller, "The Forms and Limits of Adjudication," 92 *Harv. L. Rev.* 353 (1978).

29. Henry M. Hart and Albert Sacks, *The Legal Process: Basic Problems in the Making and Application of Law,* ed. William Eskridge and Phillip Frickey (Westbury, N.Y.: Foundation Press, 1994).

30. Neil MacCormick, *Legal Reasoning and Legal Theory* (Oxford: Clarendon Press, 1978), chs. 7 and 8.

31. J. M. Finnis, "On 'The Critical Legal Studies Movement,' " 30 *Am. J. Jurisprudence* 21, 38 (1985).

32. Dworkin, *Law's Empire.*

33. Ronald Dworkin, *A Matter of Principle* (Cambridge, Mass.: Harvard University Press, 1985), p. 2.

34. Fuller, "The Forms and Limits of Adjudication," pp. 393–405.

35. Hart and Sacks, *The Legal Process,* pp. 646–647.

36. Dworkin, *A Matter of Principle,* p. 147.

37. Gerald Postema, " 'Protestant' Interpretation and Social Practices," 6 *Law & Phil.* 283, 289 (1987).

38. Dworkin, *A Matter of Principle,* p. 2.

39. Dworkin, *Law's Empire,* p. 411.

40. See Mitchel Lasser, "Judicial (Self-) Portraits: Judicial Discourse in the French Legal System," 104 *Yale L.J.* 1325, 1343 (1995).

41. André-Jean Arnaud, *Les juristes face à la société du XIXe siècle à nos jours* (Paris: Presses Universitaires de France, 1975).

3. IDEOLOGICAL CONFLICT OVER THE DEFINITION
OF LEGAL RULES

1. Universalization, as I'm using it here, is a defining characteristic of normative discourse of the type Habermas calls "practical reason," which I think well describes legal argument. See Jürgen Habermas, *The Theory of Communicative Action: Reason and the Rationalization of Society*, vol. 1, trans. Thomas McCarthy (Boston: Beacon Press, 1984), pp. 16–19.

2. See, generally, Antonio Gramsci, *Prison Notebooks*, ed. Jospeh A. Buttigieg, trans. Joseph Buttigieg and Antonio Callari (New York: Columbia University Press, 1992).

3. Four interesting takes on these phenomena are Robert Gordon, "Law and Disorder," 64 *Ind. L.J.* 287 (1989); Robin West, "Progressive and Conservative Constitutionalism," 88 *Mich. L. Rev.* 64 (1990); Jack Balkin, "Ideological Drift and the Struggle over Meaning," 25 *Conn. L. Rev.* 869 (1993); and Frank Michelman, "Property, Federalism, and Jurisprudence: A Comment on Lucas and Judicial Conservatism," 35 *Wm. & Mary L. Rev.* 301 (1993).

4. See Michel Foucault, *The Order of Things: An Archaeology of the Human Sciences*, trans. Alan Sheridan (New York: Vintage, 1973).

5. See Thomas Kuhn, *The Structure of Scientific Revolutions*, 2d ed. (Chicago: University of Chicago Press, 1970).

6. See Brian Bix, *Law, Language, and Legal Indeterminacy* (Oxford: Clarendon Press, 1993), p. 53.

7. Norberto Bobbio, *Destra e Sinistra: Ragioni e significati di una distinzione politica* (Rome: Donzelli, 1994).

8. Duncan Kennedy, "The Structure of Blackstone's Commentaries," 28 *Buff. L. Rev.* 205 (1979). Much more sophisticated than the inference of a conspiracy theory was the response of Alan Hunt: "Throughout his discussion of Blackstone, Kennedy tends to employ the idea of 'intention' more frequently than that of 'motive'; it thus seems clear that his analysis requires the imputation of an explicit or conscious intent to Blackstone in particular, and by inference to legal actors in general. The flavor of this usage of intention is caught by his characterization that it was Blackstone's 'intention to vindicate the common law against the charge that it was inconsistent with the enlightened political thought of his day' (1979:234) and later that 'his ultimate intention was to legitimate both judicial institutions and the substantive law they enforced' (1979:237). This mode of analysis rests on the imputation of intent that is not substantiated. Yet without the insertion of 'motive' the theoretical structure that seeks to move from 'doctrine' to the 'hidden political intention' is undermined. In other words Kennedy's methodology is not able, without an assumed intentionality, to establish the connection between doctrine and its historical context that critical theory promises." Alan Hunt, "The Theory of Critical Legal Studies," in *Explorations in Law and Society: Toward a Constitutive Theory of Law* (New York: Routledge, 1993),

pp. 153–154. I think Hunt misunderstood the method I was then and still am trying to deploy, because he imagines that the imputation of motive or intent (or preference— I use them all interchangeably), in the phrases he quotes, could be "substantiated" in the sense of "proven," or, for that matter, disproven. Substantiation in his sense is, first, impossible and, second, unnecessary for the analysis to work as it is supposed to. My imputation of an "apologetic" or "legitimating" motive to Blackstone was of the hermeneutic kind, although what I imputed to him and, by mere "inference," to legal thinkers in general, was neither liberalism nor conservatism. I tried to substantiate the imputation by critiquing Blackstone's explanations of the rules as unconvincing, indeed close to unintelligible, unless read in light of a motive of the type I proposed. I had and have no direct evidence as to whether his motive, if it was as I interpreted it, was conscious, unconscious, or half-conscious. See Chapters 8 and 11.

9. Although I don't find his critique persuasive (see previous note), Alan Hunt was right, I think, to see my presentation of Blackstone as at odds with the more familiar neo-Marxist way of conceptualizing ideology as an element in a theory of modern Western welfare-state capitalist societies. I will deal at some length with neo-Marxist theories addressed specifically to law in capitalism in Chapter 11.

10. See, generally, Duncan Kennedy, "The Stakes of Law, or, Hale and Foucault!" in *Sexy Dressing, Etc.* (Cambridge, Mass.: Harvard University Press, 1993), pp. 83– 126.

11. See ibid.

12. In deciding, from a particular ideological perspective, which of two rules is better, one can combine the good and the bad of the rule seen intrinsically with the good and the bad seen instrumentally, or "balance" the intrinsic good against the instrumental bad. One can say that prohibiting strikes is good, because striking is immoral, but that, on balance, the bad distributive consequences for labor would be so extremely immoral that we should allow them. Or one can balance the moral bad from the instrumental view (labor will end up with too much power if striking is allowed) against the (intrinsic) right to engage in the conduct (the right to strike).

13. See, generally, Duncan Kennedy, "Legal Formality," 2 *J. Leg. Stud.* 351 (1973); Duncan Kennedy, "Form and Substance in Private Law Adjudication," 89 *Harv. L. Rev.* 1689 (1976).

14. Duncan Kennedy, "Paternalist and Distributive Motives in Contract and Tort Law, with Special Reference to Compulsory Terms and Unequal Bargaining Power," 41 *Maryland L. Rev.* 563 (1982); Duncan Kennedy, "The Effect of the Warranty of Habitability on Low Income Housing: 'Milking' and Class Violence," 15 *Florida St. L. Rev.* 485 (1987).

15. Thomas C. Grey, "Holmes and Legal Pragmatism," 41 *Stan. L. Rev.* 787, 834– 835 (1989).

16. See Alan Hyde, "The Concept of Legitimation in the Sociology of Law," 1983 *Wisc. L. Rev.* 379 (1983).

17. See, generally, Brian Tamanaha, "An Analytical Map of Social Scientific Approaches to the Concept of Law," 15 *Oxford J. Leg. Studies* 501 (1995).

18. Karl N. Llewellyn, *The Bramble Bush, or, Our Law and Its Study* (New York: Oceana Publishing, 1960), p. 12 (emphasis in original).

19. See Tamanaha, "An Analytical Map," pp. 515–517.

20. Sally Merry, *Getting Justice and Getting Even: Legal Consciousness among Working-Class Americans* (Chicago: University of Chicago Press, 1990); Barbara Yngvesson, *Virtuous Citizens, Disruptive Subjects: Order and Complaint in a New England Court* (New York: Routledge, 1993).

21. Robert H. Mnookin and Lewis Kornhauser, "Bargaining in the Shadow of the Law: The Case of Divorce," 88 *Yale L.J.* 950 (1979).

22. See, for example, Duncan Kennedy, "Sexual Abuse, Sexy Dressing, and the Eroticization of Domination," in *Sexy Dressing, Etc.,* pp. 131–162; Molly McUsic, "Reassessing Rent Control: Its Economic Impact in a Gentrifying Housing Market," 101 *Harv. L. Rev.* 1835 (1988); Lawrence Kolodney, "Eviction Free Zones: The Economics of Legal Bricolage in the Fight against Displacement," 18 *Ford. Urban L.J.* 507 (1991).

23. Marc Galanter, "Why the 'Haves' Come Out Ahead: Speculations on the Limits of Legal Change," 9 *Law & Soc'y Rev.* 95 (1974).

24. Alice Dembner, "Female Athletes Gain in Legal Game," *Boston Globe,* October 1, 1994, s. 1, pp. 1, 20.

25. Ibid.

4. THE PARADOX OF AMERICAN CRITICAL LEGALISM

1. Agostino Carrino, *Ideologia e coscienza: Critical Legal Studies* (Naples: Edizioni Scientifiche Italiane, 1992), pp. 45–51.

2. Franz Neumann, *The Democratic and the Authoritarian State: Essays in Political and Legal Theory,* ed. Herbert Marcuse (Glencoe, Ill.: Free Press, 1957), pp. 22–68.

3. Rudolph von Ihering, "The Heaven of Legal Concepts," in Morris Cohen and Felix Cohen, *Readings in Jurisprudence and Legal Philosophy* (Boston: Little, Brown, 1951), p. 678.

4. John Dawson, *The Oracles of the Law* (Ann Arbor: University of Michigan Law School, 1968).

5. Sadok Belaid, *Essai sur le pouvoir créateur et normatif du juge* (Paris: L.G.D.J., 1974).

6. Mitchel Lasser, "Judicial (Self-) Portraits: Judicial Discourse in the French Legal System," 104 *Yale L.J.* 1325 (1995).

7. H. L. A. Hart, "American Jurisprudence through English Eyes: The Nightmare and the Noble Dream," 11 *Ga. L. Rev.* 969, 971 (1977).

8. Ibid., p. 972.

9. Ibid., pp. 972–973.

10. Ugo Mattei, "Why the Wind Changed: Intellectual Leadership in Western Law," 42 *Am. J. Comp. Law* 195, 205 (1994).

11. Rodolfo Sacco, "Legal Formants: A Dynamic Approach to Comparative Law," 39 *Am. J. Comp. Law.* 1, 343 (1991).

12. Hart, "American Jurisprudence," p. 971.

13. For example: "Following the prevailing fashion in judicial opinions, [this opinion] proceeds to its conclusions chiefly by a process of deductive reasoning from apparently fixed premises supposed to be established by prior cases. The fact that in the last analysis the decision really turns upon notions of policy entertained—consciously or unconsciously—by the members of the court is thus thrown into the background." Walter Wheeler Cook, "Privileges of Labor Unions in the Struggle for Life," 27 *Yale L.J.* 779, 783 (1918). See also Arthur Corbin, "Offer and Acceptance, and Some of the Resulting Legal Relations," 26 *Yale L.J.* 170, 206 (1917); Roscoe Pound, "Mechanical Jurisprudence," 8 *Colum. L. Rev.* 605 (1908).

14. For example, Lawrence Tribe, "The Puzzling Persistence of Process-Based Constitutional Theories," 89 *Yale L.J.* 1063 (1980).

15. Henry Terry, "Legal Duties and Rights," 12 *Yale L.J.* 185, 188 (1903).

16. George Gardner, "Observations on the Course in Contracts" (1934), reprinted in Lon Fuller and Robert Braucher, *Basic Contract Law* (St. Paul: West Pub. Co., 1964), p. 151. The father of contradictionism in law appears to have been Rudolph von Jhering, *Geist des Romischen Rechts* (Leipzig: Breitkopf und Hartel, 1852–1865). Some major works of realist and postrealist contradictionism, as I see it, are Karl Llewellyn, "What Price Contract—An Essay in Perspective," 40 *Yale L.J.* 704 (1931); Lon Fuller, "Consideration and Form," 41 *Colum. L. Rev.* 799 (1941); Freidrich Kessler and Edith Fine, "Culpa in Contrahendo, Bargaining in Good Faith and Freedom of Contract," 77 *Harv. L. Rev.* 401 (1964); Stewart Macaulay, "Private Legislation and the Duty to Read—Business Run by IBM Machine, the Law of Contracts, and Credit Cards," 19 *Vand. L. Rev.* 1051 (1966); and Grant Gilmore, *The Death of Contract* (Columbus: Ohio State University Press, 1974). The crit and quasi-crit variants are well represented by Duncan Kennedy, "Form and Substance in Private Law Adjudication," 89 *Harv. L. Rev.* 1685 (1976); Frances Olsen, "The Sex of Law," in *The Politics of Law: A Progressive Critique,* ed. David Kairys (New York: Pantheon, 1990), p. 473; Elizabeth Mensch, "Book Review," 33 *Stan. L. Rev.* 753 (1981) (reviewing P. Atiyah, *The Rise and Fall of Freedom of Contract*); Paul Brest, "The Fundamental Rights Controversy: The Essential Contradictions of Normative Constitutional Scholarship," 90 *Yale L.J.* 1063 (1981); Roberto Unger, *The Critical Legal Studies Movement* (Cambridge, Mass.: Harvard University Press, 1986); Frank Michelman, "Justification (and Justifiability) of Law," *Justification: Nomos XXVII,* ed. J. Ronald Pennock and Robert Chapman (New York: New York University Press, 1986), p. 71; Robert Gordon, "Unfreezing Legal Reality: Critical Approaches to Law," 15 *Fla. St. L. Rev.* 195 (1987); and Joseph Singer, "The Reliance Interest in Property," 40 *Stan. L. Rev.* 611 (1988).

17. Oliver Wendell Holmes, "Privilege, Malice, and Intent," in *Collected Legal Pa-*

pers (Buffalo, N.Y.: William S. Hein, 1985), p. 117 (originally appearing at 8 *Harv. L. Rev.* 1, 8 [1894]).

18. Ibid, p. 128.

19. Ibid., p. 120. "Therefore, decisions for or against the privilege, which really can stand only upon [policy] grounds, often are presented as hollow deductions from empty general propositions like *sic utere tuo ut alienum non laedas* which teaches nothing but a benevolent yearning, or else are put as if they themselves embodied a postulate of the law and admitted of no further deduction, as when it is said that, although there is temporal damage, there is no wrong; whereas, the very thing to be found out is whether there is a wrong or not, and if not, why not."

20. W. N. Hohfeld, "Some Fundamental Legal Conceptions as Applied in Judicial Reasoning," 23 *Yale L.J.* 16 (1913). See Joseph Singer, "The Legal Rights Debate in Analytical Jurisprudence from Bentham to Hohfeld," 1982 *Wisc. L. Rev.* 975.

21. Felix Cohen, "Transcendental Nonsense and the Functional Approach," 1935 *Colum. L. Rev.* 809, 820.

22. Robert Hale, "Bargaining, Duress, and Economic Liberty," 1943 *Colum. L. Rev.* 603, 625–626.

23. Duncan Kennedy and Frank Michelman, "Are Property and Contract Efficient?" 8 *Hofstra L. Rev.* 711 (1980).

24. See Cohen, "Transcendental Nonsense"; Walter Wheeler Cook, "Privileges of Labor Unions in the Struggle for Life," 27 *Yale L.J.* 779 (1918). On Holmes, see Thomas C. Grey, "Molecular Motions: The Holmesian Judge in Theory and Practice," 27 *Wm. & Mary L. Rev.* 119 (1995).

25. Jerome Frank, *Law and the Modern Mind* (Gloucester, Mass.: P. Smith, 1970).

26. Thurman Arnold, *The Folklore of Capitalism* (Garden City, N.J.: Blue Ribbon, 1941); Thurman Arnold, *Symbols of Government* (New Haven: Yale University Press, 1935).

27. Joseph Hutcheson, "The Judgment Intuitive: The Function of the "Hunch" in Judicial Decision," 14 *Cornell L.Q.* 274 (1929).

28. Max Radin, "The Theory of Judicial Decision, or, How Judges Think," 11 *A.B.A. Journal* 357 (1925).

29. For an example, see David Richards, "Constitutional Legitimacy and Constitutional Privacy," 61 *N.Y.U. L. Rev.* 800 (1986)(on Bowers v. Hardwick).

30. For example, Richard A. Posner, *Problems of Jurisprudence* (Cambridge, Mass.: Harvard University Press, 1990), pp. 124–143.

31. Karl N. Llewellyn, *The Bramble Bush, or, Our Law and Its Study* (New York: Oceana Publishing, 1960).

32. Karl N. Llewellyn, "Remarks on the Theory of Appellate Decision and the Rules or Canons about How Statutes Are to Be Construed," 3 *Vand. L. Rev.* 395 (1950).

33. Llewellyn, *The Bramble Bush*, p. 68 (emphasis in original).

34. See Chapter 10.

35. Ronald Dworkin, "Is Wealth a Value?" 9 *J. Legal Stud.* 1191 (1980).

36. Before we begin Suzanna Sherry's respectful but total demolition of Cass Sunstein's new book, *Legal Reasoning and Political Conflict* (New York: Oxford University Press, 1996), we learn that she is "working on a book about social constructivism and law." Suzanna Sherry, "Law and Order," *New York Times Book Review,* September 8, 1996, p. 17.

37. Andrew Altman, "Legal Realism, Critical Legal Studies, and Dworkin," 15 *Phil. & Pub. Aff.* 205 (1986).

38. "The language was the work of Chief Justice William Rehnquist and four other appointees of Presidents Reagan and Bush. The alignment was unfortunate, suggesting devotion to an ideological agenda rather than legal principle." Editorial, *New York Times,* March 29, 1991, S. 1, p. 22.

39. The best example I know of is Pietro Barcellona, *Formazione e sviluppo del diritto privato moderno* (Naples: Jovene Editore, 1995). For a description and critique of the American versions of these approaches, see Duncan Kennedy, "Paternalist and Distributive Motives in Contract and Tort Law, with Special Reference to Compulsory Terms and Unequal Bargaining Power," 41 *Maryland L. Rev.* 563, 575–583 (1982). For a critique of the Marxist versions, see Chapter 11.

40. André-Jean Arnaud, *Les juristes face à la société du XIXe siècle à nos jours* (Paris: Presses Universitaires de France, 1975). See also Stefano Rodotà, *Repertorio di fine secolo* (Rome: Laterza, 1992). There may be an aspiration to overcome the dichotomy, but by informal means.

41. Two European tendencies that are not "critical" but have something in common with the American viral strand are the "école de Bruxelles," see Chaim Perelman and L. Olbrechts-Tyteca, *The New Rhetoric: A Treatise on Argumentation,* trans. John Wilkinson and Russell Weaver (Notre Dame: University of Notre Dame Press, 1969)(but it is wedded to practical reason for all its preoccupation with the semiotics of topoi), and the "scuola di Sacco" in Italy, see Sacco, "Legal Formants" (but Sacco is a classic external critic in that he believes that "legal formants" determine legal rules through the vehicle of indeterminate legal dogmatics).

42. See Kennedy, "Form and Substance in Private Law Adjudication," pp. 1710–1711.

43. For a somewhat more filled out version of the critique in the text, see Duncan Kennedy, "Comment on Rudolph Wietholter's 'Materialization and Proceduralization in Modern Law,' and 'Proceduralization of the Category of Law,'" in *Critical Legal Thought: An American-German Debate,* ed. Christian Joerges and David Trubek (Baden-Baden: Nomos Verlagsgesellschaft, 1988). I critique, summarily, the distinction between private law and regulatory law in Duncan Kennedy, "The Political Significance of the Structure of the Law School Curriculum," 14 *Seton Hall L. Rev.* 1 (1983). On

the public/private distinction, see Duncan Kennedy, "The Stages of the Decline of the Public/Private Distinction," 130 *U. Pa. L. Rev.* 1349 (1982).

5. POLICY AND COHERENCE

1. Oliver Wendell Holmes, "Privilege, Malice, and Intent," in *Collected Legal Papers* (Buffalo, N.Y.: William S. Hein, 1985), p. 117 (originally appearing at 8 *Harv. L. Rev.* 1, 8 [1894]).

2. I will use the word "deduction" to denote all these versions, without meaning to take a position in the various disputes about the technical meanings of the different terms. See Thomas Grey, "Langdell's Orthodoxy," 45 *U. Pitt. L. Rev.* 1, 12, n. 37 (1983).

3. Neil MacCormick, *Legal Reasoning and Legal Theory* (Oxford: Clarendon Press, 1994), chs. 2 and 3.

4. For example, see Texas Refining and Marketing, Inc. v. Samowitz, 570 A.2d 170 (Conn. 1990).

5. Restatement (Second) of Torts, s. 936.

6. Duncan Kennedy, "Form and Substance in Private Law Adjudication," 89 *Harv. L. Rev.* 1685 (1976).

7. See, generally, Frederick Schauer, "Formalism," 97 *Yale L.J.* 509 (1988).

8. See Charles Fried, *Contract as Promise: A Theory of Contractual Obligation* (Cambridge, Mass.: Harvard University Press, 1981), pp. 18–19.

9. Lon Fuller and William Perdue, "The Reliance Interest in Contract Damages," 46 *Yale L.J.* 52 (1936), pp. 57–60.

10. Ibid., pp. 65–66.

11. Lochner v. New York, 198 U.S. 45, 76 (1905) (Holmes, J., dissenting).

12. Melvin Eisenberg, *The Nature of the Common Law* (Cambridge, Mass.: Harvard University Press, 1988), pp. 64–76.

13. W. Page Keeton et al., *Prosser and Keeton on the Law of Torts* (St. Paul, Minn.: West Pub. Co., 1984).

14. E. Allan Farnsworth, *Farnsworth on Contracts* (Boston: Little, Brown, 1990).

15. See O'Brien v. O'Brien, 489 N.E.2d 712 (N.Y. 1985), and Susan Keller, "The Rhetoric of Marriage, Achievement, and Power in Judicial Opinions Considering the Treatment of Professional Degrees as Marital Property," 21 *Vt. L. Rev.* (1996).

16. But see, for the revival of interest in analogy as a way out of the bind, Cass Sunstein, *Legal Reasoning and Political Conflict* (New York: Oxford University Press, 1996); Scott Brewer, "Exemplary Reasoning: Semantics, Pragmatics, and the Rational Force of Legal Argument by Analogy," 109 *Harv. L. Rev.* 923 (1996).

17. Rudolph von Ihering, "The Heaven of Legal Concepts," in Morris Cohen and Felix Cohen, *Readings in Jurisprudence and Legal Philosophy* (Boston: Little, Brown, 1951), p. 678.

18. Roscoe Pound, "Mechanical Jurisprudence," 8 *Colum. L. Rev.* 605 (1908).

19. Felix Cohen, "Transcendental Nonsense and the Functional Approach," 1935 *Colum. L. Rev.* 809.

20. For a terrific exposition of what formalism might mean, see Grey, "Langdell's Orthodoxy," pp. 6–11, especially n. 30. The closest thing to an American formalism is probably Langdell's theory, developed by Beale, which conceived law as a "science." Grey points out that even the legal scientists did not think they could dispense altogether with what Grey calls "acceptability," meaning policy broadly conceived. Ibid., pp. 13–14.

21. Why exactly they believed they could refute formalism in this way is by no means clear, and Grey's explanation, ibid., pp. 43–47, is unilluminating.

22. Thomas C. Grey, "Molecular Motions: The Holmesian Judge in Theory and Practice," 27 *Wm. & Mary L. Rev.* 119 (1995).

23. But see *Symposium on Legal Formalism,* 16 *Harv. J. Law & Pub. Pol.* (no. 3, Autumn 1993); Ernest Weinrib, "Legal Formalism: On the Immanent Rationality of Law," 97 *Yale L.J.* 949 (1988).

24. For example, see Lucas v. So. Carolina Coastal Council, 505 U.S. 1003, 1015–1018, 1030–1031 (1992)(opinion of Scalia, J.).

25. Thomas Grey, "Holmes and Legal Pragmatism," 41 *Stan. L. Rev.* 787 (1989).

26. Duncan Kennedy, "Toward an Historical Understanding of Legal Consciousness: The Case of Classical Legal Thought in America, 1850–1940," in *Research in Law and Society,* vol. 3, ed. Steven Spitzer (Greenwood, Conn.: Greenwood Press, 1980).

27. Kennedy, "Form and Substance," pp. 1725–1728.

28. Mitchel Lasser, "Judicial (Self-) Portraits: Judicial Discourse in the French Legal System," 104 *Yale L.J.* 1325 (1995). In Italy, it is common to refer to the "values" and "human rights" embodied in the general clauses of the Italian Constitution in a way that resembles American policy argument. See Stefano Rodotà, *Repertorio di fine secolo* (Rome: Laterza, 1992).

29. This requirement is occasionally stated explicitly in American theories of adjudication. See, for example, Harry H. Wellington, "Common Law Rules and Constitutional Double Standards: Some Notes on Adjudication," 83 *Yale L.J.* 221, 225–226 (1973); Melvin Eisenberg, *The Nature of the Common Law* (Cambridge, Mass.: Harvard University Press, 1988), pp. 29–31. On universalizability, see Jürgen Habermas, *The Theory of Communicative Action: Reason and the Rationalization of Society,* vol. 1, trans. Thomas McCarthy (Boston: Beacon Press, 1984), pp. 16–19.

30. For an amusingly "retro" version of this position, see Lino Graglia, "Do Judges Have a Policy-Making Role in the American System of Government?" 17 *Harv. J. Law & Pub. Pol.* 119 (1994).

31. See Chapter 2, n. 7.

32. Gary Peller and William Eskridge, "The New Public Law Movement: Moderation as a Postmodern Cultural Form," 89 *Mich. L. Rev.* 707, 762–763 (1991).

33. For a perceptive description and critique of this state of mind, see Pierre Schlag, "Normative and Nowhere to Go," 43 *Stan. L. Rev.* 167 (1990).

34. DeShaney v. Winnebago County Dept. of Social Services, 489 U.S. 189, 203–112 (1989)(Brennan, J., dissenting).

35. Lucas v. So. Carolina Coastal Council, 505 U.S. 1003, 1036–1061 (1992)(Blackmun, J., dissenting).

36. Benjamin Cardozo, *The Nature of the Judicial Process* (New Haven: Yale University Press, 1957), p. 98. Llewellyn's "situation sense" and "rule of the Singing Reason" are contextualized versions of the same idea. See Karl Llewellyn, *The Common Law Tradition: Deciding Appeals* (Boston: Little, Brown, 1960), p. 60. See Charles Clark and David Trubek, "The Creative Role of the Judge: Restraint and Freedom in the Common Law Tradition," 71 *Yale L.J.* 255 (1961).

37. Lon Fuller, "The Forms and Limits of Adjudication," 92 *Harv. L. Rev.* 353 (1978). See James Boyle, "Legal Realism and the Social Contract: Fuller's Public Jurisprudence of Form, Private Jurisprudence of Substance," 78 *Cornell L. Rev.* 371 (1993).

38. Henry M. Hart and Albert Sacks, *The Legal Process: Basic Problems in the Making and Application of Law*, ed. William Eskridge and Phillip Frickey (Westbury, N.Y.: Foundation Press, 1994). See Gary Peller, "Neutral Principles in the 1950's," 21 *Univ. Mich. J. Law Reform* 561 (1988).

39. Hart and Sacks, *The Legal Process*, p. 113.

40. Ibid., ch. 1.

41. Herbert Wechsler, "Toward Neutral Principles of Constitutional Law," 73 *Harv. L. Rev.* 1 (1959).

42. See Peller, "Neutral Principles in the 1950's," p. 561, John Ely, *Democracy and Distrust: A Theory of Judicial Review* (Cambridge, Mass.: Harvard University Press, 1980), p. 87.

43. William Eskridge and Phillip Frickey, "Historical and Critical Introduction," in Hart and Sacks, *The Legal Process*, pp. li–cxxxvi.

44. A dramatic example is Henry Hart and Edward Prichard, "The Fansteel Case: Employee Misconduct and the Remedial Powers of the National Labor Relations Board," 52 *Harv. L. Rev.* 1275 (1939).

45. See Henry Hart, "The Supreme Court, 1958 Term, Foreword: The Time Chart of the Justices," 73 *Harv. L. Rev.* 84 (1959) (endorsing Herbert Wechsler's critique of Brown v. Board of Education in "Toward Neutral Principles"), and see generally Morton Horwitz, *The Transformation of American Law, 1870–1960: The Crisis of Legal Orthodoxy* (New York: Oxford University Press, 1992), pp. 252–268.

46. Specifically, Ronald Dworkin, *Taking Rights Seriously* (Cambridge, Mass.: Harvard University Press, 1978); Ronald Dworkin, *A Matter of Principle* (Cambridge, Mass.: Harvard University Press, 1985); Ronald Dworkin, *Law's Empire* (Cambridge, Mass.: Harvard University Press, 1986).

47. See, generally, *Ronald Dworkin and Contemporary Jurisprudence*, ed. Marshall Ber-

man (Totowa, N.J.: Rowman and Allanheld, 1984). My favorite liberal critiques are Andrew Altman, "Legal Realism, Critical Legal Studies, and Dworkin," 15 *Phil. & Pub. Aff.* 205 (1986), and Joseph Raz, "The Relevance of Coherence," 72 *B.U.L. Rev.* 273 (1992). See also Peter Gabel, Book Review, 91 *Harv. L. Rev.* 302 (1977)(reviewing Ronald Dworkin, *Taking Rights Seriously*).

48. Dworkin, *Law's Empire*, pp. 167–168.

49. Ibid., at pp. 225, 255.

50. Dworkin, *Taking Rights Seriously*, pp. 22, 90; Dworkin, *Law's Empire*, p. 223. I discuss Dworkin's elaboration of this distinction at note 74 below. Deduction plays almost no role at all in Dworkin's theory. His view of precedent is even more radical than Llewellyn's—see *Taking Rights Seriously*, pp. 110–113, 122.

51. H. L. A. Hart, "American Jurisprudence through English Eyes: The Nightmare and the Noble Dream," 11 *Ga. L. Rev.* 969 (1977).

52. Raz, "The Relevance of Coherence," p. 273.

53. MacCormick, *Legal Reasoning*, ch. 9.

54. Dworkin, *Taking Rights Seriously*, pp. 95, 97, 102, 106.

55. Dworkin, "Liberalism," in *A Matter of Principle*, pp. 181–204.

56. Dworkin, "Law as Interpretation," in *A Matter of Principle*, pp. 164–165. Although this article appears before "Liberalism" in *A Matter of Principle*, it was first published four years after that article.

57. Dworkin, *Law's Empire*, p. 399.

58. Ibid., at pp. 45–46.

59. Ibid., at pp. 359–369.

60. Ibid., at pp. 369–379.

61. Dworkin, "Law as Interpretation," p. 160.

62. Dworkin, *Taking Rights Seriously*, p. 60; Dworkin, *A Matter of Principle*, pp. 137–145.

63. Dworkin, *Taking Rights Seriously*, p. 118.

64. Dworkin, *Law's Empire*, p. 354.

65. Ibid., pp. 269–271.

66. Dworkin, *Taking Rights Seriously*, pp. 83–85; Dworkin, *Law's Empire*, pp. 243–244.

67. Dworkin, *Taking Rights Seriously*, p. 184 ("[t]he debate does not include the issue of whether citizens have *some* moral rights against their Government. It seems accepted on all sides that they do").

68. Dworkin, *Taking Rights Seriously*, p. 88.

69. Dworkin, *Law's Empire*, p. 378; see also pp. 397–398.

70. Dworkin, *A Matter of Principle*, p. 70.

71. Dworkin, "Law as Interpretation."

72. Kent Greenawalt, "Policy, Rights, and Judicial Decision," 11 *Ga. L. Rev.* 991, 992 (1977).

73. Dworkin, *Taking Rights Seriously*, p. 294.

74. Dworkin's detailed response is to my mind perhaps the least satisfying of his writings—it seems to me a small masterpiece of equivocation in the use of the word "right"—and I know of no one who has read it who claims to understand it. I see it as the Waterloo of what we might call the First Empire, leading eventually to the Second Empire, in which the interpretive right answer based on fit, along with liberalism as legitimate political theory, largely supersede rights as the base for the discursive superstructure. It is interesting that it seems to have been the evidence for antebellum policy orientation Morton Horwitz mustered in *The Transformation of American Law: 1788–1860* (Cambridge, Mass.: Harvard University Press, 1977) that pushed Dworkin into a fruitless attempt to maintain a sharp distinction between policy arguments and rights arguments while unequivocally severing the distinction from that between consequentialist and nonconsequentialist arguments. For my view of rights argument thus divorced from nonconsequentialism, see Chapters 12 and 13. I should also add that I agree with the distinct criticisms put forward by Altman and Raz in n. 47 above.

75. Farwell v. Boston & Worcester R.R. Corp., 45 Mass. (4 Met.) 49, 58–59 (1842).

76. Duncan Kennedy, "The Structure of Blackstone's Commentaries," 28 *Buff. L. Rev.* 205, 351–354 (1979).

77. Dworkin, *Taking Rights Seriously,* p. 293.

78. Dworkin, *Law's Empire,* p. 399.

79. Dworkin, *Taking Rights Seriously,* pp. 192–193.

80. Ibid., pp. 206–222.

81. Ronald Dworkin, "Is Wealth a Value," 9 *J. Leg. Stud.* 1191 (1980); Dworkin, "Law and Economics," in *A Matter of Principle,* pp. 267–275.

82. Dworkin, *Taking Rights Seriously,* p. 273.

83. Dworkin, *A Matter of Principle,* pp. 89–90.

84. Ibid., p. 68.

85. Ibid., p. 364.

86. Ronald Dworkin, *Life's Dominion* (New York: Knopf, 1993).

87. Dworkin, *A Matter of Principle,* pp. 107–113.

88. Ibid., p. 388.

89. Ronald Dworkin, "Women and Pornography," *New York Review,* 40, October 21, 1993, p. 36.

90. Dworkin, *Law's Empire,* p. 398.

91. Ibid., p. 399.

92. Ibid.

93. See n. 46 supra.

94. Dworkin, *Law's Empire,* p. 275.

6. POLICY AND IDEOLOGY

1. Ferdinand de Saussure, *Course in General Linguistics,* trans. Roy Harris (La Salle, Ill.: Open Court, 1986).

2. Claude Lévi-Strauss, *The Savage Mind* (Chicago: University of Chicago Press, 1966).

3. Jean Piaget, *Play, Dreams, and Imitation in Childhood,* trans. C. Gattegno and F. Hodgson (New York: Norton, 1962).

4. See, generally, Duncan Kennedy, "A Semiotics of Legal Argument," 42 *Syracuse L. Rev.* 75 (1991), and the same article with "European Introduction: Four Objections," in *Collected Courses of the Academy of European Law,* vol. 3, book 2, pp. 309–365 (Amsterdam: Kluwer Academic Publishers, 1994).

5. Compare two doctrinal structures: "a voluntary invasion is a trespass unless justified by necessity," and "good faith is required in contractual performance, but a requirements contract buyer does not have to have any requirements at all." In each case we have a rule-exception structure and a rule-standard structure. But in one case the rule is a rule and the exception is a standard, whereas in the other the rule is a standard and the exception is a rule.

6. Kennedy, "A Semiotics of Legal Argument." This approach was influenced by Al Katz's unpublished manuscript "Studies in Boundary Theory: An Exploration of Thought in the Context of Responsibility and Authority" (1980). For the extension and sometimes the transformation of the argument-bite idea, see Mark Kelman, "Interpretive Construction in the Criminal Law," 33 *Stan. L. Rev.* 591 (1981); Gerald Frug, "The Ideology of Bureaucracy in American Law," 97 *Harv. L. Rev.* 1276 (1984); James Boyle, "The Anatomy of a Torts Class," 34 *Amer. Univ. L. Rev.* 1003 (1985); Jack Balkin, "The Crystalline Structure of Legal Thought," 39 *Rutgers L. Rev.* 195 (1986); Jeremy Paul, "A Bedtime Story," 74 *Va. L. Rev.* 915 (1988); Pierre Schlag, "Cannibal Moves: An Essay on the Metamorphoses of the Legal Distinction," 40 *Stan. L. Rev.* 92 (1988).

7. Note the analogy to the organization of rules into rule-exception or rule-counterrule pairs.

8. Note the analogy to the general-particular structure within doctrine.

9. There is an analogy to the subject-matter structures of doctrine.

10. The Constitution also confers general powers on Congress, e.g., the commerce power, and state legislatures are constitutionally endowed with a general "police power." These are *not* usually understood to be self-justifying here in America, since according to a fundamental legal/political argument, they exist in the service of rights and the general welfare.

11. See Karl N. Llewellyn, *The Bramble Bush, or, Our Law and Its Study* (New York: Oceana Publishing, 1960); Karl N. Llewellyn, "Remarks on the Theory of Appellate Decision and the Rules or Canons about How Statutes Are to Be Construed," 3 *Vand. L. Rev.* 395 (1950).

12. See, generally, Duncan Kennedy, "Freedom and Constraint in Adjudication: A Critical Phenomenology," 36 *J. Legal Education* 518 (1986).

13. Kennedy, "A Semiotics of Legal Argument."

14. Ronald Sullivan, "Liability Waiver Barred at N.Y.U. Dental Clinic," *New York Times,* December 30, 1990, s. 1, p. 27.

15. See Frances Olsen, "From False Paternalism to False Equality: Judicial Assaults on Feminist Community, Illinois, 1869–1895, 84 *Mich. L. Rev.* 1518 (1986).

16. See, for example, Martin Shapiro, *Freedom of Speech: The Supreme Court and Judicial Review* (Englewood, N.J.: Prentice Hall, 1966), p. 103.

17. Javins v. First Nat'l Realty Corp., 428 F.2d 1071 (D.C. Cir. 1970).

18. Escola v. Coca-Cola Bottling Co. of Fresno, 24 Cal. 2d 453, 150 P.2d 436 (1944) (Traynor, J., concurring).

19. Duncan Kennedy, "Form and Substance in Private Law Adjudication," 89 *Harv. L. Rev.* 1689 (1976).

20. Ibid., pp. 1702–1710.

21. Ibid., pp. 1766–1776. See also, Duncan Kennedy, "The Structure of Blackstone's Commentaries," 28 *Buff. L. Rev.* 205 (1979), and Duncan Kennedy and Peter Gabel, "Roll Over Beethoven," 36 *Stan. L. Rev.* 1 (1984).

7. IDEOLOGICALLY ORIENTED LEGAL WORK

1. In Dworkin's terminology, they behave as "pragmatists." Ronald Dworkin, *Law's Empire* (Cambridge, Mass.: Harvard University Press, 1986), pp. 151–164. For an introduction to the social science literature, see Sheldon Goldman and Austin Sarat, *American Court Systems: Readings in Judicial Process and Behavior* (New York: Longman, 1989).

2. I've dealt with this subject before, in Duncan Kennedy, "Freedom and Constraint in Adjudication: A Critical Phenomenology," 36 *J. Legal Education* 518 (1986), and Duncan Kennedy, "American Constitutionalism as Civil Religion: Notes of an Atheist," 19 *Nova L. Rev.* 909 (1995).

3. Owen Fiss, "Objectivity and Interpretation," 34 *Stan. L. Rev.* 739 (1982).

4. Remember that ideological projects have a collective dimension. An ideological preference is "individual" and "personal," but not idiosyncratic in the way a preference for litigants in blue shirts would be. See Chapter 3.

5. There are also "loopified" fields. They are the most "postmodern," and perhaps all fields are "really" loopified. See Kennedy, "Freedom and Constraint," pp. 68–69, and Duncan Kennedy, "The Stages of the Decline of the Public/Private Distinction," 130 *U. Pa. L. Rev.* 1349 (1982).

6. See Paul Brest, "Interpretation and Interest," 34 *Stan. L. Rev.* 765 (1982).

7. Neil MacCormick, "Reconstruction after Deconstruction: A Response to CLS," 10 *Oxford J. Leg. Stud.* 539, 553–554 (1990).

8. If he accepts interpretive fidelity, he will give up if he can't achieve what he sees as the just result, and he will be open to conversion to the other side through the experience of delving into the materials.

9. Reagan v. Farmers Loan & Trust, 154 U.S. 362 (1894).

10. DePeyster v. Michael, 7 Selden 467 (N.Y. 1852).

11. Brown v. Bd. of Educ. of Topeka, 347 U.S. 483 (1954)(school desegregation).

12. Reynolds v. Sims, 377 U.S. 533 (1964)(reapportionment).

13. Miranda v. Arizona, 384 U.S. 486 (1966)(notification of right to counsel).

14. Dred Scott v. Sandford, 60 U.S. (19 How.) 393 (1857)(citizenship of African Americans).

15. Lochner v. New York, 198 U.S. 45 (1905) (constitutionality of minimum hours laws).

16. Escola v. Coca-Cola Bottling Co. of Fresno, 24 Cal. 2d 453, 150 P.2d 436 (1944)(Traynor, J., concurring).

17. Javins v. First Nat'l Realty Corp., 428 F.2d 1071 (D.C. Cir. 1970).

18. Duncan Kennedy, "A Semiotics of Legal Argument," 42 *Syracuse L. Rev.* 75 (1991), and the same article with "European Introduction: Four Objections," in *Collected Courses of the Academy of European Law,* vol. 3, book 2, pp. 309–365 (Amsterdam: Kluwer Academic Publishers, 1994). Jack Balkin, "Nested Oppositions," 99 *Yale L.J.* 1669 (1990). See the excellent discussion in William Edmundson, "Transparency and Indeterminacy in the Liberal Critique of Critical Legal Studies," 24 *Seton Hall L. Rev.* 557, 570–574 (1993).

19. Ronald Dworkin, "The Model of Rules," in *Taking Rights Seriously* (Cambridge, Mass.: Harvard University Press, 1978), pp. 26–27.

20. H. L. A. Hart, "American Jurisprudence through English Eyes: The Nightmare and the Noble Dream," 11 *Ga. L. Rev.* 969 (1977).

21. Ibid., pp. 977–978.

22. MacCormick, "Reconstruction," p. 554 (citing no examples).

23. In Chapter 11, I give many examples of this kind of analysis. It may be that Andrew Altman's *Critical Legal Studies: A Liberal Critique* (Princeton, N.J.: Princeton University Press, 1990) contains a criticism of this version of cls, but if so I haven't been able to find it in his discussions of what he calls the "patchwork" and the "duck-rabbit" theses, neither of which seems recognizably related to what I argued in Kennedy, "Form and Substance," and think I am still arguing here. I would say the same of Charles Yablon, "The Indeterminacy of the Law: Critical Legal Studies and the Problem of Explanation," 6 *Cardozo L. Rev.* 917 (1985); Lawrence Solum, "On the Indeterminacy Crisis: Critiquing Critical Dogma," 54 *U. Chi. L. Rev.* 462 (1987); and Ken Kress, "Legal Indeterminacy," 77 *Cal. L. Rev.* 283 (1989). Nor does Edmundson, "Transparency," see the issue the way I do. I hope this version is clearer and more accurate than my earlier ones and will give rise to less misunderstanding. A view close to my own is Elizabeth Mensch, "Book Review," 33 *Stan. L. Rev.* 753 (1981)(reviewing P. Atiyah, *The Rise and Fall of Freedom of Contract*).

8. STRATEGIZING STRATEGIC BEHAVIOR IN INTERPRETATION

1. Jeffrey Rosen, "Make Up Our Mind, Justice O'Connor," *New York Times,* December 26, 1995, s. 1, p. 21.

2. I hope the reader will remember that I did not attempt to prove that legal reasoning could never produce closure or that the experience of boundness is mere illusion. My goal was only to show that there are gaps, conflicts, and ambiguities, that these are a function of legal work as well as of the materials the judge works with, that the experience of "freedom" to shape the legal field is common, and that one cannot say with certainty that when closure occurs it is a product of a property of the field rather than of the work strategy adopted under particular constraints.

3. Jerome Frank, *Law and the Modern Mind* (New York: Coward, McCann, 1935).

4. No *rationalist* version of explanation can be "saved" by interpolating a "text/event" distinction at the last minute. But that is not the goal. The point in the text is that we will sometimes reach explanatory closure, in the sense that we feel constrained, by our theory of why the case came out the way it did, to respond in a particular way. If we feel constrained to the conclusion that the judge chose as she did because she felt constrained by her understanding of her own liberalism, then it will make sense to offer her an alternative version of liberalism, to invest energy in internal critique. If we think she was bribed, or hates the particular class of plaintiffs, this strategy will appear a waste of time, *and we will act accordingly.* This pragmatist version of explanation is enough for me.

5. Sigmund Freud, "Certain Neurotic Mechanisms in Jealousy, Paranoia, and Homosexuality" (1922), in Sigmund Freud, *Sexuality and the Psychology of Love* (New York: Collier Books, 1963), p. 151.

6. Anna Freud, *The Ego and the Mechanisms of Defense,* trans. C. Baines (London: International Universities Press, 1937, 1966), p. 60.

7. See Scott Altman, "Beyond Candor," 89 *Mich. L. Rev.* 296, nn. 6, 7 (1990). My approach differs both from the earlier realist versions and from his, not in my definition of denial, but in the specification of what is being denied and why. Altman's specific psychology of judging seems to me largely vitiated by his failure to distinguish clearly between "following a rule" and "following the law" in the work of interpretation (rule choice), and by his related failure to distinguish clearly between what he calls "activism" and what he calls "manipulation." His development of the parallel between defense mechanisms and cognitive dissonance is helpful, but there doesn't seem to be enough difference between the vocabularies to merit incorporating cognitive dissonance theory into the discussion beyond the mention in the text. Altman's reconstruction of "the CLS position" on indeterminacy, id. at 333–347, is even more outlandish than his self-described "caricature" of my position, id. at n. 48. Some earlier critical discussions of denial in legal thought are Duncan Kennedy, "The Structure of Blackstone's Commentaries," 28 *Buff. L. Rev.* 205, 209–221 (1979); Mark Kelman, *A Guide to Critical Legal Studies* (Cambridge, Mass.: Harvard University Press, 1987), pp. 3, 286–290; Pierre Schlag, "Contradiction and Denial," 87 *Mich. L. Rev.* 1216 (1989).

8. Anna Freud, *The Ego,* p. 48.

9. Ibid., p. 50.

10. Jean-Paul Sartre, *Being and Nothingness: An Essay on Phenomenological Ontology,* trans. Hazel Barnes (New York: Citadel Press, 1965), pp. 89–90.

11. Henry Maine, *Ancient Law* (1861, Dent and Sons Everyman Ed., 1917), pp. 76–77.

12. Anna Freud, *The Ego,* pp. 44–50.

13. The pop psychological usage is nonetheless different from Anna Freud's in at least three important ways: for her, denial always refers to anxiety-producing external facts, whereas repression is directed at anxiety-producing internal impulses; denial is a normal mechanism of defense only in childhood, becoming sympotatic in adulthood; and she was a true believer in Freud's basic concepts, rather than agnostic in the post-Freudian mode.

14. Ronald Dworkin, "On Interpretation and Objectivity," in *A Matter of Principle* (Cambridge, Mass.: Harvard University Press, 1985), pp. 171–174.

15. Ronald Dworkin, "Liberalism," in *A Matter of Principle* (Cambridge, Mass.: Harvard University Press, 1985), p. 181.

16. Ronald Dworkin, *Law's Empire* (Cambridge, Mass.: Harvard University Press, 1986), pp. 254–266.

17. Liberal theorists sometimes seem to deny because they identify with judges, writing their law review articles as though they were judicial opinions. The discussion in the text is of investments not based on this kind of direct identification with the judge.

18. Altman, "Beyond Candor," pp. 318–327.

19. Sigmund Freud, *Introductory Lectures on Psychoanalysis,* trans. J. Strachey (New York: Norton, 1916, 1966), p. 94.

20. Anna Freud, *The Ego,* p. 60.

21. For helpful discussions of Sartre's theory, see Gregory McCulloch, *Using Sartre: An Analytical Introduction to Early Sartrean Themes* (London: Routledge, 1994), ch. 4, and Matthew Kramer, *Legal Theory, Political Theory, and Deconstruction: Against Rhadamanthus* (Bloomington: Indiana University Press, 1991), pp. 222–235.

22. Compare Altman, "Beyond Candor," n. 29.

23. See Thomas Ogden, "On Projective Identification," *Int. J. Psycho-Analysis* 68 (1979), p. 357.

24. Marc Brodin, letter to the editor, *Boston Globe,* August 28, 1995, s. 1, p. 10.

25. Sigmund Freud, "Certain Neurotic Mechanisms," p. 151.

9. THE MODERATION AND EMPOWERMENT EFFECTS

1. Robert Reich, "After the Rights Revolution: Receiving the Regulatory State," *New Republic,* January 21, 1991, pp. 38–39.

2. See Chapter 7.

3. See Richard Parker, "The Past of American Constitutional Theory—and Its Future," 42 *Ohio St. L.J.* 223 (1981).

4. Textile Workers Union v. Lincoln Mills, 353 U.S. 448 (1957).

5. Jones v. Alfred Mayer Co., 392 U.S. 409 (1968).

6. Meritor Savings Bank, FSB v. Vinson, 477 U.S. 57 (1986).

7. Southern Burlington County NAACP v. Township of Mt. Laurel, 336 A.2d 713 (N.J. 1975).

8. These are the obedience and conversion effects described in Chapter 3. See Chapter 11 for discussion of their empirical plausibility.

9. Norman Dorsen, "Talking Liberties," *Civil Liberties,* Winter 1990–91, p. 16.

10. Learned Hand, *The Bill of Rights* (Cambridge, Mass.: Harvard University Press, 1958).

11. John Donahue, *The Privatization Decision: Public Ends, Private Means* (New York: Basic Books, 1989), p. 21.

12. Laurence Tribe, *American Constitutional Law,* 2d ed. (Mineola, N.Y.: Foundation Press, 1988), pp. 10–11 (not present in latest edition).

13. Ethan Bronner, "High Court Moves to the Right on Criminal Law," *Boston Globe,* April 26, 1991, s. 1, p. 1.

14. See, for example, Thurgood Marshall, "Reflections on the Bicentennial of the United States Constitution," 101 *Harv. L. Rev.* 1 (1987); Frank Michelman, "Judicial Supremacy, the Concept of Law, and the Sanctity of Life," in *Justice and Injustice in Law and Legal Theory,* ed. Austin Sarat and Thomas Kearns (Ann Arbor: University of Michigan Press, 1996).

15. Compare Robin West, "Progressive and Conservative Constitutionalism," 88 *Mich. L. Rev.* 641, 644–645 (1990).

16. For extended speculations in this vein, see "Radical Intellectuals in American Culture and Politics, or, My Talk at the Gramsci Institute," in Duncan Kennedy, *Sexy Dressing, Etc.* (Cambridge, Mass.: Harvard University Press, 1993).

10. THE LEGITIMATION EFFECT

1. The conception of legitimation I develop in this chapter and the next is Gramscian and Althusserian rather than Weberian. See Antonio Gramsci, *Excerpts from the Prison Notebooks,* trans. Quintin Hoare and Geoffrey Smith (New York: International Publishers, 1971); Louis Althusser, "Ideology and Ideological State Apparatuses (Notes toward an Investigation)," in *Lenin and Philosophy and Other Essays,* trans. Ben Brewster (New York: Monthly Review Press, 1971), p. 127; Perry Anderson, "Origins of the Present Crisis," in *Towards Socialism,* ed. Perry Anderson and Robin Blackburn (Ithaca: Cornell University Press, 1966), p. 11. On the Weberian conception, see Alan Hyde, "The Concept of Legitimation in the Sociology of Law," 1983 *Wisc. L. Rev.* 379. The use of legitimation in cls has two important forerunners: John Griffiths, "Ideology in Criminal Procedure: Toward a Third 'Model' of the Criminal Process," 79 *Yale L.J.* 359 (1970); and Douglas Hay, "Property, Authority, and the Criminal Law," in *Albion's Fatal Tree: Crime and Authority in Eighteenth Century England,* ed. Douglas Hay et al. (New York: Pantheon, 1975), p. 17. Some representative crit works are Karl Klare,

"Judicial Deradicalization of the Wagner Act and the Origins of Modern Legal Consciousness, 1937–1941," 62 *Minn. L. Rev.* 265 (1978); Alan Freeman, "Legitimizing Racial Discrimination through Antidiscrimination Law: A Critical Review of Supreme Court Doctrine," 62 *Minn. L. Rev.* 1049 (1978); Duncan Kennedy, "The Structure of Blackstone's Commentaries," 28 *Buff. L. Rev.* 205 (1979); Robert Gordon, "New Approaches to Legal Theory," in *The Politics of Law: A Progressive Critique,* ed. David Kairys (New York: Pantheon, 1982), p. 281; Peter Gabel and Paul Harris, "Building Power and Breaking Images: Critical Legal Theory and the Practice of Law," 11 *N.Y.U. Rev. L. & Soc. Change* 369 (1982–83); Gerald Frug, "The Ideology of Bureaucracy in American Law," 97 *Harv. L. Rev.* 1276 (1984); Mark Kelman, *A Guide to Critical Legal Studies* (Cambridge, Mass.: Harvard University Press, 1987), pp. 262–295. For a review, see Carol Steiker and Jordan Steiker, "Sober Second Thoughts: Reflections on Two Decades of Constitutional Regulation of Capital Punishment," 109 *Harv. L. Rev.* 355, 429–432 (1995). I discuss crit versions in specific doctrinal areas later in this chapter and the relationship between the neo-Marxist and crit versions in the next chapter.

2. See Morton Horwitz, *The Transformation of American Law, 1788–1860* (Cambridge, Mass.: Harvard University Press, 1977), pp. 117–121.

3. James Bradley Thayer, "The American Doctrine of Constitutional Law," 7 *Harv. L. Rev.* 17 (1893).

4. Franz Wieacker, *A History of Private Law (with Particular Reference to Germany),* trans. Tony Weir (New York: Oxford University Press, 1995), pp. 431–441.

5. Sally Merry, *Getting Justice and Getting Even: Legal Consciousness among Working-Class Americans* (Chicago: University of Chicago Press, 1990), pp. 96–97.

6. Michel Rosenfeld, "Deconstruction and Legal Interpretation: Conflict, Indeterminacy, and the Temptations of the New Legal Formalism," 11 *Cardozo L. Rev.* 1211, 1245 (1990).

7. Duncan Kennedy and Frank Michelman, "Are Property and Contract Efficient?" 8 *Hostra L. Rev.* 711 (1980).

8. There is an ambiguity as to why the structure of rules is in the background in the first place. It might be because we think that they are obviously right, or that they are the natural rules to govern this type of interaction, or that they flow logically from some uncontroversial premise. But to be in the background is to be outside continuous consciousness and attention. Naturalization in this sense is not a conscious operation that people perform on the rules; it is more like an assumption. The rhetoric of naturalness and necessity comes into play only when for some reason people advert to the background, and then it is most likely a way to dismiss it and get back to the foreground. This gives rise to the question whether the rules don't get naturalized because they are in the background, rather than backgrounded because naturalized. We don't need to solve this conundrum. Even if backgrounding some elements, and naturalizing what is background, are cognitive necessities, we can still work at particular figure/ground reversals.

9. See, generally, Duncan Kennedy, "The Stakes of Law, or Hale and Foucault!"

in *Sexy Dressing, Etc.* (Cambridge, Mass.: Harvard University Press, 1993). This way of looking at the constitutive role of law in the economy also applies to conflict between firms. See Rudolph Peritz, *Competition Policy in America, 1888–1992: History, Rhetoric, Law* (New York: Oxford University Press, 1996); Kipp Rogers, "The Right of Publicity: Resurgence of Legal Formalism and Judicial Disregard of Policy Issues," 16 *Beverly Hills Bar Assoc. J.* 65 (1982).

10. Hagai Hurvitz, "American Labor Law and the Doctrine of Entrepreneurial Property Rights: Boycotts, Courts, and the Juridical Reorientation of 1886–1895," 8 *Ind. Rel. L.J.* 307 (1986); Ellen Kelman, "American Labor Law and Legal Formalism: How 'Legal Logic' Shaped and Vitiated the Rights of American Workers," 58 *St. John's L. Rev.* 1 (1983); John Nockleby, "Tortious Interference with Contractual Relations in the Nineteenth Century: The Transformation of Property, Contract, and Tort," 93 *Harv. L. Rev.* 1510 (1980).

11. William Forbath, *Law and the Shaping of the American Labor Movement* (Cambridge, Mass.: Harvard University Press, 1991).

12. Felix Frankfurter and Nathan Greene, *The Labor Injunction* (New York: Macmillan, 1930).

13. Klare, "Judicial Deradicalization," p. 62. The second foundational piece is Katherine Stone, "The Post-War Paradigm in American Labor Law," 90 *Yale L.J.* 1509 (1981).

14. Stone, "Post-War Paradigm," pp. 1514–1515.

15. Klare, "Judicial Deradicalization," pp. 309–310.

16. Karl Klare, "Critical Theory and Labor Relations Law," in *The Politics of Law: A Progressive Critique,* ed. David Kairys (New York: Pantheon Books, 1982), p. 82.

17. The labor critique was preoccupied from the start with race and gender issues, and it quickly incorporated the later cls approach to law as constitutive of sexual and racial identity. See Karl Klare, "The Quest for Industrial Democracy and the Struggle against Racism: Lessons from Labor Law and Civil Rights Law," 61 *Oregon L. Rev.* 157 (1982); Karl Klare, "Power/Dressing: Regulation of Employee Appearance," 26 *New Eng. L. Rev.* 1395 (1992).

18. Neatly summarized in Robert G. McCloskey, *The American Supreme Court* (Chicago: University of Chicago Press, 1960), pp. 144–150. See Edward S. Corwin, *Commerce Power vs. States Rights* (Princeton: Princeton University Press, 1936); Robert Stern, "That Commerce Which Concerns More States Than One," 47 *Harv. L. Rev.* 1375 (1934).

19. Summarized in William O. Douglas, "Stare Decisis," 49 *Colum. L. Rev.* 735 (1949).

20. Henry Hart and Herbert Wechsler, *The Federal Courts and the Federal System* (Brooklyn: Foundation Press, 1953).

21. Nathaniel Berman, "'But the Alternative Is Despair': Nationalism and the Modernist Renewal of International Law," 106 *Harv. L. Rev.* 1792 (1993).

22. See David Kennedy, "The Move to Institutions," 8 *Cardozo L. Rev.* 841 (1987);

Berman, " 'But the Alternative' "; Nathaniel Berman, "Modernism, Nationalism, and the Rhetoric of Reconstruction," 4 *Yale J. Law & Human.* 351 (1992); Nigel Purvis, "Critical Legal Studies in Public International Law," 32 *Harv. Int. L.J.* 81 (1991); Olivier DeSchutter, "Critical Legal Studies dans le Droit International," 31 *Droit et Société* 1 (1992).

23. David Kennedy, "Primitive Legal Scholarship," 27 *Harv. Int. L.J.* 1 (1986); David Kennedy, "Spring Break," 63 *Texas L. Rev.* 1377 (1985); David Kennedy, "The International Style in Postwar Law and Policy," 1994 *Utah L. Rev.* 7; David Kennedy, "The Sources of International Law," 2 *Amer. Univ. J. Int. Law & Policy* 1 (1987); Nathaniel Berman, "Nationalism Legal and Linguistic: The Teachings of European Jurisprudence," 24 *N.Y.U.J. Int. Law & Politics* 1515 (1992); Karen Engle, "International Human Rights and Feminism: When Discourses Meet," 13 *Mich. J. Int'l Law* 517 (1992).

24. Gerald Frug, "The City as a Legal Concept," 93 *Harv. L. Rev.* 1057 (1980); Gerald Frug, "Decentering Decentralization," 60 *Univ. Chic. L. Rev.* 253 (1993); Gerald Frug, *Local Government Law* (St. Paul, Minn.: West Pub. Co., 1988); Richard Ford, "The Boundaries of Race: Political Geography in Legal Analysis," 107 *Harv. L. Rev.* 1843 (1994).

25. Gerald Frug, "The Geography of Community," 48 *Stan. L. Rev.* (May 1996); Ford, "Boundaries of Race."

26. Derrick Bell, "Brown v. Board of Education and the Interest Convergence Dilemma," 93 *Harv. L. Rev.* 518 (1980).

27. Derrick Bell, *And We Are Not Saved* (New York: Basic Books, 1987).

28. Alan Freeman, "Legitimizing Racial Discrimination," p. 1049; Alan Freeman, "Antidiscrimination Law: A Critical Review," in *The Politics of Law: A Progressive Critique,* ed. David Kairys (New York: Pantheon Books, 1982).

29. Kimberle Crenshaw, "Race, Reform, and Retrenchment: Transformation and Legitimation in Antidiscrimination Law," 101 *Harv. L. Rev.* 1331 (1988).

30. Gary Peller, "Race Consciousness," 1990 *Duke L.J.* 758; Neil Gotanda, "A Critique of 'Our Constitution Is Colorblind': Racial Categories and White Supremacy," 44 *Stan. L. Rev.* 1 (1991).

31. See *Critical Race Theory: The Key Writings That Formed the Movement,* ed. Kimberle Crenshaw, Neil Gotanda, Gary Peller, and Kendall Thomas (New York: New Press, 1995), "Introduction," pp. xiii–xxxii.

32. Catharine MacKinnon, *Only Words* (Cambridge, Mass.: Harvard University Press, 1993).

33. *Words That Wound: Critical Race Theory, Assaultive Speech, and the First Amendment,* ed. Mari Matsuda et al. (Boulder, Colo.: Westview Press, 1993).

34. Mark Tushnet, "Corporations and Free Speech," *The Politics of Law: A Progressive Critique,* ed. David Kairys (New York: Pantheon Books, 1982); Jack Balkin, "Some Realism about Pluralism: Legal Realist Approaches to the First Amendment," 1990 *Duke L.J.* 375; James Boyle, "A Theory of Law and Information: Copyright, Spleens,

Blackmail, and Insider Trading," 80 *Calif. L. Rev.* 1413 (1992); John Nockleby, "Hate Speech in Context: The Case of Verbal Threats," 42 *Buff. L. Rev.* 653 (1994).

35. Robert Steinfeld, *The Invention of Free Labor: The Employment Relation in English and American Law and Culture, 1350–1870* (Chapel Hill: University of North Carolina Press, 1991).

36. Catharine MacKinnon, "Feminism, Marxism, Method, and the State," 8 *Signs* 650 (1983).

37. Frances Olsen, "The Family and the Market: A Study of Ideology and Legal Reform," 96 *Harv. L. Rev.* 1497 (1983); Frances Olsen, "The Myth of State Intervention in the Family," 18 *Mich. J. Law Reform* 835 (1985); Frances Olsen, "The Politics of Family Law," 2 *Law & Inequality* 1 (1984).

38. Andrea Dworkin, *Right-Wing Women* (New York: Putnam's Sons, 1983); Andrea Dworkin, *Intercourse* (New York, Free Press, 1987).

39. Olsen, "The Family and the Market."

40. See Catharine MacKinnon, *Feminism Unmodified: Discourses on Life and Law* (Cambridge, Mass.: Harvard University Press, 1987), p. 54; Dworkin, *Right-Wing Women,* pp. 21–23. See also Kennedy, *Sexy Dressing,* pp. 147–162.

41. Mary Joe Frug, "A Post-Modern Feminist Legal Manifesto (an unfinished draft)," 105 *Harv. L. Rev.* 1045 (1992); Janet Halley, "Sexual Orientation and the Politics of Biology: A Critique of the Argument from Immutability," 46 *Stan. L. Rev.* 503 (1994). Cf. Robin West, "The Difference in Women's Hedonic Lives: A Phenomenological Critique of Feminist Legal Theory," 3 *Wisc. Women's L.J.* 81 (1987).

42. Clare Dalton, "An Essay in the Deconstruction of Contract Doctrine," 94 *Yale L.J.* 999 (1985); Mary Joe Frug, "Re-Reading Contracts: A Feminist Analysis of a Contracts Casebook," 34 *Am. Univ. L. Rev.* 665 (1985); Elizabeth Schneider, "Describing and Changing: Women's Self-Defense Work and the Problem of Expert Testimony on Battering," 9 *Women's Rts. L. Rep.* 195 (1986); Vicki Schultz, "Telling Stories about Women and Work: Judicial Interpretations of Sex Segregation in the Workplace in Title VII Cases Raising the Lack of Interest Argument," 103 *Harv. L. Rev.* 1749 (1990); Lama Abu-Odeh, "Crimes of Honour and the Construction of Gender in Arab Societies," in *Feminism and Islam,* ed. Mai Yamani (Reading, Eng.: Garnet, 1996), p. 141.

43. Frances Olsen, "Statutory Rape: A Feminist Critique of Rights Analysis," 63 *Tex. L. Rev.* 387 (1984); Engle, "International Human Rights."

44. Susan Keller, "Viewing and Doing: Complicating Pornography's Meaning," 81 *Georgetown L.J.* 2195 (1993); Lama Abu-Odeh, "Post-Colonial Feminism and the Veil: Considering the Difference," 26 *New Eng. L. Rev.* 1527 (1992); Dan Danielsen, "Representing Identities: Legal Treatment of Pregnancy and Homosexuality," 26 *New Eng. L. Rev.* (1992); *After Identity: A Reader in Law and Culture,* ed. Dan Danielsen and Karen Engle (New York: Routledge, 1995).

45. For example, Susan Keller, "The Rhetoric of Marriage, Achievement, and Power: An Analysis of Judicial Opinions Considering the Treatment of Profes-

sional Degrees as Marital Property," 21 *Vt. L. Rev.* (1996. See also Chapter 11, n. 21.

46. Kimberle Crenshaw, "Mapping the Margins: Identity Politics, Intersectionality, and Violence against Women," 43 *Stan. L. Rev.* 1241 (1991).

47. Kendall Thomas, "Beyond the Privacy Principle," 92 *Colum. L. Rev.* 501 (1992); Danielsen, "Representing Identities"; Halley, "Sexual Orientation."

48. For example, Duncan Kennedy and Leopold Specht, "Limited Equity Cooperatives as a Mode of Privatization," in *A Fourth Way? Privatization, Property, and the Emergence of New Market Economies,* ed. Gregory Alexander and Grazyna Skapca (New York: Routledge, 1994), p. 267.

49. Elizabeth Schneider, "Equal Rights to Trial for Women: Sex Bias in the Law of Self-Defense," 15 *Harv. C.R.-C.L. L. Rev.* 623 (1980).

50. Merle Weiner, "From Dollars to Sense: A Critique of Government Funding for the Battered Women's Shelter Movement," 9 *Law & Inequality* 1985 (1991).

51. Gregory Alexander, "Pensioners in America: The Economic Triumph and Political Limitations of Passive Ownership," Karl Klare, "Legal Theory and Democratic Reconstruction: Reflections on 1989," and William Simon, "Republicanism, Market Socialism, and the Third Way," all in *A Fourth Way? Privatization, Property, and the Emergence of New Market Economies,* ed. Gregory Alexander and Grazyna Skapca (New York: Routledge, 1994); Katherine Stone, "Labor and the Corporate Structure: Changing Conceptions and Emerging Possibilities," 55 *U. Chi. L. Rev.* 73 (1988); Karl Klare, "Workplace Democracy and Market Reconstruction: An Agenda for Reform," 38 *Cath. U. L. Rev.* 1 (1988); Alan Hyde, "In Defense of Employee Ownership," 67 *Chi.-Kent L. Rev.* 159 (1992). For a similar approach to agricultural law, see Marjorie Benson, *Agricultural Law in Canada, 1867–1995: With Particular Reference to Saskatchewan* (Calgary: Canadian Institute of Resources Law, 1996).

52. *Words that Wound* (see n. 33).

53. Regina Austin, "Employer Abuse, Worker Resistance, and the Tort of Intentional Infliction of Emotional Distress," 41 *Stan L. Rev.* 1 (1988).

54. Gerald Frug, "Decentering Decentralization."

55. Lawrence Kolodney, "Eviction Free Zones: The Economics of Legal Bricolage in the Fight against Displacement," 18 *Fordham Urban L.J.* 507 (1991).

11. ADJUDICATION IN SOCIAL THEORY

1. See generally David Trubek and Marc Galanter, "Scholars in Self-Estrangement: Some Reflections on the Crisis of Law and Development Studies in the United States," 1974 *Wisc. L. Rev.* 1062; David Trubek, "Complexity and Contradiction in the Legal Order: Balbus and the Challenge of Critical Social Thought about Law," 11 *Law & Soc'y Rev.* 529 (1977); David Trubek, "Where the Action Is: Critical Legal Studies and Empiricism," 36 *Stan. L. Rev.* 575 (1984). David Trubek introduced me to the issues discussed in this chapter in his seminar "Law and Development" at the Yale Law School

in the spring of 1970. His and Roberto Unger's work has continued to influence mine, as is evident throughout the text that follows, in spite of their different emphases and different conclusions. Roberto Unger, *Knowledge and Politics* (New York: Free Press, 1975); Roberto Unger, *Law in Modern Society: Toward a Criticism of Social Theory* (New York: Free Press, 1976); Roberto Unger, *The Critical Legal Studies Movement* (Cambridge, Mass.: Harvard University Press, 1986); Roberto Unger, *Politics: A Work in Constructive Social Theory*, 3 vols. (New York: Cambridge University Press, 1987).

2. Susan Silbey, "Ideals and Practices in the Study of Law," 9 *Leg. Stud. Forum* 7, 10 (1985).

3. Points *a* and *b* remain part of the conventional wisdom of the school of Amherst: "By offering deconstructions of specific texts, critical legal studies tends to associate law with the textual pronouncements of judges and legal theorists. The very idea of law as rhetoric focuses almost exclusively on the discursive aspects of the law—the professional grammar invoked by those responsible for linguistically justifying the use of a legal regulation or the imposition of a legal sanction. Such linguistic justification, however, can be seen as but a small part of the law. Fitzpatrick, by contrast, reaches toward a more capacious understanding of law, one which, though never explicitly theorized, would include practices of administrators and legal 'subjects' rather than merely pronouncements of judges." We learn that Peter Fitzpatrick "begins where much of critical jurisprudence ends—by observing the deeply contradictory nature of law." Lawrence Douglas and Austin Sarat, "(De)Mythologizing Jurisprudence: Speaking the 'Truth' about 'Myth,'" 19 *Law & Soc. Inquiry* 523, 529–530 (1994) (footnotes omitted).

4. See the "implementation" research cited in Alan Hyde, "The Concept of Legitimation in the Sociology of Law," 1983 *Wisc. L. Rev.* 379, 410, n. 89.

5. Jean Braucher, "The Afterlife of Contract," 90 *Northwestern L. Rev.* 49, 80 (1995) (summarizing Robert Gordon, "Book Review," 1974 *Wisc. L. Rev.* 1216, 1223–1225).

6. Robert H. Mnookin and Lewis Kornhauser, "Bargaining in the Shadow of the Law: The Case of Divorce," 88 *Yale L.J.* 950 (1979).

7. See Duncan Kennedy, "Sexual Abuse, Sexy Dressing, and the Eroticization of Domination," in *Sexy Dressing, Etc.* (Cambridge, Mass.: Harvard University Press, 1993).

8. Braucher, "Afterlife," p. 88.

9. In other words, the sociologists are suggesting—without, lamentably, any attempt at empirical verification—a legitimation effect.

10. See, for example, Rand Rosenblatt, "Health Care Reform and Administrative Law: A Structural Approach," 88 *Yale L.J.* 243 (1978).

11. Lon Fuller, *The Morality of Law* (New Haven: Yale University Press, 1964).

12. Michel Foucault, *The History of Sexuality*, vol. 1, trans. Robert Hurley (New York: Vintage, 1978), pp. 92–96. See, generally, Duncan Kennedy, "The Stakes of Law, or Hale and Foucault!" in *Sexy Dressing, Etc.* (Cambridge, Mass.: Harvard University Press, 1993).

13. Hyde, "Legitimation," pp. 408–409 (footnotes omitted; the quote is from Hans Adamy, "Legitimacy, Realigning Elections and the Supreme Court," 1973 *Wisc. L. Rev.* 790, 808; emphasis in the original).

14. Frank Munger and Carol Seron, "Critical Legal Studies versus Critical Legal Theory: A Comment on Method," 6 *Law & Policy* 257, 269 (1984).

15. Hyde, "Legitimation," p. 383, n. 5.

16. Antonio Gramsci, *Prison Notebooks,* ed. Joseph A. Buttigieg, trans. Joseph Buttigieg and Antonio Callari (New York: Columbia University Press, 1992).

17. Louis Althusser, "Ideology and Ideological State Apparatuses (Notes toward an Investigation)," in *Lenin and Philosophy and Other Essays,* trans. Ben Brewster (New York: Monthly Review Press, 1971), p. 127.

18. See Hyde, "Legitimation."

19. See Robert Gordon, "New Developments in Legal Theory," in *The Politics of Law: A Progressive Critique,* ed. David Kairys (New York: Pantheon Books, 1982).

20. Kimberle Crenshaw, "Race, Reform, and Retrenchment: Transformation and Legitimation in Antidiscrimination Law," 101 *Harv. L. Rev.* 1331 (1988).

21. The "cultural studies" variant of cls shows that the rhetoric of opinions, say, the images of women they deploy, is a part of the general cultural discourse of identity and as such worth study. The discourse both reflects and contributes to the reproduction of widespread, culturally dominant ideas about what women and men, for example, are naturally like. Moreover, cultural imagery may weigh more heavily than either deduction or policy in influencing judicial rule choice. This is an extension of the idea that appellate adjudication is a forum of ideology, where liberals and conservatives fight it out and where the marginal, more extreme positions are "silenced." The discourse of the forum may legitimate, say, gender roles. But this is not the kind of effect I address in the text. Legitimation, as I am using the term, is an effect of the specific institutional practice of adjudication rather than of authoritative discourse in general. See Peter Gabel, "The Mass Psychology of the New Federalism: How the Burger Court's Political Imagery Legitimizes the Privatization of Everyday Life," 52 *Geo. Wash. L. Rev.* 263 (1984); Rosemary Coombe, "Contesting the Self: Negotiating Subjectivities in Nineteenth-Century Ontario Defamation Trials," 11 *Studies in Law, Politics, and Society* 3 (1991); Nathaniel Berman, "A Perilous Ambivalence: Nationalist Desire, Legal Autonomy, and the Limits of the Interwar Framework," 33 *Harv. Int. L.J.* 353 (1992); Lisa Binder, " 'With More Than Admiration He Admired': Images of Beauty and Defilement in Judicial Narratives of Rape," 18 *Harv. Women's Law J.* 265 (1995); Susan Keller, "The Rhetoric of Marriage, Achievement, and Power: An Analysis of Judicial Opinions Considering Professional Degrees as Marital Property, 21 *Vt. L. Rev.* (1996).

22. See Sally Merry, *Getting Justice and Getting Even: Legal Consciousness among Working-Class Americans* (Chicago: University of Chicago Press, 1990), p. 11; Barbara Yngvesson, *Virtuous Citizens, Disruptive Subjects: Order and Complaint in a New England Court* (New York: Routledge, 1993), pp. 11–12.

23. See Chapter 2.

24. Thomas Heller, "Structuralism and Critique," 36 *Stan. L. Rev.* 127 (1984).

25. See Joseph Singer, "The Legal Rights Debate in Analytical Jurisprudence from Bentham to Hohfeld," 1982 *Wisc. L. Rev.* 975.

26. Roberto M. Unger, *Knowledge and Politics* (New York: Free Press, 1975), p. 88.

27. Duncan Kennedy, "Legal Formality," 2 *J. Legal Studies* 351, 364, nn. 21, 22 (1973); Duncan Kennedy, "Form and Substance in Private Law Adjudication," 89 *Harv. L. Rev.* 1685 (1976).

28. This form of normative external determination is the subject of the next two chapters.

29. Richard A. Posner, *Problems of Jurisprudence* (Cambridge, Mass.: Harvard University Press, 1990), pp. 459–460.

30. Austin Sarat, "Legal Effectiveness and Social Studies of Law: On the Unfortunate Persistence of a Research Tradition," 9 *Leg. Stud. Forum* 23, 30–31 (1985).

31. Boaventura de Sousa Santos, *Toward a New Common Sense: Law, Science, and Politics in the Paradigmatic Transition* (New York: Routledge, 1995).

32. What follows is an account of an actual debate, carried out over four or five years at conferences and summer camps. The account is no doubt seriously defective as history because of the vagaries of memory and the distorting influence of narcissistic investment. The debate was only partly reflected in the writings of the participants I refer to in the course of the narrative.

33. Morton Horwitz, *The Transformation of American Law, 1788–1860* (Cambridge, Mass.: Harvard University Press, 1977); Karl Klare, "Judicial Deradicalization of the Wagner Act and the Origins of Modern Legal Consciousness," 62 *Minn. L. Rev.* 265 (1978); Peter Gabel, "Intention and Structure in Contractual Conditions: Outline of a Method for Critical Legal Theory," 61 *Minn. L. Rev.* 601 (1977); Mark Tushnet, "A Marxist Analysis of American Law," 1 *Marxist Perspectives* 96 (1978); Trubek, "Complexity and Contradiction"; Jay Feinman and Peter Gabel, "Contract Law as Ideology," in *The Politics of Law: A Progressive Critique,* ed. David Kairys (New York: Pantheon Books, 1982).

34. Evgeny Pashukanis, *Law and Marxism: A General Theory,* trans. Barbara Einhorn (London: Ink Links, 1978); Isaac Balbus, "Commodity Form and Legal Form: An Essay on the 'Relative Autonomy' of the Law," 11 *Law & Soc'y Rev.* 571 (1977).

35. Willard Hurst, *Law and the Conditions of Freedom in the Nineteenth Century United States* (Madison: University of Wisconsin Press, 1956).

36. Lawrence Friedman, *A History of American Law* (New York: Simon and Schuster, 1973). For the neo-Marxist critique, see Mark Tushnet, "Perspectives on the Development of American Law: A Critical Review of Friedman's 'A History of American Law,'" 1977 *Wisc. L. Rev.* 81.

37. Duncan Kennedy, "Form and Substance in Private Law Adjudication," 89 *Harv. L. Rev.* 1685 (1976); Unger, *The Critical Legal Studies Movement.*

38. Horwitz, *The Transformation of American Law.*

39. See Chapter 4 and the sources cited in Chapter 4, n. 16.

40. For example, Alan Freeman, "Legitimizing Racial Discrimination through Race Law: A Critical Review of Supreme Court Doctrine," 62 *Minn. L. Rev.* 1049 (1978); Alan Freeman, "Antidiscrimination Law: A Critical Review," in *The Politics of Law: A Progressive Critique,* ed. David Kairys (New York: Pantheon Books, 1982); Frances Olsen, "The Family and the Market: A Study of Ideology and Legal Reform," 96 *Harv. L. Rev.* 1497 (1983).

41. For example, Gerald Frug, "The City as a Legal Concept," 93 *Harv. L. Rev.* 1057 (1980); Mark Kelman, "Interpretive Construction in the Substantive Criminal Law," 33 *Stan. L. Rev.* 591 (1981); William Simon, "Visions of Practice in Legal Thought," 36 *Stan. L. Rev.* 496 (1984); William Simon, "The Invention and Reinvention of Welfare Rights," 44 *Md. L. Rev.* 1 (1985).

42. Robert Gordon, "Unfreezing Legal Reality: Critical Approaches to Law," 15 *Fla. St. L. Rev.* 195 (1987).

43. Hyde, "Legitimation"; Crenshaw, "Retrenchment."

44. Some examples of the underlying attitude I'm talking about are Alan Freeman, "Truth and Mystification in Legal Scholarship," 90 *Yale L.J.* 1229 (1981); Mark Kelman, "Trashing," 36 *Stan. L. Rev.* 293 (1984); Duncan Kennedy and Peter Gabel, "Roll Over Beethoven," 36 *Stan. L. Rev.* 1 (1984).

45. Duncan Kennedy, "The Structure of Blackstone's Commentaries," 28 *Buff. L. Rev.* 205 (1979); John Nockleby, "Tortious Interference with Contractual Relations in the Nineteenth Century: The Transformation of Property, Contract, and Tort," 93 *Harv. L. Rev.* 1510 (1980); Kenneth Vandevelde, "The New Property of the Nineteenth Century: The Development of the Modern Concept of Property," 29 *Buff. L. Rev.* 325 (1980); James Kainen, "Nineteenth Century Interpretations of the Federal Contract Clause: The Transformation from Vested to Substantive Rights Against the State," 31 *Buff. L. Rev.* 381 (1982); Joseph Singer, "The Player and the Cards: Nihilism and Legal Theory," 94 *Yale L.J.* 1 (1984).

46. Kennedy, "Blackstone's Commentaries," pp. 362–363, n. 56; Duncan Kennedy, "The Role of Law in Economic Thought: Essays on the Fetishism of Commodities," 34 *Amer. Univ. L. Rev.* 939 (1985).

47. Karl Klare, "Law Making as Praxis," *Telos,* Summer 1979, 123.

48. Robert Gordon, "Critical Legal Histories," 36 *Stan. L. Rev.* 57, 110–113 (1984).

49. W. N. Hohfeld, "Some Fundamental Legal Conceptions as Applied in Judicial Reasoning," 23 *Yale L.J.* 16 (1913). See Joseph Singer, "The Legal Rights Debate in Analytical Jurisprudence from Bentham to Hohfeld," 1982 *Wisc. L. Rev.* 975.

50. Kennedy, "Form and Substance"; Duncan Kennedy, "Paternalist and Distributive Motives in Contract and Tort Law, with Special Reference to Compulsory Terms and Unequal Bargaining Power," 41 *Maryland L. Rev.* 563 (1982).

51. Duncan Kennedy and Frank Michelman, "Are Property and Contract Efficient?" 8 *Hofstra L. Rev.* 711 (1980); Kennedy, "Role of Law." See generally the discussion of "contradictionism" in Chapter 4, particularly n. 16.

52. Leopold Specht, "The Politics of Property: Soviet Property as a Bundle of Rights," unpublished S.J.D. thesis, Harvard Law School, Cambridge, Mass., 1994; J. Kornai, *The Socialist System: The Political Economy of Communism* (Princeton: Princeton University Press, 1992), p. 226.

53. Kennedy, "Role of Law"; Duncan Kennedy, *Legal Education and the Reproduction of Hierarchy: A Polemic against the System* (Cambridge, Mass.: AFAR, 1983).

54. Duncan Kennedy, "Cost-Benefit Analysis of Entitlement Problems: A Critique," 33 *Stan. L. Rev.* 387 (1981); Kennedy and Michelman, "Are Property and Contract Efficient?"; Kennedy, "Role of Law."

55. See, for example, Robert Steinfeld, *The Invention of Free Labor: The Employment Relation in English and American Law and Culture, 1350–1870* (Chapel Hill: University of North Carolina Press, 1991), ch. 6; Richard Abel, "Why Does the A.B.A. Promulgate Ethical Rules?" 59 *Tex. L. Rev.* 639 (1981).

56. The progenitor of this kind of analysis was David Trubek, "Max Weber on Law and the Rise of Capitalism," 1972 *Wisc. L. Rev.* 720.

57. For example, Morton Horwitz, *The Transformation of American Law, 1870–1960: The Crisis of Legal Orthodoxy* (New York: Oxford University Press, 1992), ch. 3. But see Mark Hager, "Bodies Politic: The Progressive History of Organizational 'Real Entity' Theory," 50 *Univ. Pitt. L. Rev.* 575 (1989). See also Wythe Holt, "Tilt," 52 *Geo. Wash. L. Rev.* 280 (1984).

58. Georg Lukacs, "Reification and the Consciousness of the Proletariat," in *History and Class Consciousness: Studies in Marxist Dialectics,* trans. Rodney Livingstone (Cambridge, Mass.: MIT Press, 1971).

59. Gramsci, *Prison Notebooks.*

60. Althusser, "Ideology."

61. Jürgen Habermas, *Legitimation Crisis,* trans. Thomas McCarthy (Boston: Beacon Press, 1975).

62. On the fascist version of ideology-critique, see "Carl Schmitt Meets Karl Marx," in William Scheuerman, *Between the Norm and the Exception: The Frankfurt School and the Rule of Law* (Cambridge, Mass.: MIT Press, 1994).

63. English neo-Marxist legal sociology has gradually abandoned all four of these ideas, as Alan Hunt proudly explains in *Explorations in Law and Society: Toward a Constitutive Theory of Law* (New York: Routledge, 1993), pp. 117–138, without, so far as I can see, adopting any alternative conception. Sic transit . . .

64. The intellectual genealogy of the popular American usage includes the writers who developed the critique of "totalitarianism" (see Abbot Gleason, *Totalitarianism: The Inner History of the Cold War* [New York: Oxford University Press, 1995], for whom not Liberalism but communism and fascism are the quintessential examples), the intellectual/historical tradition represented by Karl Mannheim, *Ideology and Utopia: An Introduction to the Sociology of Knowledge* (New York: Harcourt, Brace, 1936), and the "critical" line of thought, stemming from German idealism and very much present in Western Marxism (for example, Karl Korsch, *Marxism and Philosophy,* trans. F. Halliday

[New York: Monthly Review Press, 1970]) that emphasizes the impossibility of operating without some inevitably partial cognitive framework.

65. Mark Kelman, *A Guide to Critical Legal Studies* (Cambridge, Mass.: Harvard University Press, 1987), p. 269.

66. Hunt, *Explorations,* p. 154. This formulation is meant to be responsive to Habermas's brilliant critique of structural Marxist theories in *Knowledge and Human Interests,* trans. Jeremy Shapiro (Boston: Beacon Press, 1971).

67. For a great collection, see Michael Fischl, "The Question That Killed Critical Legal Studies," 17 *Law & Soc. Inquiry* 779, 781–782 (1992).

12. RIGHTS IN AMERICAN LEGAL CONSCIOUSNESS

1. Cornel West, "The Struggle for America's Soul," *New York Times Book Review,* September 15, 1991, p. 13.

2. See Gary Peller, "Race Consciousness," 1990 *Duke L.J.* 758.

3. Mark Tushnet, "An Essay on Rights," 62 *Texas L. Rev.* 1363 (1984).

4. Peter Gabel, "The Phenomenology of Rights Consciousness and the Pact of the Withdrawn Selves," 62 *Texas L. Rev.* 1563 (1984).

5. Frances Olsen, "Statutory Rape: A Feminist Critique of Rights Analysis," 63 *Texas L. Rev.* 387 (1984).

6. Duncan Kennedy, "Critical Labor Law Theory: A Comment," 4 *Industrial Relations L.J.* 503 (1981); Duncan Kennedy, "The Structure of Blackstone's Commentaries," 28 *Buff. L. Rev.* 205 (1979).

7. Louis Schwartz, "With Gun and Camera through Darkest CLS Land," 36 *Stan. L. Rev.* 247 (1984).

8. Phillip Johnson, "Do You Sincerely Want to Be Radical?" 36 *Stan. L. Rev.* 247 (1984).

9. Staughton Lynd, "Communal Rights," 62 *Texas L. Rev.* 1417 (1984).

10. Edward Sparer, "Fundamental Human Rights, Legal Entitlements, and the Social Struggle: A Friendly Critique of the Critical Legal Studies Movement," 36 *Stan. L. Rev.* 509 (1984).

11. Michael Tigar, "The Right of Property and the Law of Theft," 62 *Texas L. Rev.* 1443 (1984).

12. Martha Minow, "Interpreting Rights: An Essay for Robert Cover," 96 *Yale L.J.* 1860 (1987); Elizabeth Schneider, "The Dialectic of Rights and Politics: Perspectives from the Women's Movement," 61 *N.Y.U.L. Rev.* 589 (1986).

13. Patricia Williams, *The Alchemy of Race and Rights* (Cambridge, Mass.: Harvard University Press, 1991); Richard Delgado, "The Ethereal Scholar: Does Critical Legal Studies Have What Minorities Want?" 22 *Harv. C.R.-C.L. L. Rev.* 301 (1987); Kimberle Crenshaw, "Race, Reform, and Retrenchment: Transformation and Legitimation in Antidiscrimination Law," 101 *Harv. L. Rev.* 1331 (1988).

14. Since the late eighteenth century, there has been a metadiscussion within con-

stitutional law about the proper role of unenacted outside rights. See Calder v. Bull, 3 U.S. (3 Dall.) 386 (1798), and Loan Association v. Topeka, 87 U.S. (20 Wall.) 655 (1875). Opponents of judicial reasoning from unenacted outside rights have insisted that there is a clear difference between being outside and being inside, and that judges should concern themselves only with the inside. Outside rights don't "really" exist; even if they exist they are too much open to ideological controversy; even if they exist and are clear they are not "law."

The opponents of a "strictly positivist" position argue the flip side: that appeal to outside rights can and should resolve gaps, conflicts, and ambiguities that arise when the judge tries to ignore the normative sources of law, and so forth. In other words, the positivists celebrate judicial method and denigrate rights theory, while the interpretivists do the opposite. This discussion remains marginal. Most of the time, the ideological intelligentsias that deploy constitutional argument confront each other in the intermediate zone. In the intermediate zone, both sides claim enacted constitutional rights *and* the objectivity of judicial method.

15. Minow, "Interpreting Rights"; Schneider, "The Dialectic of Rights and Politics"; Gabel, "Phenomenology."

16. Oliver Wendell Holmes, "The Path of the Law," in *Collected Legal Papers* (Buffalo, N.Y.: William S. Hein, 1985), p. 181.

17. Henry Terry, "Legal Duties and Rights," 12 *Yale L.J.* 185, 188 (1903).

13. THE CRITIQUE OF RIGHTS

1. Wesley Hohfeld, "Fundamental Conceptions as Applied in Judicial Reasoning," 26 *Yale L.J.* 710 (1917).

2. Compare Vegelhan v. Gunter, 167 Mass. 92, 44 N.E. 1077 (1896), with Hague v. C.I.O., 307 U.S. 496 (1939).

3. Louis Brandeis and Charles Warren, "The Right of Privacy," 4 *Harv. L. Rev.* 193 (1890).

4. Griswold v. Conn., 381 U.S. 479 (1965).

5. Lon Fuller and William Purdue, "The Reliance Interest in Contract Damages," 46 *Yale L.J.* 52, 373 (1936–37). See Chapter 5. Hohfeld is again the most important originator. Hohfeld, "Fundamental Conceptions."

6. But see Alexander Aleinikoff, "Constitutional Law in the Age of Balancing," 96 *Yale L.J.* 943 (1987).

7. Pa. Coal v. Mahon, 260 U.S. 393 (1922), Hadachek v. Sebastian, 233 U.S. 394 (1915). See Thomas Grey, "Holmes and Legal Pragmatism," 41 *Stan. L. Rev.* 787, 819–820 (1989).

8. Hohfeld, "Fundamental Conceptions."

9. Cheney v. Doris Silk Co., 35 F.2d 279 (2d Cir. 1929).

10. U.S. v. Aluminum Co. of Am., 148 F.2d 416 (2d Cir. 1945).

11. U.S. v. Carroll Towing Co., 159 F.2d 169 (2d Cir. 1947).

12. Dennis v. U.S., 182 F.2d 201 (2d Cir. 1950).

13. Learned Hand, *The Bill of Rights* (Cambridge, Mass.: Harvard University Press, 1958).

14. U.S. v. Carolene Products, 304 U.S. 144, 152–153, n. 4 (1938).

15. Powell v. Alabama, 287 U.S. 45 (1932).

16. Hague v. C.I.O., 307 U.S. 496 (1939).

17. W. Va. v. Barnette, 319 U.S. 624 (1943).

18. William O. Douglas, "Stare Decisis," 49 *Colum. L. Rev.* 735 (1949).

19. Herbert Wechsler, "Toward Neutral Principles of Constitutional Law," 73 *Harv. L. Rev.* 1 (1959).

20. Hugo Black, "The Bill of Rights," 35 *N.Y.U.L. Rev.* 865 (1960).

21. Dennis v. U.S., 341 U.S. 494, 524–543 (1951) (Frankfurter, J., concurring).

22. See, for example, Alexander Meiklejohn, "The First Amendment Is an Absolute," 1961 *Sup. Ct. Rev.* 245.

23. See, for example, Erwin Griswold, "Absolute Is in the Dark," 8 *Utah L. Rev.* 167 (1963); Paul Freund, *The Supreme Court of the United States* (Cleveland: World Pub., 1961).

24. Wechsler, "Neutral Principles."

25. Henry Hart and Herbert Wechsler, *The Federal Courts in the Federal System* (Brooklyn: Foundation Press, 1953).

26. Three quite different reactions of this general kind are Robert McCloskey, "Economic Due Process and the Supreme Court: An Exhumation and Reburial," 1962 *Sup. Ct. Rev.* 34; Jan Deutsch, "Neutrality, Legitimacy, and the Supreme Court: Some Intersections between Law and Political Theory," 20 *Stan. L. Rev.* 169 (1968); and John Griffiths, "Ideology in Criminal Procedure, or, A Third 'Model' of the Criminal Process," 79 *Yale L.J.* 359 (1970).

27. Bd. of Regents of the Univ. of Cal. v. Bakke, 438 U.S. 265 (1978).

28. Ann Freedman, "Sex Equality, Sex Difference, and the Supreme Court," 92 *Yale L.J.* 913 (1983).

29. Derrick Bell, "Serving Two Masters," 85 *Yale L.J.* 470 (1976).

30. See the discussion of Thomas Sowell in Kimberle Crenshaw, "Race, Reform, and Retrenchment: Transformation and Legitimation in Antidiscrimination Law," 101 *Harv. L. Rev.* 1331, 1339–1346 (1988).

31. Thomas Grey, "Discriminatory Harassment and Free Speech," 14 *Harv. J. Law & Pub. Policy* 157 (1991).

32. Kimberle Crenshaw, "Mapping the Margins: Identity Politics, Intersectionality, and Violence against Women," 43 *Stan. L. Rev.* 1241 (1991).

33. Martha Minow, "The Supreme Court, October 1986 Term, Foreword—Justice Engendered," 101 *Harv. L. Rev.* 10 (1987); Mary Joe Frug, *Post-Modern Legal Feminism* (New York: Routledge, 1992).

34. Even if, for one of these reasons, the realist critique of legal rights reasoning isn't very threatening to the belief that there are universal human rights, it should

still be plenty threatening to the idea that identifying them in the abstract will get away from the kind of "value judgment" that you invented them to avoid. This doesn't seem to have occurred to political philosophers outside law, but it is close to an obsession, in the form of the "countermajoritarian difficulty," of American jurisprudence.

35. Bella English, "Keeping Rights in Perspective," *Boston Globe,* July 22, 1991, s. 2, p. 13.

36. "I can engage in homosexual intercourse because I have a right to sexual freedom." "I can organize a PAC with corporate contributions because I have a right of free speech." "Slavery is wrong because it denies the inalienable rights of life, liberty, and property." "Nondisclaimable strict products liability is wrong because it denies the right of freedom of contract." "Compulsory membership in a labor union is wrong because it denies the right of free association; the banning of strikes is wrong because it denies the right to strike." "The banning of sale of contraceptives is wrong because it violates the right to privacy."

37. An exemplary critique of this kind is Jeremy Paul, "Book Review," 88 *Mich. L. Rev.* 1622 (1990)(review of Jeremy Waldron, *The Right to Private Property*).

38. Martha Minow, "Interpreting Rights: An Essay for Robert Cover," 96 *Yale L.J.* 1860 (1987); Elizabeth Schneider, "The Dialectic of Rights and Politics: Perspectives from the Women's Movement," 61 *N.Y.U.L. Rev.* 589 (1986).

39. Karl Marx, *Capital: A Critique of Political Economy,* vol. 1, trans. Ben Fowkes (New York: Vintage Books, 1977).

40. Karl Marx, *Critique of the Gotha Program* (Moscow: Progress Publishers, 1971).

41. Karl Marx, "On the Jewish Question," in *Writings of the Young Marx on Philosophy and Society,* ed. and trans. Loyd Easton and Kurt Guddat (Garden City, N.Y.: Anchor, 1967), p. 216. This essay is full of neo-Hegelian anti-Semitic ideas. I think this is one of those cases where the dross doesn't corrupt the gold. It is also typically "early Marx."

42. See, for example, Peter Gabel, "The Phenomenology of Rights Consciousness and the Pact of the Withdrawn Selves," 62 *Texas L. Rev.* 1563 (1984); Alan Freeman and Elizabeth Mensch, "The Public-Private Distinction in American Law and Life," 36 *Buff. L. Rev.* 237 (1987); Duncan Kennedy, "The Structure of Blackstone's Commentaries," 28 *Buff. L. Rev.* 205 (1979); Duncan Kennedy and Peter Gabel, "Roll Over Beethoven," 36 *Stan. L. Rev.* 1 (1984).

43. There are a number of critical analyses of the role of rights rhetoric at different stages of social movements and at different moments in American political history. See Gabel, "Phenomenology," and Alan Hunt, "Rights and Social Movements: Counter-Hegemonic Strategies," 17 *J. Law & Soc'y* 309 (1990). They aren't examples of the rights critique, although they sometimes presuppose it.

14. CONCLUSION

1. To my mind, the best statement of this way of looking at mpm is Nathaniel Berman's discussion of modernism in "Modernism, Nationalism, and the Rhetoric of

Reconstruction," 4 *Yale J. Law & Human.* 351 (1992). For an interesting interpretation of cls as left modernism, see David Luban, "Legal Modernism," 84 *Mich. L. Rev.* 1656 (1986).

2. Jeremy Paul, "The Politics of Semiotics," 69 *Texas L. Rev.* 1779, 1812–1813 (1991).

3. Jack Balkin, "The Politics of Legal Semiotics," 69 *Texas L. Rev.* 1831, 1846–1848 (1991).

4. Ibid.

5. Clare Dalton, "Book Review," 6 *Harv. Women's L. Rev.* 229 (1982) (reviewing *The Politics of Law,* ed. David Kairys); Gerald Frug, "The Ideology of Bureaucracy in American Law," 97 *Harv. L. Rev.* 1276 (1984); David Kennedy, "The Turn to Interpretation," 58 *So. Cal. L. Rev.* 1 (1985); Gary Peller, "The Metaphysics of American Law," 73 *Cal. L. Rev.* 1152 (1985); David Kennedy, "Critical Theory, Structuralism, and Contemporary Legal Scholarship," 21 *New Eng. L. Rev.* 209 (1986). I tried to counter this approach in Duncan Kennedy, "Freedom and Constraint in Adjudication: A Critical Phenomenology," 36 *J. Legal Educ.* 518 (1986), and Duncan Kennedy, "A Semiotics of Legal Argument," 42 *Syracuse L. Rev.* 75 (1991) (and same article with "European Introduction: Four Objections," in *Collected Courses of the Academy of European Law,* vol. 3, book 2 [1994], p. 309). The view I favor is close to that of Gerald Frug in "Argument as Character," 40 *Stan. L. Rev.* 869 (1988), and Matthew Kramer, *Legal Theory, Political Theory, and Deconstruction: Against Rhadamanthus* (Bloomington: Indiana University Press, 1991), p. 248: "Determinacy, for deconstructive critics, presents itself as a function or a moment in an unstoppable interweaving of fixed structures and free play. Determinacy and indeterminacy generate and exclude each other in a process that is itself both indeterminate and determinate . . . Derrida has made much the same point . . . : '[T]he production of differences, *différance,* is not astructural: it produces systematic and regulated transformations which are able, at a certain point, to leave room for a structural science. The concept of *différance* even develops the most legitimate principled exigencies of "structuralism"' (citing Jacques Derrida, *Positions* [Chicago: University of Chicago Press, 1981], p. 28)." But Kramer seems to me to fall into the error of believing that it is always possible to deconstruct, even though it may not happen in a given case, whereas to my mind deconstruction has nothing to say about its own possibility or impossibility outside a particular instance. See Part Three.

6. Frank Michelman and Margaret Radin, "Pragmatist and Poststructuralist Critical Legal Practice," 139 *U. Pa. L. Rev.* 1019, 1035–1036 (1991).

7. Jacques Derrida, *Spectres of Marx,* trans. Peggy Knauf (New York: Routledge, 1994), pp. 77–88.

8. Sanford Levinson and Jack Balkin, "Law, Music, and Other Performing Arts," 139 *U. Pa. L. Rev.* 1597 (1991).

9. Michelle Green, *The Dream at the End of the World: Paul Bowles and the Literary Renegades of Tangier* (New York: HarperCollins, 1991).

10. Pierre Schlag, "Normative and Nowhere to Go," 43 *Stan. L. Rev.* 167 (1990).

11. In law, some different efforts of this kind that I am aware of are François Geny, *Science et technique en droit privé positif: nouvelle contribution à la critique de la méthode juridique* (Paris: L. Tenin, 1914–1924); Roscoe Pound, *Jurisprudence* (St. Paul, Minn.: West Pub. Co., 1959); Harold Laswell and Myres McDougal, "Legal Education and Public Policy: Professional Training in the Public Interest," 52 *Yale L.J.* 203 (1943); Richard Posner, *Problems of Jurisprudence* (Cambridge, Mass.: Harvard University Press, 1990); Frank Michelman, "Law's Republic," 97 *Yale L.J.* 1493 (1988); Margaret Radin, *Reinterpreting Property* (Chicago: University of Chicago Press, 1993); and Roberto Unger, *Politics: A Work in Constructive Social Theory* (New York: Cambridge University Press, 1987). The last of these is full of things I agree with, for all my reconstructive unmusicality.

12. Nigel Purvis, "Critical Legal Studies in Public International Law," 32 *Harv. Int. L.J.* 81, 127 (1991)(emphasis in original).

13. Michael Fischl, "The Question That Killed Critical Legal Studies," 17 *Law & Soc. Inquiry* 779, 800 (1992).

14. Kimberle Crenshaw, "Mapping the Margins: Identity Politics, Intersectionality, and Violence against Women," 43 *Stan. L. Rev.* 1241 (1991). On the relation between mpm metaphysics and politics, see Kramer, *Legal Theory,* pp. 246–247.

15. Michel Foucault, *Discipline and Punish: The Birth of the Prison,* trans. Alan Sheridan (New York: Vintage, 1979).

16. Scientific education also involves extensive normalization but is understood to measure a much narrower band of capacities—memory and pure cognitive ability. Law school resembles the prep school I went to, where you were called on in most classes most days, took endless quizzes and tests as well as several different national aptitude and achievement tests each year, and in one class got a grade on your oral recitation in Greek every single day.

17. Duncan Kennedy, *Legal Education and the Reproduction of Hierarchy* (Cambridge, Mass.: AFAR, 1983); Duncan Kennedy, "Liberal Values in Legal Education," 19 *Nova L.J.* 603 (1986); Duncan Kennedy, "Politicizing the Classroom," 4 *U.S.C. Rev. Law & Women's Studies* 81 (1995). See also Toni Pickard, "Experience as Teacher: Discovering the Politics of Law Teaching," 33 *Univ. Toronto L.J.* 278 (1983).

18. Joseph Raz, "The Relevance of Coherence," 72 *B.U.L. Rev.* 273, 304, n. 52 (1992).

INDEX